THE PLOTS TO RESCUE THE TSAR

As President of Smith McNeal, Shay McNeal built her firm into a multi-million dollar business. After selling it she became a political consultant and retired in 1992 to pursue her passion for history and writing. She is now a highly respected historical researcher who has contributed to both the BBC and the Discovery Channel on Colonial American History.

'Shay McNeal provides a further twist to this inscrutable tale, [an] important new lead on the Romanov mystery . . . fascinating'
Sunday Times

'McNeal's sleuthing often rings true, and the long-forgotten figures who populate her story have a weird fascination'
Daily Mail

'Riveting and comprehensive, this book reveals the truth behind the disappearance of the Romanovs'
Vogue

'[A] highly readable account that throws considerable doubt on the official history'
John Crace, *Amazon*

'I can no longer accept the standard version of events as reliable or complete'
Richard Spence, Professor of History and Chair, University of Idaho

The Plots to Rescue the Tsar

Shay McNeal

ARROW

Published by Arrow Books in 2002

1 3 5 7 9 10 8 6 4 2

Copyright © Shay McNeal 2001

Shay McNeal has asserted her right under the Copyright, Designs and Patents
Act, 1988 to be identified as the author of this work

First published in the United Kingdom in 2001 by Century

Arrow Books
Random House Group Limited
20 Vauxhall Bridge Road, London SW1V 2SA

Random House Australia (Pty) Limited
20 Alfred Street, Milsons Point, Sydney,
New South Wales 2061, Australia

Random House New Zealand Limited
18 Poland Road, Glenfield
Auckland 10, New Zealand

Random House (Pty) Limited
Endulini, 5a Jubilee Road, Parktown 2193, South Africa

Random House Group Limited Reg. No. 954009

www.randomhouse.co.uk

A CIP catalogue record for this book is available from the British Library

Papers used by Random House are natural, recyclable products made from
wood grown in sustainable forests. The manufacturing processes conform
to the environmental regulations of the country of origin

ISBN 0 09 929810 4

Typeset by SX Composing DTP, Rayleigh, Essex
Printed and Bound in Great Britain by
Bookmarque, Croydon, Surrey

To Mary Ellen 'Teddi' Baird Evans, my late mother
Claude Poulin, Hethur and Paris
my loving family

ACKNOWLEDGEMENTS

There is a deep sadness attached to the very first acknowledgements of people without whom I could not have completed this work. During the compilation of the research and writing I lost my mother Teddi Evans whose tenacity first set me on this course. Then in rapid succession I lost my first two readers. Dr John Long, who was an authority on Northern Russia, after a valiant fight, succumbed to cancer. Next came the unexpected death of my other reader, Frederick Hart, the renowned sculptor whose portrayal of the Tsar's daughters, in his work the 'The Daughters of Odessa', is next only to his brilliant sculpture at the Vietnam Memorial in Washington, D.C. Rick was an aficionado of Russian history and art, and a insatiable collector of Romanov paintings and photographs. His death was soon followed by more upsetting news when Dr Bruce Lincoln, one of the most widely respected Russian historians of the twentieth century, confided to me in a telephone conversation just before he was leaving for Italy that he too was fighting cancer. He lost his battle within months of that day. I have come to call these my cold shower days. In the mornings, with a cup of coffee in hand, documents overwhelming my study at the farm and a blank computer screen beckoning me, I longed for their feedback and encouragement on this lonely journey. Their contributions were of paramount importance to me. Not long after, Richard Spence, Chair of the History Department at the University of Moscow, Idaho, and an authority on Sidney Reilly, came into my life and through him came Julian Putkowski, an interesting academic who is gifted with the ability to bring to life countless historical characters via his commentaries for radio and television. These men filled a void and inspired me again.

I would also like to express my gratitude to Kate Parkin, of

Random House, who believed in my book and bought it, as well as Anna Dalton-Knott, likewise of Random House, my editor who shepherded me and my work from start to finish, for their faith. A first time author could not have been blessed with more gracious and accommodating people to assist her in traversing the thicket that is otherwise known as publishing a book. There was also the team who helped me get the book into the hands of Kate and Anna – Gail Ross, Leslie Breed, Abner Stein, Mary Bruton, Natasha Hope, and Jenna Land. I know there were days when we all wanted to quit. I salute their perseverance and commitment.

A very special thank you is in order to the historians, researchers and family members of some of the men and women mentioned in the book for all their assistance and the encouragement they rendered. They each accepted my phone calls, listened to me weigh the pros and cons and in some cases even offered the hospitality of their homes. Warmest regards go to K.T. Anders (my last reader and sometime editor), Bob Atkinson, Manfred Bittkau, John Bescoby-Chambers, Timothy Boettger, Stephen Bruce, William Clarke, Thomas and Jo Corbin, Thomas Crane (Charles Crane's grandson), Sylvia Crane (Charles Crane's daughter-in-law) and the Bakhmeteff Archive, Rare Book and Manuscript Library, Columbia University, Sam Daniel, Josephine F. de Give (Charles Crane's great-granddaughter), Dr Marcia Eisenberg, Barbara Finlayson, (William Rutledge McGarry's granddaughter), Bruce C. Fisher (Charles Crane's granddaughter), Dr David Foglesong, Mike Gilley, Dr David Haskin and Gretchen Haskin (Henry Haskin's son and daughter-in-law), Kathleen Holt (Colt Manufacturing), Todd Huffman, Barbara Kelcey, Olga Kulikovsky-Romanov (the widow of Tihon Kulikovsky, the son of Grand Duchess Olga, Tsar Nicholas II's younger sister), Peter N. Koltypin-Wallovskoy (Russian Expert Commission Abroad), Peter Kurth, Réjean Laprade, Thomas Man (United States Library of Congress) the late Charles McLeroy, Anne Morton (Hudson's Bay Company Archives), retired Judge Mark McGarry II (William Rutledge McGarry's grandson), Robert Moshein, Greg Murphy, Dotti Nacci, Roger Nixon, Michael and Elisabeth Occleshaw, Dr Margaret Picher, Dr Richard Pipes, Dr Jane Plotke, Ed and Kristin Nute (Blitz), Dr William Shields, Anatol Shmelev (the Hoover Institution on War, Revolution and Peace), Mr. and Mrs. Wallace Starling, Dr Mark Steinberg, Anthony and Robbyn Summers, Fran and Phil Tomaselli, Sabrina Thomas

(Library of Congress) Dr Idris Traylor, Elena Tsvetkova (Blitz), Robert Warren, Doug Wicklund (National Rifle Association), Tadeusz Jaroshinsky, Dr Dino Jaroshinsky and Karolina De Mareuil (Karol Yaroshinsky's grand niece).

A special word for my father, Jack Evans, and my late mother, Teddi, as well as my grandparents, H'Earl Evans, William and Rebecca Paris Baird, who, from my first step, never let me forget that intellectual curiosity is boundless and does not recognise gender or race. My heartfelt devotion to my daughter Hethur Charlotte and son-in-law Gene and grandson Cole Charlotte, as well as my daughter Paris Smith, for their understanding of me and my endeavour. And thank you to fellow writers Terri Evans, my sister, and Lee Leslie, my brother-in-law as well as my brother Pride Evans and my sister-in-law Kristie Evans for all their inspiration. And to the superb educator and retired curator of the Chateau Ramezay, Montreal's Historical Museum, Jacques Poulin and Madeleine his wife, who have accepted me as their own, thank you for your special son Claude, who spent countless nights helping me attempt to discover the truth.

To Kathy Baldwin, Anna Dees, André Fournelle, Kenny Gilbert, Lindy Hart, Dan Jacobs, Marc Lalumière, Ruth Ann McGehee, Jim McDonald, Karen McKnew, Kathy Mizzer, Lady Angela Neuberger, Muriel and Peggy O'Callaghan, Marie and Micheline Poulin, Luc and Christiane Prévost, Steve, Hannah and Emily McMahan, Doug Pifer, Darla Rivi, Barbara Robinson, Bert Roughton and Melinda Ennis Roughton, John Scott, Peggy Schaake, David Tate, Craig Williams, all of whom assisted me in every way from compiling research to typing and proofing or simply offering encouragement at just the right time, my gratitude.

Finally, thank you to the staff and administrators of the United States National Archives, the Library of Congress in Washington, D.C., the Public Record Office in Richmond, England, the British Library in London, Chateau de Vincennes, the Bibliothèque Nationale, les Archives Nationales in Paris and the Staatsbibliothek zu Berlin in Berlin, Germany and countless universities in United States, Canada, the United Kingdom and Continental Europe/

NOTE ON DATES

The New Style calendar, already in general use on the Continent and in Great Britain, did not replace the Old Style in Russia until 1918 when thirteen days were omitted (1 February being reckoned as 14 February). In this book dates are predominantly given as New Style, except where indicated, or where cited in original sources.

CONTENTS

List of Illustrations   xiii

PART ONE   IN THE SHADOW OF THE GREAT WAR   xvii
Introduction   A Historical Enigma   1
Chapter 1   Setting the Stage   15
Chapter 2   Parties in Interest   22
Chapter 3   The Hidden Hands   39
Chapter 4   The Hidden Hands Play a Hand   56
Chapter 5   The Façade   64

PART TWO   AGENTS ON THE MOVE   73
Chapter 6   Tobolsk   75
Chapter 7   A New Cast of Characters   98
Chapter 8   Extortion   116

PART THREE   CONTRADICTIONS, ABSURDITIES
                AND IMPLAUSIBILITY   133
Chapter 9   The Tsar Was Shot   135
Chapter 10   The First Investigations   158
Chapter 11   The Messengers of Death   166
Chapter 12   Yurovsky's Revised Account   184
Chapter 13   Tsar and Family Destroyed Without a Trace   198

PART FOUR   IN SEARCH OF THE TRUTH   219
Chapter 14   San Francisco 1920   221
Chapter 15   Politics, Intrigue and Provenance 230
Chapter 16   Coming Full Circle   242

Epilogue   269
Appendix   274
Characters   278
Bibliography   284
Notes   301
Index   329

LIST OF ILLUSTRATIONS

Plate Section
The Imperial Family, *courtesy of the United States Library of Congress*
Nicholas and Alexandra, *courtesy of the United States Library of Congress*
Tsar Nicholas II and King George V, *courtesy of the United States Library of Congress*
Kaiser Wilhelm, *courtesy of the United States Library of Congress*
Rasputin, *courtesy of the United States Library of Congress*
Karol Yaroshinsky, *by permission of the Yaroshinsky Family*
Anna Vyrubova, *courtesy of the United States Library of Congress*
Nurse or Nun, *courtesy of the United States Library of Congress*
Prince Lvov, *courtesy of the United States Library of Congress*
Alexander Kerensky, *courtesy of the United States Library of Congress*
Lenin and Stalin, *courtesy of the United States Library of Congress*
Leon Trotsky, *courtesy of the United States Library of Congress*
Charles Crane, *by permission of Bruce C. Fisher*
Thomas Masaryk, *courtesy of the United States Library of Congress*
Woodrow Wilson, *with thanks to Roger Walker*
Mr and Mrs McAdoo, *courtesy of the United States Library of Congress*
Breckinridge Long, *courtesy of the United States Library of Congress*
David Lloyd George, *courtesy of the The United States National Archives*
Duke of Connaught, *courtesy of the United States National Archives*
Ipatiev House, *courtesy of the United States National Archives*
'Death Chamber,' *courtesy of the United States Library of Congress*
Living room, *courtesy of the United States Library of Congress*
Swastika, © *The Times*
Lysva, © *The Times*
Colt Letter, © *Colt Manufacturing Company, Inc*
Admiral Kolchak, *courtesy of the United States National Archives*
General Denikin, *courtesy of the United States National Archives*
Czech Legion *courtesy of the United States National Archives*
Major Slaughter, *courtesy of the United States National Archives*
Sidney Reilly, *by permission of Richard Spence*
Rescuing the Czar cover, *created by Jim McDonald*
McGarry and Romanovsky, *by permission of Barbara Finlayson and Judge Mark McGarry*

Maps
White Russian, Allied and Bolshevik/Red Forces, Moscow and Yakovlev's Activities *and* Escape Routes for the Imperial Family, *created by Lee Leslie of LeslieEvans Creative, Claude Poulin and Shay McNeal*

White Russian, Allied and Boshevik/Red Forces

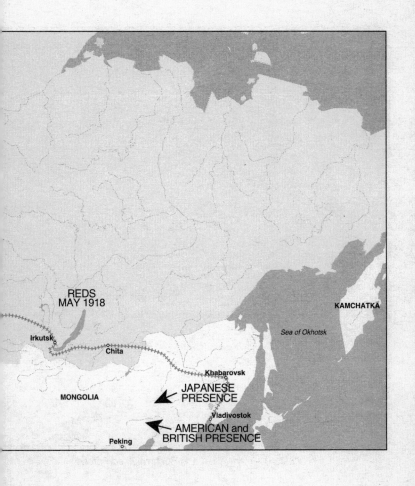

PART ONE

*In the Shadow of the
Great War*

INTRODUCTION

A Historical Enigma

Of all the victims of the Russian Revolution, Tsar Nicholas II, Tsarina Alexandra and their five children are perhaps the most famous and certainly among the most controversial. Their presumed deaths on 17 July 1918 have been the subject of several investigations and numerous books. Although the standard account of their execution by a Bolshevik firing squad was questioned from the very beginning, it has never been disproven.

Contradictions and confusion regarding their fate have reigned from the moment the Imperial family vanished from the world stage. Even after their supposed deaths, various sightings were reported. Innumerable versions of their disappearance have been floated for public consumption. The official confirmation of their 'deaths' took decades but, until now, the mystery of the last days of the Romanovs remained unsolved.

However, with the aid of new forensic evidence and heretofore undiscovered and understudied primary source material, it is possible to prove that the traditional account of the months leading up to the night, as well as during the night of 16/17 July 1918 itself, simply cannot have occurred as described. After five years of full-time research in numerous archives in various countries; after reading and scouring hundreds of books and analysing reams of unknown or understudied documents that exposed evidence never before considered interrelated, a mosaic revealed itself that differed vastly from the official story of the last days of the Romanovs. Not only was the traditional history shown to be fraught with discrepancies, but it also became apparent, by the compilation of

1

facts gleaned from disparate sources, that there were at least three and possibly four serious plans for the withdrawal of the Tsar and his family from Russia after the February Revolution in 1917. The Allies worked clandestinely, co-operating with one another at the highest level, even flirting with Bolshevik complicity, to come up with plans to pluck the Romanovs from the Bolsheviks' grasp. And they were all meticulously careful, so careful that even today some of the trails of activities and shadowy contacts twist and turn in a tantalising maze of missing files and untraceable names. This book will demonstrate that what history has told us of these events is very far from the full story, and that some 'authors' of that history may have had ulterior and hitherto unsuspected motives.

Before doing this, however, it is necessary to examine and refute one extremely important piece of evidence currently upholding the traditional view – the DNA of the so-called 'Romanov' bones.

Officially, all the speculation regarding the family's end should have come to an abrupt halt on 31 August 1995, when a team of Russian and American scientists announced the testing of the sample from the Tsar's brother, Grand Duke George, and the purported Tsar's remains had produced a match. Hence the human remains unearthed in 1991 near Ekaterinburg, Russia were those of Tsar Nicholas II, Tsarina Alexandra and three of their daughters. 'A great murder mystery spanning most of the century is solved,' said Lieutenant Colonel Victor W. Weedn, director of the United States Armed Forces DNA Identification Laboratory (AFDIL), which conducted the investigation in association with Russian DNA expert Pavel Ivanov. Upon the announcement of the 'positive' identification of the Romanovs, the officials on the Russian Governmental Commission immediately set about arranging the burial of the family, indicating that the case was now officially considered closed.

But among some contingents the findings of the commission, as well as its activities regarding the burial, were anything but clear-cut. Far from there being a universal acceptance of the evidence, as we in the West have been led to believe, in fact a veritable hue and cry went out from a number of scientists, members of the White Russian[1] community abroad and members of the Russian Orthodox Church both in Russia and the United States. Controversy continued to grow in Russia causing the ceremony to be cancelled repeatedly and then considerably downgraded from the government's original grandiose plan. Finally, the date of 17 July 1998 was chosen. President Boris Yeltsin initially announced he would not attend the funeral, only to reverse his position the day before. On the eightieth anniversary of the fateful night, the greatly abridged funeral[2] in St Petersburg would at last lay to rest the boxes of bones purported to be the remains of five of the seven Romanovs and four of their retainers.

Still, many remained unconvinced. The head of the Russian Orthodox Church, Patriarch Alexei II, refused to bow to the immense pressure the Russian government was applying to Church officials to recognise the bones, and instructed the officiating priest to refer to the remains of the five 'Romanovs,' not as Romanovs, but as 'Christian victims of the Revolution'. Father Boris Glebov, who conducted the service, is reported to have commented only days before the ceremony, 'The truth is I don't know who I am burying.'[3] In the final analysis the pressure the Russian government applied to church officials to recognise the bones failed. During the ceremony the priest did not so much as utter the Romanov name. However, this did not prevent members of the press corps from around the world who had attended the burial from filing stories calling five of the nine 'victims' spoken of in the ceremony Romanovs. But the truth is that Father Glebov never uttered the word and the Church's position remains unswayed to this day.

Yet the significance imparted by the Russian government and the media at large to the ceremony held in St Peter and St Paul Cathedral was that Russia and the world had finally brought a sordid chapter of Soviet-era history to a conclusion: the Romanovs' lives had ended on 17 July 1918, at the hands of a Bolshevik firing squad in Ekaterinburg in the Ural Mountains in Siberia. Case closed.

Interestingly, the story of how the bones first made their appearance in Russia, irregularities at the grave site and the questionable provenance of the putative Romanov samples did not find their way into the press conference or the news stories. Consequently the emphatic announcement of the conclusive DNA analysis obscured some vital facts. Among those was that, in reality, only a tenuous match at one point in the complicated DNA chain rendered the same results as a sample from Prince Philip of England, who has a familial relationship to the Romanovs.

These tenuous results were presented to the press as a match and persuaded the media, especially in the West, to announce closure to this long-running mystery. The reaction by the press and the world at large to the soundness of the DNA testing conducted in 1993, and again in 1995, is troubling, for it was surprisingly uncritical. But in several influential quarters the scientific conclusions were met with scepticism. Leading scientists, such as Dr Lev Zhivotovsky of the Russian Academy of Sciences in Moscow, raised a voice of concern. Did the bones, which had been tested for DNA, actually match the bodies of five of the seven Romanovs? Or were they merely those of nameless victims of the Revolution?

The issue at the heart of the entire controversy is that both the FSS (British Home Office's Forensic Science Service, which had been responsible for Prince Philip's DNA testing) and the AFDIL have consistently refused to release their full case file to the members of the Russian Expert Commission Abroad (RECA), so that the Commission, which has served as a watchdog committee, can release the full case file for independent peer review and the legal procedure of discovery by a truly independent body.[4]

To gain an understanding of the accepted protocol of DNA cases, I spoke to Dr Marcia Eisenberg, at Lab Corporation of America.[5] Dr Eisenberg stated that each DNA file is given a case number and that every member of the team must continually annotate the file during the life of the case. This is standard protocol to ensure that case files and their subsequent findings can stand peer review and, if necessary, face legal challenges.

In all fairness, it must be said that neither the FSS nor the AFDIL has established a reputation for exempting themselves from standard scientific protocol and it is not suggested that anyone associated with these bodies has acted inappropriately. In this case, the labs appear to have signed agreements restricting access to their notes. So the question becomes, if the positive results of the DNA test were so unambiguous, why did the Commission refuse to provide access to the RECA? Their refusal stands as a repudiation of the process of discovery that should grant open access to all parties in any legitimate judicial proceeding. After all, the Romanov affair was supposedly a multi-victim murder case and, as such, should have been subjected to all the rigours and discipline of any criminal court.

In US federal courts and most state courts, DNA evidence is admitted only if the presiding judge determines that the test procedure is scientifically valid and generally accepted by the relevant scientific community. Given that the scientific community has been denied the opportunity to analyse the Romanov raw test data, it seems very likely that a judge would throw this 'irrefutable proof' out of court. So one can only conclude that in the case of the Romanov remains, this basic criterion has never been met. To this day, the working notes are still not available to the RECA and have, as a result, been kept away from the eyes of other scientists whose analysis might lead to different conclusions than those of the Russian Governmental Commission. The failure willingly to share the working notes for a process of discovery and assessment by the RECA and its scientists arguably lowers both the legal as well as the historical bar. For the present, coming to a clear verdict on the murder of eleven 'Christian victims of the revolution' appears out of reach. Given the historical importance of this case, we should expect that judicial review and ultimately justice would be demonstrated to prevail. But this may well prove to be impossible, for the samples in question – due to difficulties in authenticating the chain of custody alone – will probably never see the inside of a courtroom.

Another problem is the simple fact that, despite widespread media acceptance, experts agree that DNA evidence alone cannot at present (nor will it in the foreseeable future) be the sole factor in identifying an individual. Unlike an actual fingerprint, which is considered unique to the individual, the DNA profile, because it uses a minuscule fraction of the total DNA 'signature', is definitely not unique. It is roughly like trying to identify someone from only a small portion of his or her fingerprint. This is why DNA experts tend to avoid the use of the word 'fingerprinting' and refer instead to DNA typing or DNA profiling. For what the lab procedure provides is literally a profile of the DNA, an analysis of the types of variations it exhibits. Since the variations are not unique within a given population, the statistical analysis seeks to establish an estimate of the probability of identification and it is only the calculation of this probability that renders DNA useful as a forensic tool.[6] (See DNA Appendix.)

To review and analyse the handling and DNA testing of the Ekaterinburg Romanov remains I consulted Dr William Shields at the State University of New York at Syracuse.[7] A noted genetics expert, he has extensive experience reviewing forensic DNA analyses and is an official consultant to the National Alliance of Families of POWs and MIAs on the forensic use of mitochondrial

DNA (mtDNA). Dr Shields pointed out to me that the commonly held view of genetic profiling does not always accord with scientific fact.

Concerning the alleged Romanov remains in particular, Dr Shields emphasised that the demonstrated mtDNA match with Prince Philip cannot be accepted as proof of the identity of the Empress Alexandra and her children:

> Even if a mtDNA sequence matches that of Prince Philip, it doesn't mean that the person is his relative. For unrelated individuals can and do match at their mtDNA sequences. So one needs to know the frequency of matching Prince Philip's sequence with the general population before one can determine what it means that a particular mitochondrial sequence matches his, and how much weight to give it in terms of making a positive identification.[8]

In the overall scheme of a forensic analysis, DNA should be considered as one element – one compelling element, but nevertheless only one – in the forensic fabric. Defence lawyers are circumspect regarding DNA evidence. The prevailing perception among jurors is that an individual's DNA match at the scene of a crime is conclusive. Unfortunately, with the uneven weight given to DNA evidence, all other traditional forensic tools have been virtually cast aside. This dynamic has made the introduction of DNA evidence dicey, unless there is an unbroken chain of custody and other substantiation of the presumed perpetrator's whereabouts, motives, etc. A person can easily be implicated in a crime by simply placing his or her used cigarette butt at the scene.

The general approach to the DNA samples in the Romanov testing seems not to have taken these limitations fully into account. A number of other elements of sound investigative and legal diligence also appear to have been set aside.

Before jumping on the DNA bandwagon, Dr Shields pointed out that we should indeed review the very curious manner in which the samples of the 'Romanov' bones literally surfaced. The truth is, the entire circumstances surrounding the collection of the Romanov bones appears strange and their subsequent DNA analysis is open to further examination.

The two men who reportedly discovered the remains tell the following story: Early in the morning of 30 May 1979,[9] armed with directions in a document, allegedly written by Yakov Michaelovich Yurovsky, the man in charge of the infamous firing squad on that night in July 1918, Geli Ryabov, a mystery writer and film maker, and Alexander Avdonin, a geologist, dug up the bones in question. Accompanied by their wives and a couple of friends, they travelled to the site previously found by Avdonin and a fellow geologist, Michael Kachurov (who accidentally drowned in a river in Siberia not long after their discovery).[10] The group opened the grave, examined some skeletons and removed three skulls. They then recovered the grave and returned to Ekaterinburg. Why they removed the skulls is a mystery. Fear should have been their constant companion as the Soviet Union had not yet embraced *glasnost* at that time and surreptitious activities by private citizens could be extremely risky, even deemed treacherous. Nonetheless, they maintain that only in the summer of 1980 did they realise the possible consequences of their actions. They then reopened the grave and reburied the skulls. It was not until almost ten years later that they went public with their findings.

Their story sounds logical except that the area where they made their astounding find had been thoroughly searched previously by investigators, who certainly must have been very unlucky – for they had all failed to find the grave. Yet these investigators who conducted the searches in 1918 and 1919 spent a substantial amount of time and resources over a nine-month period, only to come up with minimal pieces of burned jewels, corset stays, animal bones and a finger as well as a fragment of a denture. Why the unexpected discovery of human bones others had missed? The timing of their find is particularly interesting when weighed with the following circumstances. Interest in the Romanovs' fate had led to the recent publication of a number of books in the West. John O'Conor's *The Sokolov Investigation*, in 1970, was the first serious work to question and examine extensively the traditional story of the Imperial family's deaths. O'Conor, an attorney by profession, translated parts of a report on the death of the Romanovs compiled by Nicholas Sokolov (The Sokolov Report), the last official investigator appointed in 1919 by the White, anti-Bolshevik officials in Ekaterinburg. O'Conor's book appended a comprehensive assessment of many Bolshevik testimonies, as well as a detailed forensic analysis of the evidence Sokolov included in his report. O'Conor's meticulous analysis revealed the incoherence and absurdity of many of Sokolov's conclusions, including the theory that the family's remains were burned. O'Conor suggested that the family, or at least the Tsarina and the daughters, may have been secretly removed to Perm, not far from Ekaterinburg, before the night of 17 July 1918.

Later in 1970, a New York reporter named Guy Richards followed up with *The Hunt for the Czar*, a book that, for the first time, mentioned the existence of an intriguing work published in July 1920, in San Francisco, entitled *Rescuing the Czar*. This latter book details a rescue of the family and, interestingly, was withdrawn from circulation less than a year after its publication, shortly after one of its translators had met the former head of the United States Secret Service. Richards's book further shook the underpinnings of the traditional account that all seven members of the Imperial family had died in July 1918 and the foundation cracked again when Anthony Summers and Tom Mangold, two BBC journalists, published *The File on the Tsar* in 1976, arguing that the assertion by Sokolov and the Bolsheviks that the family had been burned was a fabrication. Each of these books revealed more information and raised further questions regarding the then nearly sixty-year-old Bolshevik tale that the family had been burned and their 'ashes cast to the wind'. At a minimum, they showed that Sokolov's and the Bolsheviks' characterisations of these events were fundamentally flawed. What seems more likely is that Sokolov had in fact been an unwitting participant in a closely held but elaborate cover-up.

All this international attention was followed by another curious event. In 1977, less than twelve months after the publication of *The File on the Tsar*, the Soviet government, at the instigation of KGB chairman Yuri Andropov, ordered the razing of the Ipatiev House, the site of the purported murders. The official in charge of this operation was Boris Yeltsin, at the time Communist Party chief in the Ekaterinburg (Sverdlovsk) region. A crane and wrecking ball eliminated within a few hours any hopes of extracting further secrets from the 'House of Special Purpose'. Thus, the chronology: O'Conor's book in 1970; Richards's book in 1970; Summers's and Mangold's book in 1976; and the house in ruins in 1977, at the instigation of the KGB and the Politburo. Then, in 1979, comes the discovery of the bones.

It was not long after the Ipatiev House had disappeared that Avdonin and Ryabov say they began their search for the Romanov remains. The note by Yurovsky, the head of the guards, with its description of the murders of the Romanovs and directions to the burial site, surfaced in 1979, in time to aid them in their search (the text of the note is reproduced in chapter 11). According to Massie the note had been held all those years by Yurovsky's son Alexander, a retired vice-admiral in the Soviet Navy. Alexander maintained that he gave the handwritten note to Ryabov so that he could repent for 'the most horrible page' in his father's life. But, as the RECA pointed out, why would three men – a state-employed geologist, a writer/film maker, whose success was due in no small part to his government position and contacts which would imply clearances of some nature; and a retired high-ranking Soviet naval officer – risk their careers, their pensions and potentially their lives in pursuit of a goal which, if attained, could create problems for the state and incur the wrath of the then KGB or other authorities? One possibility is that they were instructed to do so. It seems highly coincidental that they should suddenly discover the remains near Ekaterinburg just after a series of compelling books had been published in the West calling into question the traditional rendition of the Romanovs' deaths.

In 1989 the official story was questioned once again. Mark Cocker, who wrote a biography of Richard Meinertzhagen, a former British intelligence operative, cited an entry in Meinertzhagen's diary in the Rhodes House Library at Oxford University, alluding to the escape of a daughter of the Imperial family. On 10 April[11] of the same year an article was published claiming the earlier discovery of the grave and included photographs of Ryabov posing with the putative skull of Nicholas's son, Alexei. Ryabov said he was the son of a peasant and that he was now a 'monarchist'.

Two years later, in 1991, the grave site was reopened for the last time and the remains removed for analysis. Evidently lacking sufficient funds for DNA testing, officials in Ekaterinburg called in Dr William Maples, a forensic anthropologist from the United States. Dr Maples concluded that Alexei and Anastasia were missing. Significantly, Maples also expressed some doubt that the accumulated bone fragments were sufficient to make up the eleven corpses that should have been in the mass grave. Understandably somewhat possessive, the Russian Federation initially refused to send the remains abroad for testing by Western scientists, but finally agreed to send them to England.

In 1993, Michael Occleshaw, a British writer was readying a book, *The Romanov Conspiracies*. It argued that a daughter had survived and was under the watchful eye of the British until she died in 1926 at the alleged age of twenty-eight. In July of the same year Dr Peter Gill's team at the British Home Office's Forensic Science Service (FSS) revealed the DNA findings.[12]

These findings, the funeral plans and a flurry of other facts supporting the murder story emerged as another book was scheduled to appear that might challenge the traditional history of the Romanovs' deaths. It is possible it was hoped that the discovery of the Romanov remains and the thorough DNA tests to come, would settle the controversy once and for all. But there were other tests in addition to the DNA analysis that appear not to have been conducted. For example, there is no evidence in any of the published reports of the work on the bones that any of the standard tests were carried out to date the remains. It appears that determining just how long they had been in the ground by a physical examination of the bone fragments is virtually impossible, because the bones are too 'young' to be carbon dated. However the published test results would have been expected to have made reference to an amino acid racemisation test, which checks for the radioactive isotopes that are present in the bones of any person living since the beginning of atmospheric atomic bomb testing in the 1940s.

If the announcement in 1995 of the DNA results by the Russian Governmental Commission did not silence its critics, outside the scientific community there were also continuing doubts over the authenticity of the remains. Andrei Golitsyn, the leader of the Russian Noble Assembly, charged that the Government Commission that had certified the identification of the bones had 'overlooked most questions that arouse doubts' or suggested 'explanations contradicting the official one'.

Peter Koltypin-Wallovskoy, Prince Alexis Scherbatow and Eugene Magerovsky, as representatives of the Russian Expert Commission Abroad, weighed in with their questions regarding the bones in a series of memoranda addressed to President Boris Yeltsin. Among the very pointed issues the Expert Commission queried was why the DNA examination did not appear to have attempted to explore the haemophilia condition that theoretically should have been present in the Empress and possibly all four of her daughters. The memoranda also pointed out that two teeth belonging to a teenager were located in the pit where the putative Romanov bones were found and Professor Vyacheslav L. Popov MD asserted that the teeth did not belong to 'any of the skeletons located therein'. The memorandum to Yeltsin advanced the following conclusion: 'The fact [of the non-matching teeth] may possibly point to the pit being a 'collective' mass burial and thus inadvertently raises a number of questions.'[13] And finally, the memorandum by the Commission appealed for a non-politicised independent body to evaluate the remains and all forensic evidence before proclaiming the bones those of the Romanovs. Their appeals fell on deaf ears.

Dr Zhivotovsky concurred that neither the labs nor the Russian Governmental Commission charged with certifying the authenticity of the remains have published conclusive evidence of a secure chain of custody. The discovery, transportation and storage of the remains have never been convincingly documented and recorded. Dr Shields feels that the lack of documentation raises speculations concerning the provenance of the bones. He suggested that: 'It would be easy to get samples from bones of either Nicholas or Alexandra's maternal relatives and use them to salt the gravesite in Ekaterinburg.'[14]

Dr Shields raises the possibility that Prince Michael, the Tsar's younger brother, who was supposedly taken away and shot outside Perm, not too far from Ekaterinburg and whose burial site is not known in the West and remains reportedly unknown in Russia, could have been used if someone had indeed known the location of his bones. Michael's bones could produce exactly the same result as the bones of Nicholas himself. In addition, Shields notes it is more than strange that numerous anthropologists have contended that there were not enough remains to construct nine bodies. The lack of sufficient vertebrae is the most disturbing.[15] And, he says, the possibility of contamination also could loom large.[16]

In a published paper by Dr Lev Zhivotovsky in the *Annals of Human Biology*, Dr Shields's doubts are supported.[17] Zhivotovsky expertly dissects the position taken by the official Russian Governmental Commission on the authenticity of the bones. He too is troubled by many anomalies and concludes that the 'chain of custody' for the remains is dubious at best; not all appropriate measures were taken to ascertain the provenance of the bones and the grave site was repeatedly disturbed. He suggests that other hypotheses – such as the fact that the bones could have belonged to other members of the family – were discarded or not even considered. Zhivotovsky also concludes that the so-called 1920 Yurovsky note is an unsigned document that contains 'important additions about the location of the grave manually inserted at a later date by a person or persons unknown, allegedly by a top-rank historian, Dr Pokrovsky'. In addition, Zhivotovsky is concerned that the DNA studies did not appear to reference data from the Russian populations, but from the United States and United Kingdom populations. He suggests that, given the origin of the family, genetic data from Danish and German populations would also have been in order.

Dr Zhivotovsky's paper also queries why the skull of the putative Nicholas lacks any indication of the wound he had received at the age of twenty-three. Attacked by a would-be assassin in Japan, in 1891, Nicholas suffered a severe blow to his head, leaving a two and a half inch gash.[18] Zhivotovsky even states, 'There are also some indications that the grave (where the "Romanov" bones were found) had been opened by the State Security services (KGB) in 1946 (Koltypin-Wallovskoy et al, 1998).'[19] In summary, Dr Zhivotovsky offered the following view:

> The investigation should be regarded as inconclusive because critically important historical information was not taken into account either in formulating alternative scenarios or when calculating the corresponding odds and match probabilities. Among these factors were attempts to hide evidence and to develop false clues about the murders, and the fact that the grave, which contained the remains, was not intact and some skulls and other bones may have been added to the grave, possibly even those of relatives of the alleged persons.[20]

At this time, in light of excellent systematic work by Zhivotovsky and Shields, the results of the DNA tests on the purported Romanov bones should be considered inconclusive. The grave site was opened several times compromising the identity of the bones before they were taken for DNA testing. The DNA testing itself was done pursuant to a methodology that cannot yield conclusive 'positive' identification.

Furthermore, taking into account all the anomalies regarding the bones, the RECA asserts that an objective court of law would never have arrived at the same conclusion as that of the official Russian

Governmental Commission. In all likelihood the case would have been thrown out prior to reaching the courts because of unreliable evidence. Until an independent commission has reviewed the raw data, the DNA evidence cannot be considered historically conclusive.

So now we are back where we have always been: a missing Imperial family, an unconvincing account of their murder – and a new set of bones, this time human bones, that still raise unanswered questions. In the coming pages, as the absurdities pile up, we shall see that it becomes increasingly difficult to embrace the official story of the Romanov murders. 'Eyewitness' reports cannot agree on the number of people murdered, whether the bones were buried or burned and their 'ashes cast to the wind'. 'Evidence' appears and disappears.

So the question remains, what really happened to the Romanovs? And why are there so many conflicting answers? Who stood to gain by having the world think the Romanovs had been killed? Who would have benefited if the Romanovs had been rescued and kept alive?

The answers play out on the stage of world politics. England, Germany, the United States, France, Czechoslovakia and Japan all had links to the Tsar and their own reasons for wanting the Imperial family to be freed. Each faction was well aware that any overt move in the midst of the First World War and the Russian Revolution would be politically dangerous. This book will demonstrate that a number of the people who planted the assorted accounts that endeavoured to explain the disappearance of the Imperial family had ulterior motives: King George V and Kaiser Wilhelm, secretly reluctant to turn their backs on their mutual cousins; the Allies, seeking enhanced opportunity for the repayment of huge Russian government debts; Lenin, using the Imperial family as pawns for his impoverished revolution. So, as a result, the versions promulgated to the public are riddled with implausibility, contradictions and absurd embellishments. In fact, the events proffered in the standard historical explanations of the night of 17 July 1918 simply could not have occurred as described.

Yet despite all the potential political fallout, a small but extra-ordinary group of politicians, invisible diplomats, intelligence operatives, an industrialist, and several members of British, European and Japanese royalty did, in fact, formulate plans for the safe removal of the Tsar and his family. These parties in interest helped to contribute to the confusion and obfuscation surrounding the Romanovs' demise. Ultimately, these same parties were successful in planting their own versions of the events of the night of 17 July 1918 – in the shadow of the Great War while the world looked the other way.

CHAPTER 1

Setting the Stage

Chaos and Fear

At the beginning of the twentieth century, the Romanov dynasty had ruled Russia for 300 years and Tsar Nicholas II was considered one of the wealthiest men in the world. Russia was an immense country comprising one-sixth of the world's land mass. The Tsar's recent construction of a railway across Russia had met with great enthusiasm. The Trans-Siberian Railway from European Russia to Vladivostok on the Pacific Ocean was thought to be the key to unlocking the vast mineral treasures of Siberia, thereby leading to economic expansion that would be similar to that of the American west.

However, the Russo-Japanese war of 1904–5 ended disastrously for Russia. On the domestic front, the mishandling of street demonstrations resulted in the bloody massacres of December 1905 which severely damaged Nicholas's reputation. These events generated a feeling of great unease during the last years of Nicholas's reign and even caused his allies to start questioning his ability as a successful political and military leader of Russia. Yet we shall see that once the Bolsheviks had taken power, these same individuals in various governments would find themselves working secretly to save the Tsar and his family, almost as if that would have been the lesser of two evils. Some however did act out of fidelity for a loyal ally, while still others acted out of family and personal considerations. But first, to comprehend further Russia's gradual slide into revolution, the Tsar's abdication and the uncertain future of Nicholas and his family during their last days in Ekaterinburg, let us return to the years just before the February Revolution. During the war years the Russian government, as well as the personal lives of Nicholas and Alexandra, were becoming more tumultuous and contentious with each passing day.

Courtiers, Germans and Bolshevik propagandists of every ilk had launched a barrage of unrelenting criticism against the Tsar and Tsarina. Nicholas had been weakened during the Great War and the universal enthusiasm and exuberance that had greeted the announcement of the war in August of 1914 had been replaced by despair, disgust and disillusionment among those upon whom Nicholas had relied in the past. This reversal was being felt throughout Europe but even more so in Russia, where millions of soldiers, badly equipped and frequently unarmed, had been slaughtered by German 'pounders' in the horrible trenches of the Eastern front. Nicholas's decision, in August of 1915, to assume the role of commander-in-chief and more or less to exile the former military commander, his uncle Grand Duke Nicholas, to Tiflis, Georgia led to inefficiency and military disasters.

These military disasters and the intense propaganda resulted in cementing the overwhelmingly negative portrait of the Romanovs. Many Russians believed that the peasant and self-styled 'holy man' Gregory Rasputin and the Tsarina, rather than the Tsar, were now running the country. Both the Bolsheviks and the Germans used these rumours as the basis of their assaults aimed at destabilising the Tsar and Tsarina in the hope they would force Russia out of the war. All Nicholas's and Alexandra's antagonists made great use of this negative perception and prevailing atmosphere. The regime was crumbling around the Imperial family.

Nicholas and Alexandra were not without blame and their refusal to sever their relationship with Rasputin did continue to fuel the ever-increasing intrigues surrounding them. The Romanovs' image of insensitivity was seized on and enhanced. The concern over Rasputin's influence on the Imperial family had created an environment where the palace intrigues among the Tsar's courtiers, and even some members of his family, were more prevalent and vicious than at any time in his reign.

Yet Alexandra, motivated by the love of her child, and Nicholas, who appeared to want nothing more than to be a 'family man', continued to turn a blind eye and a deaf ear to most of the criticism. What the detractors did not know – and what only a few within Nicholas's and Alexandra's inner circle knew – was that the heir apparent suffered from a life-threatening illness diagnosed as haemophilia. Nicholas and Alexandra were desperate to save him – by any means – and Rasputin had convinced them that he and he alone, through God's help, could quell the tragic course of the disease that held their son in its grasp. It remains an enigma to this day as to how the 'mad monk' was able to assuage the symptoms of the disease and bring relief to a child who was obviously in physical pain and whose life was imperilled. Over the years this close relationship led to rumours that the 'holy man' had an undue political influence over, if not a sensual relationship with, the Tsarina. While there appears to be no basis in fact to the sexual innuendo, it was maintained that this 'relationship' had the tacit approval and even the blessing of Nicholas.

Ultimately the tongue-wagging and unrest were so widespread that some members of the court felt compelled to take action. Prince Felix Yusupov, scion of one of Russia's wealthiest families, masterminded a plan to murder Rasputin in order to end his perceived domination over Alexandra and the Tsar. He was aided by one of the Tsar's closest relatives: his nephew Duke Dmitrii Pavlovich. Vladimir Mitrofanovich Purishkevich, who had publicly called to 'get rid of Rasputin', completed the triangle. A letter cited by Richard Pipes in one of his many books about the Russian Revolution offers insight into the state of mind of Yusupov. His correspondence to Vasilii Alekseevich Maklakov, a Duma member, speculates about the Tsarina and in the end he asserts: 'Her spiritual balance depends entirely on Rasputin: the instant he is gone, it will disintegrate. And once the Emperor has been freed of Rasputin's and his wife's influence, everything will change: he will turn into a good constitutional monarch.'[1]

Yusupov was to administer Rasputin's death sentence on the night of 16 December, 1916. The plan was executed, but not without complications. Yusupov and his colleagues first attempted to poison Rasputin. The monk was not very accommodating and it was said he did not die of the poison he had ingested. So they shot him. Then they cast him into the icy river. With Rasputin gone, a fresh wind might have swept away the innuendoes, exaggerations, falsehoods and outright lies regarding the relationship of the family to the controversial mystic. It was not to be.

Shortly after the murder Alexandra wrote to Nicholas, 'I cannot and won't believe. He has been killed. God have mercy.'[2] From her

17

perspective the life of her only son, Alexei had been held in Rasputin's 'healing' hands. In the final analysis the Empress was mournful and fearful after Rasputin's murder. However, the plan concocted by Yusupov to demoralise her was not fully successful. She did not suffer the emotional collapse he had anticipated.

In retrospect, one of Nicholas's and Alexandra's greatest short-comings was an altogether too common human failing – the overprotection of a child. They refused to admit to his future subjects that Alexei suffered from a physical handicap, afraid that if a member of the monarchy expressed normal human emotions or suffered from a physical disability, the knowledge of the condition would somehow diminish the dynasty. The 'divine right of kings' was at play: since the heir was believed to be God's representative on earth, he could not be perceived as weak physically or mentally.

In addition, the Romanovs made tactical mistakes in their attempts to respond to the challenge that was being posed by their own courtiers. The assaults to their rule went largely unanswered. Nicholas and Alexandra appeared to be too isolated and therefore seemed uncaring, which further reduced the little sympathy they were inspiring. While alive, they were seldom forgiven for their human lapses. Perhaps history might have been different had the family made their son's weakness known. But their refusal to do so exacerbated the negative atmosphere. However, acknowledgement of Alexei's frailties could possibly have diminished the mysterious hold and emotional blackmail that Rasputin exercised over the family and therefore the empire. Certainly Russia was fraught at the time with mysticism and this atmosphere contributed to Nicholas's and Alexandra's plight.

Only two months after Rasputin's death, and just two weeks before Nicholas's abdication, he and Alexandra again came into conflict with a member of their family. A telling confrontation with Grand Duke Alexander Michaelovich (Sandro), the husband of Nicholas's sister Zenia, unmasks some of the tensions that existed. The perception throughout all social classes, including the nobility, was that the country had been run, not by an enlightened autocrat, but through the arbitrary influence Rasputin exerted over Nicholas and especially Alexandra. Now, with Rasputin gone and the Tsar supposedly free of his influence, Sandro expressed his continuing consternation over Nicholas's actions to his brother, Grand Duke

Nicholas Michaelovich, in a letter penned while on a train on 14 February 1917:

> ... In my conversation with A and N, I also touched on two subjects, which have been raised by Protopopov, the expropriation of landowners' land in favor of the peasants and equal rights for the Jews. It's typical that Alix did not voice any protest on these questions, while he [Nicholas] objected to the first and then appeared confused about the second, replying that it was equality only in the sense of a widening of the Pale of Settlement; I protested as strongly as I could, saying that concessions or new rights for the Jews were unthinkable, that we could not afford to be merciful to a race which the Russian people hate even more now because of their negative attitude towards the war and outright treason; it was noticeable that Alix didn't protest, obviously such protests do exist. Knowing the position Alix defends is that of Tsar and people, I tried to demonstrate to her that the people are not as she thinks, that it is difficult to draw a line between where the people begin and the other class ends, that the people need to be led, and consequently it is essential to have another estate to bring the people in line, otherwise leaders will emerge who will incite the people against them. She kept insisting that the people are loyal to them and that she has many proofs of this, as she did, she lay back on the cushions and rolled her eyes. The only question on which she and I were in agreement was freedom of the press with the most stringent laws against slander; here she turned to N and said: 'I always told you that such a law was necessary.' The whole conversation had taken place in English ... By the way, I strongly advised Nicky to return as soon as possible to the Stavka [at Mogilev], at which point she interrupted the conversation and said that he could not return now, as matters in Petrograd had to be settled.[3]

Sandro's dissatisfaction is revealed in another meeting where he told Alexandra that he was 'deeply upset' that their conversation had resulted in 'absolutely nothing'. He had hoped she would be an 'ally' to help him convince Nicholas that he was taking the wrong course. He said that he would continue to write to her because he was being 'driven to despair'.

Seemingly unaware of how serious the assault to his rule had become, Nicholas returned to his headquarters at Mogilev just after the encounter, obviously disregarding Alexandra's advice to stay in Petrograd. On 23 February a revolution started in the streets of Petrograd. Several thousand female textile workers protested and were immediately joined by thousands of revolutionary demonstrators. In three days, more than 250,000 working men and women filled the streets of Petrograd. The long fall into the abyss commenced on the fourth day when, instead of containing the demonstrators, or ordering them home, the Petrograd garrison – which until that time had been loyal to the Tsar – joined them.[4]

At the Tsar's headquarters at Mogilev, the first telegram describing the disorders arrived on 27 February. Nicholas called for the Imperial train to return to Petrograd, but obstacles were put in his way that prevented him from proceeding. The train was not ready before midnight and then it took six more hours to clear the line. The following afternoon the train stopped because a bridge had been destroyed. A different route was attempted and when it reached Pskov, a town south-west of Petrograd, a deputation from the Duma was waiting for the unsuspecting Tsar. Without any formalities or courtesies, they immediately asked for his abdication in favour of his son Alexei, with his brother Grand Duke Michael as Regent. Nicholas learned nearly simultaneously that all the army group commanders had declared in favour of his abdication. He asked if he and his family could leave for the Crimea, but was informed that his son Alexei would have to remain behind with his people.[5]

Once again, in the throes of an extremely traumatic moment in Nicholas's life, his concern for Alexei's welfare had been at the forefront. Pierre Gilliard, the family tutor, reported in his memoirs that on 2 March, as the Tsar wrestled with the decision to abdicate and leave the throne in the hands of Alexei, he sought the counsel of Professor Fedorov: 'Tell me frankly, Sergei Petrovich, is Alexei's malady incurable?'[6]

The response was not reassuring and Gilliard says the Tsar hung his head and sadly murmured: 'That's just what the Tsarina told me. Well, if that is the case and Alexei can never serve his country as I should like him to, we have the right to keep him to ourselves.'[7]

Faced with the demands of the leaders of what was shortly to become the Provisional Government and with a vote of no confidence by his military leaders, Nicholas turned over the reins of power to his brother Grand Duke Michael Alexandrovich on '2 March 1917 at 3.05 p.m'.[8] Grand Duke Michael, who had insisted that the Russian people and the Provisional Government approve his elevation to the throne, was also undone when his supporters reached the frank realisation that placing him on the throne at that point would be a mistake. Less than two days later, his abdication followed on 4 March. Nicholas, overwhelmed, then submitted four demands to General Alexeev (one of the generals who would later become embroiled in an Allied banking scheme, which would serve as a conduit for funds to erect a safe house for the Tsar and his family in Murmansk): allow him to proceed unimpeded to his palace in Tsarskoe Selo with his retinue; allow his family to reside safely at Tsarskoe Selo until the children's recovery from measles; allow the family to proceed unimpeded to Romanov-on-the-Murman (Murmansk) with the same persons; and finally, at the war's end, allow the family to settle in the Crimea at the Livadia Palace.[9] He received no response.

On 7 March, in Journal No. 10 of the Provisional Government, the demands of Nicholas were discussed. General Alexeev was 'instructed to assemble a detail to guard the abdicated Emperor', who was to be declared under arrest and delivered to Tsarskoe Selo. Additional resolutions included instructing members of the Duma who were accompanying him to submit a written report when they completed their assignment and to 'promulgate the present resolution'.

The tragic result of these few days of intense political manoeuvring was that the fledgling 'democracy' spun out of control. The machinations of various factions, including the German and Bolshevik propagandists as well as some of the Tsar's closest relatives, contributed to the collapse of the Russian Empire and the ultimate disruption of the texture of Russian life, which had already been tattered and torn. As we shall see, Nicholas's allies may also have had an indirect influence on the last days of the Tsar's reign, but as they eventually realised the full impact of an imploding Russia they will move surreptitiously to extract Nicholas and his family in the vain hope that a constitutional monarchy will restabilise the demoralised country.

CHAPTER 2

Parties In Interest

The International Arena

While the February Revolution and the Tsar's abdication did not come as a complete surprise to the international community, political events of this magnitude tend to reorder all participants. The word revolution implies the unpredictable and the unpredictable is often fraught with problems. So it was with the Russian Revolution, which quickly demonstrated that it was not going to play out as the many factions had expected. In addition to political circumstances, Germany, the Allies and Japan, as well as several other nations, still had ties to the Tsar that influenced their reaction to the revolution and shaped behind-the-scenes intrigues. As we shall see later, the manoeuvres, which grew from these considerations, generated a chain of activities in the various countries that have remained mysterious, and virtually untraceable until now. However, to gain an understanding of these considerations, it is first necessary to examine some of the attitudes of the leaders of these countries vis-à-vis Russia.

Most governments in the West were hoping that when the new Provisional Government seized power it would revitalise the faltering Russian war machine. In fact, the Provisional Government that took over after the Tsar's abdication did bring to power aristocratic leaders, such as Prince Lvov, who were committed to continuing the war with Germany. The Allies breathed a sigh of relief, since unfounded rumour had it that Nicholas might sign a separate peace with Germany and leave them in the lurch. But to the German government the revolution of February 1917 represented a defeat. The Germans had their own plans for Russia and those plans did not include the new Provisional Government.

For some time Germany had been scheming with various revolutionary groups to destabilise Russia and force her out of the war. The principal aim of German foreign policy was to isolate the enemy (i.e. Britain and France) and conclude a separate peace with Russia, thereby transforming the Great War into a one-front conflict. To that end the Germans found a common interest with uncommon bedfellows – the Bolsheviks: Germany believed the Bolsheviks, whose rank and file was largely composed of factory workers and some peasants, could be relied upon to throw Russia into turmoil. But since Germany, like England, was an empire, support of the Bolsheviks was not only an extreme position, but one which had to be kept cloaked from public view.

In fact, the Bolsheviks were also capable of double dealing and casting aside any scruples about relying heavily on Imperial Germany's support to fuel their proletarian revolution. But despite the two sides' distrust of each other, the Germans could find no other political group in Russia in 1917 that seemed likely to fulfil their objective of eliminating Russia from the war.

Documents discovered since the war reveal that even the Bolshevik leaders (who only months later, in October, would execute a successful coup by toppling the Provisional Government) were in the pay of the Germans. This is an allegation that was trumpeted by the Allied propaganda of the period, but one which, until recently, was thought to have been discredited. However, Dr Richard Pipes's work has comprehensively confirmed this relationship.[1] It seems that the Bolsheviks, while largely co-operating with the Germans, found subservience to them irksome and did their best to evade many of their demands. These tactics were not always successful, especially when the financial stakes were high and, in spite of all the manoeuvring, acquiescence was generally the order of the day. Working through their diplomatic legations in Copenhagen and Stockholm, the Germans used the offices of a long-time revolutionary, Alexander Israel Helphand, known as Parvus, to advise them on the situation within Russia and to form their links with the Bolsheviks.

Following the advice of Parvus, the German embassy in Switzerland began negotiating with Lenin and his fellow exiles for their return to Russia. Lenin was anxious that the Bolsheviks should not be seen as Germany's tool and drove a hard bargain:[2] the Russian émigrés were to be exchanged for German civilians interned in Russia, and the train on which they travelled was to have extraterritorial status and be free from passport controls. Lenin's party, which numbered thirty-two, left Zurich station on 27 March 1917, and reached the Baltic on the 30th. Lenin's entry into Petrograd on 3 April was dramatic. It was the final day of the All-Russian Bolshevik Conference. He was greeted by a band playing the 'Marseillaise' and crowds of supporters, whom he addressed from the body of an armoured car that was thoughtfully illuminated by a projector. The very next day the German agent in Stockholm wired Berlin, 'Lenin's entry into Russia successful. He is working exactly as we desire.'[3]

Lenin's activities continued to require funding. Bolshevik propaganda cost money. The German ties and their importance were succinctly expressed by German State Secretary von Kuhlmann who summed up the progress to date in a memorandum to the High Command of the German Army in September 1917:

> The military operations on the Eastern front, which were prepared on a large scale and have been carried out with great success, were seconded by intensive undermining activities inside Russia on the part of the Foreign Ministry.
>
> Our first interest, in these activities, was to further nationalist and separatist endeavours as far as possible and to give strong support to the revolutionary elements. We have now been engaged in these activities for some time, and in complete agreement with the Political Section of the General Staff (Capt. von Hulsen). Our work together has shown tangible results. The Bolshevik movement could never have attained the scale or the influence which it has today without our continual support.[4]

Throughout 1917, considerable sums reached the Bolsheviks through the German embassy in Stockholm, much of it via the hands of Kurt Riezler, a Bavarian career diplomat who was the Russian expert stationed at the embassy.[5] Riezler would later become a member of the German mission in Moscow under Count Wilhelm von Mirbach.[6] Just weeks before the family disappeared, von Mirbach would, at the Kaiser's request, press Lenin over the safety of the Romanov 'princesses' who were at the time in Ekaterinburg.

The diplomatic corps and the general staff were not the only entities that applied pressure on Russia to pull out of the war. Two years earlier, Germany's Crown Prince appears to have tried to negotiate with Nicholas. He wrote to the Tsarina's brother, the Grand Duke of Hesse:

> I am of the opinion that it is absolutely necessary to conclude a separate peace with Russia. First of all, it is too silly that we should hack each other to pieces only so that England could fish in dark waters, and then we would have to get all our forces back here, so that we could put the French in order, because this protracted stationary war costs much sacrifice, and it does not improve the morale of our troops. Could you not establish contact with Nikki [the Tsar] and advise him to agree with us amicably, the desire for peace is apparently very great in Russia – only we would have to get rid of that bastard Nikolai Nikolaevitch . . . [who was Nicholas's uncle].

Approaches from German members of Alexandra's family were not new. It is also believed that the Crown Prince's initiative resulted in the Grand Duke of Hesse travelling secretly to Russia in 1916 and speaking to the Tsar. While nothing came of the mission – Germany and Russia remained locked in war – it shows that secret dynastic missions could and did take place, and it led to important developments in Germany's strategy against Russia. High-stakes politics were being played out at every turn.[7]

While Germany was furiously trying to undermine the Provisional Government, many American and British officials believed the new government represented Russian enlightenment. In the initial view of the Americans and the administration of President Woodrow Wilson, the revolution of February 1917 had shifted Russia into an ideal position. By installing a progressive governing body, Russia could evolve from an autocratic country into one that could take its place at the table of democratic nations. In fact, according to the Duke of Leuchtenberg, one of Nicholas's relations and closest advisers, the revolution had been engineered with the aid of American money,[8] though not necessarily United States government money. Many Romanovs generally believed that money from the great American banking houses had financed the overthrow of the Tsar.

The international banking community, consisting *inter alia* of Kuhn and Loeb in America and the Rothschild banking house of Germany, were rumoured to have been significant supporters of the

Bolshevik efforts in Russia. The Russian autocracy had long victimised the Jews and the opportunity to deal the old regime a fatal blow would have been welcomed by some Jewish bankers in the United States. The American Jewish banker Jacob Schiff, of Kuhn and Loeb, apparently had personal reasons for supporting the overthrow of the Tsar. Trotsky had supposedly been in the company of Schiff during his stay in America and some historians, without proof, contend that the banker personally financed the fiery leader. But one thing is for certain: Schiff was in support of the Provisional Government in 1917.[9] Dominique Venner, in his book *Les Blancs et les Rouges*, published in Paris in 1997, quotes a telegram sent in April 1917 by Schiff to Paul Miliukov, then Minister for Foreign Affairs of the Provisional Government: 'Allow me as the enemy of the tyrannical autocracy that mercilessly persecuted people of my faith to congratulate you and the Russian people.'[10]

Schiff had played a large part in financing the successful Japanese war effort against Russia in 1904–5.[11] In 1915, when Lord Reading, later British ambassador to the United States, was trying to raise a loan for the Entente powers in America, Schiff had made his contribution to the loan conditional upon 'not a penny of the money going to Tsarist Russia'. The plan backfired because Reading, who was also Jewish, would not tolerate any condition that excluded an ally. Subsequently, Schiff was subjected to virulent attacks in the press for being pro-German.[12] Perhaps Schiff was initially supportive of the revolution, but we shall see that by the end of 1917 many Zionist leaders would be offering their support to overthrow the Bolshevik government.[13]

In America, Woodrow Wilson had been elected President on a platform that promised the country that the United States would continue its isolationist attitude and sit out the Great War. As America played a waiting game, one of President Wilson's closest advisers stepped forward and, as a result of his long-standing friendship with the leaders of the new Provisional Government, began to urge Wilson to modify America's policy towards Russia. As we shall see, the overthrow of the Tsarist regime and the establishment of a democratic government could also open the way for the United States to enter the war at the side of another democratic, not autocratic, power.

Charles Crane, the Chicago industrialist, multimillionaire owner of Crane Plumbing and the man who would become critical not only to America's Russian Policy but also to the Romanov saga, was considered one of the most knowledgeable Americans on Russian affairs. Although asked to assume the ambassadorship to Russia, Crane declined for personal reasons. He did, however, become the architect of Wilson's Russian policy. On the President's behalf, Crane had hand-picked Wilson's ambassador to Russia, George T. Marye of San Francisco, and Professor Samuel Harper, who accompanied Marye. At Harper's father's urging Crane had also endowed the University of Chicago with funds for a Russian Department. Crane became one of the men who helped engineer Wilson's re-election and when Marye resigned, Crane once again anointed the future ambassador, David Francis of St Louis, who was subsequently confirmed.[14]

Crane first became acquainted with the country he would come to love in 1888, when he was the guest of his cousin Thomas Smith, the son of his maternal uncle Samuel, who lived in Moscow and was close to the court. Writing from Moscow, Crane expressed his interest in many facets of Russian life.[15]

By the time of his visit in 1894 to St Petersburg, where he resided at the Grand Hotel d'Europe, Crane could write of his closeness to the inner circle of the Tsar's and Tsarina's court.[16] His friendship with Count Rostovstov, the Tsarina's private secretary who looked after the personal fortunes of the Imperial family,[17] was established around that time and would grow over the years to become his closest relationship in Russia. Crane was such a frequent guest in Rostovstov's house that pictures of Crane's family were always on the dresser to greet him.[18] In one of his letters, he reassured his wife that 'Count Rostovstoff has fully lived up to the estimate you know I have held him in and devotes himself to me and my affairs all of the time.'[19] The extent of intimacy Crane and Rostovstov would come to enjoy would have repercussions for the Imperial family in its final days. Crane's closeness to other courtiers is also demonstrated by his following correspondence from Russia:

Last evening I dined with Mr Peter Siemonoff once more and after the dinner, when we were alone in the library, he gave me a most interesting account of the most critical time in the history of the Emancipation Commission – the time of the death of the great Count Rostovtsoff [*sic*]. Mr Siemonoff and the Emperor Alexander II were present at the death at 3.00 in the morning and the Count died in the arms of the Emperor. For some days before his death the Count prepared his will regarding [the] process of Emancipation and Siemonoff wrote it. As soon as the Count had passed away the Emperor told Mr Siemonoff to come to him the next day at 10.00. At that time there were strong efforts to break up the work of the Committee. The Emperor assembled the Committee at once and made a very brief address in which he told them that Count Rostovtsoff's Will was to be made their law and the great work went on.[20]

Crane's letters continue to illuminate his flourishing associations with men such as Prince Galitzin, whom he called the 'most extraordinary man I have ever seen . . . one of the great military men of Russia and Governor of the Urals'. He was quite taken that Galitzin 'has gone all over Asiatic Russia and Western China on horseback'. He became so familiar with these fascinating men that he even travelled to Turkestan to visit Count Rostovstov and the Count's brother, when they resided there for several years.[21] The full significance of this will become apparent in later chapters but it is interesting to note here that the curious book *Rescuing the Czar* – an intriguing tome published in the United States detailing the Imperial family's survival and subsequent trek through Turkistan, China, and on to Ceylon via Japan – maintained it was in Turkistan that the family had been briefly hidden when they fled Ekaterinburg 'after the murders'.

Crane's influence and fortunes continued to grow during the construction of the Tsar's Trans-Siberian Railway begun in 1891. He became responsible for negotiating the contract for a joint venture between the Crane Company and Westinghouse for air brakes on the railway. At the height of the Russo-Japanese War in 1905, Crane persuaded the Westinghouse Company to donate a considerable sum to the Tsarina's hospital for the sick and wounded. A reply conveying the Tsarina's thanks came through her financial secretary and Crane's close friend, Rostovstov.[22] Years later, in 1917, Rostovstov, still in the family's service, would be called upon to account to the Bolsheviks for the financial position of the Romanovs. [23]

During his nearly twenty trips to Russia from 1888 to the time of the Revolution, Crane also became intimate with numerous members of the future Provisional Government. He was a Christian

Progressive in much the same mould as Woodrow Wilson, and his letters reveal that he attended meetings in Kiev with Prince George Lvov (the first leader of the Provisional Government and the one who would ask England to grant the Romanovs asylum), Alexander Guchkov (one of the Duma leaders) and an unknown Mr Romanov in the summer of 1917. Prior to the meetings, he had discussed with Guchkov the direction that the new government would take in the: '. . . organization of the land owners to prepare for the constitutional assembly and act generally together in view of the extensive social changes that are being projected . . .'[24]

From Crane's correspondence of 1916–17, it is more than apparent that the leaders of the February Revolution certainly enjoyed his support and, because of his closeness to President Wilson, the de facto support of the American government. So, from the tenor of Crane's correspondence of the period, it is not surprising that, when Nicholas abdicated and the Provisional Government assumed the reins of power, it was one of Crane's hand-picked men, David Francis, the American ambassador in Russia, who rushed through the recognition of the Provisional Government thereby allowing the United States to be the first country officially to extend diplomatic relations. Britain followed close behind.

Also later in the summer of 1917, while still in Russia, Crane gladly accepted an appointment by President Wilson to the Root Commission led by Elihu Root, which was formed to assess the new Kerensky government that had taken over after Prince Lvov's resignation. Although the other members of the commission were initially enthusiastic about the Kerensky government, Crane became disillusioned. The Bolsheviks were beginning to gain power within the second Provisional government under Alexander Kerensky and his correspondence to his daughter expressed dismay about what happened to an art school in Petrograd that he had supported:

In Petrograd I went to luncheon almost every day at Miss Schneider's really wonderful art school. The school and her sister were out in the country at the hospital they are directing. But the socialist soldiers who lived across the street from the school were very threatening and said they were going to move into the school and throw all of the art models out of the window. They said new Russia was only interested in force and not in art. Fortunately they revolted just the day they were to move in, were disbanded and for the moment the school is saved. As the graduates of the school all go to the Semstvos, or country governments, to help the people in their Koustarny (or home) art work, there is a certain amount of sympathy for Miss Schneider's work among the more enlightened of the Socialists, even though her school was built and maintained by the Empress. But generally the revolutionary movement is almost hostile to art of all kinds.[25]

After the commission departed from Russia he remained behind and his letters indicate that he was increasingly disturbed by what he was witnessing.

Like Woodrow Wilson, Crane had subscribed to the concept of self-determination for nations. But now his belief was being tested to the limit by the earth-shattering realisation of Russia's potentially doomed future and the jeopardy in which his Russian friends and the Imperial family were finding themselves. His misgivings, when shared with President Wilson, appeared to have had a great influence on Wilson's desire to become quietly pro-active in Russia. Crane's change of opinion regarding the new government had caused concern at the highest levels.

By late 1917 the situation no longer seemed as simple as it had in late 1916 and early 1917 when it was believed that Russia, under the new leadership of the Provisional Government, was on its way to democracy and a full resumption of the war against Germany and Austria. It had originally been thought that the Tsar and Tsarina could, if thought prudent, perhaps be reintroduced as constitutional monarchs or, if not, it was envisaged that they could leave quietly for England. At that time the possibility of events to come in Ekaterinburg must never have entered anyone's mind. However Crane and the United States government were still clearly becoming increasingly concerned and filled with apprehension about the future of Russia. And they were not the only ones.

If there was a city where the fall of the Russian monarchy in and of itself could be expected to cause dismay, it was London. Not only had Nicholas proved to be a loyal ally in the war against Germany, but he and Alexandra were also tied to the British in a web of familial relations. They were both first cousins of King George V. The King's mother, Queen Alexandra, was the sister of Nicholas's mother, the Dowager Empress Marie, making Queen Alexandra the Tsar's aunt. The King's father, Edward VII, was the brother of the

Tsarina's mother, Alice of Hesse, making Edward the Tsarina's uncle. Also Edward VII's sister, Victoria, had married Frederick III of Prussia, making the Tsarina's mother Alice aunt to their son, Kaiser Wilhelm. And finally the Tsar's mother, Marie, was sister to the Queen Mother Alexandra, the Kaiser's aunt. The inter-webbing of European and Russian royalty was extensive and such intimate interconnections were not ties that England or Germany wished to be scrutinised as their nations clashed.

But, in fact, that is exactly what happened. World revolution was in the wind and anti-monarchical feelings were on the rise. Negotiations for the Romanovs' safe passage to England had been undertaken by Prince Lvov, the then head of the Provisional Government (the same man who we shall see, in December 1918 spread his false first-hand account of the murder of the Imperial family) and Alexander Kerensky, its Minister of Justice, on 8 March 1917, old style calendar – 21 March, new style, after Nicholas had been arrested. The Coalition Government, under Prime Minister David Lloyd George, had reason to fear providing a safe haven for King George's, not to mention the Kaiser's, relatives. With the ever-present threat of strikes led by militant socialist workers capable of bringing industry to a standstill, Lloyd George could not act overtly to grant asylum to the Romanovs. Coupled with his fears were the misgivings of the British royal family itself. The English Civil War, which had led to the absence of a monarch for nearly a decade, along with the more recent events of the French Revolution, and now Nicholas's predicament, had demonstrated how fragile even a significant long-standing monarchical structure could become under the rapidly changing dynamics of a troubled political climate. There was absolutely no doubt in George V's mind that royalty had been and could be rapidly swept from its revered pedestal. So the negotiations for bringing the family to England were to die a slow death. For Britain as a nation, the Romanovs were a decidedly difficult and thorny issue.

Queen Alexandra's personal concern for the family was the first to show itself in the official record. Arthur Balfour, the Foreign Secretary, was moved to write a memorandum to the Queen's private secretary, Sir Arthur Davidson, on an aspect of the case which might not immediately have occurred to the King – namely, the feelings of the Queen Mother, who had been given the substance of a telegram from the British ambassador in Petrograd, Sir George

Buchanan, on the fall of the monarchy in Russia.

The Queen Mother had been sending messages of support and sympathy to her sister, the Tsar's mother, and this worried both the British government and the Russian Provisional Government. Balfour stated, 'The Government are very apprehensive lest it be thought that influence is being exerted from England in order to restore the Imperial regime.'[26] The problem was that if the Revolutionary Committee – the Petrograd Soviet – thought that a foreign power was intervening to support the old regime, then the Anglo-Russian alliance and Russia's continuation in the war might be swept away in a flood of anger. This would be a disaster without parallel. In addition to these political and military consequences, Balfour acknowledged: 'The safety also of the whole Imperial Family depends in great measure on the strictest and most careful avoidance of any form of interference or expression of opinion by England, especially from the King, the Queen and Queen Alexandra. Even the simplest messages of sympathy may easily be distorted into political views or actions.'[27]

On 19 March 1917 Paul Miliukov, the Russian Provisional Government's first Foreign Minister, asked Sir George Buchanan how the British would take the Tsar and his family out of Russia into exile in Britain, naturally assuming that the British had a plan. But no such plans existed and an embarrassed Buchanan could only reply to Miliukov that he would raise the question with the Foreign Office in London.

In London, reaction was swift. On 22 March the Imperial War Cabinet met to consider the matter and reported back the same day at another meeting attended by Prime Minister Lloyd George himself. The decision was taken to offer asylum in Britain to the Tsar and his family until the end of the war. A telegram to this effect was sent to St Petersburg the same day, with the caveat, however, that Sir George had to emphasise that the invitation had been extended at the express request of the Provisional Government. With the invitation made, everything now seemed set for Nicholas and his family to travel into dignified exile in England.

All over Europe the strain on society imposed by the war had brought many countries close to breaking point. The monstrous scale of the casualties, the shortages – leading to potential starvation – and the increasingly apparent pointlessness of the war had created a fertile soil for unrest

The spring of 1917 saw this unrest spreading throughout Europe. It had reached its climax in Russia, but rulers and masses across Europe knew that no state could hope to continue fighting the war if its people did not support it. Britain was no more immune to this trend than the rest of Europe. The Chief of the Imperial General Staff, General Sir William Robertson, wrote to the Commander-in-Chief in France, Field Marshal Sir Douglas Haig, that 'I am afraid there is no getting away from the fact that there is some unrest in the country now as a result, partly, of the Russian Revolution. There have been some bad strikes recently, and there is still much discontent.'[28]

Meanwhile the King was receiving many letters opposing the idea of Nicholas coming to Britain and his own misgivings appear to have been increasing.[29] Ultimately Buchanan was advised to avoid pursuing the matter further, on the grounds that: 'There are indications that a considerable anti-monarchical movement is developing here, including personal attacks upon the King. Part of the ground of the attacks is that he supported the ex-Emperor and King Constantine of Greece. It is thought that if the emperor comes here it may dangerously increase this movement.[30]

As if to take some of the unpleasantness out of Buchanan's position, it was suggested that it would be a better idea if the family went to France instead. On 15 April Buchanan replied that he fully agreed with the new plan. However, the French would not entertain the notion, allegedly because of stories still circulating that the Tsarina had been spying for and in league with the Germans. French public opinion held her responsible for the defeats of the Russian armies and, by association, with the fact that the French had spent a lot more blood in the effort to defeat the Germans than they otherwise would have.

Nevertheless, letters continued to be passed between the royal relatives. As Buchanan told Balfour on 9 April: 'I see no reason however why I not as in the past forward any letters which I may receive from members of the Imperial family to their relatives in England as this cannot compromise Government but recipients might be warned to keep receipt of such letters secret.[31]

Feelings were running high and in 1917, with the war at its height, the King was clearly very sensitive about his foreign relations. In July 1917 George decreed that the family name would change from the German Saxe-Coburg-Gotha to the very English Windsor. The change of name and the opposition to the Romanovs coming to

Britain were clearly an attempt on the part of George to distance himself from the Imperial family. All these machinations effectively undermined any remaining inclination on the part of the War Cabinet to keep the invitation open. In Petrograd Sir George Buchanan found himself in an awkward position. Ultimately it was felt that accepting the Romanovs in England could jeopardise the very heart of England's democracy and the monarchy as well. The offer was withdrawn.

However, there is a vast difference between publicly withdrawing an official offer of sanctuary and personally abandoning a cousin, who is the former head of an allied nation. On a familial level King George appeared to be as concerned about the Imperial family as he had always been. The correspondence between George and Nicholas, preserved in the Central State Museum in Moscow, shows that they remained personally very close.[32]

But between the time of the proposal to bring Nicholas to England and the night of 17 July 1918 in Ekaterinburg, the Imperial family is seldom mentioned in existing records of exchanges between the King and his ministers. One instance was in the summer of 1917 when George asked the Foreign Office whether it was true that Nicholas had been taken to Tobolsk, and another was in May 1918 when he asked the Foreign Office to see that the family were treated well.

However, the King's behaviour in similar situations during this period suggests that there was probably more going on than met the eye. George was a man of honour. At least three times he had extended his protection to sovereigns who were more distantly related to him than Nicholas and Alexandra. For example, he agreed to a secret Allied plan to rescue the Romanian royal family when it was threatened with capture by the victorious Germans in the winter of 1917.[33] The King's personal protection even extended to monarchs who had been his enemies during the war, as was the case with Emperor Charles of Austria-Hungary. In 1919, Charles and his family were living in desperate circumstances in the Austrian countryside. They were in physical danger as demobilised soldiers from the Imperial Army were roaming the area where they were living. George sent an officer as personal bodyguard to Charles and his family to ensure that he could leave the new Austrian republic without abdicating. As would be the case with the Romanovs, a member of royalty would seek the help of the Holy See. King George wrote to Rome for assistance.[34]

And one year earlier, in 1918, the King had attempted to get his aunt, Nicholas's mother, the Russian Dowager Empress Marie, away from danger. For much of 1918 she had been living in the Crimea. She had already been rescued once by German troops, who arrived in the nick of time as her house was under attack by Bolsheviks from Yalta, in the spring. In November 1918 she was living in a house called Chateau Kharaks, near Cape Aitodor on the Black Sea. On 1 November Vice-Admiral Calthorpe, Commander-in-Chief of the British Mediterranean Fleet, received a message from the Admiralty in London. It read:

> VERY SECRET. His Majesty the King is very anxious that steps should be taken to protect Dowager Empress of Russia and family in event of German Guards being withdrawn. It is believed they have so far being [*sic*] protecting person of Her Majesty.[35]

Plans were swiftly laid for a daring nocturnal mission in the early hours of 21 November 1918. Commander A. Turle of the Royal Navy and the Russian Lieutenant-Commander Korostovzoff went ashore from HMS *Tribune*. They were received by the Dowager Empress, but according to Turle's report: 'Her Majesty was disinclined to leave THE CRIMEA and is undoubtedly very optimistic concerning the whole situation; as an instance, she still believes that the late Tsar Nicholas is alive.[36]

Marie refused to go with the would-be rescuers and she would not even depart with another officer, 'Colonel' Joe Boyle, the Canadian millionaire and adventurer, who had rescued the Romanian royal family and was also sent to persuade her to leave that same November. When the Dowager Empress finally did consent to leave in 1919, it was aboard a British battleship, HMS *Marlborough*, which took her to the British base at Malta. On her way to Malta and while there, the Dowager Empress was in good spirits. She insisted that both her sons were alive, but she gave little away. The Marchioness of Milford Haven, one of the Tsarina's sisters, wrote that the Dowager Empress had told her that the family was hidden in the far north of Russia, which could only be reached in summer. Their guardians were reputedly 'Old Believers', a sect of the Orthodox Church that had resisted the seventeenth-century transformation of relations between Church and State under Peter the Great.[37]

In neither of these attempts to help the Dowager Empress is there any record of King George having consulted the English government. It seems he was prepared to act without the sanction of the government when occasion demanded. He even did so again in 1922 when another first cousin, Prince Andrew of Greece – allied to one of the factions Lloyd George had been supporting in the catastrophic Greek invasion of Turkey – was facing death at the hands of Greek revolutionaries. The King sent the cruiser HMS *Calypso* to Athens. Prince Andrew was saved. Given his personal intervention on behalf of his other relatives, it is difficult to believe that he would totally abandon both his first cousins and their children without raising a hand, regardless of the political implications.

Meanwhile, Nicholas and his family continued under house arrest at Tsarskoe Selo, where the Provisional Government had first confined them. During their early months in the palace their lives had not been severely altered. But the decision by the Provisional Government to place them under house arrest became the defining moment that would cause their lives to hang in the balance for the next sixteen months. Many who had a role in the initial decision to confine the family have said that the Provisional Government, under the leadership of Prince Lvov, feared for the family's safety. Kerensky stated in his book, *The Road to the Tragedy*, that Lvov's words were, 'It was necessary to shield the former Supreme Ruler from the possible excesses of the first surge of the Revolution.'[38]

Because of the widespread propaganda that the Tsar and Tsarina entertained German sympathies, Kerensky, prior to moving the Imperial family to Tobolsk, investigated these charges on behalf of the Provisional Government. He found nothing to substantiate the stories that Alexandra, or anyone in the family, had betrayed Russia to the Germans. The charges were deemed to be groundless. However, Russian author Edvard Radzinsky attempts to implicate both Nicholas and Alexandra by asserting, without revealing his sources, that, for some reason, they burned their papers at that point, while Alexandra consigned her diaries to the flames as well.[39]

Kerensky addresses the question of who was actually responsible for the refusal of sanctuary in England. He asserts that Michael Tereshchenko, Minister for Foreign Affairs, received a letter in late June or early July 1917 on this very subject, delivered by Ambassador Buchanan. It supposedly said that 'due exclusively to considerations of internal politics' the family had been refused asylum. Additionally, Kerensky said the letter contained the following, 'The Prime Minister was unable to advise His Majesty to offer hospitality to people whose pro-German sympathies were well known.'[40] As a result of England's refusal, Kerensky claims he was assigned by Lvov to make new arrangements for a relocation of the family to a safer locale.

Regardless of whose account we believe, the Imperial family was moved in the still hours of the morning, under a veil of secrecy, to Tobolsk in Siberia. Tsar Nicholas II, Tsarina Alexandra, Grand Duchesses Olga, Tatiana, Maria and Anastasia, and the Tsarevich Alexei boarded two trains flying Red Cross flags. The date was 31 July 1917. The family's sleeping cars were supplied from the rolling stock of the Chinese-Eastern Railway. In total, two trains were required to move the large contingent of retainers, as well as the Tsar's aide-de-camp, General Tatishchev; Prince Valia Dolgorukov; the children's tutors, Pierre Gilliard and Charles Sidney Gibbes; the court physician, Eugene Botkin; the Tsarina's personal lady-in-waiting, Anastasia Gendrikova; the Tsarina's reader, Ekaterina Schneider; another lady-in-waiting, Baroness Sophie Buxhoeveden; parlour maids, Anna Demidova and Elizaveta Ersberg; Ivan Sednev, the children's servant; the cook, Kharitonov; a valet, Alexander Volkov; and Alexei's companion, N. G. Nagorny, a sailor. Thus began the Imperial family's spiralling descent that would lead to the night of 17 July 1918, in Ekaterinburg.[41] But, as we shall see, there are clues that George did take steps to rescue the family after their exile and even continued to do so once the Bolsheviks seized power.

On the other side of Russia the Japanese were also concerned for the safety of the Tsar. Japan had signed a secret treaty with Nicholas just prior to the February Revolution.[42] The two countries had promised mutual aid and support as well as important railway concessions, particularly with respect to the Chinese-Eastern Railway, which was in the rump of the trade routes. In light of the treaty and other considerations, the Japanese were concerned, now that the government had been overthrown, about the integrity of the treaty and unsure as to whom they should grant official recognition.

Japan was also confronted with another difficulty that involved Nicholas II personally. In 1891, while on a visit to Japan when he was still the Tsarevich, Nicholas had been injured when a would-be assassin lunged forward and swung his sword across his face.[43] The wound was serious and left a deep scar embedded in the right side of Nicholas's forehead. The embarrassment of the Japanese Emperor was profound. The dicta of Japanese culture, combined with the deep bond felt by all royalty, resulted in the Emperor feeling a strong moral and personal obligation towards Nicholas.

Thus, for their individual reasons, various top-level members of the Allies were rapidly coming to the conclusion that the safety of the Imperial family had to be taken into their hands. Since the King of England and the German Kaiser were both involved in a war and closely related to the Russian Imperial family there was a need for secret action if they were not to be accused of putting family ties before loyalty to their countries. In America, Crane had ties both to Russia and the family, and favoured their protection. Japan's Emperor had several compelling reasons, from political to personal, for protecting the Tsar. France's interests were pressing – their Russian loans were a significant part of their debt and over fifty per cent of French households at that time held Tsarist bonds.[44] But for any of the Allies or Japan to offer support overtly would have been tantamount to committing political suicide. The propaganda that had been mounted so effectively against Nicholas and his family had made any public support of the Tsar all but impossible.

The political situation required careful, calculated manoeuvres if the Romanovs were to be snatched from their Siberian exile. And the only conceivable method of doing this would require the involvement of what the intelligence community regarded as the 'hidden hands'.[45]

CHAPTER 3

The Hidden Hands

Invisible Diplomacy

The international community was experiencing growing concern over the future of Russia and in some quarters the future of the Imperial family was also on the agenda. As events in Russia continued at a breathless pace, a series of coincidences in the autumn and winter of 1917 – people in the right places, memos full of innuendo – led to the conclusion that plans, far from the public view, were in the making regarding Nicholas and his family. The first indications of an international rescue operation began to take shape. A politically daring attempt by the Allies to fund counter-revolutionary forces under the very noses of the Bolsheviks themselves was also being formulated.

Under the Provisional Government there had been no danger to the Imperial family. But complications soon arose which appear to have made some leaders among the Allies apprehensive and increasingly desirous of surreptitiously intervening on the family's behalf. Trotsky had returned from America on 5 May 1917. The First All-Russian Congress of the Socialist Revolutionaries Party was organised on 25 May. By 16 June Kerensky had ordered the Russian armies to take the offensive against Germany and consequently the Allies were pleased that Russia was once again active as an ally.[1] The diary generally accepted to be that of Nicholas, indicates that on both 19 and 27 June he was following the military action closely. His 19 June entry contains a blow-by-blow description of a battle in the Zolochovsk sector and concludes with obvious satisfaction: 'Thanks be to God! May God grant good luck! I felt entirely different after this joyous news.'[2]

Unfortunately his joy was short-lived. The first part of July brought the collapse of Kerensky's offensive and the Germans broke through the Russian lines at Tarnopol. By mid-July there was turmoil within the various factions of the new government. A Bolshevik coup was narrowly avoided. Kerensky had been intriguing to accuse Lenin publicly of German complicity. His objective was to inspire Russian men to join the effort to defeat the Germans, but it backfired: the Bolshevik Central Committee refuted the accusations against Lenin as 'bourgeois press'.[3] Kerensky mishandled the situation; he failed to seize the moment and as a result the Bolsheviks were only temporarily neutralised. Soon after, Lvov resigned and asked Kerensky to form another government. Even after the resignations of Lvov, Guchkov and Miliukov, who were Crane's friends, the family had enjoyed the protection of Kerensky.

In mid-July Boris Savinkov, Kerensky's aide and the man who would later figure in attempts to save the Imperial family, advised Kerensky to appoint General Lavr Kornilov Commander-in-Chief of the Army, replacing General Alexei Brusilov. Kornilov, after executing a list of demands, assumed the post at the end of July.[4]

Nicholas followed these events throughout the summer and continued to make notations about the political and military situation including the following: 'The New Provisional Government has been formed with Kerensky at its head. We'll see whether his affairs will go better. The very first task concerns tightening up army discipline and lifting the army's spirits and also putting Russia's domestic situation into some kind of order!'[5]

It was not to be, for shortly thereafter Kerensky's poor judgement would help bring Lenin to power. General Kornilov, who appears to have become dismayed with the state of affairs under Kerensky, sent troops to Petrograd and demanded civil and military control. He was under the impression that Kerensky would quietly acquiesce, but instead he found himself accused of treason. Kerensky, now the head of the Provisional Government, was certain that Kornilov was bent on destroying his government. Kornilov, however, convinced that the 'Bolshevik majority and the Soviets act in complete accord with the plans of the German Staff Headquarters', thought Kerensky should have taken action against the Bolsheviks and Lenin the previous month when the Bolsheviks attempted a coup.[6]

Kerensky, on the contrary, chose to do the opposite in what would be a tactical mistake of incalculable consequences. For the first time he actually involved the Bolsheviks in the government, seeking help from the Central Executive Committee of Soviets. He freed the now imprisoned Bolshevik leaders on the assumption that only they, with the aid of armed Petrograd workers, would have sufficient influence to resist Kornilov. And so Kornilov was defeated, and the Bolsheviks were set on the road which would ultimately lead them to power just three months later.

In the meantime, as mentioned in chapter 2, Kerensky, in order to protect them from the first 'surges of the revolution', had quietly removed the Tsar and his family, as well as fifty retainers, to Tobolsk for safe keeping. Gilliard, the Tsarevich's tutor, later maintained he heard the Tsar say, upon learning the news of Kornilov's defeat, that he regretted his abdication.[7] The lines of communication had remained open to Nicholas in Tobolsk and he was able to follow both political and military events. While the family were being relocated to Tobolsk, a foreshadowing of future trouble had already appeared from Ekaterinburg. A telegram arrived from the Ekaterinburg District Soviet to the Petrograd Soviet, signed by M. Medvedev, Secretary and S. Derzhabin, on behalf of the Chairman of the Executive Committee of Soviets of Workers' and Soldiers' Deputies, enquiring about the family's train journey passing through Ekaterinburg on its way to Tiumen on 4 August while being transferred to Tobolsk: 'The rumor is going around that the train is under orders to go to Novo-Nikolaevsk and on to Harbin. The rumor is exciting ferment in the population . . . if they are accurate then measures to be taken.'[8]

Medvedev[9] and Derzhabin asked if the Central Executive Committee and the Workers', Soldiers' and Peasants' Deputies had participated in the decision. Already the Ekaterinburg Soviet was using innuendo to imply a threat to the family by saying, 'measures to be taken'. Whether the Ekaterinburg Soviet received a response from the Petrograd Soviet is unknown.

By the end of September Kerensky formed his last coalition government with himself at the head. The family's protection continued under the compassionate care of Colonel Eugene Kobylinsky, who had been the Commander at Tsarskoe Selo and had journeyed with them to Tobolsk. Kobylinsky had now been assigned an assistant, Vasily Pankratov, a geologist and a socialist revolutionary (SR) hand-picked by Kerensky,[10] who had once been exiled for murdering a policeman.

But in October, with Kerensky's fall about to come, the tone of the government was to change dramatically. The Petrograd Soviet voted to form the Committee for Revolutionary Defence and the Bolshevik Central Committee adopted Lenin's resolution on 'armed insurrection as an immediate task'. Shortly thereafter, the Kiev Soviet in the Ukraine and the Minsk Soviet in Byelorussia formed the Northern Regional Soviet Congress, and on 19 October the Ural Regional Soviet Congress declared for Soviet power.[11] On 24 October Kerensky was to make his last speech. The October Revolution began on 25 October, and the Council of Republic was closed by troops at twelve noon. The Petrograd Soviet saw Lenin make his first appearance at three o'clock that same afternoon. The Winter Palace operations, where Kerensky's ministers were huddled, ceased to function at nine that night and the Provisional Government fell at two the following morning. The All-Russian Soviet passed decrees on peace and land, and set up a new government – the Council of Peoples' Commissars. The Congress adjourned at 5 a.m. on 27 October.[12]

As always, the Tsar heard about 'the Revolution' and noted in his diary on 17 November, 'It's nauseating to read the newspaper's description of what happened two weeks ago in Petrograd and Moscow.'[13] What little security Nicholas might have felt in Tobolsk, far away from the action in Petrograd and Moscow, proved only to be superficial and temporary. The atmosphere throughout the major population centres of Russia was becoming increasingly violent. At this time Tobolsk was still run by Mensheviks, who were the most conservative of the Social Democrats, and by Socialist Revolutionaries, who were more liberal than the Constitutional Democrats or Kadet party, but less extreme than the Bolsheviks. Other cities like Moscow, Petrograd, Ekaterinburg and Omsk were already in the hands of the Bolsheviks but Tobolsk would remain under the control of its more moderate contingent for a few more months.[14]

Tensions continued to build. Germany sent a division under Graf von der Goltz to Helsinki to help Baron Carl Gustave Mannerheim win Finland's independence from the Soviet government. Germany's intention was to move across the Finnish border and to utilise the Russian Arctic ports of Murmansk and Archangel for submarine bases.[15] Finland proclaimed its independence on 6 December, to the consternation of the Allies, who realised that

Germany could now move its troops west to fight France and Britain and as we shall see this presented a particular problem – it could potentially interfere with plans that were brewing in England to free the Romanov family.

In the latter part of December the Allied Supreme War Council began its work in France. The Four Powers – Britain, France, Italy and the United States – charged the Council with the responsibility of co-ordinating strategies to win the war. Permanent Military Representatives, who were chosen from the ranks of the generals of each Allied army, would convene twice a week. This body took the step of recognising the thousands of Czechoslovak soldiers who were being held as prisoners of war in Siberia as an autonomous army. The intention of the Council was to enable approximately 40,000 Czech soldiers to leave Russia in order to join the Allies in France, on the Western front, after the successful negotiation of their release. This crucial step would prove to be one of the pivotal factors in what would become known as the Siberian intervention that was to play out just miles from the Romanovs' house of confinement the following July.

The four generals who comprised this committee wrestled with numerous difficult issues and the debates were frequently contentious. British Prime Minister Lloyd George and General Henry Hugh Wilson believed that the war could be won not on the Western Front but elsewhere in Gallipoli or in the Dardanelles. They pushed the idea of intervention in Russia more aggressively than French General Maxime Weygand or General Luigi Conte Cadorna of Italy, or even American Lieutenant-General Tasker Bliss. The notion was:

> The British had a gem to guard – India – and they would guard it with the same ferocity as they guarded the home islands. They knew that what happened in Moscow affected Bokhara and what affected Bokhara affected Bombay. The British wanted to depose the Bolsheviks, who were calling for a world-wide proletarian revolution, and in late 1917 the British began supplying money and arms in unending quantity to Cossacks in Transcaucasia and to anti-Bolsheviks mobilizing armies along the Don in southern Russia.[16]

Interventions cost money. Money was something the opposition in Russia did not have. Historically it has been stated that the British and the other Allies wanted to create conditions that would lead to the overthrow of the Bolshevik regime, and they certainly had strong financial reasons for doing so. By mid-December, the Bolsheviks had already made noises about repudiating all debts owed to foreign nations. This naturally gave the Allies immense concern. In the balance lay huge war debts owed to the various nations by the Tsarist government, as well as significant debts owed by the Kerensky government. According to the figures cited in the *Atlas of the First World War*, as of July 1917, Russia owed: Britain, £2,760,000,000; France, $760,000,000; United States, $280,000,000; Italy, $100,000,000; Japan, $100,000,000 in currencies of the time.[17] Large quantities of armaments had previously been shipped to the Tsarist and Russian Provisional governments and stockpiles of armaments sat idle while great sums of receivables were being carried as assets, which would soon turn to liabilities, in the financial ledgers of industrial giants operating in the United States, Britain, France and even Japan. But in the event that the Allies were successful and did manage to overthrow the Bolsheviks, the pressing question remained of who would step forward to govern Russia?

Documentation presented later in this chapter will demonstrate that a few people at the highest levels of the Allied governments decided that the Tsar should be freed and that he and his family should take up residence in northern Russia to await the outcome of the war. Then the option would be available, at the appropriate time, to consider a reinstallation of the monarchy, perhaps in the form of a constitutional monarchy, with, if acceptable, Nicholas as its head. This argument is further supported by a piece of correspondence forwarded later, in December 1918, by Charles Crane's friend and another of Crane's nominees, American ambassador to China, Paul Reinsch, to the State Department. Reinsch was responding to a request that had apparently been sent by the State Department regarding the political atmosphere and the possibility of a restoration of the monarchy in parts of Russia:

Report on monarchical reaction in Transbaikal, Siberia and Ural district. Résumé of reports upon this subject from all consular officers under my direction . . . Ekaterinburg district. 80% of the inhabitants would not oppose monarchy . . . Dheliabins district. General consensus of opinion there is a strong reaction in favour of monarchy, especially among peasants who are tired of disorder . . .

there appears to be no one in the Dheliabins district who wishes to return to Tsardom, as all realize that Russia has moved far beyond that, but there is certainly a large and growing class regard [*sic*] a constitutional monarchy with liberal tendencies as the only means of securing a strong United Russia in the present state of education and development . . . Omsk district, all classes who possess sufficient intelligence to think practically about Government problems that the salvation of Russia lies in a constitutional monarchy. They do not believe, however, that at the present is the moment to change . . . Novo Nikolaevsk district, Some peasants talk in favour of Monarchy. A majority army officers favour Monarchy. Russian church continues in favour of Monarchy . . . Irkutsk district, It is probable that 60% of the population favour constitutional monarchy. This is caused by the Kerensky and Bolshevik failures . . . Liberal leaders who were keen on revolution two years ago are no longer enthusiastic in that direction and in contact with Bolsheviks is making them behave like persons awakening from a nightmare.[18]

Ernest Harris, who had been the American consul in Irkutsk in Siberia, conducted this remarkable assessment for Reinsch. Harris concluded by saying that it could be six months to two years before a monarchy of some description could take hold in Russia but he was unwilling to speculate on how long one would last.[19] One of the more noticeable aspects of this report is that it was filed from Omsk, where Harris was in the company of Supreme Ruler Admiral Alexander Kolchak, the man under whom the Romanov investigation had just fallen.

Days after this interesting communication, another series of intriguing telegrams mentioning 'Urgent . . . verify family seven times' had been forwarded from America to London and Paris on 29 and 30 December.[20] These telegrams will be examined in full much later in Chapter 16 but are mentioned here because the 18 December timing of the Harris communication, querying a possible restoration, becomes even more suggestive when we consider that the 'verify family seven times' telegrams to London and Paris followed on 29 and 30 December at the very time President and Mrs Wilson were guests of King George and Queen Mary. That all these communications should occur around the same time is difficult to explain, unless the family, who were presumed to have died, were perhaps about to reappear (as the 'urgent . . . verify family seven times' telegram could have signalled) and the water was being tested as to a time-frame for the possibility of a reinstallation of the Romanov monarchy.

Part of the answer as to whether or not this could be a plausible explanation of the telegrams lies in the largely untapped archives of the Hudson's Bay Company files in Winnipeg, Canada. The Hudson's Bay Company was, in late 1917, and still is today, one of the oldest operating companies in the world. During World War One the Hudson's Bay Company was the purchasing agent for France, Russia and Romania, even though its headquarters was on Lime Street, London. In its files resides one of the clues that the family were not forgotten. There is proof that a residence was being built for the Tsar and that the Allies were planning a rescue attempt.[21]

In late November of 1917, Charles Crane left Russia to travel to England via France. In a letter to his son, Richard Crane, United States Secretary of State Lansing's secretary, Crane conveyed that he was on his way to England, where he was to receive his mail 'in care of Sir Courtney Ilbert [Clerk of the House of Commons] at Palace Westminster.'[22] It is doubtful that it was a coincidence that while Crane was in England work began on a most interesting house in northern Russia. Its assembly and construction fell under the auspices of the Hudson's Bay Company. Assembled in Archangel, the plan was for it to be constructed and erected in Murmansk by the end of November 1917 and its construction paid for by the British Admiralty.[23] It now appears that it was intended as a safe house for the Tsar and his family – the first hard evidence of there ever being any building outside Tobolsk or Ekaterinburg to house the Imperial family. This house was referred to in a British telegram, sent in October 1918, relayed from the Admiralty in Archangel:

Following received from Mr Browd on behalf of the Murmansk Scientific Industrial Society the offer of a building to be erected on the Dvid Company's land near the British Consulate Murmansk formerly intended for the late Tsar and now offered for occupation by General Poole or Admiral Kemp. Buildings complete with heating light utensils etc. and now in charge of Kambolin Engineer erecting them . . .[24]

Could the telegram's usage of the expression 'late Tsar' be a necessary obfuscation? Although the message indicates that the house was, at that time, to be utilised by the British general and admiral, the Hudson's Bay archives indicate that this was not its original function when it was being assembled at Murmansk in late November 1917. Parts of the payments for construction of the structure were to be paid to the Makarov Construction Company. Strangely, a Brussov and Makarov Construction Company is mentioned in *Rescuing the Czar*, the book that alleged the survival of the Imperial family.

The house detailed in the Hudson's Bay Company files was provisioned with dishes, food, beds, blankets, etc. in quantities of seven. Additionally, the provisioning list called for most provisions also in quantities of seven, and stressed luxury items that according to Barbara Kelcey, an expert on the Hudson's Bay Company during this time period, were strikingly different from a normal provisions list.[25] Additionally, the British Admiralty was paying not just for the construction, but also for all the expenses related to furnishings and provisioning, even though most telegrams indicate it was supposed to be a building housing Hudson's Bay Company employees – yet again a most unusual arrangement. There are no other records indicating that the Admiralty paid for Hudson's Bay employees' provisions or living quarters. Such financial transactions and preparations are inexplicable for a remote outpost like Murmansk unless the Allies were going quietly to see to it that Nicholas finally got the wish he had voiced when he abdicated – to go to Romanov-on-the-Murman.

The mystery of this house 'intended for the late Tsar' deepened in 1975 with the publication of *Life with Lloyd George: The Diary of A. J. Sylvester, 1931–45* by the former Prime Minister Lloyd George's secretary.[26] In it Sylvester revealed that King George V had expressed great concern over the impending publication of a book by Lloyd George concerning events in Russia during World War One. In fact, according to Mr Sylvester, King George V censored portions of the Prime Minister's book and refused to allow Lloyd George to write about a residence for the Tsar. Moreover, the King insisted that the entire chapter regarding British activities in northern Russia be excised. It now appears that the house alluded to in the Hudson's Bay files was part of a plan to bring the family out of Siberia.

Charles Crane, Wilson's Russian adviser, is also linked to the overall plans to overthrow the Bolsheviks and free the family. Prior to going to England Crane, as usual, had stayed at the home of his long-time friend Count Rostovstov, the Tsarina's financial secretary and guardian of the Grand Duchesses' trust funds.[27] During the preceding months in the summer of 1917, Crane had visited Kiev where he had met two men who would play important roles in the events to come in 1918: his long-time friend, Thomas Masaryk, the future President of Czechoslovakia and soon to be the father-in-law of Crane's daughter, as well as the man who would negotiate the release of the Czech soldiers, and General Alexis Kaledin, the White Russian, who would be funded by an Allied banking scheme and on whom much hope, from the Allies' point of view, would be pinned.[28]

It is from Masaryk that we know about the Kiev meetings, as they were never mentioned in Crane's papers. Crane, Wilson's 'fixer', appears to have gone to England on one of his missions, as he would do again a year later in December 1918, when he travelled on a 'secret mission' to China for the President.[29] Plans were in the works and Crane was the United States point man. Just after he left England, in November 1917, the building of the house was accelerated and the banking scheme, which would finance Kaledin's anti-Bolshevik forces, began to take shape.[30] The fact that Crane was deeply involved in the activities that comprised the banking scheme developed to support Kaledin and subsequently General Alexeev is partly substantiated by assertions that Crane was contributing financial aid from his own personal fortune to Kaledin and his forces.

Just after Crane returned from England he met Secretary of State Lansing. In his book George Kennan indicates how deeply he felt Crane was involved in the intrigues:

When Mr Crane came to see the secretary on December 11, he had only recently returned from Russia. He had been one of the members of the Root mission, and the only one – be it said to his credit – who failed to share Root's optimism over the prospects of the Provisional Government. This does not mean, however, that he was necessarily pessimistic about Kaledin's fortunes. There was some suspicion among American officials then serving in Russia that Mr Crane himself was at that time giving private financial support to Kaledin. However that may be, Milyukov whom Crane knew well was one of those conservative figures who appeared at Kaledin's headquarters in the weeks following the Revolution, and such an arrangement would have been in no way surprising. In any case it would not be unreasonable to suppose that Crane, too, urged governmental support for the Kaledin-Alekseyev movement, closely connected as it was with Milyukov and the Kadet party . . .[31]

Crane may have been financing the movement with private funds, but he also was about to become the United States point man for a banking scheme being formulated in England that included an unstated plan to rescue the Tsar and place the family in safe keeping until the outcome of the war had been determined. The proposed banking scheme was to be utilised to gain control of a number of banks, including the Siberian Bank, through which to channel Allied funds. When the new evidence in the Hudson's Bay Company is coupled with what we are to learn, it can now be suggested that the object of the banking scheme was not just to create a financial infrastructure so that it would be possible to separate Siberia from European Russia (which was largely controlled by the Bolsheviks) for an interim period until Great Russia re-stabilised after the fall of the Bolsheviks. But it was also an avenue to save the Tsar so that he could possibly return to power in some fashion or other should the time be ready. As a result of the financial aid expected to be distributed through the banking scheme, DeWitt Poole, the American consul in Moscow, stated in mid-January that 'clandestine preparations' were under way to 'counter B [Bolshevik] attacks at opportune moments in Moscow and other cities'.[32]

This banking scheme and the Hudson's Bay Company's personnel acted in concert. The fact that the company was not only the provisioner for the Russian government as well as the French forces, but was also operating in London made it the ideal paymaster of intelligence operatives in northern Russia as well as of the house in Murmansk. And as we saw evidenced by the Harris telegram on pages 44 and 45, plans for a constitutional monarchy could have been in the making which, had the conditions been right, might have led to a restoration. We shall also learn from the letters and diary entries of men in Siberia and Murmansk at the time that the Kara Sea and Murmansk definitely figured in attempts to remove the family from captivity.

By the end of 1917 a sense of urgency had seized the Allies. With the realisation of the true spirit of the Bolsheviks' agenda, with huge debts[33] hanging over numerous Allied corporations, and with the threat of the Bolsheviks siding with the Germans and sitting out the war, the Allies began to solidify their plans. On 27 December the Allies' greatest fear was confirmed – the Bolsheviks officially repudiated all 'foreign debts'. Fortunately, by then the Allies had already begun to take steps to avoid the loss of the Russian front as well as to avoid potential financial disaster.

Throughout the rest of December Crane met Wilson numerous times, apparently refining America's Russian strategy.[34] The development of a two-track policy was in the making. The British had initiated the design but needed the support of other Western governments. However, in order to be successful it was essential their plans remained secret. On the surface the policy proposed telling the Bolsheviks through unofficial agents that the British wanted to work towards establishing relations with them and that the notion that the British wanted to overthrow them was absurd. This deliberate distraction was planted to throw the Bolsheviks off the true intent of the two-track policy. The British hoped to use as political capital their co-partner America's mantle of democratic idealism to keep the Bolsheviks from being suspicious. The British further stated that they would explain any contact with the White armies in the Ukraine or the Cossacks as simply a necessity.

The other track was the true intention of the banking scheme, which was to 'pay the Cossacks and Caucasians to bribe the Persians' to overthrow the Bolsheviks, with the United States assisting in the payment of these bribes. Additionally, agents would be dispatched to support the provisional governments and their armies against the Bolsheviks. The British War Cabinet hoped 'to avoid the imputation as far as we can that we are preparing to make war on the Bolsheviks, thereby hoping to influence the Soviet Regime to resist Germany in Northern Russia'.

Wilson wrote on the proposal that he thought it was sensible but he did not want to 'bribe the Persians'.[35] By 11 December Wilson had already reached a decision to give covert aid to Generals Kaledin and Alexeev against the Bolsheviks, but hesitated to participate in paying off the Persians. He had based his decision on American consul Maddin Summers's glowing reports and Crane's trip to the south – both indicating that Alexeev and Kaledin were 'the salvation of Russia'. Realising that the morale of the troops in south Russia was at an all-time low due to lack of funds and munitions, Secretary of State Robert Lansing felt that he could propose, 'Only a conditional pledge of assistance'. He thought that ' "the situation may be saved by a few words of encouragement". '[36]

Wilson, who had fretted over what to do about Russia since he had publicly endorsed a policy of non-intervention, also met Lansing on the night of 11 December 1917. Lansing praised the Russian Generals Kaledin, Alexeev, Brusilov and Kornilov, as well as the 'strength of the Kaledin movement'.[37] Lansing, receiving a positive reaction, met Treasury Secretary and head of the United States Secret Service William G. McAdoo the next day. McAdoo was Wilson's son-in-law and anything but dispassionate – his daughter was married to the Second Secretary to the ambassador of the Provisional Government (the United States would not recognise the Bolshevik Government or grant them an embassy until the 1930s). As Wilson's son-in-law agreed regarding 'aiding Kaledin', Crane's hand-picked man to overthrow the Bolsheviks, the President wrote on a telegram received from Lansing contemplating supporting Kaledin in the south: 'This has my entire approval.'[38]

The telegram sent the next day to Oscar Crosby, the US Treasury representative in London, revealed the hidden hand of America. After praising the Kaledin and Kornilov contingent, Lansing expressed the American position:

> It would seem unwise for this government to support openly Kaledin and his party because of the attitude which it seems advisable to take with the Petrograd authorities . . . Without actually recognizing his group as a de facto government which is at present impossible since it has not taken form, this government cannot under the law loan money to him to carry forward this movement. The only practicable course seems to be for the British and French governments to finance the Kaledin enterprise insofar as it is necessary, and for this Government to loan them the money to do so.[39]

The Secretary of State therefore instructed Crosby to confer with the US ambassador and Allied authorities, then report whether they were willing to adopt the US proposal. Then Lansing stated: 'And if so, to what extent financial aid will be required.'[40]

Lansing closed by reiterating the 'importance of avoiding it being known that the United States is considering showing sympathy for the Kaledin movement, much less for providing financial assistance'.[41] Knowledge of the activities in Russia was confined to a tight group of men. The plan for indirect, covert financing of anti-Bolshevik armies in southern Russia was very sensitive, since it was essentially illegal and would be a political disaster if it became known that Wilson and Lansing left some of their closest aides at the State Department out of the loop. William Phillips knew that a message had been sent to Crosby, but he noted in exasperation: '. . . neither Polk nor I have seen it, although both of us are handling the Russian situation. It is too absurd.'[42]

On 17 December, Wilson met Colonel House, his de facto Secretary of State and Robert Lansing, the de jure Secretary, about the Russian situation. House, who was close to William Wiseman, head of British Intelligence in the United States, telegraphed:

> PRESIDENT believes it is essential to give whatever aid is possible to the Polish, Cossacks, and others that are willing to fight Germany, and while he has no power to lend money direct to such unorganized movements he is willing to let France and England have funds to transmit to them if they consider it advisable.[43]

Neither Crosby nor the US ambassador, Walter Hines Page, wanted America to be involved because they felt that the anti-Bolshevik movement had not demonstrated its staying power and it seemed unnecessary to take such a risk. John Maynard Keynes, a British Treasury official (later to become one of the most influential economists of the twentieth century) suggested that Lord Robert Cecil, a member of the Russia Committee as well as the British War Cabinet, attempt to secure America's support in writing. On 21 December a telegram was received from Colonel House confirming Wilson's willingness to have the money transferred via France and England.[44] As David Foglesong points out in his *America's Secret War Against Bolshevism*, the reason Wilson structured the United States support as he did was to pass 'money through America's allies to get around legislative restrictions on presidential authority'.[45]

Soon afterwards, Lord Cecil, accompanied by Lord Alfred Milner, another member of the Russia Committee, went to the Quai d'Orsay in Paris, where they decided that the French would finance the Ukraine and the British would find money for the other regions, with the understanding that the United States would provide additional financial assistance. The French government had authorised a 100-million-franc endowment to General Alexeev to lead the effort against the Bolsheviks. Shortly thereafter American consul DeWitt Poole travelled to Rostov under the guise of assessing the 'commercial situation', while his real objective was to meet Kaledin and assess the military situation. He likewise felt the US should support the Kaledin contingent.[46] Kiev and Rostov were centres of activity Crane, Masaryk and DeWitt Poole had all visited.

Dark clouds continued to gather on the horizon. Phillips, Crosby, Page and House, who had all initially opposed the financing of the two-track policy, now appeared to support it. Phillips noted on the day after Christmas:

> Our policy in Russia seems at last to be clearly defined. We have secretly telegraphed Crosby to inform the British and French governments that this Government is willing to advance sufficient credit to those governments so that they may send whatever cash may seem necessary to the leaders in southern Russia opposing the Bolshevik regime. It is not considered wise for all the Allied governments to step into the boat at once and the United States is keeping completely in the background so that should the southern Russian developments fail, one of the Allies at least would not be in bad.[47]

Obviously there was some fear that all would not go well, and it appears that the United States would have the high moral ground in the event of any disastrous outcome. When the pieces all came together in the summer of 1918, it was apparent that this is in fact what happened. For historically, the United States escaped the harsh criticism that both the French and the English received for the fiasco.

The man who tipped the scale and won the battle in favour of supporting Kaledin and the other White Russian leaders was Charles Crane, friend of the nobility and Provisional Government leaders, who had influenced Wilson during their December meetings.[48] Again, Foglesong sums up the United States posture: 'Hence, the United States planned "to maintain a neutral and expectant attitude" in public while privately working with the British and French along a different line.'[49]

As a result of the efforts of Secretary McAdoo and Wilson,

Crosby was co-operating with the scheme by early January. In late January, however, Crosby was still having difficulty with the logistics of the money transfers. There is no evidence that America did not come through with the money they had agreed to provide but it is difficult, if not impossible, to trace the repayments in forms of credits, meaning the 'American loan' was not intended to be a loan.

Quite possibly the money was funnelled through various United States government agencies, as had been done with the money a Michael Gruzenberg would take to Europe from the United States in May 1918, while travelling to Russia on a mission at the request of Lenin.[50] These funds were sent through the Information Agency run by George Creel, a close associate of Wilson's.[51] Or perhaps the War Trade Board was the agency, since it had functioned as a conduit for erasing the part of debt owed to America by the Tsarist and Provisional governments. And some may have been channelled, in a still unrevealed fashion, through the Russian Tsarist embassy. A connection for this supposition exists: Treasury Secretary William G. McAdoo's son-in-law was the Second Secretary to the Russian ambassador, Boris Bakmetieff and would have been the ideal candidate to handle covert financial transactions.[52]

Russia Committee member Lord Cecil's attitude about difficulties the scheme would encounter were capsulated when he said, 'We must be prepared in the desperate position in South Russia to take risks.'[53] The Bolsheviks were gaining power and influence, and the only identified forces the British felt they could rely on were the volunteer White forces in the south. The 'risk' will be better understood when we discover that once the money was in Russia it was moved through the banking scheme, fronted by the English, that was established in December 1917, which had at its head a close friend and loyal supporter of the Tsar and his family.

By 22 January the British consul in Petrograd revealed that there was now, in the form of the banking scheme, a method for transferring funds to south Russia. But by this time Kaledin's Cossack forces were ready to fall. Profoundly depressed as a result of all the delays, Kaledin shot himself on 11 February, purportedly because he felt he was surrounded by deception, added to which the situation in south Russia was deteriorating dramatically. The 'method for transferring funds', utilising the banking scheme, had encountered difficulties in terms of converting Western currencies to roubles. DeWitt Poole, the American consul, suggested he personally could ' "draw dollar drafts" and "buy considerable amounts of roubles locally".'[54]

Under the watchful eye of British Major Terence Keyes, of the Indian Army (only one month after the assignment he became a Colonel and later Brigadier-General and Sir Terence Keyes), in whose hands control of the banking scheme had been placed, the Allies had worked quickly to establish the banking infrastructure and make the currency conversions easier. However, the logistical problems were immense. The banking infrastructure was illegal from the start and once in place all documents were backdated, with Lenin's knowledge, to indicate that the transactions for the various ownership transfers of numerous Russian banks, including one in Siberia, had taken place prior to Lenin's nationalisation of these same banks.[55] The rapidity with which the scheme was implemented was the result of heroic effort and the constant attention of Keyes, for there were many loose ends to his secret operation. One of those was a huge pay-off to Lenin to come.

With the illegal banking scheme in place, the Allies had indeed taken some of the risks mentioned by Lord Cecil, including but not limited to reaching a secret agreement with Lenin, and the beginning of construction of a safe house for the family that would be supervised by men who were also active in the banking scheme. The stage was set for the hidden hands.

CHAPTER 4

The Hidden Hands Play a Hand

Desperate Times

Throughout December of 1917, as the Bolsheviks tightened their grip on power the pace of high-level foreign clandestine activity was quickening. From the new evidence, it appears that the house in Murmansk was being assembled and the logistics for the banking scheme were likewise finalised. At the same time, from a British diplomatic telegram we learn that there were also foreign groups outside mainstream governmental and military organisations who were considering measures to oust the new Russian leadership. The widespread abuse of power by the Bolsheviks, and in many cases their violations of the most basic rules of civilised government, as well as cruelties they inflicted on any individual or group loosely related to the previous regimes, had unnerved many civic and governmental leaders in Western democracies. It appears some began to take action:

> TELEGRAM 4006 from Spring-Rice
> [British ambassador to the US]
> Washington
> TO WAR CABINET and King.

Secret
Certain Zionist leaders have informed me in strictest secrecy that they have arranged with US State Department to send agents to Russia to overthrow Bolsheviks. Some of the Jewish activists from New York City. Mission will be quite unofficial.[1]

If Spring-Rice's telegram is accurate, the hand of Jacob Schiff might be at work again. As we saw, Schiff had harboured much ill will towards Tsarist Russia and had without a doubt helped the Japanese to win the war against Russia in 1905.[2] Schiff hated the way he felt Jews had been treated and believed that if the Japanese defeated Russia there might have been an eventual evolution to a more liberal constitutional government. But by late 1917, even though he may have previously financially supported Trotsky,[3] Schiff was definitely having second thoughts about the Bolshevik regime. According to Priscilla Roberts: 'The Bolshevik revolution of November 1917 more than confirmed [Schiff's] misgivings, precipitating a swift and dramatic change in Schiff's attitude toward Russia.'[4]

Schiff's changing attitude was apparently representative of many of his peers. The information in the telegram sent by Spring-Rice could render insight into how disparate groups can suddenly find a commonality. While the Bolsheviks early on might have convinced some that they would not be autocratic, the very men in the United States who had been persuaded by their espoused ideals were now seeing the lack of freedom the new regime was enforcing and were questioning the godlessness and cruelty of the Revolution and its leaders.

Spring-Rice's telegram might also explain how British intelligence agent Sidney Reilly came to return to Russia. Reilly, commonly known nowadays as 'the Ace of Spies', had been living in New York City prior to the war where he had been negotiating multimillion-dollar business contracts as a Russian war contractor. It has been maintained that he had been inducted into the British intelligence community many years before 1918. However, the first official record of Reilly having been connected to British intelligence was in 1917. Born Salomon (Sigmund) Grigorevich Rosenblum to a Jewish family in Russian Poland in March 1874, he changed his name to Sidney George Reilly (supposedly because that was his first wife's maiden name) in 1899 when he acquired a British passport. As far as can be ascertained, Reilly received his passport without going through any official channels.[5]

Reilly had been skilfully negotiating his way in and out of Russian business and court circles for years. His business endeavours in America during the war made him financially independent. Early in the war he had been the agent of record in a contract for a shipment of 1.2 million rifles for the Russian government to be manufactured by the Remington Arms Company, a name which we shall see become significant later.[6] When it was thought that Hugh Leech, one of the original members of the banking scheme inner circle in Moscow, was becoming indiscreet, a fixer was selected in the person of Reilly, who was sent to Russia by the British to replace Leech in April 1918. A former Tsarist government official, engineer Beloi, whom Reilly knew before the war and had met again in Russia in 1918, is quoted in Vladimir Krymov's book, *Portraits of Extraordinary People*. Beloi recalls a conversation with Reilly:

> It was known to me that in Moscow and Petersburg one Leech, an Englishman who spoke Russian well, was selling checks on English banks for large sums and that proceeds of this exchange were going to support the Denikinist Army. I asked Reilly if this was true and was astonished that Reilly completely and openly confessed this to be so but that English Government circles were dissatisfied with Leech's activities and had ordered Leech to be dismissed and that all the affairs were to be taken over by Reilly.[7]

Reilly's involvement in the banking scheme, and the plan to overthrow the Bolsheviks as part of the two-track policy, is further supported by the correspondence of Churchill's secretary, Archibald Sinclair. His memo refers to Reilly as 'the right-hand man' to Karol Yaroshinsky,[8] the banking scheme's Russian point man who was also a close friend and benefactor of the Romanovs while they were in confinement in Tobolsk.

During the time that secret agents were being sent to Russia in November and December 1917, the Hudson's Bay Company was continuing the assembly of the house and secret funds were beginning to find their way into Russia to support the agents' actions. The timing seems more than just coincidental and, in fact, all of the activities regarding the house, the banking scheme and the covert intelligence operations had players in common who comprised a small circle of men.

Concurrently the Tsarina had managed to smuggle a note out of Tobolsk, that included a floor plan of the house, intended for King George, but which was addressed to her old governess, Miss Margaret Jackson. Whether the note was in response to a communication from the British royal family, or was initiated by the Tsarina, remains unknown. However, in light of the new evidence, it now appears that it was most likely in response to a message from King George who was taking steps to free his cousins.

The family's English tutor, Charles Sidney Gibbes, who was also in Tobolsk, retained a copy of the note with the floor plan in his personal papers. Were it not for the copy we would not have knowledge of the existence of the note for the original has yet to be located.[9]

Another common link between the house, the banking scheme and the Romanovs was the Ukrainian Karol Yaroshinsky, mentioned by Churchill's secretary, who had been selected to act as front man for the banking scheme inside Russia. Before the Revolution Yaroshinsky had been quite successful, working in association with his assistant, Boris Soloviev, a young Tsarist sympathiser and member of the Guardian Mounted Artillery Brigade who had also been a courier for Nicholas and Alexandra[10] and was the son of Nikolai Vasilevich, who had been a member of the Tsarist government's Economy Department attached as the Treasurer of the Holy Synod and a councillor of state under the Tsar. Together Yaroshinsky and Soloviev had built several successful enterprises.

With the permission of the Tsar, Yaroshinsky had also acquired numerous banks in St Petersburg. Depending upon the perspective, he was described by some as a speculator, while others saw in him a sophisticated businessman who utilised stock in one bank to mortgage and leverage the purchase of the stock of other banks, ultimately obtaining controlling interests in several Russian banks. Clearly this was someone with sophisticated insider knowledge of the Russian banking system.

In addition to his banking interests, Yaroshinsky owned shares in a Siberian railroad and oil companies in Baku. His original wealth came from his agricultural interests near Kiev, in the Ukraine, where he had extensive grain and sugar operations.[11]

A benefactor to the pianist Artur Rubinstein, his largesse was well known, but so was his penchant for Monte Carlo. Available documents generally indicate that Karol Yaroshinsky was faithfully loyal to the Allies,[12] even though at one point an English reporter[13] and an English official[14] who had been out of the loop on the banking scheme attempted publicly to discredit him. But on 25 September 1918 a report from the US Director of Military

Intelligence revealed the official Allied view: 'An unconfirmed report from Stockholm stated under date of June 5, 1918 that the Russian Bank for Foreign Trade and the Petrograd International Bank were owned by one Charles Yarochinsky. It was further stated that Yarochinsky was pro-Ally.'[15]

Yaroshinsky's loyalty and his knowledge of the Russian banking system were two very strong assets, but he possessed yet another – his close relationship to the Imperial family. Yaroshinsky was well known to the Romanovs[16] and was, himself, of noble background.[17] He had been one of the largest benefactors of the hospitals that had been under the patronage of Grand Duchesses Maria and Anastasia.[18] In a letter dated 22 January 1918 to Anna Vyrubova, one of the Tsarina's closest confidantes prior to the imprisonment of the Romanovs, the Tsarina thanked Anna for money sent to the family:

> So unexpectedly I received the letter of the 1st and the card of the 10th. I hasten to reply. Tenderly we thank through you, Yaroshinsky. Really it is touching that even now we are not forgotten. God grant that his estates should be spared. God bless him.[19]

Whatever the note from Yaroshinsky or Anna had conveyed to the Tsarina, it is apparent from her effusive reply that she was moved as a result of hearing from him. The tone of her note also implies that he had revealed something to her that she felt required a warm expression of gratitude. Since at this juncture he was already involved in the banking scheme, and we shall see that he was also involved with a Hudson's Bay employee, Henry Armitstead, who at this very time was in charge of building the house in Murmansk, the Tsarina may have been advised that there were plans to rescue them and move them to northern Russia; hence, 'even now we are not forgotten'.

Murmansk was certainly the ideal location to protect the family since it was remote, sparsely populated and already possessed an Allied presence. It would also be easier to remove them from here if necessary. And, indeed Romanov-on-the-Murman was the destination that the Tsar had originally requested for his family following his abdication.

After the events of 1918 the activities of the various people involved in the banking scheme, as well as Henry Armitstead, who was not only involved in the banking scheme but was also in charge of the assembling of the house in Murmansk,[20] were described in a number of often conflicting documents. Not only did different individuals provide different versions of the events that occurred, but also the same person's descriptions often varied over time.

Shortly after the decision was made to implement the two-track policy and formulate the banking scheme, Keyes had been introduced to a group of ex-Tsarist officials headed by V. M. Vonliarliarskii, a former business partner of Grand Duke Alexander Michaelovich[21] in an earlier Manchurian business venture. Interestingly, Sidney Reilly, Yaroshinsky's right-hand man in the banking scheme, was also extremely close to the Grand Duke Alexander Michaelovich.[22] The group comprised Vonliarliarskii, N. N. Pokrovsky,[23] a former foreign Minister, and M. Krivoshein, formerly the Minister of Agriculture. Krivoshein was a constitutional monarchist and a member of the conservative Right Centre[24] while Vonliarliarskii was a cousin of Michael Rodzianko, former leader of the Duma. Rodzianko voiced the desire to stay in the background, as he knew he had offended the Cossacks and other generals.[25]

This group of men had been responsible for bringing Karol Yaroshinsky into the scheme for aiding the Allies in funding the anti-Bolshevik activities. And this circle of men had remained fiercely loyal to the Tsar.

What is more than apparent, however, after careful comparative analysis and study of myriad pages of documents kept in the Public Record Office in England, is that the official *raison d'être* of the banking scheme, i.e. the financial support of the South-Eastern Confederacy, was only part of the reason for its existence. Later, in 1928, when both the 'loan', as the money passed through the scheme was characterised, and Yaroshinsky came under fire from high-ranking political officials in London, Colonel Keyes registered his concern in an affidavit. He began his report with an interesting statement that is full of nuance:

There has been much misunderstanding about the loans made to Russian banks, as the transaction has become to be called, that I think I ought to write down what I remember of the circumstances of the policy of which the *so-called loan* [author's italics] formed a small part.[26]

Keyes's comment regarding the 'so-called loan' to Yaroshinsky is revealing since we now know it was never intended to be a loan but was instead a front for funding Allied intelligence actions relating to the two-track plan. However, the banking scheme and all its implications have yet to be fully understood and the difficulties faced by researchers are immense. The transactions took place under the Bolshevik regime, after they had declared such transactions illegal; therefore, the documents had to be backdated. To prevent them from falling into the hands of the Bolsheviks or Germans, many were destroyed that would have shed considerable light on the nature of the banking business. Holes in existing documentation, the presence of backdated documents (according to their authors' own admissions) and the absence of dates on most documents mean that even the considerable work done by the English journalist Michael Kettle and others ultimately raises as many questions as it answers.

The difficulties are further exacerbated by the fact that the left hand often did not know what the right hand was doing. Or as R. H. Hoare, the banking auditor later in charge of investigating the bank scheme said, there was a 'double thread' to follow. The double thread he alluded to was a euphemistic way of referring to the two-track policy. As an example, Hoare stated, 'certain difficulties were encountered' since the banking scheme was not considered purely from an economic standpoint. 'They were indeed authorized by the Foreign Office mainly on political grounds'[27] – the implication being that the banking scheme had ramifications that were more political than economic in nature.

The new evidence will suggest that one of the political ramifications was the extraction of the family. For like other missing or classified files pertaining to the Imperial family and activities in northern Russia, there are, even now, in the Templewood Papers in Cambridge University, placed there by MI6 agent and head of British Intelligence in Petrograd in 1916–17 Sir Samuel Hoare, some files pertaining to Russian affairs that are restricted until 2005.[28] Why restrict such files if the banking scheme and other actions were not tied up with a possible rescue attempt of the family?

All the correspondence that remains available today indicates that Colonel Keyes was initially dealing with three men, first identified by the initials Y, X and Z. Mr Yaroshinsky, who was stated to be in need of £500,000 to implement the bank takeovers, was initially given the 'loan' at an interest rate of 3½ per cent. The stated purpose of the loan was to buy out some pro-German directors of the Russian banks in order to remove them from the boards. This course of action is alluded to in a telegram sent by Keyes on 10 February 1918.[29]

However, logic seems to desert the scenario at this point. Since, as mentioned earlier, Lenin had nationalised the banks the previous month there was no need to buy out pro-German stockholders. Legally there were no longer any stockholders, German or otherwise. Later it was openly admitted by the participants that they had antedated the documents so that they would appear to concern a bank deal struck before the nationalisation. Further, the documents state Keyes was 'meeting with Bolsheviks'.[30] So the Bolshevik leadership knew about the banking scheme and its supposed pay-off of pro-German stockholders through Lenin. If the money really was for its stated purpose, why would the Allies be interested in safeguarding the interest of pro-German stockholders? To pacify Lenin does not seem reason enough. Why was it necessary to pass secret money to Lenin? Was this a way to camouflage some sort of payment to him? It remains unclear even today whether any money ever reached the 'pro-German stockholders'. In fact, it is unclear if there were any 'pro-German stockholders' at all. So what was the real purpose of the payment to Lenin?

CHAPTER 5

The Façade

Secret Plans

By February 1918, some members of the banking scheme were experiencing difficulties as evidenced by the following telegram:

(No. 411): 10/2/1918

. . . Keyes (ref. 369) says figures in bank scheme are 'Y' (Yaroshinski), 'X' and 'Z' (two anonymous persons) Poliakoff. Scheme delayed because (1) 'X' was in prison. (2) Poliakoff could not be informed of political objects. Having seen X, P has come in wholeheartedly. Y continues policy of acquiring Bank, but is in need of £500,000 at once. Following agreed: We pay Y in London £500,000 as loan at 3½%. He transfers to X, shares worth r 35 m. Board controlling all banks etc. to consist of Y and X (or Z) plus two of us. Interest 5¼ instead of 3½ so as to give commercial appearance.[1]

The 'X' that Keyes had referred to as being in prison was Pokrovsky, who was chairman of the Siberian Bank, one of the banks that were to be included in the banking scheme and one of the individuals who had first approached Keyes and Yaroshinsky. He was now jailed by the Bolsheviks for his refusal to relinquish Russian Red Cross funds. Krivoshein, the 'Z' referred to by Keyes in his telegram, could not be located.[2] Keyes notified the Foreign Office that 'scheme delayed'.[3]

As a consequence of the non-involvement of Pokrovsky and Krivoshein, the Home Office in England suggested that Mr Poliakov, who had been associated with the Siberian Bank, be brought into the arrangement. General Frederick Poole, the British commander in northern Russia, having made the acquaintance of Poliakov, insisted on bringing him into the scheme but that notion was resisted by Terence Keyes as we have seen in the above telegram when he openly stated Poliakov could not be informed *of political objects* . . . (author's italics). The political grounds and goals that Keyes did not want Poliakov to know about may indeed have been related to the upcoming overthrow of the Bolsheviks and the potential rescue of the Romanovs. Keyes needed to contain all transactions in as low a profile manner as possible. But Poole's insistence on bringing in Poliakov inadvertently compromised the operation, for we shall see that even General Poole at that point appears to have been unaware of certain political objectives of the British Foreign Office regarding the banking scheme.

Poliakov, just after his inclusion in the scheme, brought unwelcome scrutiny to the venture from parties back in London who had previously known nothing about the scheme, by his vociferous insistence on a higher interest rate, since he thought the transaction was actually a loan to Yaroshinsky.[4] That scrutiny led to disastrous consequences. Had General Poole been fully apprised of the political objectives, surely he would not have proposed Poliakov for participation in the arrangement. This assertion will be further supported when later in the spring of 1918 Reilly is sent in to replace Hugh Leech, the British operative who had begun to talk too much about the scheme. Now it is certain that General Poole was out of the loop since shortly after Reilly arrived in April Poole received a telegram informing him that Reilly was on a secret mission. The telegram read:

> The following two officers are engaged on special secret service and should not be mentioned in official correspondence or to other officers unless absolutely unavoidable. Lieutenants Mitchelson and Reilly.[5]

The original plan had been for Yaroshinsky to purchase the Russian Commercial and Industrial Bank, the Russian Bank of Foreign Trade, the Kiev Private Bank, the Union Bank and the International Bank. Keyes, with the obvious consent of the British Chargé d'Affaires Sir Francis Lindley, who was attached to the Petrograd embassy and had been party to the two-track policy from its inception, co-ordinated the funnelling of money through the London City and Midland banks in the name of Hugh Leech. According to telegram 910 of 13 February 1918: 'Lindley ask us to pay to account Mr Leech £285,715.5s.8d at London City and Midland.'

Only a week before these transactions a telegram to England stated, 'Keyes is working out with Poole and the Bolsheviks on the banking scheme.'[6] Even though Poole only knew about the financial and military aspects of the banking scheme at this point, he was not the only one uninformed about the political objectives. Amazingly, the 'Bolsheviks' and Lenin (most undoubtedly) were party to setting up a banking structure that in fact was intended to be utilised to overthrow them after the successful removal of the family: (telegram 522, 19 February 1918):

> Keyes reports German attempts to buy up Siberian Bank. Y [Yaroshinsky] therefore with assistance of our board has secured control. Y had to buy out certain holder in Moscow Bank at request of Lenin £500,000 did not suffice to acquire Anglo-Russian Keyes promised him another £500,000 if he acquired Siberian.

Now, once again Lenin was demanding another £500,000 after he had already been given £500,000 to pay the 'pro-German stock-holders'. And just days after Lenin received the money, the Bolsheviks signed the Treaty of Brest-Litovsk with the Germans on 3 March thereby taking Russia out of the First World War. Soon afterwards they began to form their own Red Army. At this time some 40,000 Czechs had been prisoners of war, and since Russia was officially out of the war, Thomas Masaryk, Charles Crane's close friend, started negotiating with the Bolsheviks for the Czech Legions' safe passage through Siberia to join the Allied armies in France. This development would soon play an important role in the events surrounding the Romanovs in Ekaterinburg the following July.

Shortly after 3 March the Foreign Office wired to postpone any additional funding until Colonel Keyes returned to London. Five days later Lindley said, 'Transfer already made necessary there should be no delay in payment.' By 6 March there was a telegram with no number reporting a 'campaign being opened in England against Russian Commercial and Industrial Bank in which HMG [His Majesty's Government] is interested under K's [Keyes's] scheme.'[7]

The scheme that had been put into effect to fund the overthrow of the Bolsheviks and free the family was now under intense scrutiny by people who knew nothing of its real purpose and who thought Keyes and/or Yaroshinsky had been inappropriately utilising government money. During this time there were many more machinations required to acquire the Russian banks as well as the Siberian Bank needed to complete the banking infrastructure. Even Yaroshinsky operated with the code name Livewire. It is apparent from the surviving correspondence that secrecy was essential.

Within a few months a representative of the British Treasury, Dominick Spring-Rice, would be attempting to understand what actually happened to the funds that were transferred[8] and in a letter another query from W. H. Clarke, Leslie Urquhart (a British industrialist who held mining interests in Siberia) and Henry Armitstead in the latter part of 1918 also went unanswered. They asked 'in the light of existing conditions' why did the members of the banking scheme continue to try and purchase the Siberian Bank since 'the political aspect of the case had to all intents and purposes *disappeared* [author's italics]?'[9] This statement is intriguing since the Russian civil war would continue for at least two more years with Allied financial assistance. Certainly the forces opposing the Bolsheviks who were being supported by the money sent through the scheme had not disappeared, nor had the Allies' objective to overthrow the Bolsheviks. On the other hand, by this time one element of the two-track policy had indeed disappeared – the Imperial family.

Even years later, British authorities could not sort out the transactions. A Mr S. N. Tchayeff attempted to sue His Majesty's government for funds he lost based on his involvement in these transactions, but he was not successful as the government had distanced itself from the events and many of the people involved were dead.[10] At almost the same time as the banking scheme came under scrutiny in London, 160 British Marines, along with a French contingent, landed at Murmansk, supposedly to protect military stores. The local Murmansk government is said to have made an agreement with the Allies on its own, but in light of the payment to Lenin, as well as General Poole's and Keyes' involvement with the Bolsheviks, it now seems more than peculiar that Lenin would have had no knowledge of the events in Murmansk.

Furthermore it is difficult to believe that in an important port like Murmansk the local Bolsheviks did not know that a house was being constructed by foreigners and that no report mentioning construction of the structure to Moscow has survived. However, we now know from the Hudson's Bay files that foreigners had in fact brought a structure to be assembled in Murmansk. And that the same men involved in the construction of the house paid for by the British Admiralty were also the men linked to the banking scheme. Therefore, the £500,000 payment to Lenin may have served as ransom for the family that would be relocated from Siberia to Murmansk. It is also clear that after Lenin had extorted £500,000 from the Allies he was expecting another £500,000. Was this money to ensure Bolshevik co-operation with the Allies and the safe keeping of the Imperial family?

Amazingly, the two-track policy managed to persist even after the banking scheme came under scrutiny. Still only a few people knew what was actually planned, as is demonstrated by a very interesting telegram that was sent on 15 March by Roger Tredwell, American consul in Petrograd, jointly to United States ambassador Francis, Crane's appointee, and Colonel Ruggles, then located in Vologda, north-east of Moscow, where some Western diplomats had sought to escape what was rumoured to be the advancing German Army's occupation of Petrograd. Consul Tredwell states he has just seen 'L' (Robert Bruce Lockhart, Britain's special envoy to the Bolsheviks, who had been left in charge when Francis Lindley had been called back to London, most likely for the same reason that Keyes had been – to clarify the banking scheme) who hopes to join 'redbreast' (Raymond Robins of the American Red Cross, who was acting as the de facto American representative to the Bolsheviks) in Moscow but that he has been detained in Petrograd as 'T' (Trotsky) has not left and he plans to make the Moscow trip with him. Tredwell says Lockhart thinks things are taking a 'very serious turn' and the telegram continues: ' "L" was advised from London that we have agreed to the plan of action in the east [meaning that Lockhart had learned from the British that the United States had agreed to intervention in Siberia with the Japanese to defeat the Bolsheviks] as "L" hopes that is not true.'

Lockhart further informs Tredwell that he has had quite a lot of concessions made provided that our friends out there do not proceed with plans that he says he's 'heard persistent rumours about in Petrograd' during the last two weeks. Lockhart says, 'Our help out there will be welcome and the British can go in at the Northern port.' Then within the telegram are quote marks around the following words: 'But it seems that all this may be too late if there is agreement by all the umpires that the next game is to be played in the bush. L hopes that everything will be done to prevent this, for the present at least, as it is more than likely that we may all have to join the "outlaws" and our position would be serious.'

Tredwell says Lockhart will see 'T' and will communicate with him afterwards when Lockhart will inform him of the results of the interview. The last part of the telegram indicates a sense of urgency: 'L feels that the whole situation now depends upon the question which I had Prince telegraph for me 10 days ago when we discovered that our message to the Governor had not reached him. L is telegraphing Red Breast [Robins of the Red Cross] to wait for him.'[11]

On the following day, 16 March 1918, another telegram was sent by Tredwell: 'Sixteenth. This message is for the Ambassador. Instructing to inform the Ambassador that Lockhart left on the morning of the sixteenth for Moscow supposedly in company with Trotsky who is now the minister of war. Petrograd is quiet but the general opinion including that of the British Consul seems to be that the Germans will arrive on Sunday.'[12]

From the telegrams it is evident that these men were still negotiating in good faith and in a diplomatic posture, and had absolutely no knowledge of the two-track policy, just as their respective governments had planned. The two-track policy was initially designed with the objective of closeting the very men who were at that time negotiating with the Bolsheviks, thereby assuring the purity of their actions. Clearly the subterfuge of the two-track policy was effective. On the surface, the United States and England were working with the Bolsheviks. But at this point agents like Robert Bruce Lockhart, Raymond Robins and Roger Tredwell were mere pawns. They were uninformed as to the real agenda the Allies were working towards and were sincerely concerned about an impending intervention, for example an Allied and Japanese intervention in Siberia. In fact that situation would not materialise for several more months and by that time Lockhart had been made knowledgeable about the true intentions of the Allies to overthrow the Bolsheviks, and had become a proponent of intervention.

Consul Tredwell was also at the time urging the United States not to support intervention by Japan on the side of Ataman Semenov, a warlord in eastern Siberia opposed to the Bolsheviks. Both Lockhart and Tredwell felt that the concessions Lockhart had obtained from Trotsky would allow the Allies to go into the northern port to forestall the Germans who were pressing on northern Russia and were rumoured to have had submarines in the vicinity. Agents like Tredwell, Robins and Lockhart, at this point still seem to hope the Bolsheviks would invite Allied intervention in Russia to defeat the Germans. But Tredwell said that if the Allies (umpires) did not act quickly the 'next game would have to be played in the bush [Siberia]'.

Shortly after this Tredwell telegram, with Russia out of the war, on 21 March 1918 General Eric Ludendorff of the German High Command had launched the first of five 'hammer stroke offensives' on the Western Front. These military operations stunned the Allies by their force. The first offensive alone drove the British Fifth Army back thirty miles and left 120,000 casualties.[13]

However, crushing though they were, the German victories increased the resolve of the Allies to execute their plan for overthrowing the Bolsheviks and restoring the Tsar so that Russia could legitimately re-enter the war on their side. Just days after the German assaults on 26 March 1918, a telegram was sent from Lenin and Stalin to A. M. Yuriev, the Chairman of the Murmansk Soviet, chastising Yuriev for his actions pertaining to the Allies, because a British ship was in Murmansk. Was Lenin not aware of the conversations Lockhart had been engaging in with Trotsky? That hardly seems plausible. The purpose of this communication was, in all probability, to cover the actions of the leadership in the event their complicity ever became known. Lenin and Stalin insisted that Yuriev's reports 'should be entirely official but secret – that is, not subject to publication'.[14] It is likely that Moscow not only knew what was afoot but had actually engineered the activities in Murmansk and wanted to be kept more fully informed. On 10 April a telegram demonstrates that Moscow did have knowledge regarding the Allies' presence in Murmansk and it also once again confirms Lenin's willingness to double deal:

Comrade Stalin speaking.
Receive reply:
Accept aid.
Regarding the minesweepers, inquire at the institutions you have mentioned; there are no obstacles on our part. The scheme should be

absolutely unofficial. We will treat this matter as if it were a military secret; safeguarding it is your responsibility as well as ours. It seems clear; if you are satisfied, I consider the conversation closed.
Lenin, Stalin[15]

Lockhart, who had assisted in gaining the concessions regarding Murmansk, would not be made aware of the real agenda of the two-track policy until he was informed of the plan for the first uprising against the Bolsheviks, scheduled for 1 May 1918 (May Day).[16] In any event, as we shall see in a later chapter, the counter-revolution scheduled for that date did not materialise because the Bolsheviks somehow learned there was a coup in the offing. The Allies had been planning to overthrow the Bolsheviks by backing the Social Revolutionary Boris Savinkov and his followers. The coup was postponed.

Heretofore, this has been the only reason stated for the delay in implementing the uprisings. However, we may come to understand in the next chapter that the postponement of this uprising was also linked to one of the first attempts to turn over the family to the Allies, since Lenin had now received the money through the banking scheme. A 'Mission of Special Purpose' led by Vassily Yakovlev, apparently a Bolshevik who had been sent by Lenin to relocate the family to a more secure situation, failed on 27 April, four days before the planned uprising. With the rescue plan having failed so disastrously, which resulted in the family falling into the hands of the rogue Ekaterinburg Soviet, the Allies had no choice but to cancel an attempted coup for the present.

PART TWO

Agents On The Move

CHAPTER 6

Tobolsk

The First Attempt?

The 'Russian Situation' during the months leading up to July 1918 was characterised by deception. All too often the record reflects documents and activities deemed 'secret' and 'unofficial'. During the latter months of 1917, while the Imperial family was being held in Tobolsk, they had enjoyed a reasonably civilised confinement under Colonel Eugene Kobylinsky, who had first taken charge of the family in March 1917, at Tsarskoe Selo palace.[1] Pierre Gilliard, the Swiss tutor who was also confined with the family in Tobolsk, confided in his diary: 'Never was the situation more favourable for escape, for there is yet no representative of the Bolshevik Government at Tobolsk. With the complicity of Colonel Kobylinsky, already on our side, it would be easy to trick the insolent but careless vigilance of our guards.'[2]

According to Gilliard, the Tsar was urged to 'prepare for any turn of events', but the Tsarina said, 'I wouldn't leave Russia on any consideration, for it seems to me that to go abroad would be to break our last link with the past, which would then be dead for ever.'[3]

The Tsarina was expressing her reluctance in a profound way. She must have realised that their leaving Russia would have made it difficult, if not impossible, to return as constitutional monarchs. Furthermore, their departure might have intensified the rumours that she and Nicholas had been intriguing with Germany. And contrary to popular belief she was a patriotic woman who would have found it difficult to leave behind her adopted country that was now in the grip of a civil war. A network had also been established in Tobolsk for the purpose of rescuing the family and removing them to safety somewhere that would not necessitate them leaving Russia. Yaroshinsky's assistant, Boris Soloviev, was in charge of the Brotherhood of St John of Tobolsk, an organisation we now know was formed to wrench the family from there. Boris had been utilised by Alexandra to courier confidential packages to Nicholas just prior to his abdication. Further, during the time the logistics of the banking scheme were being formulated, Soloviev had conveniently married the deceased Rasputin's daughter, Maria.[4] Therefore his links to the Tsarist regime were more far-reaching than generally known. There may have been some confusion between Boris Soloviev and a Soloviev who was an active Bolshevik.

Now in Tobolsk, Soloviev was once again acting as a courier to the family with messages from relatives and friends, employing the secret symbol of the brotherhood – the reverse swastika, a good luck symbol from Tibet. Enigmatically, the same sign was found in the Ipatiev House after the presumed deaths.

According to sources who collected them, the Tsarina seems to have been fond of the sign and affixed it to postcards and other personal items belonging to her. Two of Soloviev's co-conspirators who were said to have plans to save the family were Madame Vyrubova and Lily Dehn, both of whom had been close friends of the Tsarina.[5] Another courier who was transferring money as well as messages from Yaroshinsky and the family's friends was a former officer in the Tsar's army by the name of Sergeiv Vladimirovich Markov.[6] Markov had also been a friend of a member of the Duma, Yevgeny Markov II, and to avoid confusion was called 'Little Markov' by the Tsar's circle.

Anna Vyrubova, through whom the Tsarina had thanked Yaroshinsky when she received his communication a few weeks earlier, had sent Little Markov to Tobolsk, where upon his arrival he made contact with Soloviev and Father Vasiliev, a priest who conducted services for the family during their confinement. Both Father Vasiliev and Bishop Hermogen were similarly engaged in passing messages, and in some cases money, to the family. But it has been maintained by some that Father Vasiliev compromised the family and that he occasionally kept funds for himself.[7]

According to Little Markov, Soloviev as well as Gilliard maintained that Colonel Kobylinsky would not attempt to prevent a rescue effort but felt that they should wait until the time was right.

However, during February and March, as the regime in Tobolsk began to show signs that it might harden, Little Markov and Soloviev spoke often about a plan to rescue the family.[8]

By March 1918 the political atmosphere in Tobolsk had indeed become less supportive of the Imperial family and the struggle for control of Tobolsk and the family began. The contenders were the relatively moderate West-Siberian Soviet based in Omsk against the more extreme Bolsheviks of the Ural Regional Soviet based in Ekaterinburg. The upshot of all this manoeuvring was that both Soviets sent commissars to Tobolsk and attempted to take control of the family. The Ekaterinburg Soviet was thought to be more militant and potentially violent, while the Omsk Soviet was a more moderate contingent. The situation was rapidly changing. A new commissar from Omsk named Dutzman took control of the House of Detention on 24 March, effectively replacing Kobylinsky. Dutzman was little known in the West for his position did not last long but, like other lesser-known personages, he too would later be identified in the curious book *Rescuing the Czar*.

During these turbulent times another Red Army detachment arrived and a minor scrimmage for control of the family ensued. Pavel Hokhriakov (Khokhriakov) was in charge of the detachment, along with a Bolshevik named Kaganitsky (who is likewise identified in *Rescuing the Czar* but was not of record in the Western world in 1920 when the book was printed). They soon gained power over the Tobolsk Soviet and replaced the Chairman, Ensign Alexander Nikolsky, who had arrived as part of the Kerensky government representatives and who was serving as assistant to Eugene Makarov, the man who had conducted reconnaissance with Prince Valia Dolgorukov when they first arrived in Tobolsk to prepare the house there for the Imperial family.[9] Could it be an ironic twist that Eugene Makarov bore the same surname that would find its way into the Hudson's Bay files where the Makarov Construction Company was the firm of record regarding another house intended for the Romanovs in Murmansk.[10] The irony does not end there, for the Makarov Construction company that was said to be owned by a close friend of Kerensky's also appears in *Rescuing the Czar*.

Later, the Makarov in Tobolsk referred to Ensign Nikolsky as one of his more reliable men. And reliable he must have been for it appears he may have found his way into the Ipatiev House in the last days of the family's stay as one of the new guards who also bore the name Nikolsky.[11] Could the deposed Ensign Nikolsky have got back into the good graces of the very hardliners who had thrown him out in Tobolsk and then gained access to the Ipatiev House and the family? Considering the facts, the scenario on its face seems unlikely but, as we shall see, many other forces were at work.

All the changes that took place in early 1918 in Tobolsk resulted in the living conditions of the family seriously deteriorating. The guards at the house itself had not been paid regularly and the contest for control had placed the family in dubious circumstances. With the hardliners pressing for control, the more moderate factions were becoming demoralised.

At this very time there were also plans being laid for an internationally led rescue attempt to save the family. We learn from the book *File on the Tsar* by Anthony Summers and Tom Mangold that a Norwegian businessman named Jonas Lied, who had been given an honorary citizenship by the Tsar for opening up the new trade routes from Siberia to Western Europe and America, had been approached by British intelligence (now MI6) and was 'vetted [*sic*]' around London with his friend Henry Armitstead, to discuss Lied's participation in a rescue plan. The authors quote Lied's diary: 26 February 1918: Wire from Armitstead to Kria [Oslo] asking if he gets us visa, I would come to London to discuss expedition from England to Siberia. I wired consent . . .'[12]

Summers and Mangold note that four days later Lied was bucketing across the North Sea on a steamer to Aberdeen. They again quote his diary of 3 March: 'Arr. London. Colonel Browning arranged a suite of rooms at the Savoy. Met Armitstead and discussed expedition. Saw Sole [*sic:* Sale, Armitstead's boss][13] Gov. of Hudson Bay . . .'[14]

Two days later Lied's diary contains the following: '5 March: Saw Mitchell-Thompson, who was not very helpful. Had interview with Arthur Balfour, Foreign Minister at Foreign Office. Seeing Lord Robert Cecil tomorrow.'[15]

And three days later: '8 March: Had dinner at Sir Reginald Hall's [Director of Naval Intelligence][16] house with his wife and daughter and Armitstead. What is all this about?'

Twelve days later he entered: '20 March. Saw Sir Francis Barker and Grand Duke Michael [Grand Duke Michael Michaelovich, the Tsar's cousin][17] at Vickers house about saving Nicholas II from

Tobolsk by fast motor boat through Kara Sea . . .'[18]

Sir Francis appears to have listened, but we do not know what action he may have taken for he asked that his name be kept out of it.[19] Years later Lied's friend, Ralph Hewins, a former English diplomat and specialist on Scandinavia, remembered what Lied admitted to him:

> He told me he was asked by Metropolitan-Vickers (or anyway a Vickers outfit) to berth a British boat at his sawmill depot at the mouth of the Yenisey and to transport the Imperial family from Tobolsk downriver in one of his cargo boats. The plan was feasible. The torpedo boat was to take a course far north into the Artic [*sic*], through Novaya Zemlya, so as to avoid wartime minefields and possible Bolshevik pursuit.[20]

At the beginning of the war the representative of the Vickers Company, where Lied says the meeting was held, was none other than Sidney Reilly, the man the British would have in transit to Russia at exactly this time, in the latter part of March 1918, to sort out the banking scheme. It should be additionally noted that Armitstead, who was squiring Jonas Lied around London, was at this point also functioning as the head of the Archangel and Murmansk Hudson's Bay operations and had been placed in charge of the assembly of the house, that had been paid for by the Admiralty, intended for the Tsar in Murmansk.

Jonas Lied, the man who had pioneered the Siberian trade routes leading to the Kara Sea, just may have been one of the few men in the world who could assist in freeing the Family from their exile in Tobolsk. By utilising one of his cargo boats they would be taken via first the Irtysh river, then to the Ob river that flows north into the Kara Sea, where the British torpedo boat coming from the mouth of the Yenisei river would rendezvous with the cargo boat. Any statement of Lied's about an intended rescue and any contact with British intelligence has, in the past, been difficult to prove since there were attempts by some British officials in 1920 to discredit him. Aside from his diary there has never been any proof he had worked either directly or indirectly for the Secret Service. That is, until now. As early as February 1918 Lied, who owned the Siberian Trading Company Ltd, had been in contact with Henry Armitstead.[21] And Armitstead, the man who brought Jonas Lied to

London, was definitely working for the British Secret Service, as evidenced by a letter signed on 21 May 1918, by Mansfield Cumming who was head of MI1c (later to become MI6):

Dear Sir [Sale, Governor of Hudson's Bay Company]:

As Mr. E A. Armitstead, the representative of your Company for Russia, has, with your kind permission, temporarily placed his services at my disposal for a journey through Russia, I wish to put on record that I will refund to you all Mr Armitstead's expenses on the journey from the time of leaving London until his return to this town. I am agreeable, owing to the nature of his journey and in accordance with Mr Armitstead's usual agreement for travelling expenses with your Company that his accounts shall be presented in a similar manner to those you have previously received from him.

May I take this opportunity of thanking you for your courtesy in this matter, which I much appreciate.

Yours very truly,
Signature
Mansfield Cumming
Mansfield Cumming, Captain, RN
Copy To: M. Jones[22]

Not only did Mansfield Cumming put Henry Armitstead's 'mission' on paper, he also signed it with his famous green ink. Later, the 'mission', of which Armitstead was a member, was interpreted to be a trade mission. However, it hardly seems conceivable that the head of the British Secret Service would retain the services of as well as fund Armitstead merely for a trade mission and feel compelled to pay him through a third party if the mission was simply of a commercial nature. Now it seems very persuasive that the house in Murmansk was funded through the Hudson's Bay Company by the Admiralty while Armitstead and Lied were being paid by Cumming, also through Hudson's Bay where the 'accounts payable' entry relative to Jonas Lied carries the following phrase: *'See under Armitstead . . .'*[23] Later we shall see that the mission 'C' spoke about Armitstead participating in will coincide with an attempt to free the family.

Since Lenin had received £500,000 only weeks before through the banking scheme and Armitstead was most certainly aware of plans brewing to rescue the family, as he had apparently discussed them with Admiral Hall and Mansfield Cumming, Sidney Reilly's boss, it now comes as no surprise that Reilly was on his way to Russia. He arrived on Russian soil, via Murmansk, just prior to 5 April and with the assistance of General Bonch-Bruevich, a relation of Vladimir Bonch-Bruevich, the secretary of the Sovnarkom and one of Lenin's closest associates, assumed the role of a Bolshevik by the name of Relinsky.[24] Can it be that Reilly was given his position as Comrade Relinsky so that he could be the liaison between Lenin and the British for the operations to come? There is no doubt that Yakov Sverdlov, Chairman of the Central Committee and one of Lenin's closest associates, would have known about Reilly's position and probably also that Relinsky was not his real identity, since Sverdlov's brother Benjamin had been a business associate of Reilly's in New York City prior to the war.[25] After the initial meeting with General Bonch-Bruevich that took place some time during the first week in April, Reilly started work as Comrade Relinsky and shortly thereafter began a relationship with Olga Dimitrievna Starzhevskaia, one of the secretaries in the Central Committee office who worked alongside Sverdlov. She was arrested and questioned regarding her affair with Reilly.[26] What became of Olga Starzhevskaia remains a mystery but it was rumoured she was executed after her involvement with Reilly.[27] Nonetheless, it can be said with reasonable certainty that with Reilly's close connections to the Central Committee the Allies had an ear to the ground.

As we saw, by this time the Tobolsk Soviet had become caught in the midst of intense political struggles and an unidentified member of the family's house guard had gone to Moscow to meet with Vladimir Bonch-Bruevich, who wrote a memorandum containing the following:

> Memorandum by Vladimir Bonch-Bruevich, secretary of the Sovnarkom, to the Secretariat of the All-Russian Central Executive Committee of Soviets (VTsIK) on receiving a delegate from the detachment guarding Nicholas (no later than 1 April 1918).
>
> A com. [comrade] soldier from the detachment guarding the former tsar came from Tobolsk. There are many disturbances there; many have left the detachment, don't get salaries, etc. Talk with him in depth and find out everything. This is a serious matter. Sverdlov asked that this soldier be sent to him.
>
> Vlad. Bonch-Bruevich[28]

Since the Germans had kept pressure on the Bolsheviks to protect the family, Bonch-Bruevich sent the soldier to Sverdlov.

Meanwhile, the power struggle in the Urals had reached its zenith. The Omsk Soviet, now under the control of Degtiarev, was opposed by a contingent that had arrived from the Ekaterinburg Soviet, which was under the control of Semyon Zaslavsky. And both Soloviev and Little Markov had been arrested and imprisoned for aiding the family. During their confinement they were able to scratch notes to each other and exchange them on the way to the bathroom, signing them with the symbol of the Brotherhood of St John, the reverse swastika.[29] The new political climate was far less tolerant of Tsarist sympathisers than was previously the case.

Adding to the utter chaos in Tobolsk was the arrival from Moscow of Sverdlov's and Lenin's hand-picked man Vassily Yakovlev, at the head of 150 Red soldiers with his own private telegraph operator in tow. Yakovlev presented paperwork to Colonel Kobylinsky indicating that he was on a 'mission of special importance'. Ostensibly this mission was to take the family to Moscow for the show trial that had been demanded by Trotsky. Kobylinsky assembled his men and Yakovlev made a speech promising payment of past due wages to the unhappy guards. After that first meeting, Zaslavsky tried to incite the guards against Yakovlev by spreading talk of secret tunnels and subversive activities designed to remove the family (later, *Rescuing the Czar* would maintain that the family was removed via a tunnel). Zaslavsky's remarks were targeted at discrediting the Omsk leader, Degtiarev, in order to gain control of the Imperial family. But Yakovlev was finally successful in imposing his ascendancy over Zaslavsky, thereby restoring order in the house in Tobolsk.[30]

On 21 April, Filipp Goloshchekin, the Military Commissar of the Ural Regional Soviet and a man who was later to be closely involved in the fate of the Romanovs, telegraphed his dissatisfaction regarding the conduct of some of the local Ekaterinburg Soviet men and their lack of support of Yakovlev:

To the Chairman of the Tobolsk S. [Soviet], Khokhriakov I found out [about] your conversation yesterday with Ditkovsky. Your mildness is not permissible . . . Announce to the whole town that artillery is to be used and the nest of counter-revolutionaries mercilessly razed upon least resistance or insubordination to Yakovlev's orders. 2225.

Military commissar of the Ural Region,
Goloshchekin[31]

Following Goloshchekin's order Yakovlev insisted that Khokhriakov, whom he had known previously, must accompany him on his 'mission of special importance'. Khokhriakov had recently become the Chairman of the local Tobolsk Soviet that was much less militant than the Omsk, or the very militant local Ekaterinburg Soviet, due to the fact that it did not have a very large Bolshevik presence. However, the local Ekaterinburg Soviet continued to demand that Yakovlev bring the family to Ekaterinburg, ignoring the regional commissar Goloshchekin's order and threatening that if Yakovlev did not comply they would brand him a traitor and take immediate action to hang him, the family and his soldiers.

While all this was occurring Soloviev and Little Markov remained in prison following their arrest by a Bolshevik called Gustev. Yet shortly after removal of the family from Tobolsk, both men were mysteriously released. At the least, Little Markov seems to have been unaware of this plan to remove the family from Tobolsk. It appears that he came close to compromising it unwittingly by talking to various people about an impending rescue. As a result he had been arrested by Gustev, who also had to arrest Soloviev, who may have been knowledgeable about the impending transfer, to retain the air of legitimacy necessary for the successful removal of the family. Later, in his book, Little Markov lamented how he wished he had not been in jail when Yakovlev left with the Romanovs, for he was planning to wait along the roadside to attempt to grab them.[32] But now in light of all the evidence it looks as if Gustev had closeted both him and Soloviev on purpose for fear Little Markov might have inadvertently exposed the 'mission of special importance'. Later on 8 July, a 'Gustev' would be the one to relay a message about an uprising that resulted in a train intended to transport the Imperial family, which figures in one of the rescue attempts, being sent back to Ekaterinburg.[33]

The route to Moscow that Yakovlev and his party followed from Tobolsk began overland, by rural carts, to the nearest railway station at Tiumen. There, on 27 April, Yakovlev telegraphed Moscow: 'To

Goloshchekin. Your detachments have only the single wish of destroying that baggage for which I was sent. The initiators: Zaslavsky, Khokhriakov, and Kusiatsky [Gusiatsky] . . .'[34]

During the exchange of telegrams that followed, Yakovlev explains that Zaslavsky had incited men in a couple of detachments to attempt to attack his train carrying the Imperial family but that he and his men had defeated them and had taken a prisoner who had informed him of Zaslavsky's plan. He informs Goloshchekin that the men who are causing him trouble are 'mocking' Goloshchekin as well. Yakovlev says he has learned they had planned to 'finish off the whole detachment, along with me'. He insists to Goloshchekin that the Ekaterinburg detachment has a 'strong inclination to destroy the baggage [code word for the Imperial family]'. Then he concludes:

. . . Do you guarantee the preservation of this baggage? Remember that the Council of Commissars vowed to keep me safe. Answer in detail personally. I am sitting at the station [in Tiumen] with the main part of the baggage [Nicholas, Alexandra and Maria], and as soon as I get an answer, I depart. Make a place ready.

Yakovlev, Guzakov[35]

Yakovlev's apprehensiveness continues and while still in Tiumen he next enquires of Sverdlov in Moscow about the route:

The route remains the same, or did you change it? Inform Tiumen Immediately. I am going by the old route. An immediate answer is necessary.

Yakovlev[36]

Still on 27 April, Moscow responds:

The route is the old one; tell me whether you are carrying the baggage [Nicholas] or not.

Sverdlov [VTsIK chairman – Central Executive Committee of All Russian Soviets.][37]

And in the telegrams that follow on the same day we get a clearer understanding of the 'old route':

Sverdlov at the Apparatus. Is Yakovlev at the apparatus? (Interval) Let me know if you are too nervous; perhaps fears are exaggerated and the old route can be retained. Waiting for answer?? (Interval)

Yes, yes, I read it. (Interval) It's quite clear. (A small interval) Do you consider it possible to go to Omsk and wait there for further instructions? Go to Omsk, telegraph when you get there. Appear before the chairman of the Soviet, Vladimir Kosarev. Transport everything secretly; I'll give further instructions in Omsk. Get going. Out. (Interval) It will be done; all instructions will be given. Out. Good-bye.[38]

Even though the next telegram from Yakovlev was transmitted the same day it is difficult to tell if it came before or after the previous transmission. It is compelling in that Yakovlev wants to drive home the point to Sverdlov, as he had previously informed Goloshchekin, that the Ural forces are not to be trusted:

I have just brought part of the baggage [Nicholas, Alexandra and Maria] here. I want to change the route because of the following extremely important circumstances. Certain people arrived in Tobolsk from Yekaterinburg before I did in order to destroy the baggage. The special purpose detachment repulsed their attack – barely avoiding bloodshed. When I arrived, the Yekaterinburg people hinted to me that the baggage need not be delivered to its destination. I rebuffed them.

He continues by informing them that he 'took measures' and 'they decided not to tear it away from me'. However, he says they told him not to sit next to the Tsar while travelling because he might be killed. Yakovlev did so anyway. He then conveys to Moscow how he found out that the Ekaterinburg detachment had planned to lie in wait and ambush them between Tobolsk and Tiumen, and how he managed to arrest a member of the Ekaterinburg detachments who turned informer and warned Yakovlev of the plans to destroy the 'baggage'. Yakovlev further reveals:

Yekaterinburg, with the exception of Goloshchekin, has one desire: to finish off the baggage at all cost. The Fourth, Fifth, and Sixth Red Army companies are organising an ambush. If this conflicts with the thinking from the centre [Moscow], then it is mad to transport the baggage to Yekaterinburg.[39]

Yakovlev recommends taking the 'baggage' to the Simsky Gorny district (in central Siberia), 'there are good places in the mountains that are exactly and purposely suited for this'. Clearly Yakovlev knew that the plan was not to take the family to Moscow for a show trial following which they would be executed. Hence we now realise that Yakovlev's mission was to remove them from a potentially dangerous situation in Tobolsk and put them in a safer place. For to be sure, if killing the Imperial family was what Sverdlov and Moscow wanted to achieve – the Ekaterinburg contingent appears to have had that goal and its ultimate fulfilment well in hand – Yakovlev would surely have been ordered instead to proceed straight to Ekaterinburg. However, Yakovlev continues to emphasise the dangers:

> . . . I cannot vouch for the consequences. If the baggage falls into the hands [of] the Yekaterinburg detachment, then of course the end result will be the same. So answer: do I go to Yekaterinburg or through Omsk to Simsky Gorny district? I'm waiting for an answer. I'm at the station with the baggage.
> Yakovlev, Guzakov[40]

Sverdlov was communicating with Vladimir Kosarev, Chairman of the Omsk Soviet. Kosarev received very clear orders on 28 April:

> To Vladimir Kosarev, chairman of the Soviet, Omsk. Yakovlev, [about] whose powers I informed you, will arrive [in] Omsk with the baggage; trust [him] completely. Follow only our orders [and] no one else's. I place full responsibility on you; conspiracy is necessary. Yakovlev is acting in accordance with our direct orders. Send an order immediately up the Omsk-Tiumen line: assistance must be rendered in every possible way to Yakovlev.
> Sverdlov[41]

At almost the same time as Sverdlov was directing the Omsk Soviet to render assistance to Yakovlev, another communiqué was received in Moscow on 28 April from its rival competitor for the family, the

Ekaterinburg Soviet. This time the telegram is addressed not just to Sverdlov but also to Lenin:

> Your commissaire Yakovlev brought Romanov to Tiumen, put him on the train, and made for Yekaterinburg. Having driven halfway to the nearest station, he changed direction. He went back. Now the train with Nicholas is near Omsk. We do not know what the purpose of this is. We consider such an act traitorous. According to your letter of 9 April, Nicholas is supposed to be in Yekaterinburg. What does this mean? In accordance with the decision adopted by the regional soviet and the regional party committee, an order has been given to hold up Yakovlev and the train at all costs, to arrest and deliver both him and Nicholas to Yekaterinburg. We are waiting by the apparatus for an answer.
>
> Beloborodov and Safarov.[42]

The above telegram was prompted by the fact that Yakovlev had indeed set out towards Ekaterinburg. But suddenly, with all lights doused, the train had slipped back through Tiumen and had taken the line to Omsk in the opposite direction of Moscow. But then, for some reason, the train had stopped short of Omsk.

On 29 April another series of exchanges began between Ekaterinburg officials, Yakovlev and Moscow. The situation was grim indeed. Yakovlev had been accused of treason and, by implication, so had Moscow. The Ural Soviet was challenging Moscow's hand. This time the telegram came only from Beloborodov to Sverdlov. He continues to insist that Yakovlev is conducting himself in a treasonous manner and queries who gave Yakovlev permission to take the route east towards Omsk. Further, Beloborodov reminds Sverdlov that on 9 April, Moscow had intended to send the family to the Urals and that the officials in the Urals had not been informed of any change in the decision. He states:

> Ural Regional Soviet of Workers, Peasants, and Soldiers, by unanimous verdict, sees [in] him [Yakovlev] outright betrayal of the revolution, a desire to transport the former tsar [beyond] the bounds of the revolutionary Urals for reasons unknown and contrary to the exact written instructions of the TsIK chairman.

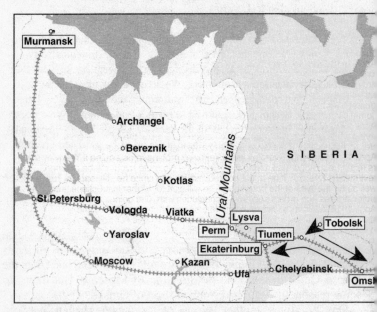

Moscow and Yakovlev s Activities — April 1918

1. **Moscow**
   - 28 March, 1918 Omsk Soviet asks Lenin and Trotsky to replace the guard in Tobolsk and put Nicholas under their control
   - No later than 1 April, 1918 Vladimir Bonch—Bruevich* states, in a letter to VTsI a soldier from Tobolsk has arrived and reported chaos in detachment guarding Nicholas — Yakov Sverdlov** responds by asking to see the soldier
   - 1 April, 1918 Moscow issues orders to protect the family or transport them immediately to Moscow. Declares orders not to be made public
   - 6 April, 1918 The Presidium of the VTsIK charges Sverdlov to order the transfer all the arrested to the Urals
   - 9 April, 1918 Sverdlov informs Ekaterinburg Soviet that Vassily Yakovlev will bri Nicholas alive; they can decide to place him in prison or a mansion

2. **Tobolsk**
   - 22 April, 1918 Yakovlev arrives in Tobolsk
   - 23 April, 1918 Yakovlev realises Alexei is ill and cannot move entire family — Yakovlev is accompanied by Pavel Matveyev and Alexander Adveyev, who will initially be placed in charge of the family in Ekaterinburg
   - 24 April, 1918, while in Tobolsk, Yakovlev receives permission from Moscow to remove only some of the family — Nicholas, Alexandra, Maria and one retainer Demidova — the trip begins with the first stop being Tiumen

en

April, 1918 From the train station in Tiumen Yakovlev informs Filipp
oshchekin*** your detachments [including Khokhriakov] have attempted to
troy the baggage [Nicholas] and are mocking you [Goloshchekin] as well as
atening the life of the family and me [Yakovlev] . Yakovlev asks Goloshchekin if
guarantees the preservation of the baggage and reminds Filipp that the Council
Commissars vowed to keep me safe — Answer in detail personally
April, 1918 (8.50 p.m.) Again from Tiumen, Yakovlev wires Sverdlov in Moscow
rying whether route has now been changed or remains the same — immediately
rdlov responds — route is the old one; asks if he has the baggage
April, 1918 (evening) Sverdlov wires Yakovlev probing to determine if Yakovlev s
s might be exaggerated, trying to decide if the old route might still be retained.
ovlev asks Sverdlov if he might go to Omsk instead since he still fears for his life
well as for the lives of the baggage — he will wait for further instructions (interval)
rdlov agrees and orders secrecy — concludes with Get going.
April, 1918 Yakovlev s wire reveals that there had been a plot by some
terinburg men to kill him and the baggage and they have captured one of the
n who has told all — then Yakovlev says, Ekaterinburg, with the exception of
oshchekin, has one desire: to finish off the baggage at all costs — I offer my
ices as permanent commissar for guarding the baggage right up to the end but
doesn t trust some in Ekaterinburg — says will take them to Simsky Gorney — if
baggage fall into the hands of [Ekaterinburg] it will be destroyed

April, 1918 Alexander Beloborodov and Georgy Safarov of the Ural Regional
iet wire Lenin and Sverdlov demanding to know why Yakovlev went to Omsk
ead of Ekaterinburg — they consider this an act of treason and inform Lenin and
rdlov they have ordered the arrest of Nicholas and Yakovlev
April, 1918 Sverdlov wires Omsk Soviet that Yakovlev should be trusted adding —
nspiracy is necessary and assistance must be rendered
April, 1918 Beloborodov wires Sverdlov and again accuses Yakovlev of treason
ne requests Sverdlov direct all parties to arrest Yakovlev [telegram was sent by
oborodov as top military priority]
April, 1918 Sverdlov wires to Ekaterinburg for Beloborodov and this time to
oshchekin as well, that Yakovlev is under orders — Once again, no interference
Yakovlev is to be trusted completely — Details by special courier
April, 1918 Sverdlov wires to Yakovlev — Immediately go back to Tiumen [hence
terinburg] I reached an understanding with the Uralites [Ural Regional Soviet]
n convinced that all orders will be precisely fulfilled.
April, 1918 With reservation, Yakovlev agrees to deliver the baggage to
terinburg, after assurances from Sverdlov that an agreement had been reached
he adds, One more thought: *if you send the baggage to Simsky district, then*
can always transport it to Moscow or wherever you want. .(Author s italics and
erline) I ll hand over the baggage. [Then] I ll go for the other part of it.

of the Sovnarkom (Council of People s Commissars)
of the All-Russian Executive Committee of Soviet (VTsIK)
ommissar of the Ural Regional Soviet and District Military Commissar
ocuments were cited in *The Fall of the Romanovs* by Mark Steinberg and Vladimir Khrustal v, pp. 229—52

Then he insists on a change of escort for the Imperial Family and forthrightly informs Moscow of the following:

> We propose not to pay attention [to] various documents that Yakovlev will present or cite, since all his former steps indisputably attest [to] the criminal scheme Yakovlev implemented, possibly on the instructions of other persons. The regional committees of the parties of Communist Bolsheviks, Left SRs, and Maximalists consider the fulfilment of the regional soviet's resolution obligatory for members of these parties. We ask [you] to immediately telegraph the regional Soviet in Yekaterinburg [about] adopted measures, [as well as about] the consequences.
>
> Chairman of the Ural Regional Soviet of Workers', Peasants', [and] Soldiers' Deputies,
> Aleksandr Beloborodov[43]

This time the formality of Beloborodov's signature and the tone of the message are both strident and defiant. As the stand-off continues, Sverdlov responds directly to Beloborodov and Filipp Goloshchekin, the man Yakovlev said was the only man in the Urals who did not want to see Nicholas and his family dead. Sverdlov excludes Safarov. His tone is unyielding:

> Everything being done by Yakovlev – concerning Preobrazhensky, Didkovsky, Safarov – is in direct fulfilment of an order I have given. I will inform [you] of the details by special courier. I issue no orders concerning Yakovlev. He is acting in accordance with an order rec. [received] from me today at 4 o'clock in the morning. Undertake absolutely nothing without our agreement. Yakovlev is to be trusted completely. Once again, no interference.
>
> Sverdlov[44]

Sverdlov's position must have been trying. He was a man unaccustomed to being questioned, and from the content of his next communiqué he seems to have assumed that his orders would be followed without a doubt, for he telegraphed Yakovlev to reverse his direction and head back towards Ekaterinburg:

> Immediately go back [to] Tiumen; I reached an understanding [with the] Uralites; they adopted measures [and] guaranteed that they will

be personally responsible for the actions of the regional men; hand all the baggage over [in] Tiumen to the chairman of the Ural regional committee; this is essential. Go together [with them] yourself; render the chairman assistance. The mission stays the same. You accomplished the main thing. [In] Yekaterinburg you will receive a detailed proposal, [also] inform me [of] your departure [from] Omsk to Tiumen [with] a copy to Beloborodov, Ural regional committee; if necessary, take reinforcements from Vladimir Kosarev, chairman of the Soviet in Omsk; I am convinced that all orders will be precisely fulfilled.

   Regards.
   Sverdlov[45]

With these orders in hand Yakovlev had one last go at his superior when he telegraphed his final transmission from Omsk on 29 April:

Without question I submit to all orders from the centre. I will deliver the baggage wherever you say. But I consider it my duty to warn the Council of Peop. Commissaires once more that the danger is entirely well founded, which both Tiumen and Omsk can confirm. One more thought: if you send the baggage to Simsky district, then you can always *transport it to Moscow or wherever you want* [author's italics]. If the baggage is taken by the first route [to Yekaterinburg], then I doubt that you will be able to drag it out of there . . . Thus, we warn you one last time and free ourselves from any moral responsibility for the future consequences. I am going by the first route. We are departing at once. I remind you there are constant misunderstandings during negotiations over the [telegraph] apparatus . . .[46]

Yakovlev's telegram continues by informing Sverdlov, who apparently feels he has regained control over the Ekaterinbug contingent, that even the people's commissaire of post and telegraph did not allow negotiations over the telegraph because the telegraph reception was unreliable and prone to misunderstandings. He then requests that Moscow wire all the appropriate personnel to grant the train speedy passage and that he will go by the first route back towards Ekaterinburg where he will hand over the baggage. The most telling part of his last communication is the phrase, *then you can always transport it to Moscow or wherever you want* [author's italics]. It seems clear that Yakovlev knew that the family was not destined for a 'show trial' and even tells us they could send them somewhere other than Moscow.

The statement of Aleksander Nevolin, a member of the Ural detachment of the Red Army and the prisoner and informant Yakovlev mentions in his telegrams, survived and supports Yakovlev's assertions. In his own words he tells of having come with the Ekaterinburg detachment to Tobolsk. He recollects seeing the detachment of Yakovlev arrive and that then he spent two nights in Tobolsk waiting to return with the family to Ekaterinburg, but that a Gusiatsky, who was aide to the chief of staff and the same one Yakovlev stated in his telegram to Goloshchekin was not to be trusted, came to him and said: 'So commissaire Yakovlev has arrived here and wants to take Romanov to Moscow, and then it seems they've decided to send him abroad. We have the following task to deliver him to Yekaterinburg at all costs.'[47]

Nevolin's statement is full of details that coincide with Yakovlev's telegraphed situation report. He says there were meetings to determine when and where to ambush the family, and that he, Nevolin, was the only one to object – then he was warned:

> And say nothing to anyone. If anyone starts asking which detachment this is, say that it's Moscow's and don't say who your chief is, because this must be done by bypassing the regional Soviet and in general all Soviets. Then I asked one question: ['] So we're to be brigands? I myself am not in agreement with your plans. If you need to kill Romanov, then you may make that personal decision, but I won't allow such a thought to enter my head.'[48]

Either this is self-serving testimony or it has a ring of truth. It is impossible to believe that all members of the Soviets wanted the Tsar dead and were willing to lend a hand to the effort. Nevolin says that when the debate escalated, he took the position that Moscow knew better what to do with Romanov but that he felt his life was in danger for disagreeing: 'Looking for a way out, I finally decided to flee with Yakovlev's detachment.'[49]

It now seems evident from this episode that Moscow was trying to move the family to safety – either the safety of another part of Russia or into the hands of a foreign power. Both the Imperial family and Yakovlev were targets of the rogues from Ekaterinburg. What is obvious is that Moscow suddenly found itself powerless against the Ekaterinburg Soviet. Not only were the Central Committee's orders ignored but it was peremptorily informed that any intervention would be viewed as treason. Quite effectively, the men from the Urals had checkmated the Central Committee. To understand how this could have occurred it is important to recall that Lenin was shepherding a fragile governmental structure that had only been established for six months. The Ekaterinburg crowd appears to have been beyond his control. They had their own agenda.

One aspect of the Yakovlev episode is constant throughout – the crying need for speed. Yakovlev continually pressed for haste in removing the family from Tobolsk. Much to Yakovlev's surprise when he arrived, he found that Alexei had been suffering from a haemophilia attack. But in spite of this Yakovlev decided not to wait for the Tsarevich to recover his health. The realisation that Alexei was not well must have been stunning. Having somehow managed to convince them to leave Alexei and the other daughters behind, he wasted little time and had set off with only Nicholas, Alexandra and Maria. Alexandra is said to have spent a tortured night trying to decide whether to stay with the rest of the family or accompany her husband. It was later recalled that she said, 'You know what my son is to me and I must choose between him and my husband. But I have made up my mind. I must be firm. I must leave my child and share . my husband's life or death.'[50]

Something must have been pressing indeed to convince Alexandra and Nicholas to take such a step. The Tsarina's turmoil could have been a result of intelligence Yakovlev had shared with her and her husband. Her decision must have been wrenching on every level as leaving her children behind would have caused her anxiety beyond description. Facing the unknown in the hands of Yakovlev, she and her husband could not have known if they would be delivered into safety or die at the hands of the Bolsheviks.

Whenever this strange episode is alluded to, the haste is usually explained by the fact that the approaching spring thaw would make the roads and rivers impassable for a time. Yet if the spring thaw would inhibit the transport of Nicholas to Moscow, it would surely have also inhibited moving the rest of the family to Ekaterinburg and that was clearly not the case for they were transported there just weeks later. And, in any case, what was so urgent about returning Nicholas for trial? An escape, by contrast, would depend on the most careful timing, since other people would have to be in the right place at the right time.

There has been much speculation about Yakovlev and his motives, and about whether he was in British or even German pay, but little reliable information is available. Soviet archival material suggests that he was an extreme Bolshevik called Konstantin Miachin, whose revolutionary past had included operating as a terrorist, complete with shootings and the robbery of a gold train. This record states that after transporting the family to Ekaterinburg, he was placed in command of the Soviet Second Army fighting against the Czechs and Whites in Siberia. The archives allege that in July 1918 he changed allegiance and went over to the Whites, and issued an appeal to the soldiers of the Red Army exhorting them to abandon the Bolsheviks. Traditionally he is supposed to have been shot by the Whites in 1919.

But Edvard Radzinsky discovered that a Yakovlev surfaced in China calling himself Stoyanovich and acted as adviser to Sun Yat-sen, a Chinese political leader; he was also said to have been spying for the Cheka (the first secret police of the Bolshevik government, later known as GPU, NKVD and the KGB). According to the official version, this Yakovlev returned to the Soviet Union in 1927 and was arrested and sentenced to work on the White Sea–Baltic Canal. Two years later he was released, but was arrested again in 1938 and shot.[51] Steinberg and Khrustalëv follow much the same path in their account of Yakovlev's subsequent life. Other archives they consulted tell us that Yakovlev returned from China in 1928 but was freed in 1933 rather than in 1929.[52] So the Soviet archives are at odds. Are they talking about the same man – and was that man the Yakovlev who was forced to take Nicholas, his wife and daughter to Ekaterinburg?

Virtually all recorded accounts of the relocation of Nicholas, Alexandra and Maria indicate that Yakovlev exhibited polite behaviour and solicitous concern towards the symbols of a regime that would have been hated by any extreme Bolshevik. Obviously this behaviour does not square with Yakovlev's official Soviet record as a revolutionary with violent tendencies. However, strangely enough, another Yakovlev appeared in files in America, in 1920. While the name Yakovlev was somewhat common, this file referred to a Mikhail Yakovlev who was supposedly in a British camp for Russian refugees in Egypt (a British protectorate) and was the holder of Russia's most coveted award for bravery, the Cross of St George. According to the paperwork, located in the Russian consulate in San Francisco, dated 1920, he was brought to the United States with the avowed objective of being reunited with his brother in Hawaii. Negotiations for his move to New York were conducted at the ambassadorial level and the normal visa requirements, usually so strict in the United States, were waived in his case. Clearly he was someone of importance and not only to the American government. He died shortly after reaching Hawaii from complications of surgery.

Just after this Yakovlev's death, the Russian consul in San Francisco, George Sergeyevich Romanovsky, who was one of the translators of *Rescuing the Czar*, wrote to Yakovlev's brother referring to the 'epic' service Mikhail had rendered to his country. While he lay dying from a bullet wound, the French, as if to underline the point, had furnished him with a free hospital bed and arranged for the best doctor in Hawaii to attend him. Additionally, the Russian embassy in Washington then paid for a full military funeral, replete with a salute over the coffin of this 'epic' soldier.[53]

He must have been special indeed. The Americans, the English, the French and the Russians all took more than a passing interest in his final days and made sure that he was laid to rest in an honourable fashion. Why? This man, to merit such treatment and the use of the word 'epic', must have done something absolutely extraordinary. Was this the Yakovlev who might have made an attempt to take the Romanovs to freedom and had he been in the service of the Allies?

The cordial conduct of the Yakovlev who appears in Soviet history is usually explained by depicting him as the dupe of Yakov Sverdlov, the chairman of the Central Committee, the body that ostensibly governed Soviet Russia. This version depicts him as obeying orders from Sverdlov to take Nicholas to Moscow to face trial there, while we are to believe that Sverdlov intended all along to have Nicholas delivered into the hands of the Ekaterinburg Soviet. Yet the Soviet archives do not mention any deception of Yakovlev, though as we have seen, Moscow most likely lost control of the situation. There is considerable evidence to suggest that Yakovlev and Sverdlov were close friends and also that Yakovlev was a Bolshevik. So why was there a need to dupe him?

This is often explained by claiming that it was done to deceive the Germans by showing that every effort had been made to take the

Imperial family to the relative safety of Moscow but that the excesses of the local Soviet had thwarted the effort.

Can the adventure be explained by the conflicting Soviet archives, or by the notion that he may have been attempting to take the family to Moscow or elsewhere? It would seem fair to say that the following scenario is more likely: Moscow wanted to relocate the family until such time as it could send them 'wherever' since the evidence indicates that Lenin was using them as bargaining chips and they would not be exchanged until he received the money and the terms he was demanding for them. He had originally intended to send them to Ekaterinburg, but as we saw in Tobolsk, the local Soviet in Ekaterinburg had developed a more radical view than the one Moscow wanted to impose. Sverdlov and Lenin, finding themselves checkmated by the Ekaterinburg Soviet, took a chance and allowed Nicholas, Alexandra, and Maria to be taken to Ekaterinburg, feeling that they and Filipp Goloshchekin could control the situation. But this was not to be. Later, in July 1918, just before the night of 17 July, Moscow would even be forced to remove the local guard to regain control.

It is interesting to note how the Yakovlev episode was treated in later books on the subject. He is given the utmost respect by authors Kerensky, Robert Wilton, a journalist for *The Times* of London, who was an operative in the pay of the British Foreign Office; Captain Paul Bulygin, formerly in command of the personal guard of the Dowager Empress; and the lady-in-waiting to the Tsarina, Baroness Buxhoeveden[54]. Such soft treatment was never afforded by a Tsarist sympathiser to any Bolshevik who had dealt with the Imperial family before or since.

The evidence presented in this book so far suggests that Yakovlev might have been charged with the responsibility of delivering the family to Moscow or 'wherever' so that it could be handed over to the British in exchange for the money that had been paid to Lenin by the Allies in February through the banking scheme. But Lenin, as will be examined later, was still double dealing and while the British may have thought it was possible that they would receive the Romanovs, so too did the Germans.

One thing is certain, however: when Yakovlev was communicating by private telegraph to Moscow he was speaking only to one of Lenin's closest advisers, Yakov Sverdlov, and Lenin himself for his instructions. In yet another interesting coincidence, one of

Sverdlov's brothers was in the French Army, assigned to intelligence duty, and, as mentioned earlier, his other brother, Benjamin, had been in business with Sidney Reilly in New York before the War.[55]

The events in April no longer appear so inexplicable since we now understand that Lied and Armitstead were part of a plan to receive the family and deliver them to Murmansk, where the Hudson's Bay Company was erecting a house provisioned for seven individuals and paid for by the British Admiralty; the Allied banking scheme had begun to function but had run into troubled waters resulting in Sidney Reilly's appearance as the Bolshevik Comrade Relinsky; and the pay-off of £500,000 to Lenin just weeks before Yakovlev's 'mission of special importance' had ended with the Ekaterinburg Soviet checkmating all plans laid by the Central Committee. It is this last factor that is going to up the stakes and have Lenin, the Allies and the Germans working overtime.

CHAPTER 7

A New Cast of Characters

Royalty Makes Another Move

The success of the Ekaterinburg Soviet in taking control of the family prompted the Allies to formulate additional plans of action that would result in the emergence of an array of new characters. A telegram, sent from Washington by the Third Under-Secretary of State, Breckinridge Long, to a close associate of President Wilson's, Gavin McNab, in San Francisco, queried the readiness of a Jerome Barker Landfield to serve in the State Department.[1] During the two years prior to 1918 Landfield had repeatedly written to the State Department offering his expertise for service in Russia, only to be, not so politely, ignored. Perfunctory notes were returned to him each time with a rejection of his offer of service.[2] However on 21 May, less than a month after the Yakovlev episode, with the family now clearly at risk in the hands of the hardline Ekaterinburg Soviets, all that changed. Long cabled McNab relative to using Landfield, stating, 'There seems now to be an opportunity.'[3]

The man enquiring about the availability of Landfield was characterised by Colonel House, Wilson's de facto Secretary of State, when he stated in his memoirs that Breckinridge Long essentially ran his own State Department known only to the President. Later, when Long wrote his memoirs, he allowed that President Roosevelt called him back during the Second World War to handle, among other important tasks, the 'evacuation of important refugees'.[4] It is also known that Long served as a courier between

Colonel House, Sir William Wiseman, head of British Intelligence in North America, and the British Foreign Secretary, Arthur Balfour, for Wilson in 1918. Long's relationship with Balfour had become so close that Balfour generally resided in the Under-Secretary's home while he was visiting the United States. From Long's correspondence it is evident that he enjoyed the deepest confidence on matters of great magnitude from Wilson, House and Balfour.

Gavin McNab, to whom Long wrote in California asking for Landfield's help, will also become an important player in the Romanov saga. He had headed Wilson's campaign organisation in the West, as well as being a national committee man for the Democratic Party, and was present, after Wilson's election, as a participant in an important labour conference.[5] Even Breckinridge Long, when writing to Gavin McNab speaks of 'your special relationship to the President'.

But it is Jerome Barker Landfield's background that is particularly engaging. Born in New York in 1871, Landfield had received his education at Cornell University and in St Petersburg. He was fluent in Russian and had explored parts of Siberia on horseback while mapping the Ural Mountains. Landfield was also familiar with both the natives and the local dialects. Having filed the first mining claim by an American in the Urals, he was one of only a handful of Westerners who could boast any expertise in the region, and as such he would have been an invaluable asset to the Allies had they needed a man who knew the Urals, and in particular Ekaterinburg and its environs. Landfield had visited the mining engineer, Professor Ipatiev, who was the owner of the Ipatiev House.[6] What's more, Landfield was a man who would have been fully sympathetic to the Tsarist cause.

After he completed his graduate work at the University of St Petersburg, Landfield married, in 1907, Princess Louba Lobanoff-Rostovsky, a lady-in-waiting to the Tsarina. Louba's sister, Olga Nikolaevna, had married, in 1895, Sir Edwin Egerton,[7] who served as British Minister in Athens and ambassador in Rome. One of Egerton's relatives served as lady-in-waiting to the Duchess of Connaught, mother of a man who would undertake a trip to the United States in 1918 at the request of King George V, which had implications for the Tsar's and Tsarina's fate. Landfield's marriage had linked him not only to the Russian Court but also to the Court of King George V.

While the suggestiveness of this information is all too apparent, it seems that Landfield's pleas to be of service were not acted on by the State Department until King George's cousin, Prince Arthur of Connaught, may have finally succeeded in having him pressed into service via Breckinridge Long. For on 21 May, the same day that Long's night telegram was sent to McNab, Prince Arthur arrived in New York, where the same Breckinridge Long met him. It was the height of the war and the King himself had pressed Prince Arthur to return from military service on the battlefields to undertake the voyage. Connaught enjoyed such a close relationship with the King that often he stood in for him at official functions when King George was otherwise engaged. And, of course, the Prince was similarly closely related to the Imperial family, for he was a grandson of Queen Victoria and, as such, was a first cousin to Alexandra. Therefore he was not a stranger to the plight of the Tsar and the Tsarina.

The Prince was delivered by a British destroyer, the official explanation being that he was on the way to the Orient to present a baton to the Emperor of Japan.[8] What has become known as the 'Baton Mission' seems legitimate on its face, but closer inspection reveals the journey as more than peculiar. Was Connaught – as has been historically argued – merely attempting to ease the way for Japanese intervention in Siberia, a policy that supposedly Wilson was uncomfortable with? Or was there an additional agenda that could embrace all the unusual circumstances occurring at the time, including the desire to induct Landfield into the State Department?

Prince Arthur's trip to America was presented as if he were simply stopping over on his way to Japan. However, if he was only there to present the baton, could not any other highly decorated military officer have performed this task? Why would George V's close relative be needed? Prince Arthur, on the other hand, with his ties to the King and the Tsar, made the perfect conduit between the King and President Wilson. Let us not forget, it is the King who had Wilson as his guest on the very night the 'urgent . . . verify family seven times' is queried the following December from London. The subject of Connaught's subsequent meetings with American officials remains unknown and although the English Baton Mission has been studied, it, like the banking scheme and the Czech uprising in Siberia to come, has not been fully understood. It now seems likely that the Baton Mission was actually in part a front for communications between King George, President Wilson and the Emperor of Japan regarding the rescue of the family. Connaught's arrival and the recruitment of Landfield were part of the new plan to rescue the family, following the failure of Yakovlev's 'mission of special importance' a month before.

We get our first clue as to what these plans could have entailed from a very interesting meeting that was taking place in Moscow just two days after Prince Arthur's arrival in America. According to documents brought from the Soviet Union by a defector in the 1960s[9] and published in Paris, there was a meeting of the Central Executive Committee on 23 May just weeks after the Ekaterinburg Soviet had wrenched control of the family from Yakovlev, during which the fate of the Romanovs was once again discussed.

The commonly accepted notion that all members of the Central Committee were united in their desire to exterminate the Imperial family at this time is, as we are about to find out, quite false. In fact, there was a deep split in their ranks. Under pressure from the Germans,[10] a heated debate was being conducted regarding the fate of the family. The conflict boiled down to whether or not to bring Nicholas back to Moscow for a show trial, as Trotsky was insisting, or leave him tucked away in Siberia. On this occasion Lenin did very little of the talking, but then he was hardly likely to make public his policy of double dealing and extortion by continuing to use the Romanovs as pawns. Lenin's strategy seems to have been to persuade the Germans not to occupy the Soviet heartland and to relax the burden of the 300 million gold rouble indemnity imposed by the Treaty of Brest-Litovsk the previous March. In return for his delivering the Romanovs into their hands, he was at the same time leading the Allies to think he was also co-operating with them following the £500,000 paid to him the previous February, ostensibly to buy out pro-German stockholders in banks he had already nationalised.

Much of the debate hinged on the foreign debts incurred by the Tsarist government and Trotsky was adamant in maintaining that these debts should continue to be renounced. During the discussions Trotsky was still desperately pushing for a show trial in which Nicholas would be judged, condemned and then executed. The discussions were heated and the intervention of Karl Radek, an Austrian citizen who had come back to Russia with Lenin the previous summer and was now a senior member of the Foreign

Office recently returned from Stockholm, sabotaged Lenin. Radek told the Committee:

> My Swedish informers have learned quite recently that close interest in the butcher Nicholas is being shown on the other side of the Atlantic. If the City of London is mainly concerned with hundreds of gold buried in the cellars of Kazan, Wall Street is showing a . . . philanthropic interest in a thoroughly devalued personality . . . the head of the Romanovs. The National City Bank is financing the operation; the broker is Thomas Masaryk, a professor who is preparing to install himself as liberator in the Hradshin [the castle] in Prague. He is the man who has remote control over the Czech legions in Siberia, and he it is who has promised his associates to free the ex-Tsar. All the deliveries made on credit to the Whites by 'Remington Arms' and the 'Metallic Cartridge Union' depend on the speed with which the Czechs approach Ekaterinburg and the prisoners in the Ipatiev house. Three million gold dollars, machine guns and rifles in exchange for the puppet Nikolachka is how Masaryk sees the piece of business proposed to him by the American bankers.

He then secured the game by announcing that he also knew: 'The American cargo ship *Thomas*[11] which is expected at Vladivostok in mid-July, is due to land 14,000 rifles, as well, doubtless as embarking the Romanov family . . .'[12]

Radek, as we shall discover in the course of this chapter, appears to have been alarmingly well informed. As we have seen, there is evidence upholding his assertions regarding a US (Allied)/Czech plot to rescue the Tsar. The *Thomas* was, in fact, in the months from May to July sailing a circuit that included San Francisco, Honolulu, Seattle, Washington, Honolulu and back to San Francisco. But by 14 August the route has changed to include Vladivostok, much as Radek had anticipated. The new circuit was from San Francisco to Vladivostok, Siberia, Nagasaki, Japan, to Manila, Philippines, Guam Island, to Honolulu, then to San Francisco. It is also worth noting that his comments regarding the Remington Arms Company allow us another glimpse into the twists and turns of the Romanov saga. It should be remembered that Sidney Reilly at this very time was disguised as the Bolshevik Relinsky. But as we saw, Reilly, as Reilly, had been an agent for the Remington Arms Company and had arranged huge rifle deals in the recent past. In fact, it may well be that the rifles Radek was referring to were rifles Reilly had arranged for while serving as the agent for Remington.

To return to the tense Central Executive Committee meeting, Radek went on successfully to quash any idea Lenin might have had for delivering the family to the Germans and, on the night in question, Lenin was forced to concede. But from what we know of Lenin, the skilled statesman and conspirator, he most likely did not take this decision as final. He had another two months before the night of 17 July in Ekaterinburg, as we shall see, to work with select colleagues to trade the family to the highest bidder. Edvard Radzinsky's view that 'as always in Bolshevik history . . . the obvious concealed the hidden', corroborates that the picture of a man whose dictum was 'one step backwards to take two steps forward'. Lenin would have ignored the realities of the political situation in favour of what he described to Trotsky as 'your romantic attitude'. The fiery Trotsky might have sought to ignore the realities as he had done in the Brest-Litovsk negotiations, but Lenin had to take a longer view.

Lenin continued to regard the family as bargaining chips. At this same time the Germans were receiving assurances from Adolf Joffe, the Bolshevik ambassador in Berlin, that the Bolsheviks had every intention of safeguarding the family and bringing them to Moscow. This is supported by the fact that German State Secretary von Kuhlmann raised the question with Joffe and von Kuhlmann wrote of this meeting:

> The Russian representative replied he had been perfectly clear about it and multiple telegraphic messages referred to it, it was important to them to look after the Tsar's family and put them in a suitable place. The decision to let them come to Moscow is also fundamentally ready and prepared when the interruption of the railway line by the Czechoslovakians is cleared. The Soviet republic is not in a position to do anything in this respect now.[13]

There were other assurances from George Chicherin, the Commissar of Foreign Affairs, in Moscow; so the plan to take the family to Moscow at the Germans' behest would look to the Germans as set as anything could be in the climate of chaos, duplicity and fear. However, time passed and neither Nicholas nor his family appeared in Moscow. Lenin it seems, was still biding his time and refining his plans. In fact, there is every probability that Trotsky's subsequent promotion to run the Red Army and his departure from Moscow to Tsaritsyn (later called Stalingrad), on the Volga river to the south was engineered by Lenin so that one of the main obstacles to his plan was removed. Stalin was even sent with Trotsky and may have acted as a 'minder', because Trotsky later wrote to Lenin that Stalin was interfering with his intention to advance on the Urals. Was it possible that Trotsky had a plan to remove the family without Lenin's agreement?

But now Lenin, with Trotsky away, could work with Sverdlov, president of the All-Russian Soviet, and Filipp Goloshchekin, leader of the Ural Bolsheviks, to effect the release of the Romanovs in typical conspiratorial fashion. Sverdlov, Goloshchekin and Stalin – who was one of Lenin's most capable administrators and the man most involved with the Czechoslovak evacuation negotiated by Masaryk – were all comrades who had been exiled together in Turukhansk and had consequently remained close.[14] Sverdlov and Goloshchekin had both already been involved in Yakovlev's earlier attempt to rescue the family. And in July they will both be implicated in the events in Ekaterinburg, while Stalin minds Trotsky.

In fact, at the very time Radek revealed his intelligence regarding Masaryk, the Czech Legion did begin an uprising. And in the United States Masaryk was preparing to speak officially to President Wilson, in a meeting that was being arranged by Charles Crane – for public consumption. This confluence of events suggests that the Czechs, under the guidance of Thomas Masaryk, certainly appear to have been more closely involved with the attempted overthrow of the Bolsheviks and the extraction of the family than conventional history would have us believe.

On 25 May 1918, in the same week as the Czech uprising began, a second telegram originating from Breckinridge Long, while Prince Arthur was still in the United States, was sent once again to Gavin McNab referencing Jerome Barker Landfield and conveying a real sense of urgency: '. . . we need him now.'[15]

Hours earlier and thousands of miles away in Russia, also on 25 May, there was other American activity. In a recent book, *Michael and Natasha*, authors Rosemary and Donald Crawford state that Grand Duke Michael Alexandrovich, the brother of Nicholas II, was on 25 May 1918 under house arrest in Perm and received an after-dinner visit from two unexpected Americans, Mr O'Brien and Mr Hess. The authors speculate that they 'were the kind of people the Cheka looked upon warily as possible messengers for plotters intent on rescuing Michael'. Were the two Americans sent to inform Grand Duke Michael of the plans being finalised by Prince Arthur in America.'[16]

Whatever the 'opportunity' to use Landfield was that Long had mentioned in his telegram to McNab just after Prince Arthur of Connaught arrived in America, it now seemed to be quite pressing and appears to have been created by the presence of Prince Arthur. Landfield immediately wrapped up his affairs in California and the State Department just as quickly pulled strings to manage to pay Landfield by manipulating the department's budget.[17] Landfield arrived in Washington on 31 May. But even today his resultant State Department records do not reveal much information as to his activities until 1919.

However, there is one captivating index card regarding Landfield's involvement with General Alexeev, one of the generals whose anti-Bolshevik forces were supported by the banking scheme. While the original document no longer exists, the synopsis reads to the effect that General Alexeev should hold on until the doctor arrives. This reference to a 'doctor' has a ring of familiarity to it, for when Sidney Reilly's memoirs were published in 1933 one of the entries also read 'the doctors have operated too early and the patient's condition is serious.'[18] One of the 'doctors' Reilly was referring to was his friend Boris Savinkov, the former terrorist and ex-Kerensky aide who was now being courted by the Allies. Savinkov was the military leader of another secret planned uprising against the Bolsheviks scheduled for mid-July 1918; however, he was betrayed and as a result initiated the fighting prematurely, resulting in a failure. Savinkov would have been joined by other 'doctors'/[military leaders of Allied forces] if the plan had not been penetrated.

DeWitt Poole, the American consul in Moscow, later testified in Congress in 1920 and he 'repeatedly and categorically denied that he had any knowledge of or connection to any plot against the Soviet regime [1918]'.[19] However David Foglesong's work on the 'secret war' has demonstrated that Poole did in fact send a telegram to Washington conveying the expected date for an uprising, which was to be mid-July.[20]

As Jerome Barker Landfield, in company with the State Department, appears to have been fully informed of the activities of Boris Savinkov and of the situation in Russia in July 1918, it is safe to assume that Landfield was also in communication with various other key individuals in Russia at this critical time in June and July 1918. Even Thomas Masaryk thanked Landfield for being 'deeply interested in all Russian matters' and 'devoted to us'.[21] The depth of his devotion and the scope of his activities will most likely never be known for all other files in this series dealing with the summer of 1918, especially June and July in Russia, were destroyed in 1929, by 'order of the executive officer'. But it can now be suggested that the Czechs were indebted to him for his covert activities on their behalf as well as their Russian counterparts.

The fact that Savinkov was betrayed and, based on false information, began the uprising at the end of the first week in July, compromised the orchestrated confluence of events. Events that Landfield and others were fully aware of, as is now clear from the destroyed document telling Alexeev to hold on until the 'doctor' arrived. The 'doctor', Boris Savinkov, would also be mentioned in a document supposedly left by one of the Tsar's manservants, Parfen Domnin, that found its way into the American Military Intelligence files in 1921. The Parfen Domnin document, which we shall see later, narrates an entirely different outcome for the Tsar and his family from the accepted version of the events of the night of 16/17 July 1918.

The new evidence suggests that there was in actuality a strategy to have the Czechs, Savinkov's forces and Alexeev from the south, the Japanese from the east, as well as the British, who had entered northern Russia under the command of General Poole, all converge in an effort to overthrow the Bolsheviks in the spring and summer of 1918. The code names for the British operations were 'Syren' and 'Elope'.[22] With whom did the British think they would be eloping? The Imperial Family remains the only likely candidate and all the new evidence unequivocally points to that conclusion.

In fact, while in New York in the middle of May at almost the same time as the arrival of Prince Arthur, Charles Crane had written a letter to President Wilson's secretary Tumulty[23] thanking the President for his recent decision to support the efforts of the Slavic people. No evidence remains that Crane met Long or Prince Arthur during his New York stay to discuss the events occurring in Russia, but it would be likely as Crane and Breckinridge Long were close friends and often lobbied Wilson for the same agenda, as well as the fact that Crane was well enough connected in England to have received his mail at 'Palace Westminster'. The letter to Wilson's secretary implies that he had met Wilson in the early part of May, which was not uncommon, as the President and his wife were often guests of the Cranes, and Wilson had decided to become more involved in the fate of the Czech Legion in Russia prior to their uprising at the end of May. Crane's masterful hand appears to have been at work once again.

Charles Crane's efforts on behalf of Czechoslovakia most likely stemmed from the nature of his relationship with Masaryk – a relationship that was so close that Jan, Masaryk's son, had been living in the Crane household in America as a young man and eventually married Crane's daughter, Frances. Once again Crane had been instrumental in setting up communications and meetings with the President for Masaryk, his friend and confidant. As mentioned earlier and as alleged by Karl Radek in May 1918, under the guidance of Thomas Masaryk the Czechs do indeed appear to have been more closely involved with the fate of the Romanovs than conventional history would have us believe.

When we consider Karl Radek's intelligence report to the Central Committee that Masaryk had promised his associates to free the ex-Tsar, and all the new information regarding operatives like Landfield and Reilly and the operations such as the building of the house in Murmansk and the banking scheme, we come to realise that there is far more to the traditional record of the period. Did Thomas Masaryk, with the help of his long-time friend Charles Crane, secretly co-operate with the Allies to have the Czech Legion 'revolt' and was a Czech agent by the name of Emanuel Voska the line of communication? With this new insight, coupled with the comment of Radek who spoke of the intelligence he had picked up in May in Stockholm regarding the trade of the Remington rifles for the 'puppet' Nicholas, as well as the fact that Reilly was the agent of record for the Remington Arms Company, the happenstance nature of the revolt appears to deserve more scrutiny with respect to the involvements of the actions of underground agents and 'invisible diplomats'.

The Allies' financial and political interests in Russia, including the interests of America's large financial institutions, were at risk. In fact, National City Bank, J. P. Morgan and Company, Kuhn and

Loeb, and Guaranty Trust were also at risk for large loan defaults. As a result of the Bolsheviks' repudiation of all foreign debts, the comments of Karl Radek regarding Wall Street and Thomas Masaryk, which had put Lenin and Trotsky at odds, now take on more significance.

It must be remembered that Stalin had assisted in setting up the terms for the Czechs' exit from Russia in the spring of 1918, after the Bolsheviks signed the Treaty of Brest-Litovsk, which took Russia out of the war. Stalin had taken part in the arrangements negotiated by Masaryk and Eduard Beneš on behalf of the Allies for the Czechs to exit Russia. The Czech soldiers, travelling across Russia with their passports signed by Stalin, were to join Allied troops on the European front to continue the fight against Germany.

When the Czech forces broke out in open revolt against the Bolsheviks in May, the incident was attributed to a brawl between the Czechs and Hungarian former prisoners of war at Chelyabinsk in western Siberia. While there seems little room for doubt that the Bolsheviks were trying, at German insistence, to disarm the Czechs and prevent their transit across Siberia, it also seems impossible that the actions of multiple Czech echelons, comprising over 40,000 men, stretching from Penza on the Volga to Vladivostok, a distance of approximately 7000 kilometres, could have been so well co-ordinated without prearrangement. It would seem that such a daring military action would have required the most careful preparation and could hardly have been accidental.

As has already been discussed, any plan on behalf of the Allies or America for sorting out the complex situation in Russia most likely hinged on using the Czech forces to assist in overthrowing the Bolsheviks with the view to an eventual restoration in the form of a constitutional monarchy. Hence Masaryk's extremely brief reference in his memoirs that the Czech revolt did not include a plan to rescue Nicholas is not convincing. Even Carl Ackerman, who was the first American journalist to arrive in Ekaterinburg in the autumn of 1918, while ostensibly working for the *Saturday Evening Post* and the *New York Times*, believed otherwise. Ackerman enjoyed close contact with the Czechs and subsequently wrote: 'The Czecho-Slovaks, despite their revolutionary tendencies, were bent upon snatching the Czar from the Bolsheviki. There were independent Russian and foreign business interests in Ekaterinburg which wanted him released.'[24]

Ackerman's sentiments echoed those of Karl Radek, who announced in the meeting on 23 May that 'the National City Bank was financing the operation' to free the Tsar and that the Czechs under Masaryk would facilitate it in exchange for arms and gold. In fact, National City Bank was at risk for large loan defaults and its Board of Directors, which included both Charles Crane and Jacob Schiff, must have been quite apprehensive. Ackerman mirrored some of the same sentiments in an article he published in December 1918 in the *New York Times*, about the family and Parfen Domnin. Stranger still, these same notions appeared in the book *Rescuing the Czar*. What was Ackerman's role in the entire matter? Evidence has come to light that Ackerman was far better informed than he has been given credit for, as is indicated in the following telegram:

Received from Berne, 9 May 1918

To the Honorable Secretary of State, Washington.

Sir:

I have the honor to transmit under separate cover a leather case belonging to Mr Carl W. Ackerman of the *Saturday Evening Post*. This case contains Mr Ackerman's private papers and material for his writings. In view of the fact that Mr Ackerman made his trip to Switzerland with the acquiescence of the Department, I venture to hand the Department the package for delivery to Mr Ackerman upon his arrival in Washington if there is no objection thereto.

I have the honor to be, Sir,

Your obedient servant,

Under Separate Cover: Leather briefcase.[25]

As we can see, Ackerman, like numerous journalists during this time period, actually acted as a spy, having a close relationship with the State Department while supposedly travelling as a journalist for the *Saturday Evening Post*. While he was not in Russia when Savinkov's July uprising occurred, he was on his way to Russia via the Far East by 7 September when another State Department telegram read:

You are authorised to accept for transmission by cable or pouch to the Department or to Colonel House through the Department, messages from Carl Ackerman who is now en route the Far East.

Lansing (US Secretary of State)[26]

If anyone was well briefed it must have been Ackerman. Consequently his conclusions should, at least, be entertained leading us to suspect that the Czechoslovak Legion was not a loose cannon rolling all over Siberia, but may have been operating as part of an orchestrated effort in conjunction with a shadow White government. It has been said that there were no 'shadow governments [i.e. governmental structures that were secretly operating in the background and, in this case, had as their goal the toppling of the Bolsheviks]'. Traditional history holds that various White governments independently sprouted in Siberia but only after the liberation facilitated by the Czechs. Supposedly these governments resolved themselves into two main centres of power, one in Samara, where a Socialist Revolutionary government (Komuch) held sway, and another in Omsk, where the self-styled Provisional Siberian Government (PSG) attempted to operate. The assertions that Komuch and the PSG, which supposedly came into being after the Czech Legions had liberated Central Siberia, were the only governmental structures operating in 1918 are now questionable. In a telegram sent on 24 July 1918, Major Homer Slaughter, a US military attaché in Ekaterinburg, made the following statement:

> . . . New government composed mostly inexperienced men who frankly admit lack experience and express desire receive sound advice. America can control this government and in all its policies if prompt action is taken send advisers. Government declares itself to be temporary . . . this duma met last *January (1918)* and was closed by the Bolsheviks at once, after which secret meeting held selected present government, whose membership became known only after Bolshevik defeat . . .[27]

As a result of this communication it can now be suggested that this shadow government may have been in contact with leaders of the Czech Legion before May of 1918. However, if the government that Homer Slaughter was referring to was in fact either Komuch or the PSG, then it may have been operating secretly and in a more sophisticated manner than we have heretofore recognised. Again we must question what were the overall objectives of the Czech uprising?

Slaughter's activities were very detailed in his various reports from Siberia. Interesting, though, is the glaring absence of reports for the time period of 16 July through to 24 July not only with respect to his activities on behalf of the Czechs but even on his whereabouts[28] (he maintained he was in Omsk with US Consul Ray who was ill, but no reports substantiate this explanation) suggesting that, like many other files missing for this period, either his file has been purged, or he did not commit his activities to paper. The gap in his records is not the only gap pertaining to the activities of agents in Siberia, for we shall see that Sidney Reilly has a similar gap in his personnel file for the same period of time.

Yet the presence of another person in Siberia in June 1918 suggests that the Czechs were being used by the Allies to overthrow the Bolsheviks and help the Romanovs. During the war Emanuel Voska had been directed by Thomas Masaryk to approach Sir William Wiseman, the head of British intelligence in the United States. Voska was working at the time at the Austro-Hungarian legation. As a result, he supplied the British, through Sir William Wiseman, with intelligence of incalculable worth. He arranged a service that intercepted confidential telegrams and official mail from Germany and Austria, and unmasked one of their spies within the Russian embassy in Washington. He also tapped the telephone lines to the German embassy. This intelligence was shared not only with Wiseman, but also with President Wilson and Colonel House.

In a book called *The Final Memoranda*, edited by Ralph E. Weber, about the activities of Major-General Ralph H. Van Deman, we learn that he was sent on an intelligence mission to Europe on 5 June 1918. Van Deman makes reference to his 'special mission' several times, but he never revealed its nature.[29] From what we have now learned it is possible that Van Deman was sent abroad to co-ordinate operatives for the uprisings planned in the summer of 1918. During that time various operatives like Voska and Homer Slaughter in Ekaterinburg were reporting to Ralph Van Deman, often called the 'Father of US Intelligence'. At the time, Van Deman was being 'mentored' by General Kuhn, the companion of Prince Arthur of Connaught during the American portion of his May mission to Japan only weeks before.[30]

According to Weber, Van Deman held Voska in high esteem and utilised him throughout the war:

Voska had been an editor of a newspaper in Austro-Hungary and had gotten into trouble politically and had because of this come to the

United States some twelve years before the war broke out in 1914. He was the real organizer of the Bohemian National Alliance in the United States. He worked for the British Intelligence in 1914–15 and 16 and did some exceedingly clever work himself . . . All of the expenses incident to these agents were borne by the Alliance. When the United States entered the war, Voska stopped the activities of the Alliance in the United States because he said that now he felt its activities should be directed by the United States and that meant military control.[33]

In 1918 at the direction of Van Deman, the United States formally recognised Voska: '. . . we then commissioned Voska and six others and sent him and five of his men to France . . .'

While Voska did go to France, there are other reports that he was also in Russia. Again we learn from Van Deman the extent to which Voska was involved: '. . . it was decided at this talk with Voska that he should continue as in the past with his work, keeping in close contact from time to time with Mr Beneš and Mr Thomas Masaryk, the first President of Czechoslovakia.'[32]

It can now be entertained that Boska may have been in contact with the Czech Legion in the Ekaterinburg area under Masaryk's instructions.

When we consider that the Czech forces appear to have pressed on to Ekaterinburg not just for military tactical reasons, it is conceivable that they were involved in attempts to rescue the family.

Some historical accounts conveyed that after the spontaneous uprising of the Czech Legions, the family were murdered largely because the Czechs were approaching Ekaterinburg and the Bolsheviks panicked, fearing that the Romanovs were going to be taken out of their hands. But then Masaryk maintained in his memoirs that the Czechs had no intention of liberating the former Tsar.[33] If Masaryk was as active in covert affairs in general as he appears to have been with Voska, Sir William Wiseman and Charles Crane, then it would stand to reason he would consider the knowledge of the activities he was involved in as state secrets to be retained by him as a head of state. Consequently this statement, like many others made about this period, appears to be obfuscation.

The evidence we have seen thus far suggests that British, American, Czech and French secret agents worked in unison towards the overthrow of the Bolsheviks as well as a rescue of the family. To do so would require both the military and the diplomatic branches of the various governments to act in concert.

On 24 July 1918 Homer Slaughter sent a situation report referring to 'larrabee', a code that was being utilised in the vicinity of Ekaterinburg. This particular code was developed in 1913 and was to be employed during any 'secret' communication between officers of the Army, Navy, Diplomatic and Consular services whenever they were jointly involved in a mission. Otherwise they were to use their own codes for their respective services.[34] Slaughter said:

> Note Wireless message from American consul Tashkent was received here perhaps you may reach us same way. New larrabee code words not [then not is scratched through] for telegraph—— and——.
>
> Signed Consul Ray and Major Slaughter.[35]

Additionally, in light of the new evidence it is indisputable that a British agent, Captain Kenelm Digby-Jones, who coincidentally had been recommended by Sir W. H. Clarke for his duty in Siberia[36], (the same man who had accompanied Armitstead on the 'trade mission') was bringing orders to the Czechs that they should take Perm and Viatka, and effect junction with the Allies at Vologda as soon as possible. A telegram from General Poole in Archangel:

> Decipher. Mr Lindley (Archangel) [the British chargé d'affaires – the same man connected to the banking scheme]. 27 August 1918
> D. 7.12 p.m. 27 August 1918
> R. 3 December 1918
> No. 104 (R)
>
> My Telegram 101 . . . Polish Officer brought with him cypher messages from British, American and French consuls at Ekaterinburg. We cannot decypher ours but United States Ambassador has given me copy of his which contain additional information. Early in July Bolsheviks shot 73 persons among them three women whom they had arrested in the town and surrounding villages. Captain Digby-Jones whom I sent from Vologda about July 10 has reported that the time had arrived and informed Czechs they should make every effort they should join our forces at Viatka.[37]

But Digby-Jones would never tell his own story because in a

communication marked secret it was ascertained that he died 'on 25 September at Chelyabinsk from meningitis and heart failure'[38]and 'all particulars were in possession of Eliot'. (Sir Charles Eliot, British High Commissioner in Siberia[39] who would be sent to Ekaterinburg officially to investigate the disappearance of the family.)[40]

British records also reveal that General Diterikhs, a former officer of the Tsar's army who commanded another Czech faction advancing from Vladivostok, was in British pay.[41] With these additional facts, as we have seen, the characterisation of the Czech revolt as having been spontaneous must be re-examined. The answer may be found in the heretofore unstated secret American involvement in the two-track policy.

Within weeks after the initial uprising the Czech legions had fought their way along the Trans-Siberian Railway, thereby taking a large part of Siberia from the Bolsheviks. It is possible that the 'spontaneous' uprising was in fact a planned effort to separate Siberia from greater Russia and free the family. But for the lack of supplies and more substantial Allied assistance, it might have been successful.

The mission of Prince Arthur, who appears to have come to the United States to co-ordinate plans relating to the intervention and the next attempt to free the family, was completed by mid-June. While journeying through the United States he was accompanied by Major-General Kuhn, who was at the time the commander of the 79th Division at Fort Meade, near Washington DC. The Prince, travelling incognito, via arrangements that had been made by Breckinridge Long, who had again utilised Gavin McNab in San Francisco to ensure that there was not to be any press coverage, was on his way to Japan. General Kuhn returned to Washington, but Kuhn's military records do not account for his whereabouts from the beginning of June to 28 July 1918 when he finally reappeared and rejoined his division in France, which had shipped out during his absence.[42]

The cloud of secrecy continued as the Prince crossed the Pacific and it intensified during his sojourn in Japan. Interestingly enough, Prince Arthur presented the baton to the Japanese Emperor on 24 June, then took several 'holidays', still surrounded by a wall of secrecy in Japan and later in Canada, where he was subsequently taken by a Japanese cruiser. The Prince did not surface until 27 July.

At the time, even Sir Conyngham Greene, the British ambassador in Japan, could not penetrate the shield and lamented that he had to depend on the brief official programme and scanty press reports for his information. Greene was present at a meeting between the Prince and the Japanese Prime Minister, and reported: 'His Excellency added that it was evident in dispatching Prince Arthur to Japan the King had something more in mind than the ceremonial handing of a Field Marshal's baton.'[43]

Whatever the 'something more' was, it has remained secret. There was no shortage of opportunity for the Prince to play whatever part was needed in making the necessary arrangements for the Romanovs' safety and for confirming details with the Emperor of Japan. A statement dated 10 July in the file on his mission at Windsor Castle was removed by Colonel Clive Wigram, understudy and later successor to Lord Stamfordham, the King's private secretary. As with numbers of other critical documents pertaining to events that were occurring during this time-frame, it is unfortunate we shall never know its content.

After the failure of the Yakovlev mission, the Allies had worked quickly during the month of May to reformulate additional plans to successfully withdraw the Romanovs from Siberia. The help of the Czech Legions was essential to the success of the uprisings that were being planned for the defeat of the Bolsheviks and the freedom of the family because by now they constituted an Allied army in Siberia, since England, France and the United States could not spare troops from the Western Front. But the actions also required the support of Japan. The logistics of an escape of the family, housed in the Ipatiev House and guarded by the rogue Ekaterinburg Soviet, demanded the knowledge and skill of numerous men like Henry Armitstead, Jonas Lied and Jerome Barker Landfield. Prince Arthur's trip had been essential to lay the groundwork for the next move on the chessboard.

CHAPTER 8

Extortion

Bids for 'Gold' and 'Platinum'

The intense activities that occurred in Russia, England, America and
Japan in May 1918 were not coincidental – these were desperate
times and the dangerous environment in which the Romanovs were
confined was growing more threatening by the day. Prince Arthur's
visit to the United States and Japan at the behest of King George V
becomes more understandable when we accept that the political
situation was spiralling out of control. Talks of an escape plan which
would remove the family to northern Russia were taking shape. As
we saw, Jonas Lied wrote in his diary that he had been vetted around
London with Henry Armitstead of the Hudson's Bay Company to
discuss a potential escape operation for the Imperial Family.[1] In fact,
evidence suggests that Henry Armitstead, along with Leslie
Urquhart, a close friend of Jonas Lied's,[2] and Sir Francis Lindley (of
the banking scheme) would participate in June 1918 in an attempt to
extricate the family while they were operating out of Murmansk
under the guise of the commercial trade mission.

The trade mission was supposedly being conducted without the
knowledge of the Foreign Office, but it now appears unlikely that
this was the case. Its stated purpose was to advise on trade relations
and try to block German economic penetration of Russia. However,
its real activities have never been fully understood. Richard Ullman,
one of the authorities on the British intervention, noted: 'The
circumstances surrounding this economic mission are still not
entirely clear . . . It seems to have nothing to do with the Foreign
Office.'[3]

On 25 June 1918, from Murmansk, Armitstead penned a letter to

116

his superior, C. V. Sale, the head of the Hudson's Bay Company and the other individual Lied said he met in London in regard to a rescue attempt. Sale had done business extensively in Japan and had served as an agent to the Baldwin Locomotive Company, which was also represented by Sidney Reilly.[4] It should be remembered that it was to Sale that the head of the British Secret Service, Mansfield Cumming, had written to thank him for the use of Henry Armitstead on the 'Russia Mission'. In his letter Armitstead expressed great concern and frustration:

> As you can see we are still at Murmansk this owing partly to exceptional ice conditions at the entrance to the White Sea partly owing to circumstances I am not at liberty to write about . . . As far as I can judge, and Urquhart is more or less of my opinion, our whole mission will be a failure in a commercial sense on lines you suggested. Clarke [Sir William] is very nice but a typical bureaucrat and like all of them his personal career goes before everything else . . . the arrangements for the plan are far from being adequate and Urquhart and myself have been quite outspoken on the subject. Lambert,[5] the third member of our mission is the only salaried one and consequently cannot open his mouth . . . I am afraid Paris [later General Paris, at the time head of the French forces in Siberia] will be much disappointed when he comes out . . . and so our mission is complete waiting for orders to continue *their journey* [author's italics]. I will write to you again as soon as I can see more light.[6]

Henry Armitstead, the man in charge of the house in Murmansk, who had taken Jonas Lied to meet Mansfield Cumming, the famous 'C', Admiral ('Bubbles') Hall, Director of Naval Intelligence (whose naval operations were involved in efforts to save the family) and one of the Romanov Grand Dukes, was now sitting in Murmansk while the mouth of the White Sea was 'unseasonably' blocked. He was awaiting orders to continue, not 'our journey', but 'their journey'. 'Their journey' could clearly point to the fact that he was waiting to hear about the arrival of the Imperial family.

What was happening in Ekaterinburg at that time? According to the accepted story of the fate of the Romanovs, it was on 19 or 20 June, almost a week before the Armitstead letter, that a letter in French was passed to the family informing the Romanovs that their 'friends no longer sleep'. The letter contained a hopeful message indicating that if the family could supply a drawing of their house of captivity, help would be coming to free them. It was signed by: 'someone who is ready to die for you, Officer of the Russian Army'.[7]

A few days later, between 21 and 23 June 1918, a second letter, also in French, was sent back stating:

> From the corner up to the balcony, there are 5 windows on the street side, 2 on the square. All of the windows are glued shut and painted white. The little one is still sick and in bed and cannot walk at all – Every jolt causes him pain. A week ago, because of the anarchists, we were supposed to leave for Moscow at night. No risk whatsoever must be taken without being absolutely certain of the result. We are almost always under close observation . . .[8]

Romanov historians and aficionados who analysed this letter believe that either Nicholas or his daughter Olga had penned the responses, for both spoke and wrote French. From the dates of these two letters it can be speculated that 'someone' had planned to take the family away within a night or two of 19 June. But once again the rescue was delayed because of Alexei's illness. If all had gone according to plan, the trip to Murmansk would have been completed around 25 June. Two reasons appear to have caused the delay, Alexei's illness and the unseasonable ice at the mouth of the White Sea.

Three more letters follow during this period wherein the family expressed their concern about the 'Doctor, a maid, two men and a little boy' saying, 'It would be ignoble of us (although they do not want to inconvenience us) to leave them alone after they have followed us voluntarily into exile.'

In this same letter they note that there are fifty men (guards) in a little house across the street. The letter from the family also mentions that Alexandra and Nicholas have crates in the shed and that they are especially worried about crates AF (Alexandra Feodorovna) number 9 and NA (Nicholas Alexandrovich) 13. In the closing lines of the letter they ask how they can be sure that if their people are left behind, nothing will happen to them. They even add that: 'Dr Botkin begs you not to think about him and the other men, so that your task will not be more difficult. Count on the seven of us and the woman, May God help you; You can count on our "sang froid [calmness amid trying circumstances]".'

The response on 26 June again reassured them and asked them if they could make a rope, but in the response to the 'officer' they said they did not want to nor could they 'escape' – 'We can only be carried off with the use of force, just as force was used to carry us from Tobolsk. Thus do not count on any active help from us.'[9]

The language of this response by the family seems to imply that the 'force' with which they were removed from Tobolsk was pre-planned and that the same appearance of force would need to be enacted this time as well. Nicholas and Alexandra would not want to give the impression that they were voluntarily fleeing because they could have felt that the propagandists would use this against them in the future if they were ever restored. Moreover, they had insisted that they wanted to stay in Russia so someone must have implied to them directly or otherwise that Murmansk was their ultimate destination. In this letter they intimate the fear that the plan does not sound very workable – an echo of Armitstead's concerns expressed to Sale and written on 25 June from Murmansk when he said, '. . . the arrangements for the plan are far from being adequate and Urquhart and myself have been quite outspoken on the subject'.

They say their surveillance has been increased and they even fear to stick their heads out for risk of being shot in the face. From these exchanges it appears that on 27 June Nicholas was still waiting for the would-be rescuers when he stated in his diary: 'We spent an anxious night and stayed awake fully dressed. This was because, a few days ago, we received two letters, one after another, which informed us that we should prepare to be rescued by some people devoted to us! But the days passed and nothing happened, only the waiting and the uncertainty were torture.'[10]

According to any number of reports, around 25 June, in Ekaterinburg, an officer named Rostovstev was shot when the Bolsheviks put down a counter-revolutionary movement.[11] (The search for this Captain Rostovstev and his connection to Count Rostovstov, Charles Crane's friend and the family's financial secretary, has been fruitless.) The logistics of another attempt to transfer the family appear to have gone awry and once again their hopes must have been shattered.

In the meantime, the members of the trade mission had gone into Moscow to meet Lenin. But not before Yaroshinsky, the family's friend and benefactor as well as the point man for the banking scheme, had offered to make his way through 'dangerous territory' to meet members of the 'trade mission' to assure himself that he was still in their good graces.[12] After the meeting with Lenin, the members of the mission left Moscow quickly, making their way to Vologda where most of the Western diplomatic corps were now in residence. Were they waiting in Moscow for the deliverance of the family and did the rogue Ekaterinburg Soviet once again interfere with Lenin's plan when they foiled Rostovstov's rescue attempt? Clearly Lenin's hand had been tipped or there was once again confusion in the highest ranks of the Bolshevik government – resulting in the near arrest of Urquhart. Some time later Urquhart's secretary confided that: 'Orders were issued by the Secret Police for his arrest but that by good fortune Mr Urquhart was able to leave Moscow before these orders were carried out . . . The orders to arrest Mr Urquhart had been issued without Lenin's knowledge.'[13]

This incident could have potentially blown all the Bolshevik complicity with the Allies regarding the Romanovs wide open. The fact that the mission escaped their impending arrest and were allowed to return to their ship via Vologda would indicate that the rescue attempt in Ekaterinburg had been spoiled by the uprising that took the life of Captain Rostovstev. Moreover, the family they might have been in Moscow to receive from Lenin would not be coming.

With respect to Reilly's role in the Murmansk attempt, it is important to understand the part he played in the banking scheme and the funnelling of money for the various pay-offs. There is no doubt that he was central to all the Allied intrigues and was playing multiple roles. His role as a Bolshevik gave him an opportunity to move freely in Bolshevik circles, while his other operative name, Massino, a foreign businessman, allowed him freedom in various circles of commercial endeavours. His involvement in the banking scheme and connection to Yaroshinsky, and in turn Soloviev, was not only recorded by Engineer Beloi but, also by Winston Churchill's assistant, Archibald Sinclair. In 1919 Sinclair identified Reilly as Yaroshinsky's right-hand man. In a letter to Mr Tilden-Smith, Sinclair observed: 'William Wiseman, who is well connected to Yaroshinsky's scheme, and with Mr Reilly who is Yaroshinsky's right hand-man, Reilly at Wiseman's suggestion was present at recent discussions between Lord Reading and Yaroshinsky.'[14]

Certainly Reilly had worked with Yaroshinsky on the banking scheme when he had been sent into Russia in April 1918, but now it is also certain that Reilly had been privy to and very much a part of the two-track policy that had at its heart the banking scheme to be utilised to overthrow the Bolsheviks and free the family.

On 28 May 1918, just one month before the second Murmansk rescue attempt, the Director of Military Intelligence wired Brigadier-General Poole in Murmansk regarding Reilly, who had already been in Russia for at least two months posing as a Bolshevik: 'The following two officers are engaged on special secret service and should not be mentioned in official correspondence or to other officers unless absolutely unavoidable, Lieutenants Mitchelson and Reilly.'[15]

As noted earlier, Reilly had arrived in Russia in early April 1918 and had assumed the identity of the Bolshevik Relinsky. But the summer of 1918 remains a chapter in Reilly's life that is virtually unknown. Most notably, over the decades his involvement in the so-called 'Lockhart Plot' of August 1918 has received the most scrutiny. While its details may vary from one version to the next, the Lockhart Plot, supposedly engineered by British envoy Robert Bruce Lockhart and the Allies with the help of Sidney Reilly, was intended to overthrow the Bolshevik government. But, in fact, it represented an attempt finally to pull off one of the most important elements of the two-track policy. Since the previous uprisings near the urban centres had failed in May and July, the Allies were trying again. But this attempt would also be exposed.

In Moscow, just two weeks after the family vanished, it was revealed that Robert Bruce Lockhart of England, Consul General Grenard of France and Consul General DeWitt Poole of America, as well as the American secret agent Xenophon Kalamatiano, had all been involved in a plan to overthrow the Bolsheviks. There is no doubt that Reilly and his cohorts had been set on accomplishing just that, but now it appears that Reilly was involved in more than the Lockhart Plot, and indeed the banking scheme, before August 1918.

What little is known about Reilly is that in the summer of 1918 he was dividing his time between Moscow, Petrograd and Vologda, where he was once again in correspondence with Sir Francis Lindley, one of the members of the 'trade mission' and one of the men who had vetted Jonas Lied while Lied was in London only two months before. And four days after the night of the Romanovs' alleged murders on 17 July, Reilly was granted a travel pass to Moscow via Petrograd by the Vologda Executive Committee of Bolsheviks, containing the notation, 'not to be bothered'.[16] When deals were in the works between the Allies and the Bolshevik government, it now seems safe to speculate that Reilly was frequently acting as a go-between.

Interestingly, his secret 'messengering' during this period was not confined only to corresponding with Lindley, but he also was arranging for a large sum of money to be given to the Russian Orthodox Church. Supposedly this action was taken because he was convinced that a strong Church represented a rampart against Bolshevism. His go-between was the prominent Russian churchman K. M. Aggeeff, who was the Church's go-between with the Bolsheviks. Aggeeff was also President of the Financial Department of the Church and as such was presumably close to Boris Soloviev's father who had been treasurer of the Holy Synod. Additionally Aggeeff was one of the closest advisers to Patriarch Tikhon, the head of the Russian Orthodox Church.[17]

Whatever the fate of the Romanovs, it is safe to assume that the Church would have made its best efforts to assist the former head of the Church, as in the eyes of the Church the Tsar was God's representative on earth. In Tobolsk the Church had been involved in passing messages to the family and now the actions of Reilly, who ostensibly was taking money to the Church for propaganda purposes, might have been actions that were instead involved in taking money to the Church to assist in hiding the family for a time before they were to be moved or restored. To be sure, the efforts of both the Church and Reilly had to be closeted from the public view, just as all Allied intervention on behalf of the family also had to be in that turbulent, chaotic summer of 1918.

When we recall Nicholas's mother, the Dowager Empress Marie's statement that her sons had been saved by the Old Believers – which it is reported she believed to her dying day – Reilly's activities in relation to the Church take on even more significance. Did the Empress possess facts that have yet to come to light?

The collection of Anthony Summers contains an interview with the daughter of British Major William Peer Groves in which she maintains her father told her that the family had escaped from the cellar with the aid of British Secret Agents and loyal guards and had then been taken to Japan and Canada.[18] This is very nearly the scenario outlined in *Rescuing the Czar*. In 1919, Peer Groves was assigned to British intelligence in Odessa at the same time that Reilly and another intelligence officer, Captain George Hill, were posted there. His duty was to escort members of royalty out of Russia.

During this time Peer Groves made a trip to Malta in April 1919, where he and his wife visited the Tsar's mother, Dowager Empress Marie, at the San Anton Palace while she awaited transport to Britain. In fact, the visitors' book shows that Peer Groves was a guest at the palace on 23 April 1919. It was during this visit that he is reported to have assured the Dowager Empress that her sons were alive and given her some token which confirmed this fact to her.

In January 1919, three months prior to this visit of Peer Groves, Marie had sent Captain Paul Bulygin, in the company of Grammatin, Soloviev's fellow courier of messages between Nicholas and Alexandra, to assist in the investigation of the Romanov family's disappearance then being conducted by Nicholas Sokolov.[19] Yet after Peer Groves's visit she refused even to review the Sokolov findings in the early 1920s. Perhaps after meeting Peer Groves, who is said to have shared intelligence with her that her sons were alive, she felt no need to read the Sokolov Report; or she knew that the deaths had been fabricated and had contributed to the obfuscation by paying for Sokolov's endeavours while he was under the influence of Bulygin, her hand-picked man. Later we shall see that Bulygin had made a trip to England and returned to see the Dowager Empress just before he travelled via India where he had a one-week stay prior to continuing to Russia to present himself to Sokolov as an assistant sent by the Tsar's mother. He also was carrying a secret message from London for Admiral Kolchak, the man under whom the Romanov investigation had just fallen.

The failure of the second attempt in Murmansk on behalf of the Allies to gain the family's freedom increased the pressure on Lenin and the Bolsheviks to continue to protect the family. And, of course, it was not only the Allies who were trying to secure the Romanovs, the German General Staff also recognised their value and were bargaining with Lenin as well, and might have increased their ante. A couple of months before the attempt the Germans had signed the Treaty of Brest-Litovsk with the Bolsheviks in March 1918 and Lenin thought that the exchange of the family would lessen some of the harsh terms of the yoke that had been placed around both his and Russia's neck. Even the King of Denmark was willing to assist the Germans and offered aid to the Kaiser in rescuing the family. Wilhelm's reply emphasised the humanitarian motives that lay behind so many of the attempts to help the Imperial family: 'I cannot deny the Imperial family my compassion from the human point of view, and when it lies in my power I will gladly do my part to ensure that the Russian Imperial family has a safe and suitable situation.'[20]

Keeping the Allies' activities in Siberia quiet was becoming increasingly difficult and Lenin had to do quite a lot of manoeuvring to keep his double dealing from view. But it was not until 26 June that George Chicherin, the Commissar for Foreign Affairs, admitted that a counter-revolutionary attempt in Ekaterinburg had been crushed and told Ambassador von Mirbach that no harm had come to any of the Imperial family.[21] Obviously Chicherin (who later maintained that the family did not die) feared von Mirbach would find out about the Bolshevik involvement in the failed Murmansk plot and felt the need to prevent any political fallout as well as any suggestion that the Bolsheviks were double dealing. Since the family had to appear to be taken by force, the failure of the plot surely complicated matters from a diplomatic point of view.

In June, offers of safety from the family's German relatives certainly reached Nicholas, if Queen Olga of Greece is to be believed. After speaking to Crown Princess Cecile of Germany, she said that Nicholas had refused to be saved by Germany at any price.[22] Nicholas and Alexandra were keenly aware that many of their subjects had accepted as fact the propaganda that had been floated accusing the Tsarina of being a German sympathiser, or worse, a German spy. While accepting a guilt-ridden relative's offer of help might have been personally appealing, the Tsar must have known that acquiescing to the Kaiser would have been tantamount to acknowledging there was truth to the rumours and would leave no hope that Russia could ever aid its allies in winning the war. Moreover, to accept help from the enemy would obstruct for ever any effort to restore the monarchy. The Kaiser had been so greatly disturbed by this response that he spent sleepless nights brooding over the Romanovs' predicament.[23]

In fact, in late June, just as reports that Nicholas had been killed started circulating, Lenin was personally taking steps to ensure that nothing of the sort happened. The commander of the Red Third Army, based in Ekaterinburg, was a Latvian revolutionary named Reinhold Berzin. He inspected the Ipatiev House and, at five minutes past midnight on 27 June, just two days after the uprising that thwarted the attempt to move the family to Murmansk, sent a telegram to Moscow assuring the Central Executive Committee that all members of the family were alive and well. If Lenin's assistance had not been involved in the effort to release the family he could have simply telegrammed the efficient Ekaterinburg Soviet guards who had spoiled the attempt.

It has often been claimed that the rumours of Nicholas's death were a Communist ploy to test public reaction to his demise in order to assess the danger that might arise when their alleged plan to murder the Romanovs became known. It is an argument that does not stand examination. Had that been true, there would have been no need for the commander of the Third Army personally to check to see if Nicholas was alive, nor to inform the Central Executive Committee of this fact – a body that would certainly have been aware of any 'kite-flying' of this nature.

In the politically charged atmosphere of late June 1918, Lenin's desire to retain the family as his political pawns led him to take charge personally. Three telegraph operators at the Ekaterinburg post office were later to tell White Russian investigators that they had witnessed a direct telegraph exchange between Lenin in Moscow and Berzin in Ekaterinburg in which Lenin 'ordered Berzin to take under his protection the entire Imperial family and not to allow any violence towards them whatsoever; if there was any such violence, Berzin would answer for it with his own life.'[24]

The fact that Lenin made Berzin, like Yakovlev, responsible with his own life for the safety of the Imperial family indicates how much importance he attached to them as negotiation devices. It now appears more than coincidental that a week after this exchange the original Ekaterinburg guard under the brutal Avdeyev was replaced on 4 July when Lenin sent in Yakov Yurovsky. Yurovsky had been a medic and had also had photographic training. Years before, having lived in Germany he supposedly converted to Lutheranism, the former religion of the Tsarina, even though he was Jewish by birth.

When Yurovsky entered the Ipatiev House at the head of a new detachment, his guards were described by all witnesses as 'Letts', hand-picked men who were utterly loyal and disciplined. They replaced the previously undisciplined Red Guards who are said to have engaged in excessive drinking and pilfering of the Romanovs' belongings, and were now on direct orders from Moscow not to enter the house. Why did Yurovsky replace Avdeyev, the dedicated

Bolshevik who had led the cause in the Urals and had murdered the owner of the Zlokazov factory where he had worked?

The usual answer is that Moscow feared that the guards under Avdeyev were becoming too friendly with their prisoners, and this was shown by Avdeyev permitting milk and eggs to be brought into the house from the local monastery for the sick Alexei. However, on the contrary, sneering and loutish behaviour were the hallmarks of Avdeyev's command. Drunkenness among the guards and the theft of the family's property are said to have been the reasons for their dismissal. These were hardly convincing reasons to cause grief to a leadership in Moscow that would later take credit for killing the family. The Soviet archives have not produced a single document to substantiate the claim that Avdeyev was on dangerously good terms with his prisoners. In stark contrast to Yurovsky, Avdeyev's character and history mark him as the ideal man to humiliate and slaughter the family, if that was what Moscow wanted.

So we must ask why such profound changes took place at this particular date, less than a fortnight before the Romanovs disappeared. And why would the former guards be barred from the house? It is significant that after the change had taken place, Moscow was informed that there was 'no cause for alarm'. In terms of the concern shown by Lenin and his instructions to Berzin, the only cause for alarm could have been for the safety of the family while under the custody of Avdeyev.

If any of these moves were made on behalf of the Romanovs they might be linked to dealings with Russian monarchists in Kiev. Count Hans Bodo von Alvensleben was one of Germany's top diplomats in the nominally independent Ukraine. On 5 July he met, at his own request, two Russian monarchists, Prince Alexander Dolgorukov, and Fyodor Bezak, a member of the Ukrainian State Council. According to Dolgorukov, Alvensleben: '. . . warned us that between 16th July and the 20th rumors would be spread about news of the death of the tsar, and that this rumor or news should not alarm us; like the rumor of the murder of the tsar, which was current in June, it would be false, but it would be necessary for certain reasons, namely for the tsar's rescue.'[25]

Was this another example of the Bolshevik-German negotiations that were taking place simultaneously with the Allied-Bolshevik negotiations for the family? When presented with an opportunity to double deal, the Bolsheviks never hesitated. They had already involved themselves in a secret manner with the Allies when Lenin and Stalin ultimately agreed with the Murmansk Soviet to allow the British into Murmansk in April 1918, although the Bolsheviks wanted nothing said about Moscow's complicity.[26] Lenin never played just one game but entertained parallel intrigues working simultaneously. He was still secretly courting both the Allies and Germany. The family remained his trump cards. When Count von Mirbach was assassinated in early July, Lenin had feared it would trigger a German invasion: 'There is ample opportunity for it, now at any price we must influence the character of the German report to Berlin.' Within days Lenin had many leaders of the Left Socialist Revolutionaries (LSR) responsible for the assassination arrested and shot as a reprisal. To be sure this was not the time to displease the Germans even more by allowing harm to come to the Kaiser's cousins.

The Bolsheviks could take extreme risks without the fear of having to answer to their constituency. With virtually no governmental oversight, since the Revolution was in its infancy and it was not, nor would it become, democratically driven, the Bolsheviks were certainly capable of conducting secret negotiations with any government relative to the Romanovs in that fraught summer when expediency, rather than principle, ruled everybody's actions. The Bolsheviks, from October 1917 through to July 1918, were staying alive by extortion, blackmail and money from what appears to be ransoms.

In a report filed in August 1918 regarding a prisoner named Weinberg, we gain a better understanding of the additional money the Bolsheviks had extorted and the fact that they definitely did not want proof of their activities floating around, since it could become apparent they were locked in a bidding war. An unknown prisoner sent a report to Britain regarding a man named Weinberg, whom he calls the 'German chief secret service agent'. The prisoner had befriended Weinberg and every night Weinberg was beaten because 'Dzergenski [*sic*]', who was the head of the Bolshevik Secret Service, was demanding receipts indicating that Weinberg had paid 12 million roubles from the account of the German Government 'to Lennin [*sic*], Trotski [*sic*] and Dzergenski [*sic*]' in January 1918. The payments had been made against receipts that Weinberg had forwarded to Mendelsohns bank, in Berlin. Weinberg had received 540,000 roubles from Count von Mirbach's representative (at almost the same time that Keyes and Lindley appealed to London for the money to buy out pro-German stockholders). The objective was to recover 'the receipts signed by Lenin and Dzergenski held by Weinberg' so they would never become public, thereby furnishing proof that the Bolsheviks were in the pay of the Germans. Dzerzhinsky failed to recover the receipts, since in all likelihood they were already in Berlin and 'eventually Weinberg was taken down . . . stripped and flogged . . . and dragged out and shot'.[27] Obviously Lenin had a lucrative couple of months in January and February 1918. The Allies had paid him at least £500,000 and Germany had rendered another significant contribution in what appears to have been a bidding war.

Bargaining of one sort or another continued on into the summer. As early as 10 June Henry Palmer, the American consul in Ekaterinburg, forwarded a telegram from Sir Thomas Preston, the British consul in Ekaterinburg, to the American consulate in Moscow for the attention of the British consul. It alerted London to the imminent danger of the 'gold' and 'platinum' being removed, and asked, 'Telegraph me what quantities purchased by British Government in order that I may endeavour withhold mineral here. Could also purchase on open market as formerly provided you provide me credit.'[28]

Gold and platinum? The records show that the gold and platinum that had been in Ekaterinburg had already been removed.[29] So why would the American consul be involved in the matter? Whatever Palmer's role was, he seems to have been a man trusted by all parties, for Major Slaughter stated in an intelligence report that he was the only consul the Bolsheviks trusted and would deal with. What was he negotiating? The British files disclose that the head of munitions who normally sanctioned this type of purchase of gold or platinum was queried, and he said he knew nothing of any approval to purchase these items at that time and that the price was far too high. Even though the British and the US were inclined to purchase platinum as a hedge against future scarcity, there is no record of any inclination to speculate in gold by paying inflated values, without the knowledge of the government, at this juncture.[30]

However it is interesting to remember that the larrabee code, being utilised by the men in the Ekaterinburg area at that time, was employing two key words —— and ——, which remain unknown to this day. Earlier in the war the first word was to be the day of the month but by this time the protocol had changed. Could 'gold' and 'platinum' have been code words for the Tsar and his family? The words appear numerous times in a context which would make that thought a plausible supposition.

Shortly after this series of events the Allies requested a United States passport control officer from Vladivostok to be seconded to the Ekaterinburg area for an unusual assignment – to participate in a purchase of gold and platinum.[31] Why would the United States be asked to move one of their passport control officers to the area to purchase gold and platinum? To cast more light on these events, I requested the records of the United States consul in Ekaterinburg for July 1918 but, according to archivists at the National Archives in Washington DC, they are not of record.

What is significant about Consul Preston's telegram is that it suggests the Allies could now have been trying to bid against the Germans for the Imperial family, as can be interpreted from Preston's suggestion to 'purchase on open market [meaning to go to the highest bidder]'. Bearing in mind the debate of 23 May in the Central Committee and how it revolved so much around gold, it can be seen that the Bolsheviks must have thought they could turn the 'thoroughly devalued personality' of Nicholas into a bargaining chip and some among them were inclined to do just that. The Bolsheviks provide the link between this plan and the change of guard at the Ipatiev House through another telegram sent on 4 July from Beloborodov to Nicholas Gorbunov, Lenin's personal secretary, in Moscow, where Goloshchekin had been staying with Sverdlov: 'Syromolotov has just gone to organise matter in accordance with instructions of centre. No cause for alarm. Avdeyev replaced. His assistant Moshkin arrested. In place of Avdeyev Yurovsky. Internal guard entirely changed, replaced by others.'[32]

So what was Syromolotov going to organise? It must have pertained to the family for the rest of the communication speaks of the change of guard at the Ipatiev House. Again, it is Beloborodov, who also now seems to be in Lenin's confidence, who establishes the link by telegraphing Syromolotov at Perm on 7 July, 'If Matveyev's train not yet dispatched, detain it, if dispatched take all measures to detain it en route so that it will not in any case reach place indicated by us. In event risk at new place of holding, return train to Perm. Await coded telegram.'[33]

Matveyev had been an Ensign in the Tsar's Lifeguards at

Tsarskoye Selo[34] and was now head of the 'Special Purpose Detachment' after Yakovlev had left. He had accompanied Yakovlev, which links him to the possible attempt to remove the Romanovs to the safety of 'Moscow or wherever'. After his service with Yakovlev he was based at Perm and was in charge of a train that appears to have been destined to take the family to safety – if it could be arranged. The replacement of Avdeyev and his local Bolsheviks was part of the same plan, a fact that is suggested by the next telegram from Beloborodov to Syromolotov on 8 July, 'If possible to replace train guard detachment with unconditionally reliable personnel replace all send back to Ekaterinburg. Matveyev remains commandant of train. Discuss train with Trifonov.'[35]

Any plan that sought to continue to move the family around, in relative safety and well away from the grasp of the Ekaterinburg Soviet until Lenin confirmed his highest bidder, was thwarted by events outside Bolshevik control. Much like the previous attempts to hand over the family to the Allies, the best-laid plans were falling apart. Beloborodov had to follow up his last telegram with another to Gorbunov later in the day, 'Gusev of Petrograd advised white guard uprising in Yaroslavl we returned train to Perm consult with Goloshchekin how to proceed further.'[36]

Perm is near the town of Lysva which is possibly the town whose name was found by investigators scribbled in reverse on the wall of the Ipatiev House after the disappearance of the Romanovs.[37] When the symbol is placed in front of a mirror there is every probability that the word is Lysva, without the 'a', as if someone were hurried and did not have any opportunity to finish the message. Were the guards attempting to take the family to Lysva, where the country estate of Count Paul Benckendorff, the last Grand Marshal of the Tsar's court, stood waiting to be used as a safe haven until Lenin could get them to Moscow or 'wherever'? The train returned to Ekaterinburg.

The 'white guard uprising' mentioned in Gorbunov's last telegram was in fact the premature uprising led by Boris Savinkov, the trusted friend of Sidney Reilly who had been betrayed. As we saw earlier, Reilly stated in his memoirs that the doctor operated on the patient too early. That the family may at that time have been on a train to relocate them is plausible but it was not to be, due to the interruption of the rail lines because of the Yaroslavl uprising.

A short time after the machinations pertaining to the train that may have attempted to move the family, the purported assassination of the Romanovs took place on the night of 17 July 1918 and they vanished for ever. Within days the Bolsheviks were driven from Ekaterinburg by the Czechoslovak Legion and White Russian troops. In America the diary of Will Starling,[38] a United States Secret Service agent, assigned to the White House, who had become a friend of Charles Crane as well as President Wilson, recorded that on the night of 25 July the President cancelled a trip due to the 'Russian situation'. This was an unprecedented step by Wilson. Even with battles raging on the Marne, he had always continued to meet his scheduled commitments. What other news could there have been from Russia to cause the President to take a step that he never took at any other time?

The Czechs had encountered the Red Army near Lake Baikal in the latter part of June and the Allied diplomatic corps at Vologda was retreating to Archangel on the 25th, but it is unclear whether the President would have known about those problems on that night since telegram traffic between the United States and Russia could take from one day to a week. He had not cancelled engagements as the diplomatic corps was on the run from Moscow in the earlier part of the year when there was supposed to have been an advancing German Army. However, *Rescuing the Czar*, the curious McGarry/Romanovsky manuscript, does allude to the fact that the family was taken out of the Ipatiev House through a cistern, by an English intelligence agent, after an independent agreement had been reached between King George V and Kaiser Wilhelm. The agent, Charles James Fox, purportedly committed to his diary that he and the family remained inside a tunnel leading from the Ipatiev House to the nearby British consulate for a number of days before surfacing in the consulate. He maintained he had infiltrated the guard when the new guard had been installed and had been aided in doing so by Bolshevik officials.

Was Wilson on 25 July anxiously awaiting confirmation of a successful mission that had begun on the night of 17 July – a confirmation that must be for his eyes only? And were the Romanovs finally in the hands of the Allies, where they would begin a journey to another life? Or is the traditional story of their death by a firing squad, comprised of eleven men on the night of 17 July, the answer to one of the great mysteries of the twentieth century?

PART THREE

Contradictions, Absurdities and Implausibility

CHAPTER 9

The Tsar Was Shot

Or Was He?

Part of the explanation for the ready acceptance of the traditional account of the death of all seven Romanovs and the dismissal of any plausible escape scenarios is based on the fact that historians maintain that King George V did not act to save his relations. His advisers are said to have convinced him because of the 'anti-monarchical movement' that prevailed at the time to withdraw the offer of asylum he had extended to the Romanovs shortly after Nicholas's abdication in March 1917. As a consequence, until now we have been encouraged to believe that thereafter, while the seven members of the family remained under guard, neither blood relations nor the Allies' financial interests, nor simple human compassion motivated any serious attempt to assure the survival of the family.

In the first part of this book we have seen that George V was not averse to aiding his royal relatives in distress and, since he and Kaiser Wilhelm II of Germany were both cousins of Nicholas as well as Alexandra, it is hard to believe that neither monarch made any moves to liberate the family. Additionally, given that Imperial Russia owed the equivalent of billions of dollars to Allied banks and corporations, it is equally implausible that these same groups would not move to protect their financial interests.[1]

Considering all these dynamics, it would seem to defy logic that the family would have been relegated to nonentities. But just as surely the plans to save them could not have been effected openly. Successful or not, it would have been imperative for all traces of any such operation to disappear from the pages of history to avoid embarrassment to the governments that had been involved in the arrangements for their release or to protect the operatives who would have been hunted down and eliminated. Moreover, the family would also have to disappear. To avoid speculation or conjecture, they would have to remove themselves from public view until Russia was free of Bolshevism and then perhaps the story could be told. For decades after these events the records of the British operatives in Russia during this era remained sealed, for fear they or their families would be hunted down and annihilated. The authorities, with all good reason, would have been even more convinced that the family would meet the same fate.

And so, until now, we have been left with the official version of the family's demise: in the early hours of the morning of 17 July 1918, the Imperial family of Russia – Tsar Nicholas, Tsarina Alexandra and their five children – were unceremoniously herded down the steps to the basement of the Ipatiev House, in Ekaterinburg, where they had been imprisoned. Along with the seven unsuspecting members of the last Tsar's family were the Tsarina's personal physician, her lady-in-waiting, their cook and a manservant – all of whom had willingly accompanied them to Siberia. They had been awakened and told they were being moved to another location so their captors could better protect them. Shortly after their arrival in the stonewalled room that measured a mere fourteen by seventeen feet, eleven armed men crowded through the double doors. Under the command of their commissar they took aim and unleashed a furious hail of bullets. So ended the lives of Nicholas's family, the 300-year reign of the Romanov dynasty and the life of the man portrayed as 'Bloody Nicholas'.

However, increasingly the discoveries over the past decades and the new information revealed in this book, erode the already fragile structure of the standard account. Until now, the period from March 1917 to the middle of 1918 has generally been portrayed as a time when the Romanovs were largely ignored, forgotten souls whose only hopes for survival were the hare-brained rescue schemes of hapless junior officers who had belonged to the former Imperial army. Yet, findings presented in this book demonstrate that, on the contrary, there was a small, multinational cadre of powerful politicians, diplomats, intelligence operatives, religious leaders and several members of European royalty who worked at the highest level to attempt the safe removal of the Imperial family. The assembly and construction[2] of the house on the Tsar's property[3] beginning in late autumn of 1917 while the family were imprisoned at Tobolsk, in Siberia, suggests that a staging house was being readied for the Romanovs in northern Russia, by the very people who have always been described as 'heartless' relatives and Allies.

In late 1917 and 1918, behind-the-scenes helpers such as Charles Crane, Karol Yaroshinsky, the Polish-Russian banker and close friend of the Romanovs, as well as Sidney Reilly, the erstwhile Russian double agent, who was operating on Britain's behalf, were involved in the formulation and execution of various attempts to snatch both Russia and the family from the Bolsheviks. Evidence also shows that the players involved in the various schemes loosely operating under the auspices of an ad hoc task force of the British government, officially called the Russian Committee, were attempting to execute numerous objectives orchestrated by the Allies, which have appeared nebulous until now.

Earlier chapters have demonstrated how the real objectives of this group were cloaked in policies that were intentionally designed and executed as two distinct tracks: the first, as stated before, intended for public consumption and dealing in general terms with the potential control by the British of a large portion of the Russian banking system, which in turn would be utilised to support White Russian military activities in the southern part of Russia. The second policy track encompassed quite a different, and secret, agenda.[4] It appears that the reason for the second track was twofold: the heretofore known objective, i.e. the overthrow of the Bolsheviks by the Whites and Czechs in the summer of 1918, and an even more clandestine unstated operation – unsuspected until now – the rescue of the Romanovs.

As we have seen, the hidden agenda was extremely complicated and faced numerous obstacles. However, its ultimate success may have been announced by the anomalous telegrams issued by the United States State Department and forwarded to London and Paris at the very time President Wilson and King George were meeting. On 30 December 1918, just five months after the family had vanished, a coded telegram containing the words 'Urgent . . . verify . . . family seven times' was issued from the American embassy in London[5] in response to a telegram received the preceding day from the United States Department of State, which had used, in code, the term 'family' also seven times. Marked 'confidential' and 'urgent,' and written in one of the highest-level codes, the 'Green' cipher ostensibly about the East-China Railroad, the mention of 'family' seven times appeared to be out of context and forced. Especially since the code term 'family' was used in already enciphered documents.

Initially the telegrams seemed to defy logical explanation as they were marked 'urgent' and 'confirm family seven times' for no apparent reason. Until, that is, they were put in the context of the events that we have seen played out over the preceding nine months, when contact between the Americans and British concerning the fate of the Imperial family was, despite appearances to the contrary, anything but illogical. In chapter 16 the details and importance of this telegram regarding the ultimate fate of the Imperial Family will be examined.

The family's disappearance spawned rumours of their survival from the first day that their 'execution' was announced. From the very beginning, confusion about the fate of the Romanovs lingered beyond the announcement of the death of only the Tsar on 18 July 1918 by Yakov Sverdlov, Chairman of the All-Russian Central Executive Committee of the Soviets (VTsIK) and one of the men involved in Yakovlev's April rescue attempt, through the official communist press bureau: '. . . The Presidium of the Ural Soviet decided to shoot Nicholas Romanov, and this was carried out on 16 July. The wife and son of Nicholas have been sent to a safe place.'[6]

For some reason it then took two days for the report of the death of the Tsar to make the headlines in the Soviet newspaper *Izvestiya*.

Moscow, 20 July 1918
[Quoted from Izvestiya News Agency]

Chairman Sverdlov announced receipt by direct wire of advice from Ural Regional Soviet of shooting of ex-Tsar Nicholas Romanov. In recent days danger of approach by Czechoslovak bands posed serious threat to Ekaterinburg, capital of Red Urals. At same time, fresh plot by counter-revolutionaries exposed, aimed at tearing crowned executioner from hands of Soviet power. In view of these circumstances presidium of Ural Soviet decided shoot Nicholas Romanov. Execution carried out 16 July. Wife and son of Nicholas sent to safe place. Documents concerning plot sent to Moscow by special courier . . . It had recently been proposed put former Tsar on trial for crimes against the people. However, current events prevented trial from being held. Presidium having discussed reasons that led Ural Soviet to take decision to shoot Romanov, Central Executive Committee, through its presidium, decided to accept decision of Ural Regional Soviet as correct.

By this act of revolutionary punishment, Soviet Russia has given a solemn warning to all its foes who dream of restoring the former Tsardom, or who even dare to attack us.[7]

After the story broke, the initial version – indicating only the death of the Tsar and the safety of Nicholas's wife and son – was to change rapidly. Subsequent versions would come from baffling sources and through most unusual channels. Each time a new account of the fate of any or all of the Romanovs found its way into the public arena it had metamorphosed into something somewhat different from any earlier description. We shall see that the various versions will reveal that one died, one or two escaped, or all lived. It would appear that the Bolsheviks did not yet know what version of the Romanovs' deaths they wanted to propagate to the world.

On 5 October 1918, Sir Charles Eliot, British High Commissioner who had been appointed by his government to proceed to Ekaterinburg on a 'fact-finding mission regarding the Imperial family', sent a report from Ekaterinburg to Arthur Balfour, the British Foreign Secretary.[8] The report left open the possibility that at least some members of the Imperial family survived:

Ekaterinburg, Russia
5 October 1918

It [the Ipatiev House] was quite empty; . . . On the wall opposite the door and on the floor were the marks of seventeen bullets or, to be more accurate, marks showing where pieces of the wall and floor had been cut out in order to remove the bullet holes, the officials charged with the investigation having thought fit to take them away for examination elsewhere. They stated that Browning revolver bullets were found and that some of them were stained with blood. Otherwise no traces of blood were visible. The position of the bullets indicated that the victims had been shot when kneeling and that other shots had been fired into them when they had fallen on the floor. Mr Gibbes thought that for religious reasons the tsar and Dr Botkin would be sure to kneel when facing death. There is no real evidence as to who or how many the victims were but it is supposed that they were five, namely the tsar, Dr Botkin, the empress' maid and two lackeys. No corpses were discovered, nor any trace of their having been disposed of by burning or otherwise, but it was stated that a finger bearing a ring believed to have belonged to Dr Botkin was found in a well. On July 17 a train with the blinds down left Ekaterinburg for an unknown destination and it is believed that the surviving members of the Imperial Family were in it.

It will be seen from the above account that the statement of the Bolsheviks is the only evidence for the death of the tsar, and it is an easy task for ingenious and sanguine minds to invent narratives giving a plausible account of His Imperial Majesty's escape. It must indeed be admitted that since the empress and her children, who are believed to be still alive, had totally disappeared, there is nothing unreasonable in supposing the tsar to be in the same case.

The marks in the room at Ekaterinburg prove at most that some persons unknown were shot there and might even be explained as the result of a drunken brawl. But I fear that another train of thought is nearer to the truth . . . There is some evidence that they [the Bolsheviks] were much alarmed by an aeroplane flying over the garden of the house and I fear it is comprehensible that in a fit of rage and panic they made away with His Imperial Majesty.

It is the general opinion in Ekaterinburg that the empress, her son and four daughters were not murdered but were dispatched on 17 July to the north or west. The story that they were burnt in a house seems to be an exaggeration of the fact that in a wood outside the town was found a heap of ashes, apparently the result of burning a considerable quantity of clothing. At the bottom of the ashes was a diamond and as one of the grand duchesses is said to have sewn a diamond into the lining of her cloak, it is supposed that the clothes of the Imperial Family were burnt there. Also hair, identified as belonging to one of the grand duchesses, was found in the house. It therefore seems probable that the Imperial Family were disguised before their removal. At Ekaterinburg I did not hear even a rumour as to their fate, but subsequent stories about the murder of various grand dukes and grand duchesses cannot but inspire apprehension.

I have the honour to be with the highest respect, Sir,

Your most obedient, humble servant.

C. Eliot.[9]

Sir Charles's report actually alludes to the Tsar and four retainers as the victims. Furthermore, he states that there was 'no trace of their having been disposed of by burning or otherwise'. Yet ironically, the burning theory would become the basis of the Sokolov report, which would be published in 1924. Another of the more puzzling aspects of the events surrounding the night of the presumed deaths of the family is that no one, except those involved, saw or heard anything suspicious on the night of the murders.

The commonly held notion that Ekaterinburg, one of the most important cities in the Urals and place of confinement for the Imperial family, would not have been crawling with Allied intelligence agents seems highly unlikely, given what we have seen of Allied activities in the Ekaterinburg area. In the margin of Sir Charles's report is the name 'Jones'. This reference indicated that someone named Jones was in some way connected with the Imperial family, or at the very least with the events in Ekaterinburg in the summer of 1918. A cryptic note bearing the name 'Jones'[10] is also found in the margin of a separate correspondence by another official, Sir Thomas Preston, the British consul in Ekaterinburg, who sent the telegram regarding the purchase of gold and platinum. Additionally Preston indirectly informs us of the whereabouts of Digby-Jones when he noted in his memoirs that around the night of 15 July 'a British officer in plain clothes, who had come through the lines from General Poole's expeditionary force at Archangel arrived in Ekaterinburg.'[11]

This man and the 'Jones' Sir Charles Eliot referred to in the marginalia were almost certainly British officer and intelligence agent Captain Digby-Jones who, as we saw in chapter 7, arrived somewhat conveniently on 16 July itself and was apparently billeted at the British consulate, a stone's throw from Ipatiev House and well within earshot of any sound of gunfire. While Preston's sister-in-law, who was staying at his home, later said she heard some shots, she resolutely maintained she only heard a few. The recently declassified records of Digby-Jones, of the British Royal Engineers, state that Ekaterinburg was his destination in early July and that he had recently departed from Archangel.[12] The very fact that his records remained classified all those years supports the evidence we have already seen that he was likely to have been more than just an engineer. Given that Digby-Jones the egineer was almost certainly a British intelligence operative, and was staying opposite the Ipatiev

House, why is it that not one report filed by him resides in any Allied government archives relating any observations of the house or even his commentary of what must have been a most newsworthy announcement of the death of the Tsar in the city where the Imperial family was imprisoned? The few reports that existed in America are missing pages. Whole documents that appear in the index do not exist now. Therefore it is safe to assume that more records relating to the activities surrounding the night of 17 July 1918 did at one time exist and may have been part of several hundred documents regarding 'northern Russia' that were destroyed 'by order of Executive Officer' in 1929.[13]

That the name 'Jones' was a part of Sir Charles's communication in October is not surprising, since Sir Charles Eliot was privy to knowledge regarding the activities of agents connected to the British intelligence service in Russia. The following telegram to British General Knox from the War Office in London, on 24 September 1918, establishes that Eliot was in a position to know about intelligence activities in Ekaterinburg. (It should be remembered that 'C' in the telegram designated Captain Mansfield Cumming, the man behind the building of the safe house in Murmansk while head of MI1c, also known as the Secret Intelligence Service – SIS – still later as MI6.)

Dispatched 11.30 p.m. 24 September 1918

67072 cipher: Your 73 of 21 September

. . . C has at the present time a secret organisation based at Vladivostok temporarily under Shaw from Hong Kong who is in touch with Sir Charles Eliot.

Was Sir Charles truly on a fact-finding mission for the British government or was his role to plant misinformation that could eventually cut both ways because it was deliberately ambiguous? Depending on the situation, Eliot's report could, in the future, become useful to the Allies, especially the British, for it left room for a completely different outcome, if a rescue mission had taken place and the family was yet to surface.

In addition to Sir Charles Eliot's communication of his interpretation of the circumstances surrounding the night of 17 July, the American Military Intelligence agent, Captain Homer Slaughter, also filed an extremely intriguing report. Slaughter, who had originally been detailed as an assistant military attaché to Romania, had arrived in Vladivostok, then paid a brief trip to Tientsin, China and, on 17 February 1918, was redirected to report to Russia also as an assistant military attaché.[14] Slaughter's wife almost cost him his assignment when she wrote a curious letter to his mother that Homer and another West Pointer were 'going to stand-in for the Bolsheviks'.[15] What her statement meant remains unknown but, as we saw in chapter 7, by July Slaughter was deeply involved in the area of Ekaterinburg, acting as the American liaison to the Czech forces.[16] Like Digby-Jones, Slaughter's July reports strangely do not mention any news regarding the Tsar or his family's fate. Conveniently, Homer Slaughter's reports state that he withdrew from the Ekaterinburg area only a few days before the night in question. The reason? His file says another nearby diplomat, American Consul Ray, was ill and Slaughter had to accompany him on a trip. However, the State Department always kept records for missed days due to illness. (Amazingly, even in those difficult times in Russia, there are countless personnel records with very specific dates recorded as sick days.) Consul Ray's personnel file is maddeningly vague, dates and travel records missing.[17]

Another personnel file with irregularities is that of Sidney Reilly. From correspondence that has survived, we now know that Reilly was shuttling back and forth from Moscow and St Petersburg to Vologda, north-west of Ekaterinburg, at that time. Yet Reilly's personnel file is literally blank during the period from May to October 1918.

There are other mystifying discrepancies. During the summer, while Slaughter was on duty in the region, he was also in touch with the American consul Roger Tredwell, then in Tashkent, Turkistan (now Uzbekistan) – the city in which Count Rostovstov, the Tsarina's financial secretary and Charles Crane's friend, had resided. Tredwell, who had been part of the two-track policy personnel in Moscow, was communicating with Slaughter utilising the larrabee code.[18]

Whatever Slaughter and Tredwell were in touch about, it had to be a mission that involved neither just the military nor the diplomatic corps. More bewildering is how Slaughter and Tredwell were communicating at all, since Tredwell's State Department file indicated that just after the enigmatic telegram we saw earlier, where Tredwell was reporting on Lockhart's and Trotsky's negotiations just prior to the Treaty of Brest-Litovsk, a message was communicated that had originated in London, which was meant to cover Tredwell's activities for the next few months: '. . . a Albert W. Stickney, bearer of Dep't of State passport number 52115 and now in Cyprus, telegraphs that when he left Petrograd in February Roger Tredwell was in that city and was in poor health and that subsequently he was advised by Consul Skinner at London that Tredwell died in March 1918 . . .'[19]

Tredwell's presumed death in March 1918, said to be in Moscow, served as a cover for him to go to Turkistan on a special mission. Six months later a letter from Tredwell's mother to President Wilson in November 1918 revealed even more. She wrote the letter after she learned from a Moscow newspaper, repeated in a *New York Times* report in October 1918, that the Bolsheviks had arrested her son in Tashkent. She apologised to the President for troubling him during such a stressful time for both Wilson and the country, but continued by reminding him that when her son volunteered for 'this mission', it was stated that if anything happened to him the 'country would stand behind him'.[20]

Slaughter, working for Military Intelligence and diverted to Ekaterinburg from his initial assignment to Romania, and Tredwell, on a special mission with assurances that the country would stand behind him, were clearly co-ordinating some kind of mission. Obviously Tredwell, who had been thought to be deceased, was anything but dead as had been reported. Instead, he had been quietly moved to Turkistan where he was later arrested. Whatever his and Slaughter's mission, it was steeped in covert actions.

Major Slaughter also divulged in his reports the names of other intelligence officers in the area of Ekaterinburg, including the French intelligence agent Major Guinet.[21] But conspicuous by its absence, since Slaughter and Digby-Jones would have been among a very small cadre of Allied officials, is any mention of the British officer Digby-Jones – the Jones presumably scribbled in the margin of Sir Thomas Preston's and Sir Charles Eliot's reports, who we know was in Ekaterinburg liaising with the Czech forces. Digby-Jones's activities later became the subject of enquiry in both the United States and Great Britain in July 1920 when the activities of the Allies and Czechs, during the spring and summer of 1918, came under scrutiny. In a telegram from Van S. Merle-Smith of the United States State Department to Richard Crane, Charles Crane's son who was then ambassador to Czechoslovakia, a request was made to ascertain information from the Czech archives regarding incidents which led the Czechs to fight the Bolsheviks and, more specifically, Digby-Jones's involvement. The reason given for this enquiry was that the various embassies in London, Paris and Prague were instructed to gather all information on the subject 'to be used in the preparation of a memorandum on the Diplomatic Correspondence with Russia'.[22] The beginning of the enquiry came only weeks after *Rescuing the Czar* was published in San Francisco in July 1920. These documents definitely corroborate, contrary to the traditional version of history, that Ekaterinburg in July of 1918 was the centre of previously unsuspected activities involving several Allied agents like Major Homer Slaughter and French Major Guinet. And if that was so, it seems logical to assume that the Ipatiev House would have been one of the main focuses of this interest.

In all probability Carl Ackerman, the *New York Times* reporter who, as we saw earlier, was actually working for United States intelligence and who later wrote that the Ipatiev House was being watched by foreigners, may have been referring to these men. Ackerman's subsequent book stated forthrightly that the Czechs, who along with the Whites were approaching Ekaterinburg in July, were bent on defeating the Bolsheviks and snatching the Tsar.[23] So again it must be asked, with the large number of intelligence operatives present in the area surrounding Ekaterinburg and in the city itself, how can it be that not one report detailing observations of the house on the night of 17 July 1918 survived? Seeking clarification, I sought the consulate files for Ekaterinburg in the United States, England and France as well. All that exists are a few rather vague, after-the-fact reports, including one from Sir Thomas Preston. In fact, all consulate files as such are non-existent. Consequently nothing filed on the night of the 16th or the morning hours of the 17th regarding activities at the Ipatiev House has emerged from members of the Allied intelligence or diplomatic community on the ground at the time.

However, one of the few surviving after-the-fact documents is a strange dispatch from Major Slaughter to General William Graves, Commanding Officer of the American Expeditionary Force in Siberia and the same man who sent the 'family seven times' telegrams, five months after 17 July. It adds more intrigue than clarity to an already clouded picture. Much of what you are about to read was also revealed to the world in a 23 December 1918 front-page article in the *New York Times*, after reporter-intelligence agent Carl Ackerman spent $6000 to wire the much abridged story to his editor.[24] Major Slaughter's intelligence file states that he obtained the document from American consul Palmer in Ekaterinburg, who had received it from the local monastery where its author, 'Parfen Domnin', the man mentioned in *Rescuing the Czar*, had lived after leaving the Ipatiev House. (In the interest of historical review, this document is presented, misspellings and all, in its entirety, just as it appeared in Slaughter's intelligence file.)

[12 December 1918]

THE LAST DAYS OF THE FORMER CZAR
N I K O L A I R O M A N O F F[25]
(before his murder)

PARFEN ALEKSEIVICH DOMNIN, the Tsar's personal attendant and Major Domo. The lackey or major-domo Parfen Alekseivich Domnin, who had been serving the former Czar for 22 years permanently and who voluntarily had followed him into his exile, gives some very interesting details of the last days of the former Tsar's life. Parfen Alekseivich Domnin is 60 years old and was born in the village Domnin, of the Kostroma Government and district and leads his origin from the so called peasants belopashtsy, the descendants of Ivan Sussanin.

BEFORE THE ADVANCE OF THE
CZECHO-SLOVACS

Beginning with the first days of July areoplanes were appearing over Ekaterinburg every day, they flew low and were bombarded, but always without result. With regard to these flights, it was rumored that the Czecho-Slovacs were making reconnaissances and intended to occupy the town. One evening the former Tsar returned from his usual walk in the garden unusually excited and aftera fervent prayer before the icon of the HolyNikolai, The Thaumaturgist, he lay down on his bed without taking off his clothes. This never occurred before. 'Please allow me to undress you and to make the bed for you,' asked the Parfen Alekseivich of the former Tsar.

'Do not trouble, old man,' replied the former Tsar. 'My heart feels that I shall live only a short time longer. Perhaps already today—' The Tsar did not end the sentence.

'God bless you what are you saying.' The former Tsar began to explain to Parfen Alekseivich, that just now, during his evening walk, he had received news that therewas being held a Special Council of the Ural District Soviet of Workmen, Cossack and Red Army Deputies, who were to decide the fate of the former Tsar. As they say, he is suspected that he will escape and run to the Czecho-Slovacs, who were advancing towards Ekaterinburg, and who had promised 'To tear him out of the hands of the Soviet Powers'. 'I do not know anything [blank space with apparent erasure] at all,' finished the former Tsar.

THE REGIME OF THE FORMER TSAR

According to the words of Parfen Alekseivich, the confinement of the former Tsar was very strict; he was not allowed to buy newspapers or journals; he was not allowed to walk longer than a certain time, and the servants were thoroughly searched when coming or going. Once the old lackey Parfen Alskseivich Domnin was forced to take off all of his clothes because the Commissair of the Guard theought he was carrying letters for the former Tsar.

The food was very scarce, generally herring and potatoes; bread was given at the rate of half a pound a day for each.

THE SUCCESSOR to the THRNOE

The successor to tye imperial throne, Aleksey Nikolaivich, was ill all the time, once he was even spitting blood. Once in the evening Aleksey Nikolaivich came running into the room of the former Tsar quite out of breath and loudly crying, and, falling in the arms of his Father, he said through his tears, 'Dear papa, they want to shoot you.' 'It is the will of God for everything,' lowly answered the Father. 'Be quiet, my sufferer, my songet quiet. Where is mama?' Mama weeps. 'Ask mama to be appeased, with weeping one cannot help; it is God's will for everything. Papa, dear papa, with ardor said Aleksey Nikolaivich, you have suffered enough already, why do they want to kill you? That is not just

Aleksey, I want to ask you one thing – go and appease mama. Aleksey left and the former Tsar knelt down before the icon of the Holy Nicolai and prayed for a long time. During the last days Nikolai Alexandrovich became very devout. It occurred that when he awoke in the night because of some nightmare, that the former Tasr did not sleep any more but spent the rest of the night inprayers.

ALEXANDRA FEODOROVNA

From time to time Nicolai Alexandrovich was allowed to meet his wife Alexandra Feodorovna, or as he called her, Alice, but his son he could see whenever he liked. Once Alexandra Feodorovna came into the room of the Nikolai Alexandrovich weeping and said; Koko, write down your last directions; that is necessary in any case and you should put all your papers and documents in order. Letters. Afetr these words Nikolai Alexandrovich was writing all the night through. He wrote many letters and among them those to all his daughters; to his brother. Miehail Alexandrovich; to his uncle Nikolai Nikolaievich; to general Dogert; Duke Gendrikoff; to CountOlssufieff, Prince of Oldenburg; to CountSumarokoff-Elston, and to many others. He did not seal the letters, as all his correspondence was controlled and censored by the Soviet and oftenletters were returned with the pencil remark 'Are not to be forwarded'.

TROUBLESOME FEELING AND HEARTSICKNESS . . .

For whole days Nikolai Alexandrovich was eating nothing, but fell down and was only praying. Even for a man who had not the gift of observation it was evident that the former Tsar was highly troubled and feeling heartsick.

THE 15th OF JULY

It was on July 15 late in the evening when suddenly in the room of the former Tsar appeared the Commissair of the Guard and announced: 'Citizen Nikolai Alexandrovich Romanoff, will you follow me to the meeting of the Ural District Soviet of Workmen and Cossack and Red Army Deputies.'

'Tell medear, freely, are you leading me out to be shot?' asked Nikolai Alexandrovich in a begging tone.

'You must not be afraid. Nothing will happen until the very death. You are wanted at the meeting,' said the Commissair smiling.

Nikolai Alexandrovich got up from his bed, put on his greay soldier blouse, his boots, fastened his belt and went with the Commissair.

Outside the door were standing two soldiers – Letts with rifles. All three surrounded Nikolai Alexandrovich and for some reason began to search him all over. Then one of the Letts went ahead. Nikolai Alexandrovich was forced to go behind him, next to the Commissair, and the third one went behind them.

Nikolai Alexandrovich did not return for a very long while – about two hours and a half At last he returned quite pale and with his chin quavering.

'Old man give me some water.' I brought him the water. He at once emptied a large cup. 'What had happened?' I asked him. 'They have informed me that I shall be shot within three hours.'

THE FORMULATION OF THE REASON FOR THE EXECUTION.

During the meeting of the Ural District Soviet of Workmen, Cossack, and Red Army Deputies was read in the presence of the Tsar a rather minute act of trial on the charge of a counter-revolutionary plot by a secret organization under the name of 'Association ofor the Defense of the Native Country and Freedom'.

The counter-revolutionaries have the intention of suffocating the workmen and peasants revolution by instigating the masses to rise against the Soviet power, accusing it provocatively and in the lump for all the hard consequences which have been caused by the world war and slaughter, as famine, want of work, downfall of trans-portation, advance of Germans etc.

To reach this aim the organization is trying to join all non-soviet political parties. This block would conjoin socialistic parties as well as distinctly imperial ones. The materials thus received at the trial show that the staff of this counter-revolutionary organization could not carry out his instructions fully on account of dicord of views regarding tactics between the right and left parts of this band. The materials of the trial show that at the head of this plot stands the personal friend of the former Tsar, General Dogert. In this organization work also representatives of the Duke Krapotkin, Colonel of the General StaffShkart [Eckhart], Engineer Ilinsky [Relinsky or Sidney Reilly] and others. There are reasons to believe that Ssavenkoff [Savinkov] also was in direct communication with this organization, and that he is supposed to be the head of the new Government, as a military dictator. All those leaders have estab-lished a very strong conspiracy. In the Moscow fighting gropup there are about 700 officers who afterwards are transferred to Samara, where they were to await reinforcements from the allies with the purpose of establishing the so called Ural Front, which would separate Great Russia from Siberia. Later on when the results of this viz: – famine – would show itself, they were to mobiliz all who sympathized with the overthrow and after the turnover of the Sovit power, to advance against Germany. There are documentary proofs that in this plot are taking part, socialistic parties, such as the peoples socialists, the right social revolutionaries, and sometimes the Mensheveki, who are acting in full harmony with the constitutional democrats. The Chief of Staff of the organization is in direct communication with Gneeral Dutov and General Denikin and in the last few days has been found a new plot of the counter revolutionaries which has for its object, with the help of General Dutov, to take the former Tsar out of the hands of the Soviet power . .

Besides this it has been proved that up to now the former Tsar Nickolai Romanoff did continue a secret correspondence with his personal friend General Dogert, who in his letters has been urging him to be ready to be freed.

In view of the above mentioned and also of the troublesome situation, caused by the decision of the Ural District Soviet of Workmen, Soldiers and Red Army Deputies, to evacuate Ekaterinburg for a short time, the further trouble with the former Tsar especially in view of the time of war, is absolutely not to be justified, and is even harmful. The Soviet has made the decision: the former Tsar Nickolai Romanoff has to be submitted without delay to an execution.

'Citizen Nikolai Romanoff,' said the cairman of the Soviet to the former Tsar, 'I inform you that you are given three hours to make your last orders.' 'Guard I ask you not to let Nikolai Romanoff out of view,' ordered the chairman.

THE LAST FAREWELL

Soon afetr Nikolai Romanoff had returned from the meeting his wife called on him with Alexis Alexandrovich, both of the weeping. Alexandra Feodorovna fainted often and the Doctor had to be called. When Alexandra Feodorovna recovered from her fainting, she knelt down before the soldiers of the guard and asked for mercy. The soldiers answered that it was not in their power to render mercy.

'Be quiet for Christ's sake, Alice', repeated Nikolai Alexandrovich severak times in a very low voice, and he made the sign of the cross over his wife and son. Afet this Nikolai Alexandrovich called his former majordomo, kissed him and said 'Old man do not leave Alexandra Feodorovna and Aleksey. You see that there is nobody with me now. There is nobody to appease them and I shall soon be led away.'

Later it proved that nobody except his wife and son, of his beloved were allowed to bis farewell to the former Tsar. Nikolai Alexandrovich, his wife and son remained together until there appeared still five other soldiers of the Red Army with the chairman of the Soviet and two other members of it – workmen.

'Put on your overcoat' resolutely commanded the chairman of the Soviet. Nikolai Alexandrovich, who did not lose his self possession, began to dress, kised his wife, son the lackey, once more made the sign of the cross over them, and then addressing the men who had come for him, said in a lod voice 'NOW I AM AT YOUR DISPOSAL'.

Alexandra Feodorovna and Aleksey fell in a fit of hysterics and both fell down on the floor. Parfen Alekseivich made an attempt to bring mother and son to their sense but the Chairman said 'Wait, there should not be any delay, and you may do that after we have gone.'

'Permit me to accompany Nikolai Alexandrovich,' the old lackey began to ask. No accompanying. Nikolai Alexandrovich was taken away, nobody knows where and hass been shot in the night of the 15th of July by a group of soldiers of the Red Army consisting of twenty men.

AFTER THE EXECUTION

Before the dawn of day the Chairman of the Soviet again came to the room, where Nikolai Alexandrovich had been held, with him some soldiers of the Red Army, a doctor and the Comissaire of the Guard. The Doctor gave assistance to Alexandra Feodorovna and to Aleksey Romanoff. Then the Chairman of the Soviet asked the doctor 'is it possible to take them at once'. 'Yes.'

'Citizen Alexandra Feodorovna Romanova and Aleksey Romanoff – get ready, you shall be forwarded from here. You will be allowed to take with you, only the most necessary things; not over thirty or forty pounds,' said the Chairman.

Mastering themselves but tumbling from side to side, mother and son soon got ready. The Chairman did not permit them to bid farewell to their beloved ones (Tsarinas daughters) only hurried them all the time. 'And you old man, also, get away from here now, there is no one for you to serve any more.'

'Tomorrow you will get out of here', commanded the Chairman of the Soviet, addressing the Commissaire of the Guard. Alexandra Feodorovna and Aleksey Nikolaivich were at once taken away in an automobile it is not known where. In the morning of the next day appeared again the Commissaire of the Guard and ordered Parfen Ivanovich immediately to get out of the room, taking with him some of the property of the former Tsar. But all letters and documents of the former Tsar were taken by the Commissaire of the Guard. With great trouble Parfen Ivanovich procured a railway ticket at the station as as the station and the cars were filled with soldiers running about recklessly from the Red Army who were evacuating the precious things of the city.

EPILOGUE.

The Tchelabinsk paper 7549 UTRO SIBERIA, notes that the execution of Nikolai Romanov is certified by a special government declaration. All his papers were seized.

At a place 10 versts from Ekaterinburg, on the 30th of July as the paper stated, was found a heap of ashes left from a burned house, in which was found metal things belonging to the family of the Tsar ans also burned Corpses to the number of the Romanov family. The authorities detailed to investigate the dissapearance of the Tsar have gone out to this palace. Thus it is probable that the members of the Romanoff family have been burned.

As hoastages the were taken from the City of Ekaterinburg, the Grad Duchess Elena Petrovna, the Countess Hendrikova and still a third whose name is not known. The total number od hostages amounted to 80. The Bolsheveki fled in the direction of Verkotrie.

SUPPLEMENT FROM THE HISTORICAL SOCIETY OF EKATERINBURG

A memebre of the Russian Historical Society has had the opportunity of seeing absolutely in the secret archives of the Russian Senate a proof sheet of the 'Collection of Laws and orders of the Government', of the 17th October 1905 in which was printed the following manifest. 'Disturbances and riots in the capitals and in manynparts of our great empire are filling my heart with painful grief. The welfare of the Russian Emperor is indissoulbly joint with the welafre of the people, and the affliction of the people is his grief. From the distrubances now arisen may proceed a deep disorder among the population and a threat to the unity and integrity of our state. In these days when the fate of Russia is determining we as our duty of conscience to facilitate among our peope a close union and the joining of all parts of the population for the highest prosperity of the state and therefore we have decided to abdicate the throne of the Russian Empire and to lay down the high power. Not wishing to separate from my beloved son, we surrender the succession to my brother, Duke Mikhail Alexandrovich, and we bless him on his ascention to the throne of Russia.' Follows the signature Nikolai Romanov and the counter Signature of Court Baronet Frederiks. Then the date October 16, 1905, Novy Peterhov.

On the text of the manifest is the following note in red pencil 'Hold up printing' Hofmister Kedrinsky, Manager of Typography. Hofmeister A. A. Kedrinsky, who was the manager of typography for the Senate in 1905 gives the following details in regard to the delay in printing the manifest

At 8 o'clock in the evening on October 16 I received from a courrier a packet from the Minister of the Court Baronet Fredriks, in which I found the above mentioned maifest and a letter by Frederiks asking me to publish the manifest in the next number of the collection of laws. As the manifest was not received in the usual way through the Minister of Justice, Kedrinsky gave the manifest to the typographer to prepare for printing and at the same time informed Shtsheglovitoff by telephone of the receipt of the document. At first the minister of Justice only directed delay in printing, but at eleven p.m. Kedrinsky was vistited by a functionary for special commissions from Shtsheglovitoff, who who asked him to hand him the original of the manifest and ordered the proof sheet transmitted to the archives of the senate.

NOTE: [by Slaughter]

The above manuscript was secured by the American Consul in Ekaterinburg from the Moanstery in Ekaterinburg where Parfen Ivanovich Domnin stayed for some days after he left the service of the Tsar and where he later returned and remained for some weeks. At this Monastery also resides the sister who took milk to the Tsars house daily. She has nothing to tell which would be of any interest except the fact that on July 17 she was told not come any more. She was never allowed to see any of the family and did not know how they lived. Actually this is the best piece of evidence I have seen which at all bears any relations to the final end or disposition of the Tsar and family. Everything else is rumor and hearsay. The bodies. The bodies of five of the Royal family were found in a well at Alopaievsk [Grand Duchess Elisabeth, the Tsarina's sister; Grand Duke Sergei Michaelovich, three sons of Grand Duke Constantine and a son of Grand Duke Paul] during the latter part of November and the Grand Duchess Elena Petrovna was thensick in a Hospital in Perm.

[Major Homer Slaughter's signature]
Major Infantry, U.S. Army
Ekaterinburg December 12, 1918.
HEADQUARTERS AM. EXP FORCES
VLADIVOSTOCK, SIBERIA
RECORDED
MAR 29 1919
[War Department Stamp – Office Chief of Staff – MIL. INTEL. DIV. Date stamped – March 22, 1921]

The Parfen Domnin document is troubling on numerous fronts. First, its tone and style seem to indicate a change of voice from time to time. The document swings from compassion to strident revolutionary rhetoric when it is quoting what went on at the meeting of the Bolsheviks. But Slaughter appears to have followed up the report, for he says he has questioned the nun, who apparently had nothing more to add to the account of Parfen Domnin.

After Slaughter filed this report in December and Ackerman's newspaper story relating an abridged version of the Parfen Domnin story appeared a week later, the name Parfen Domnin itself became a bone of contention. Those familiar with the Tsar's entourage quickly pointed out that no one by the name of Parfen Domnin had ever served Nicholas II. While this may be true, many White Russians, like their Bolshevik counterparts, were living under assumed names to protect themselves. During the Ekaterinburg phase of imprisonment there was only one manservant of record present in the 'House of Special Purpose' – Terenty Ivanovich Chemodurov and one footman, Trupp, who was alleged to have been shot with the family. The Tsarina recorded in her diary on 24

May that Chemodurov was stripped and searched and had been hospitalised.[26] Yet the guard's log, two days later, still lists him as a resident of the house.[27] If he was in the house, then *Rescuing the Czar* has another ring of truth since Charles James Fox says Domnin was present there on the night in question.

After the night of 16/17 July, the nervous old valet maintained to Colonel Kobylinsky (who had been in charge of the family during their imprisonment at Tsarskoe Selo and in Tobolsk) that the family did not die. Sadly, Chemodurov himself died only a few months after the events were reported. Many, including Summers and Mangold, believe Parfen was an alias for Chemodurov.[28] If so, how did he come up with such a story and why did he pass it along to the monastery, where the nun gave it to American Consul General Palmer who in turn passed it on to Slaughter?

Whoever wrote the Parfen Domnin story may have been intending to leave a significant message by indicating that Parfen Domnin was a descendant of Ivan Sussanin and a resident of the village of Domnin in the Kostroma government region. Several hundred years earlier, Ivan Sussanin had saved Nicholas's ancestor (the first Romanov) from the Poles by hiding him in the Ipatievsky Monastery in Kostroma and pronouncing him dead, only to have him reappear when the threats to his life had abated. Other descendants of Sussanin had not only kept Alexander II from assassination but also attended Nicholas's and Alexandra's wedding.[29]

Since little is known about the ancestry of Nicholas's men-servants, it is impossible to ascertain whether one really descended from the illustrious peasant hero. If this detail was not intended to have deeper meaning but was purely coincidental, then it was certainly a cruel irony. Or was it a clever way to pass a message along to the American War Department where a staff member would recognise the special significance of the words 'Ivan Sussanin' and then pass on the information to the other Allies? And how did Ackerman, who published an abridged version of the Parfen Domnin story in the *New York Times*, gain access to it?

In fact, Ackerman had been in the company of Major Slaughter from the time he arrived in Siberia in the autumn of 1918. And as we have seen, he himself frequently served as an intelligence operative for the United States State Department. During the previous years he had been operating under the cover of various publications, including the *New York Times*[30] and the *Saturday Evening Post*, as also shown in the following telegram.

'Green Code'
14 (18) August 1917
AM legation:
Berne:

The Department is considering sending Carl W. Ackerman, well known to your legation, to Berne to cooperate with you in American publicity work and in gathering intelligence regarding Germany. He has sources of information in German which would doubtless prove valuable to the legation. He would go ostensibly as correspondent for the *Saturday Evening Post* but would work in close cooperation with you. Please cable your views as to advisability of this step.

Signed by Secretary of State Lansing[31]

Not only had Ackerman worked frequently for the State Department in the past, but he was also being paid by the State Department. In January, just after publication of his *New York Times* article, he would be paid $1500 through the State Department office in Japan and on the document itself it is noted in pencil 'Special agent'.[32] Why would such responsible and bright men as Slaughter and Ackerman pass along the Domnin description of the night of 15 July (though the rest of the world believed it to be the 16/17th) to be lodged in military intelligence files and printed in one of the most respected papers in America?

Shortly after Slaughter received the document, complete with rhetoric of this purported descendant of Sussanin, it was logged into the headquarters of General Graves, head of the American Expeditionary Forces, only days before the puzzling 29 December 1918 telegram mentioning the word 'family' seven times was sent to the State Department by Graves with instructions to forward it to Paris and London. Stranger still, Slaughter dated his report 12 December 1918 in Ekaterinburg, but it was not officially stamped into headquarters in Vladivostok until 29 March 1919 even though Carl Ackerman had travelled back to headquarters in late December. We only know of the Parfen Domnin document's existence because Congress requested all documents pertaining to Russia from Homer Slaughter and consequently the Domnin story became of record in the War Department, Office of Chief of Staff, Military Intelligence

Division on 22 March 1921. Yet in 1920, prior to Slaughter relinquishing his records to Congress, the book *Rescuing the Czar*, containing a tale of survival – replete with allusions to Parfen Domnin – would appear in the United States. However this time Parfen appears only briefly unlike the central role he had in both Ackerman and Slaughter's reports. The details of this curious book are yet to come.

What is now evident is that at the close of 1918 it was unclear from the public perspective what had really happened to the Tsar and his family, for the whole matter had received very little attention in the press because of the war and its aftermath. However, Ekaterinburg had been the scene of intense manoeuvring in July 1918, when intelligence operatives and the military advance on the city were at the forefront of the Allies' strategy as part of the two-track policy.

CHAPTER 10

The First Investigations

A Glimmer of Hope that the Family Survived

The Parfen Domnin account was not the only version that chronicled a scenario that would conflict with what has become the accepted view of the events of the night of 17 July 1918 in Ekaterinburg. Various contradictory stories of the family's status evolved from the day the Bolsheviks fled Ekaterinburg. When the city, following a fierce thrust by the Czechs, fell on 25 July just over a week after the fateful night in the Ipatiev House, many White officers on the ground did not accept the belief that the family had been killed.

It is important to realise that, at the outset, no one was simply conducting a murder investigation. The Romanovs had disappeared – and while it was certainly not excluded that they had been murdered, a number of investigators were also accumulating evidence that they had escaped or been moved elsewhere.

The first investigators, both military and civilian, who handled the case were always met with criticism and in some cases mysteriously disappeared. Within days of the alleged executions and the Bolsheviks' retreat from Ekaterinburg, Prince Galitzin, a close friend of both Tsar Nicholas II, and Charles Crane, ordered the local commandant, Prince Riza-Kuli-Mirza, to form a special commission of officers to look into the fate of the Romanovs. The army's Criminal Investigation Division began a separate inquiry. The military also asked that the local judiciary provide its own team of investigators. Since the public prosecutor was absent, his deputy, on 30 July 1918, appointed Alexander Nametkin, Coroner of Justice of Special Affairs, to begin the investigation. The situation faced by Nametkin and the other investigators was anything but helpful to a proper inquiry. Rumours of all kinds were circulating in Ekaterinburg, there were no reliable witnesses and life itself was a struggle for survival during these difficult times as a result of the civil war.

One of the first men to be interviewed was Fidor Nikitin Gorshkov.[1] According to Gorshkov, the entire family died in the Ipatiev House. As Summers and Mangold point out, Gorshkov was a Communist whose testimony was 'supplied to investigator Nametkin by the prosecutor's office as "the basis on which to begin a preliminary inquiry".[2] Gorshkov's story was utter hearsay, but unfortunately this very first interpretation survived for years. Who was Gorshkov and how did he come into possession of the facts about what happened that horrible night in the Ipatiev House? Fidor Gorshkov stated he learned what he knew from an acquaintance who had been told by the sister of Anatole Yakimov, one of the guards, who had been told by Yakimov himself. So Gorshkov received his information fourth-hand. Because of the weight given to Yakimov's testimony, one would think he must have witnessed the scene. But alas, Yakimov, a thirty-one-year-old metal turner, had only posted the watch that night and then gone to bed. Yakimov, described as 'head of the guard', apparently on the outside, testified that he was awakened at four in the morning and told by other guards, Ivan Kleshchev and Nikita Deryabin, that they had witnessed the shooting after Pavel Medvedev and Konstantin Dobrynin had warned them that the shooting would take place.[3] Clearly this initial testimony should be deemed highly questionable since neither Gorshkov nor Yakimov had witnessed the deaths themselves, but had merely passed on what they had been told by two men who were supposed to have witnessed the murders.

From 2 through to 14 August, first Nametkin and then Ivan Sergeyev investigated and searched the house, completing a meticulous inventory of each room on the upper floor. Nametkin was accompanied by Captain Malinovsky (Captain of the body-guard to Nametkin),[4] the Tsar's valet, Terenty Chemodurov who, if he was indeed Parfen Domnin, was helping to lay a false trail and Dr Vladimir Derevenko, who had been the physician attending the Tsar's haemophiliac son Alexei.

It should be noted that no evidence of any sort had been found until just days after the Czechs had taken Ekaterinburg, when an odd character named Lieutenant Sheremetevsky arrived mysteriously on the scene. Reporting to White Russian and Czech military officials a few days after the fall of Ekaterinburg, Sheremetevsky said that he had been hiding in the nearby village of Koptiaki, disguised as a peasant, when some villagers on their way to Ekaterinburg on the morning of 17 July had been chased away by Bolshevik soldiers. Later these villagers, together with Sheremetevsky, returned to the site where the soldiers had been, known as the Ganin Pit after the prospectors who had worked it. There they had found charred clothing and jewellery, some of which the Lieutenant collected and brought with him to Ekaterinburg. Sheremetevsky led Nametkin and others to the site. The items found there, together with additional remnants of clothing and jewellery subsequently found at the same site by the investigators, were promptly identified by the valet and the doctor as belonging to the Imperial family.

Sheremetevsky soon disappeared, as quickly and as mysteriously as he had come on the scene. He was never clearly identified nor was it ever confirmed that he was a White officer. Various authors have described him only as the 'mysterious Sheremetevsky'. However, my research revealed that in a book by Baroness Buxhoeveden, who was one of the Tsarina's closest confidantes and had been with the family in Tobolsk, she mentions Madame Dehn, née Scheremeteff, who, she states, is a 'distant relation of the Emperor's', and one of the Tsarina's closest and most loyal friends.[5] It appears that Madame Dehn's husband, Captain D. V. Dehn, was an aide-de-camp to the Tsar. It is unclear whether Captain Dehn, using an alias borrowed from his wife, was in fact the mysterious White officer 'Sheremetevsky', who first led the investigators to the evidence of the 'murders'. We have seen evidence that Lily Dehn, along with Anna Vyrubova, another member of the Tsarina's entourage, and Boris Soloviev, Yaroshinsky's assistant, whom the Tsarina had used to send messages to Nicholas just prior to his abdication,[6] had planned and participated in escape strategies in the spring and summer of 1918. The Brothers of St John of Tobolsk, with Soloviev at their head, were utilising their secret Tibetan reverse swastika sign, when they were providing information as well as funds for the group that included the family's closest confidants working together with Yaroshinsky of the banking scheme.

While the name Sheremetevsky is slightly different from Scheremeteff, it was not uncommon in those trying times for people to alter their names slightly by adding 'sky'. In fact, we saw Sidney Reilly operating in the summer of 1918 in Russia under cover as the

Bolshevik Relinsky. It does seem more than a coincidence and extremely convenient that this mysterious Sheremetevsky, or if he was in fact the Tsar's relative Scheremeteff, should be the first to point out the remains of the Romanovs that were immediately identified by loyal servants of the Tsar, one of whom may have been laying a false trail, only to disappear.

However, if some parties were attempting to feed the idea of the Romanov murders there were, at the same time, others telling a quite different story. Ivan Starkov, a senior guard at the Ipatiev House, told his guard comrades Philip Proskuryakov and Pavel Medvedev's wife that the Imperial family had been 'taken away'. Some testified that Starkov was seen immediately after the family's disappearance in the room of Yurovsky, head of the Ipatiev detail, where he was observed in conversations with Chaya (Filipp) Goloshchekin, Ural District Military Commissar and member of the Presidium of the Ural Regional Soviet Executive Committee and the same man involved with Yakovlev's attempt to take the family from Tobolsk to 'wherever', and Alexander Beloborodov, Chairman of the Ural Regional Soviet. In such lofty company it would seem that Starkov would have been privy to the truth, but we shall never know because he was 'killed at the front'.[7]

In any case, the military investigations ended without issuing a final report. Captain Malinovsky, a member of the officers' commission who had first investigated the family's disappearance, did later offer an explanation and registered his conviction that the family were alive. As Summers and Mangold cite in *File on the Tsar*, Malinovsky, one of the first on the scene, had this to say:

As a result of my work on this case, I became convinced that the Imperial Family was alive. It appeared to me that the Bolsheviks had shot someone in the room in order to simulate the murder of the imperial family, had taken them away in the night along the Koptiaki road, also with the purpose of simulating a murder, changed them into peasant clothing, then taken them from there to some other place, and burned their clothing. These were my impressions as a result of my observation and considered thought. It seemed to me that the German Imperial House could in no way permit such evil. It could not allow it. That is how I thought, and it also seemed to me that everything I had observed during the investigation was a simulation of murder. [For some strange reason, this testimony found in Sokolov's report was excised from his published report.] [The previous bracketed statement is that of Summers and Mangold.][8]

In September 1918 Alexander Samoilov, a conductor on the Omsk Railway who gave testimony, reported that his friend, Alexander Varakushev, also an Ipatiev House guard and a worker at the central staff headquarters of the Red Army in Ekaterinburg, said that Filipp Goloshchekin was spreading the story of the deaths, but that the Tsar, his wife and his family were still alive. Later Varakushev was severely reprimanded by Sergei Mrachkovsky, a Bolshevik commissar, who ordered him to 'say nothing about it or I would be severely punished'. Summers and Mangold assert that Varakushev may have had information that was valid because of his position at the central staff of the Red Army and they noted he was a bona fide guard of the Ipatiev House whose name appeared on the staff list.[9]

When the public prosecutor, Alexander Kutuzov, eventually returned to Ekaterinburg, he decided that the case was too important to be entrusted to an examining magistrate. Nametkin was therefore dismissed, leaving behind his case file, but no record of his own opinion about the Romanovs' fate. He later went missing, reputedly shot by the Bolsheviks for investigating the case. Kutuzov eventually appointed Judge Ivan Sergeyev, who took over the investigation on 7 August.

It was under Sergeyev's jurisdiction that most of the important forensic discoveries were made. He completed Nametkin's work in the Ipatiev House, examining the lower floor, which Nametkin had not thoroughly investigated. One room in particular showed unmistakable signs of violence and it drew most of Sergeyev's attention. He spent five days analysing this room alone. There were twenty-seven bullet holes and traces of human blood in some of the holes as well as on the floor, which Sergeyev felt had obviously been carefully scrubbed. Eventually the judge would conclude that perhaps the Tsar and some of his suite had been murdered at the Ipatiev House, but he did not believe that the Empress, the Tsarevich or the Grand Duchesses had been shot.[10]

Sergeyev's scepticism is understandable. A mass execution appears unlikely considering the dimensions of the room, which measured just fourteen by seventeen feet – hardly space for as many as twenty-four people (eleven or twelve victims and eleven or twelve murderers – depending on whose testimony one reads).

Proponents of the official account have attempted to escape the confines of this cramped space by having the execution squad stand in the doorway. But the double doors were only five feet wide; twelve men could not have squeezed themselves into such a narrow space, even if, as some have suggested, they were arranged in three rows. Besides, Yurovsky, head of the guards, was by his own account, as we shall see in the next chapter, in the room. How did he manage to avoid being hit by the hail of bullets coming from the doorway?

Then there is the curious matter of the proliferating number of bullet holes. Sergeyev is supposed to have counted twenty-seven – but this figure was provided in a later account by Nicholas Sokolov, who would replace Sergeyev. Sir Charles Eliot, the British investigator who filed his report on 5 October 1918, from Ekaterinburg (and who, as we saw previously, left room for either interpretation – death or escape), would report that Sergeyev said he had found seventeen holes. Another eyewitness, who claimed to have been in the room even before the arrival of the Czechs and Whites in late July, said he saw just three holes. Sokolov, finally, would eventually tally thirty. Given the care with which Sergeyev studied the room, it now seems likely that additional bullets could have been fired into the walls between July 1918 and the winter of 1919 when Sokolov's investigation would begin.

The location of the bullet holes raises another series of questions. Yurovsky stated that he ordered the shots to be aimed at the victims' hearts. Strangely, most of the bullets were found within two feet of the floor – meaning that the guards would have been aiming no higher than the thighs of even their shortest victim. This has been conveniently explained away by saying everyone dropped to their knees. Even using the females as models, and assuming the victims had been kneeling, the height of their hearts would be approximately three to three and a half feet. Yurovsky claimed that the bullets ricocheted, 'jumping around the room like hail'.[11] One would expect ricocheting bullets to come to rest throughout the room, rather than being concentrated along the foot of one wall even if the victims ducked or fell immediately. And it is more than a little miraculous that none of the guards was seriously injured in this storm of ricochets.

Most of the accounts from the former Soviet archives agree that the guards fired furiously. The impression from the alleged eyewitnesses is of a frantic expenditure of ammunition. Yurovsky later wrote: 'My assistant spent an entire clip of bullets,' and of his own weapons, 'The remaining bullets of the one loaded clip for the Colt, as well as the loaded Mauser, went to finish off Nicholas's daughters and the strange vitality of the heir.'[12]

Some interesting questions also arise about Yurovsky's gun. According to Edvard Radzinsky's *The Last Tsar*, Yurovsky used a Colt 45 to kill the Tsar. Its serial number was 71905. In tracking down the weapon, I obtained additional information from the Colt Company historian Kathleen Holt. If the serial number 71905 were followed by a letter, then the gun would have been part of a Colt shipment to Russia, possibly through France. But if there was no letter following the serial number, then the history of Yurovsky's gun would be quite different. Colt's archives indicate that the gun model 1911 serial number 71905 (without any letter tagged on at the end) was manufactured in 1914 and was sold to the United States government. It was delivered to the Ordnance Officer at Fort Thomas, Kentucky on 30 April 1914, one of 150 weapons received. The 45s were issued to officers, military police and pilots only.[13]

Thus the self-proclaimed leader of the assassins, at least according to the serial number Radzinsky gave, was using an American army issue gun. Yet America was not supposed to have a military presence in Russia in July 1918. The US finally sent troops to Siberia approximately six weeks later under the command of General William Graves. If the serial number Radzinsky quotes is right, then how did the Colt 45 from Kentucky end up in the hands of Yurovsky?

The investigators continued work at the abandoned mine, although Sergeyev did not feel the need to visit it himself. Water was pumped out of the shaft and a more thorough search of the surrounding area was made. The results were meagre and disappointing, particularly for anyone who wanted to make a case that the bodies of the Imperial family and their retainers had been disposed of at that location. Finally, the only human remains to be found were a fingertip, two pieces of skin and the top section of a set of false teeth.

By early November 1918 Imperial Germany had collapsed. But as the European war was winding down, the turmoil in Russia was becoming more intense. Almost at the same time as the Armistice, a coup took place among the White Russian leadership, bringing

Admiral Alexander Kolchak to power in Omsk. He was promptly proclaimed Supreme Ruler of all the Russias on 18 November, exactly one week after the Armistice. Under Kolchak, the investigation in Ekaterinburg would change dramatically. Whatever the strategy was that the Allies and Kolchak were to employ behind the investigation, it is interesting to note that Consul Harris's assessment of the return of a constitutional monarchy reproduced in chapter 3 was sent from Omsk just one month earlier.

Shortly after Admiral Kolchak's ascendency, General Mikhail Diterikhs, a member of Kolchak's high command, instructed Judge Sergeyev to turn over to him all of the effects of the Imperial family that had been found, together with all the materials relating to the investigation. On 23 January 1919 the judge surrendered his material and his authority in the case to Diterikhs at Omsk in Siberia, where Kolchak had established his headquarters. Like Nametkin before him, Judge Sergeyev was never credited with having voiced the definitive opinion that the family died at Ekaterinburg.

By January 1919 murder stories were suddenly abounding everywhere and these prepared the public to anticipate and accept the belief that the family had indeed been slain on the night of 17 July 1918. General Diterikhs needed a dutiful investigator. On 23 January 1919 he appointed Nicholas Sokolov. Now it remained for Sokolov, Official Investigator for Cases of Exceptional Importance, to provide the judicial proof that would eventually demonstrate that the family's death had been at the hands of the Bolsheviks. If Sokolov was not a part of what was almost certainly a cover-up, he was at least its unwitting accomplice. Within weeks of his replacement by Sokolov, Sergeyev, like Nametkin before him, disappeared. General Diterikhs said Sergeyev was later executed 'by the Bolsheviks'. Apparently he was another victim of the rather strange end to befall the various investigators of the Romanov mystery.

CHAPTER 11

The Messengers of Death

Manipulation and Obfuscation

In December 1918, the fact that all family members had died was still inconclusive but it was rapidly becoming the accepted version. However, a different version of the murder story was being promoted by the Bolsheviks, as well as the United States State Department's intelligence operative Carl Ackerman, who was touting the story of the Tsar's death as told by the valet Parfen Domnin.

The Bolsheviks needed the family to die since the feeling among the majority of their rank and file was that if the Tsar were alive he would represent a rallying point for all monarchists and that would further hinder the takeover of Russia by the Communist party. If the Whites and Allies could prove the family died it would help in demonstrating the true violent and bloodthirsty character of the Bolsheviks – that would soon be exposed in any case by the Red Terror.

Next to take the misinformation stage was Prince George Lvov. Following the Tsar's abdication, it was Lvov who had seized the reins of the government and had become premier of the Provisional Government. However, the Bolsheviks overthrew the Provisional Government in October 1917 after less than nine months in power. Contrary to widely held beliefs, the Provisional Government did not simply melt away; indeed, some of its members attempted to re-establish it in exile in Peking, where it was said to be awaiting an invasion of Japanese troops through Vladivostok. Purportedly, Lvov and members of his former regime planned to link up with the Cossacks of Ataman Semenov and the Japanese to drive the Bolsheviks from Siberia.[1]

In October 1918 Lvov, then in Japan, wrote to President Wilson making it known that he was waiting for a visa to enter the United States. The clear impression the correspondence leaves is that arrangements for his entry into the United States had already been made but had encountered some delay. The letter was sent to President Wilson via Richard Crane, the son of Charles Crane. Richard was serving as secretary to US Secretary of State Robert Lansing, who had signed the telegrams confirming Ackerman as an agent of the State Department. Lvov's letter to Wilson recounts in detail his imprisonment by the Bolsheviks in Ekaterinburg, at the end of February 1918. He states that he escaped and was then on the run for five weeks before going directly to Vladivostok. Lvov later told General Knox, head of the British Military Mission in Russia, that the Imperial family had been murdered in the prison just next to him while he was in Ekaterinburg. Yet when he wrote to Wilson in October he makes no mention of the family in his lengthy letter. Particularly interesting is the chronology Lvov set out in his letter to the President. It simply does not allow for him to have been in prison in Ekaterinburg in the middle of July. Three months in prison, beginning at the end of February, then five weeks on the run while proceeding to Vladivostok, places him in Japan around the beginning of July.

Furthermore, with a visa on the line it is unlikely that Lvov would have failed to mention to President Wilson that he had been in Ekaterinburg when the family were murdered or that he would have lied about the timing of his movements. The letter also showed marked impatience at the delay of the visa, prompting him to demand enigmatically whether this was 'due to the observance of formalities', or to 'the essence of the matter'.[2] Based upon the statement he was to make in France at the end of December about the murder of the Imperial family, it seems quite possible that 'the essence of the matter' was regarding a role he was now to play – this time, not physically protecting them as he had earlier in St Petersburg – but spreading the story of their deaths.

Once in the United States, Lvov visited Samuel Harper, a man who had often acted as aide to Charles Crane. Lvov then proceeded to a meeting Crane had arranged for him with President Wilson. From Washington Lvov travelled to London, where he met Vladimir Nabokov, a Russian lawyer who had written the abdication statement for the Tsar's brother, Prince Michael, which came only hours after the Tsar's and his son Alexei's abdications.[3]

On 29 December 1918, less than a week after the *New York Times* had published the Ackerman piece that first brought Parfen Domnin to the public front, Lvov was in Paris where all the Allies were meeting to negotiate the Treaty of Versailles. There he told a startling new story: he had personally witnessed the executions of the entire Imperial family in Ekaterinburg. At this same time Wilson was a guest of King George in London and the 'family seven times' telegram was being received at the American embassy there and forwarded to Paris. Whether the French foreign minister, Stephen Pichon, was privy to the telegram or not remains unknown, but Pichon did turn his attention to the Romanovs when he announced to the Chamber of Deputies in Paris on 29 December 1918:

> Prince Lvov was in a cell next to the one the members of the imperial family were in. . . . They brought them together into the one room, and having made them sit down in a row, they spent the entire night inflicting bayonet blows on them, before finishing them off next morning, one after the other, with revolver shots; the emperor, the empress, the grand duchesses, the tsarevich, the lady-in-waiting, the empress' female companion, and all the people with the imperial family, so that according to what Prince Lvov has told me, the room was literally a pool of blood.[4]

Had Lvov simply forgotten to include this detail in his October letter to President Wilson? Did it somehow slip his mind that he alone had the answer to an important question being examined by numerous investigators throughout the end of 1918? Lvov, who had initially been responsible for arranging the removal of the family from Russia to England, now appeared to have been delegated the task of spreading the word of their deaths.

It soon became obvious when Lvov's story spilled into the newspapers that he was promoting an outrageous fabrication. He had been held at the city prison, not at the Ipatiev House, which of course had no 'cells'. When I discovered his self-described chronology in the October letter to President Wilson, in which he asserts that he had left the city five weeks before the family were supposedly murdered, I realised that it was more than unlikely that Lvov even caught a glimpse of any member of the Imperial family while they were in captivity in Ekaterinburg.

Nevertheless Lvov tried to bolster his earlier story by recounting how he had spoken to a judge who was investigating the crime. According to Lvov, the investigator told him, 'the chances are 99 out of 100 that the Imperial family was massacred'. Another fabrication: Sergeyev was still in charge of the inquiry at that time and there is no record of him ever having voiced the definitive opinion that the family died.

Murder stories continued to tumble forth. Soon, other distinguished Russians took up the chorus, Count and Countess Tolstoy among them. Count A. A. Tolstoy, for example, confidently announced in late January 1919 that the entire family had been destroyed by fire and acid.[5] This is even more curious, since investigator Sokolov would not reach that conclusion until months later and his view would not become public until years later.

In the spring of 1919 Commandant Joseph Lasies, a former member of the French National Assembly and of the French Military Mission stationed in Ekaterinburg, was travelling by train with White Russian General Bogoslovsky. According to American intelligence files, Bogoslovsky was held in high regard by Major Homer Slaughter,[6] Ackerman's companion and the deliverer of the Parfen Domnin document. Bogoslovsky served as Chief of Staff for Czech General Gaida who had helped lead the assault on and subsequent takeover of the Trans-Siberian Railway, and who was now headquartered at the Ipatiev House. On the train journey from Glazov to Perm, Commandant Lasies was stunned when the General confided in him that the Imperial family had not been murdered. Afterwards, in his book *La Tragédie Sibérienne*, Lasies put forth a convincing case that no murders occurred in Ekaterinburg. Furthermore, Lasies conveyed that he had met a Japanese officer who he felt knew the real story about the events in Ekaterinburg.[7]

In May 1919, Lasies encountered Robert Wilton, a correspondent for *The Times*, on a platform at the Ekaterinburg train station. Wilton, who was also on the payroll of the British Foreign Office, had developed what local British officials considered an overly intimate and compromising relationship with investigator Sokolov and various White Russian officials. While on the platform, Lasies confronted Wilton and pressed him on how fire and acid could have destroyed the family. Wilton, becoming uncomfortable, said he would return in a few minutes and when he did return stated:

> Commandant Lasies, even if the tsar and the imperial family are alive, it is necessary to say that they are dead!'[8]

Lasies responded, 'It sounds like British diplomatic acid to me.'[9]

Wilton was giving voice to a version of events that was clearly formed much earlier in December 1918. Consider the context: at the end of 1918, when a still-doubtful Judge Sergeyev was about to be relieved of duty by the White Russian military, it appears someone was anxious to spread the story of regicide. Lvov, a credible Russian politico, was in Europe telling a strangely evolving murder story about the last days of the Imperial family. What had motivated him to bend the truth? Whose interest was he assisting?

Finally, it is necessary to consider the last and most damning evidence supporting the murder account, namely the testimony of the Romanovs' alleged murderer, Yakov Yurovsky, head of the execution squad of the eleven (or twelve) men who shot the Imperial family. Yurovsky professed to know all the details of the brutal murders. His purported account was contained in the 'Yurovsky Note' supposedly written in 1920.

It surfaced publicly in 1989, but was supposedly written in 1920. It contains an account of the events in Ekaterinburg surrounding the night of 16/17 July 1918 and is alleged to have been written by Yurovsky himself. This note, unavailable to Sokolov and the other investigators at the time, is said to have led to the discovery of the bones in a Siberian forest. Before then the lack of the victims' bodies and the absence of a confession (or even the capture of an actual participant in the crime) persistently mocked the efforts to make a clear-cut case for murder, and may help account for the more fantastic aspects of the stories spread by Prince Lvov and others.

Yurovsky left behind two full narratives of the execution and burial of the Romanovs and their retainers. The first of these allegedly dates from some time in 1920, the second is the text of a speech he made to a gathering of old Bolsheviks in Ekaterinburg on 1 February 1934. (There was also a brief 'notice' that he wrote to the Museum of the Revolution in 1927, accompanying the donation of two pistols he claimed to have used that night in Ekaterinburg.) The

1920 document, which has come to be known simply as the 'note', has become the source of ongoing controversy.

In his official Soviet era history, Pavel Bykov, a member of the Ural Soviet in 1918, is at odds with the account of the Soviets' own man on the scene – Yakov Yurovsky. Yurovsky's note, as we shall see, varies from Bykov's account on some crucial points, such as how many executioners were present at the time. When Yurovsky's own two accounts are closely compared, there are also notable discrepancies – discrepancies so serious that they cannot be explained away as mere lapses of memory over a fourteen-year period.

Yurovsky's 1920 Note[10]

On 16 July [1918], a telegram in previously agreed-upon language came from Perm containing the order to exterminate the R-ovs [Romanovs]. At first (in May), the intention was to bring Nicholas to trial, but this was prevented by the advancing Whites. On the 16th at 6 o'clock in the eve., Filipp G-n [Goloshchekin] decreed that the order be carried out. A car was to arrive at midnight to take away the corpses. At 6 o'clock, the boy [Leonid Sednyov] was taken away, which very much upset the R-ovs and their people. Doctor Botkin even came to ask why this was called for? It was explained that the boy's uncle, who had been arrested, had escaped and then returned and wanted to see his nephew. The boy was sent the next day to his birthplace (in Tula province, I think). The truck did not arrive at 12 o'clock; it came only at half past one. This delayed carrying out the order. By that time everything was ready: 12 people with revolvers (including 5 Latvians) were selected who were supposed to carry out the sentence; 2 of the Latvians refused to shoot at girls.

Everyone was asleep when the car came. Botkin was woken up, and he woke up all the rest. The explanation was as follows: 'The R-ov family must be moved from upstairs to downstairs as all is not calm in town.' They dressed in half an hour. A downstairs room was selected that had walls of plastered wood (to prevent [the bullets from] ricocheting); all the furniture was removed. The detachment was at the ready in the next room. The R-ovs suspected nothing. The comm. [commandant] went to get them personally, alone, and led them downstairs to the room below. Nich. was carrying A. [Aleksei] in his arms; the rest carried little pillows and other small things with them. Walking into the empty room, A.F. [Alexandra Feodorovna] asked: 'What, there isn't even a chair? One isn't even allowed to sit down?' The comm. ordered two chairs to be brought. Nich. seated A. on one, and A. F. sat down on the other. The commandant ordered the rest to stand in a row.

When they had taken their places, he called in the detachment. When the detachment came in, the commandant told the R-ovs that, in light of the fact that their relatives in Europe were continuing their aggression against Soviet Russia, the Ural [Regional Soviet] Executive Committee had decreed that they were to be shot. Nicholas turned his back to the detachment, his face toward his family, then, as though collecting himself, turned to the commandant with the question: 'What? What?' The comm. hurriedly repeated his statement and ordered the detachment to get ready. The detachment had been given instructions earlier on whom to shoot and were ordered to aim directly for the heart to avoid a large amount of blood and to finish them off more quickly. Nicholas, again turning to the family, said nothing more; the others made a few incoherent exclamations; this all lasted a few seconds. Then the shooting started; [it] lasted for two to three minutes. Nich. was killed on the spot by the comm. himself. A. F. died immediately after that and the other R-ovs (altogether 12 people were shot [in fact, later it was officially stated that 11 people were shot]); N., A. F., four daughters (Tatiana, Olga, Maria, and Anastasia), Doctor Botkin, the footman Trupp, the cook Tikhomirov [actually, Kharitonov], another cook, and a lady-in-waiting whose last name the commandant has forgotten [actually, Alexandra's personal maid, Anna Demidova]. A., three of his sisters, the lady-in-waiting, and Botkin were still alive. They had to be shot again. This surprised the comm. because they had aimed for the heart. It was also surprising that the bullets from the pistols ricocheted off something and jumped about the room like hail. When they tried to finish off one of the girls with bayonets, the bayonet could not pierce the corset. Thanks to all of this, the entire procedure, including 'verification' (feeling the pulse, etc.), took around 20 minutes.

Then they started carrying out the corpses and putting them into the car, which had been covered with heavy blankets so the blood wouldn't seep out. At this point, the stealing began: three reliable comrades had to be assigned to guard the corpses while the procedure continued (the corpses were brought out one by one). All of the stolen goods were returned under the threat of execution (a gold watch, a cigarette case with diamonds, and so on). The comm. was only assigned to carry out the sentence; the removal of the corpses and so on was comrade Yermakov's [Ermakov's] responsibility (a worker from the Upper Isetsk factory, a party comrade, ex-prisoner). He was supposed to come with the car and be admitted by using the agreed-upon password, 'chimney sweep'. The car's late arrival caused the commandant to doubt Ye-v's [Yermakov's] thoroughness, and the comm. decided to stay with the whole operation to the end.

Around 3 o'clock in the morning, we departed for the place that Y-ev was to have prepared (beyond the Upper Isetsk factory). First it was assumed that they [the corpses] would be brought by car and then, beginning at a certain point, on horseback, since the car could go no further. The place selected was an abandoned mine. After driving a little more than 3 miles past the Upper Isetsk factory, we bumped into a whole encampment – about 25 people – on horseback, in light, horse-drawn carts, etc. These were workers (members of the soviet, of the Executive Committee, etc.) whom Y-ev had prepared. The first thing they exclaimed was: 'Why didn't you bring them to us alive?!' they thought the Romanovs' execution would be entrusted to them. They began to load the corpses into the light carts, but wagons were needed. This was very inconvenient. They immediately began to clean out [the corpses'] pockets – it was necessary to threaten them with being shot and to post sentries here as well. Then it was discovered that Tatiana, Olga, and Anastasia were dressed in some kind of special corsets. It was decided to strip the corpses bare, but not here, only at the place of burial. But it turned out that no one knew where the mine was that had been selected for this purpose.

It was growing light. The comm. sent men on horseback to find the place, but no one found anything. It turned out that nothing had been readied at all; there were no shovels and so on. The car had gotten stuck between two trees, so it was abandoned, and, after the corpses were covered with blankets, the carts moved in single file. We drove about 11 miles from Yekaterinburg and stopped a mile from the village of Koptiaki; this was around 6 or 7 o'clock in the morning. In the forest, an abandoned prospector's mine about eight feet deep was found (gold was once mined there). The mine had a couple of feet of water. The comm. ordered the corpses undressed and a fire built so that everything could be burnt. Men on horseback were posted everywhere to drive away all passersby.

When one of the girls was being undressed, it was noticed that the bullets had torn the corset in places, and diamonds could be seen in the holes. The eyes of those all around began burning brightly. The comm. immediately decided to dismiss the whole group, leaving on guard a few men on horseback and five of the detachment. The rest dispersed. The detachment began to undress and burn the corpses. A. F. was wearing a whole pearl belt made of several strands sewn into cloth. Around each girl's neck, it turned out, was a portrait of Rasputin with the text of his prayer sewn into the amulets. The diamonds were instantly removed. They (things made of diamonds, that is) amounted to about eighteen pounds. These were buried in the cellar of one of the little houses at the Alapaevsk factory; in 1919 they were dug up and brought to Moscow.

After we put everything valuable into bags, the rest of what was found on the corpses was burnt and the corpses themselves were lowered into the mine. While this was going on, a few of the valuables (someone's brooch, Botkin's dentures) were dropped, and in the effort to cave in the mine with the help of hand grenades, it was evident that the corpses were damaged and that certain parts were torn off some of them – that is how the commandant explains how the Whites (who discovered it) came to find a ripped-off finger and so forth at this spot. But it was not planned to leave the R-ovs here – the mine had earlier been designated only a temporary burial spot.

Having completed the operation and left the guard, around 10 to 11 o'clock in the morning (already 17 July), the comm. went to report to the Ural [Regional Soviet] Executive Committee, where he found Safarov and Beloborodov. The comm. told them what had been found and expressed his regret that they had not allowed him to conduct a timely search of the R-ovs. The comm. found out from Chutskaev (chairman of the Executive Committee of the city soviet) that at mile 6 along Moscow highway there are very deep, abandoned mines suitable for burying the R-ovs. The comm. left for that spot but did not arrive immediately because his car broke down. He [eventually] reached the mines on foot and actually found three very deep mines filled with water, where he decided to submerge the corpses by tying rocks to them. Guards were there who served as inconvenient witnesses, so it was decided to send, together with the truck containing the corpses, a car with Cheka security officers, who would arrest everyone there under the pretext of a search. To make his way back, the comm. appropriated a pair of horses that happened to come along. Those who had been by chance detained [for being in the area] were sent on. After setting out [for town] on horseback, together with another Chekist [member of the Cheka], to organize the whole matter, the comm. fell from his horse and badly hurt himself (afterwards, the Chekist fell as well). In case the plan with the mines didn't work, it was decided to burn the corpses or to bury them in clay pits filled with water, after first disfiguring the corpses beyond recognition with sulfuric acid.

Finally, having returned to town around 8 o'clock in the evening on the 17th, everything necessary began to be gathered: the kerosene, the sulfuric acid. Horse-drawn carts without drivers were taken from the prison. It had been planned to leave at 11 o'clock at night, but the incident with the Chekist held things up, and we left for the mine, together with ropes to drag out the corpses and so on, only around 12.30 on the night of the 17th to the 18th. In order to isolate the mine (the first prospector's mine) for the duration of the operation, it was announced to the village of Koptiaki that Czechs were hiding in the first, that the forest would be searched, and that on no account should anyone from the village go anywhere. It was ordered to shoot on the spot anyone who happened to break the cordoned-off area.

Meanwhile, dawn came (this was already the third day, the 18th). The thought was to bury some of the corpses right then and there by the mine. We began to dig a pit and almost finished digging it out. But just then a peasant acquaintance of Yermakov's drove up, and it turned out he had been able to see the pit. That effort had to be abandoned. It was decided to take the corpses to the deep mines. Because the carts were flimsy and falling apart, the comm. left for town to get motor vehicles (a truck and two motorcars, one for the Chekists). The carts had broken down earlier, and the vehicles could not make it to the place of temporary burial and that was why the carts still had to be used. When the vehicles arrived, the carts were already moving – the vehicles met them a quarter of a mile closer to the Koptiaki. We could not begin the trip until 9 o'clock at night. We crossed the railroad tracks and, a quarter of a mile later, we moved the corpses on to the truck. We drove with difficulty, paving the hazardous places with railway ties, but we still got stuck a few times. Around 4.30 in the morning of the 19th, one of the vehicles got completely stuck. Since we had not reached the mine, it was necessary to either bury or burn the corpses. One comrade, whose last name the comm. has forgotten, promised to take the latter upon himself but left without carrying out his promise.

We wanted to burn A. [Aleksei] and A. F., but by mistake the lady-in-waiting [the maid Demidova] was burnt with A. instead. We then immediately buried the remains under the fire and lit the fire again, which completely covered up traces of the digging. Meanwhile we dug a common grave for the rest. A pit around 6 feet deep and 8 feet square was ready by around 7 o'clock in the morning. We piled the corpses in the pit, poured sulfuric acid on to their faces, and generally all over their whole bodies to prevent them both from being recognized and from stinking as a result of decomposition (the pit was not deep). Having thrown dirt and brushwood on top, we put down railroad ties and drove over them a few times – no traces of the pit were left. The secret was completely safe; the Whites didn't find this burial place.

Koptiaki is 12 miles from Yekaterinburg. The R.R. crosses mile 6 between Koptiaki and the Upper Isetsk factory to the northwest [of town]. The burial place is 700 feet closer to the U. Isetsk factory from the point of intersection.

The existence of Yurovsky's note was for many years only a tantalising rumour, a kind of holy grail for Romanov researchers. This document, recording the events of July 1918 while they were still fresh in Yurovsky's memory, could potentially verify or debunk other accounts and perhaps precisely identify the Romanovs' burial site. The Russian writer Edvard Radzinsky asserts that he finally tracked down the note in 1989, at a time, as he says, 'when the [Soviet] archives were just starting to be declassified'.[11] At the end of a set of files, Radzinsky recalled, 'there were two poorly typed copies of a document that had no title or signature'. One of the copies had been corrected by hand. Radzinsky, who was familiar with Yurovsky's handwriting, recognised it immediately and concluded, 'Yes, he was the author!' At the end of the corrected copy Radzinsky found 'the terrible address . . . the location of the grave where the corpses of the tsar and his family had been secretly buried'.[12]

There is no reason to doubt Radzinsky's truthfulness, but as mentioned before, the details and timing of the discovery are striking. In April 1989, Geli Ryabov made the first public announcement that he and Alexander Avdonin had opened the Romanov grave in 1979.[13] In mid-May 1989, Radzinsky published the note. It appeared to be another one of those strange coincidences that have aided the execution theory from the very beginning, whereby an additional piece of key evidence emerges when it is most needed. Radzinsky's fortuitous discovery and publication of the note at the time of Ryabov's announcement helped to corroborate the story and substantially advanced the likelihood that the remains were authentic. Later, Ryabov and Avdonin would maintain that the handwritten copy of the note they obtained from Yurovsky's son in 1978 only confirmed that Avdonin had already pinpointed the site. However, Radzinsky asserts that the son's copy did not even contain the 'address'.[14]

Moreover, Yurovsky's supposed handwriting on the note does not settle the question of its origin and authenticity. According to a 1997 article in a Moscow newspaper, the Russian historian Vitaly Olpokov located the original typed note while working on documents seized from Admiral Kolchak's White Army in 1919. The article suggested that the Yurovsky note was found among other spurious 'testimonies' invented by Kolchak's counter-intelligence service for White Russian–anti-Bolshevik propaganda purposes. It seems possible that the note did originate with Yurovsky – in the sense that he participated in its fabrication. Or alternatively, if its creation in 1920 is accurate, that it was a calculated response to some other event, for example, the debut in July of the same year of the baffling book *Rescuing the Czar*.

Definitive conclusions simply may not be drawn from available evidence concerning the origin of the note, but what is equally intriguing and important is the content of Yurovsky's testimony. For the purposes of analysing his stories, it will be assumed that the note was written in 1920 by Yurovsky.

The significant variations between the note and the speech he was to make in 1934 after he had had access to the Sokolov Report are impressive. The account Yurovsky renders is, of course, horrifying, vicious and tragic. For a dedicated Bolshevik, it may have been perceived as somewhat noble and heroic. And for the modern reader, at least, it is not a little sad, absurd and comic. Here is a selective summary of some key events, drawn almost exclusively from the 1920 note:[15]

The first thing to strike the reader when examining the 1920 account is that it is written in the third person singular – that is to say, Yurovsky never refers to himself as 'I', but always says 'the commandant' – usually abbreviated to 'the comm.' – or 'he'. To say the least, this is very odd. Why should Yurovsky have taken such an unusual course? Radzinsky writes, 'Yurovsky proudly referred to himself in the third person as "commandant". For on that night there was no Yakov Yurovsky, there was a terrible commandant – the weapon of proletarian vengeance. The weapon of history.' It is an ingenious attempt to explain something unnatural, something that does not fit. The more we look at this the more unconvincing the explanations appear. Russian historians continue to debate the validity of the infamous note. In some quarters it has been put forth that Yurovksy dictated his note, which was subsequently transcribed in the third person.

Again, according to Dr Lev Zhivotovsky's article in *The Annals of Human Biology*, the note was added some time after the original body of the text had been written. Dr Zhivotovsky states that the alleged author was historian M. N. Pokrovsky.[16] The surname Pokrovsky was also associated with the saga of the Romanovs and the banking scheme as we have seen earlier. Interestingly, an M. Pokrovsky[17] was one of the initiators of the banking scheme who would bring in Karol Yaroshinsky, the friend of the Tsar and his family, as the front man in Russia for the banking scheme designed to establish a banking infrastructure to overthrow the Bolsheviks and rescue the Tsar and his family. It is also striking that the abbreviations and initials for individuals spoken about in the Yurovsky note, the Parfen Domnin manuscript and *Rescuing the Czar* all bear a strong stylistic resemblance.

The second surprising aspect of Yurovsky's testimony is the fact that in 1920 he stated that twelve people instead of eleven were killed on the night of 17 July. He adds a cook called Tikhomirov to the victims. Nowhere else, in any other document or testimony, is there a mention of that name.[18] The only other unexplained servant's name associated with the events of July 1918 was the elusive manservant, Domnin.

In this case it might be argued that Yurovsky was confusing the cook with Terenty Chemodurov, who may have later referred to himself as Parfen Domnin for his safety's sake. However, Yurovsky was said to have been head of the guard in the Ipatiev House with the family for thirteen days. Surely he would have come to know the prisoners reasonably well in that time. As guard commandant, it would have been his duty to know precisely how many prisoners he was responsible for and who they were. Perhaps he could forget or confuse a name, but surely, too, he would recall the total number of prisoners under his charge so he could accurately render reports to his superiors. While minor discrepancies might arise in the course of retelling a story, significant facts like the number and identity of the victims are unlikely to fall into that category.

According to the Yurovsky note the disposal of the bodies had been entrusted to Pyotr Ermakov, a Bolshevik leader and long-time associate of Filipp Goloshchekin. The plan was to remove the bodies to the forest and dump them into a deep abandoned mine shaft under cover of darkness. The truck to be used for transporting the bodies was to arrive at the Ipatiev House at midnight. Inexplicably, it did not show up until 1.30 a.m. Doubting Ermakov's competence, Yurovsky decided to 'stay with the whole operation to the end'. But the end would be a long time coming.

In the forest, Yurovsky's party encountered a group of about twenty-five men whom Ermakov had enlisted to help with the burial. The men were disappointed to learn that the Romanovs were already dead; Yurovsky was appalled to see that many of them were drunk and that they had brought only light carts rather than heavy wagons. The carts could transport only a few bodies at a time and they would frequently break down as the operation proceeded. 'This was', Yurovsky said, 'very inconvenient.'

But it got worse. No one had thought to bring even a single shovel, indeed, 'nothing had been readied at all'. In the darkness, Yurovsky and Ermakov could not locate the deep mine they had supposedly chosen earlier as a disposal site. Then the truck became stuck between two trees and was abandoned. Finally, 'at about 6 or 7 o'clock', in the full light of the Siberian summer morning, the group came across an old mine shaft, only eight feet deep. Yurovsky ordered the corpses stripped and the clothing burned. The guards then discovered the 'armor' that had protected some of the women: diamonds and other jewels sewn tightly into their corsets. Dismissing most of the men and posting armed guards to turn away passing peasants, Yurovsky ordered the naked bodies lowered into the mine. Eleven bodies, however, occupied so much space that some of the corpses were still clearly visible. (And it could have been twelve bodies according to his statement.) An attempt to collapse the mine with grenades failed and attracted more passers-by.

Having returned to Ekaterinburg in the late morning of 17 July, Yurovsky learned about some very deep mines 'along the Moscow road' that would be a more suitable burial spot. He set out with one or more Chekists to investigate, but the car broke down and they had to cover the last mile or more on foot. In order to return to town and make arrangements for the transfer of the bodies, Yurovsky commandeered two horses from a peasant. While on his way, he fell from his horse, severely injuring his leg. Some time later 'the Chekist fell as well'.

Yurovsky determined that he needed not only a plan (submerge the bodies in the flooded mines 'by tying rocks to them') but also a back-up plan ('to burn the corpses or to bury them in clay pits filled with water, after first disfiguring the corpses beyond recognition with sulfuric acid'). Back in town, he gathered the necessary materials and left again at around 12.30 a.m. on 18 July.

At the original burial site, Yurovsky ordered the guards to cordon off the area and shoot anyone who entered. It was now dawn of the second day. Perhaps hesitant to transport the bodies to the deep mines by daylight, or possibly realising the general state of exhaustion among the men, Yurovsky decided 'to bury some of the corpses right then and there by the [shallow] mine'.

'We began to dig a pit,' he recalled, 'and almost finished digging it out. But just then a peasant acquaintance of Ermakov's drove up, and it turned out he had been able to see the pit. The effort had to be abandoned. It was decided to take the corpses to the deep mines.' To avoid having to use the carts, which were 'flimsy and falling apart', Yurovsky returned to Ekaterinburg again, and picked up a truck and two cars. But the vehicles could not get to the shallow mine and the carts had to be used after all. The trip to the deep mines began at 9 p.m. on 18 July. The truck became stuck at least twice, requiring the group to unload the bodies and supplies (including tanks of kerosene and sulphuric acid), push the truck free and then load everything up again.

Finally, 'around 4.30 in the morning of the 19th, one of the vehicles got completely stuck. Since we had not reached the mine it was necessary to either bury or burn the corpses.' For some reason Yurovsky determined that Alexandra and Alexei should be burned, 'but by mistake the lady-in-waiting [actually the maid, Demidova] was burned with Alexei instead'. Their remains were buried and another fire was lit to obscure the traces of digging. Meanwhile, a shallow pit was dug. The remaining corpses were piled in, doused with sulphuric acid and covered with railroad ties. More than fifty hours after the execution, the 'secret' burial was complete. Since Yurovsky states that they burned Alexei and the maid, we must ask why the Russian Commission says Alexei and either Maria or Anastasia are still missing. According to Yurovsky, all the daughters' bones should have been with the rest of the bones found in the Koptiaki forest.

In any case, it is precisely Yurovsky's meticulous and seemingly 'realistic' reconstruction that often exposes the implausible if not outright impossible aspects of his story. To take another obvious example: assuming that Yurovsky awoke at 6 a.m. on 16 July, we are asked to believe that he remained awake for over *seventy-five* hours, until the morning of 19 July. During much of this time he was supposedly engaged in arduous physical labour and subject to tremendous psychological stress – not to mention suffering from a 'severe' injury to his leg. One has to conclude that Yurovsky could not possibly have carried out all the actions he describes in his story.

Or consider Yurovsky's remark regarding the effort to collapse the mine: 'In the effort to cave in the mine with the help of hand grenades, it was evident that the corpses were damaged and that certain parts were torn off some of them – that is how the commandant explains how the Whites . . . came to find a ripped-off finger and so forth at this spot.' But a ripped-off finger and two small pieces of skin were the only human remains found at the site. Which requires us to accept that these were the only fragments torn off the bodies by the numerous explosions, or that Yurovsky's otherwise inefficient crew was able to locate and collect every other tiny piece of human tissue. Neither scenario seems very plausible.

Finally, Yurovsky grants that, aside from his original detachment, dozens of individuals witnessed some part of the burial process, including the twenty-five men who were enlisted by Ermakov. It is very strange that, of all those witnesses, few came forward to the Whites and no one knew where the graves were, or at the very least helped to identify the vicinity of the burials. Moreover, from Sokolov's report we know that he and numerous others walked the very ground where the bodies were later found – systematically pushing metal poles into the earth. It is hard to conceive that Sokolov would not have discovered the burial site. Yet his exhaustive searches in the late spring and early summer of 1919 remarkably yielded no results.

At least one other member of the guard gave testimony about the events that took place in the Ipatiev House. Pavel Medvedev's story became a part of the Sokolov records when he surrendered to the Whites in Perm shortly after the events in Ekaterinburg. Medvedev was frequently cited as an eyewitness to the events of that terrible night. If he is to be taken seriously, we must then question if Yurovsky was with the burial party at all in the early hours of 17 July. Medvedev states Yurovsky went back to his office at 3 a.m. after ordering the murder room to be cleaned up. Medvedev's testimony might be regarded as unreliable because he had once been a Bolshevik, but since it was thought to be sound enough to be added to the former Soviet archives and is still cited by writers working from those archives, the implication is that it is meant to be taken seriously.

Of course, Medvedev might have been mistaken about Yurovsky's movements, but there is another testimony in the former Soviet archives which demonstrates that the differences in timing, actions and responsibilities are not confined to him. The other witness was Pyotr Ermakov, the Upper-Isetsk commissar. His description of the murder is radically different from Yurovsky's. Ermakov testifies it is he, not Yurovsky, who gave the orders. In his account Ermakov tells the Romanovs to leave their bedrooms, the victims were seated, not standing, and Ermakov attributes to himself the honour of killing the Tsar – and not only the Tsar, but Alexandra, one of the daughters and Alexei. The wild discrepancies between these two accounts have been explained away by Edvard Radzinsky who argued that, as well as being a braggart, Ermakov was so drunk that he did not know what was going on. It is a weak explanation. No source has been discovered that supports this theory, nor any that reports Ermakov as drinking heavily. Moreover, those few that comment on his behaviour the next day do not leave us with the impression of a man who is suffering from a hangover or does not know what he is doing.

It is not as if Ermakov was discreet about his claims; he advertised them as much as he could. Yet Yurovsky never openly contradicted him, nor did any of the rest of the detachment. It was not as if killing 'Bloody Nicholas' were a minor episode that could easily be forgotten. It was a once-in-a-lifetime event, which would have filled a revolutionary with pride. What happens to Yurovsky's pride when faced with the claims of Ermakov? It disappears. One, or both, of these men were lying. This night should have been embedded in the mind of a revolutionary to its smallest detail. Yet there were glaring discrepancies. Bykov and Yurovsky differ on the most fundamental element – how many executioners were there. Starkov, one of the senior guards, claims to have seen Yurovsky in conversation with Filipp Goloshchekin at the very time Yurovsky says he was on the road to the Koptiaki forest with the burial party. Starkov further stated that Filipp Goloshchekin, who as we saw previously was stated to be the only man in the Urals who did not want to see the family die, was the one who had spread the untrue story that the family died. How is it that these extremely troubling disparities have always been explained away or dismissed? Suspicions about Yurovsky's story multiply when the note is compared with his 1934 speech before the group of old Bolsheviks.[19]

CHAPTER 12

Yurovsky's Revised Account

What Do We Believe?

Delivered at a meeting of old Bolsheviks, Yurovsky's second account can be decisively dated to 1934. It was a remarkable year, for it marked the beginning of Stalin's purges that were to be responsible for eliminating many of the 'old Bolsheviks' including those who had been close to the events in Ekaterinburg in 1918. The discrepancies between his 1920 Note and this speech fourteen years later are striking.

> . . . it was presumed that a trial would have been organized for them had time permitted. But as I have already said above, the front had been moving closer and closer since the beginning of July and was then only about 25 miles away, inevitably hastening a denouement.
>
> This was a question of great political significance then and could not be resolved without a decision by the center, because the situation at the front also depended not only on the Urals but also on the center's possibilities (by this time, you see, the Red Army was becoming more and more centralized and concentrated). There were continual contacts and conversations with the center about this. Around 10 July, the decision had already been made about what to do if abandoning Yekaterinburg became unavoidable. You see, only this can explain why execution without a trial was put off until 16 July, with Yekaterinburg being finally abandoned on 25–26 July; moreover, Yekaterinburg's evacuation was conducted in a

completely, so to speak, orderly and timely way. Around 10 or 11 July, Filipp [Goloshchekin] told me that Nicholas would have to be liquidated and that it was necessary to prepare for this.

When it came to liquidation methods, we had no experience in such matters, since we hadn't engaged in such things before, and thus it was no wonder that there was a lot that was rushed in putting this matter into effect, especially because all sorts of dangers in the proximity of the front intensified the problem. He told me that individual comrades thought that to pull this off more securely and quietly it should be done at night, right in their beds as they sleep. That seemed inconvenient to me, and I said that we would think about how to do it and would get prepared.

On the morning of 15 July, Filipp arrived and said that things had to be finished off tomorrow. Sednyov the kitchen boy (a boy of thirteen) was to be taken away and sent to his former birthplace or to somewhere in central Russia. It was also said that Nicholas was to be executed and that we should officially announce it, but when it came to the family, then perhaps it would be announced, but no one knew yet how, when, and in what manner. Thus, everything demanded the utmost care and as few people as possible – moreover, absolutely dependable ones.

On the 15th I immediately undertook preparations, for everything had to be done quickly. I decided to assemble the same number of men as there were people to be shot, gathered them all together, and told them what was happening – that they all had to prepare themselves for this, that as soon as we got the final order everything was going to have to be ably handled. You see, it has to be said that shooting people isn't the easy matter that it might seem to some. After all, this wasn't going on at the front but in a 'peaceful' situation. You see, these weren't bloodthirsty people, but people performing the difficult duty of the revolution. That is why it wasn't mere chance that, at the last minute, the situation arose that two Latvians refused [to participate] – they didn't have it in them.

On the morning of the 16th, I sent away the kitchen boy Sednyov under the pretext of a meeting with his uncle who had come to Sverdlovsk. This caused anxiety among the arrested. Botkin, the devoted intermediary, and then one of the daughters asked where and why they had taken Sednyov and for how long. Aleksei missed him, they said. Having gotten an explanation they left, seemingly calmed. I prepared 12 Nagant revolvers and determined who would shoot whom. Comrade Filipp warned me that a truck would arrive at 12 o'clock at night. Those who arrived would give a password; they would be allowed in and would be given the corpses, which they would take away for burial. Around 11 o'clock at night on the 16th I gathered the men together again, gave out the revolvers, and stated that we would soon have to start liquidating the arrested. I warned Pavel Medvedev about the thorough check of the sentries outside and in, about how he and the guard commander should be on watch themselves in the area around the house and at the house where the external guard was lodged, and about how they should keep in contact with me. Only at the last minute, when everything was ready for the shooting, were they to warn all the sentries as well as the rest of the detachment that if they heard shots coming from the house they shouldn't worry and shouldn't come out of their lodgings, and that if something was especially worrysome they should let me know through the established channel.

The truck did not show up until half past one in the morning; the fact that we waited longer than expected couldn't help but create anxiety, in addition to the anxiety of waiting in general, but the main thing was that the [summer] nights were so short. Only after the truck came – or after I learned by telephone that the truck was on its way – did I go to wake the arrested.

Botkin was asleep in the room closest to the entrance; he came out and asked what the matter was. I told him that everyone had to be woken up right away as the town was uneasy, that staying upstairs was dangerous for them, and that I would transfer them to another place. Preparations took a lot of time, around 40 minutes. When the family was dressed, I led them to a room previously selected in the downstairs part of the house. We had thought this plan through with comrade Nikulin. Here I have to say that we didn't think in advance about the fact that the windows could not contain the noise; second, that the wall against which those [who] had to be shot were to be lined up was made of stone, and, finally, that the shooting would take on a chaotic character, but this was impossible to foresee. This last thing wasn't supposed to occur because each man was going to shoot one person, and so everything was to be orderly. The reasons for the chaos – that is, disorderly and confused shooting – became clear later. Although I warned them through Botkin that they didn't need to bring anything with them, they nevertheless gathered up various little things – pillows, little bags, and so forth – and I believe, a little dog.

Once they descended to the room (at the entrance to the room on the right is a very wide window, almost the size of the whole wall), I suggested they stand by the wall. Apparently, at that moment they still did not imagine anything of what was in store for them. Alexandra Fyodorovna said: 'There aren't even chairs here.' Nicholas was carrying Aleksei in his arms. And he continued to stand with him like that in the room. I ordered a pair of chairs to be brought. Alexandra Fyodorovna sat on one of them to the right of the entrance, almost in the corner and by the window. Next to her, toward the left side of the entrance, stood the daughters and Demidova.

Here Aleksei was set down beside them on a chair; after him came Doctor Botkin, the cook, and others, and Nicholas was left standing opposite Aleksei. Simultaneously, I ordered the people to come down and ordered that everyone be ready and that each be at his place when the command was given.

Nicholas, having seated Aleksei, stood so that he was blocking him. Aleksei sat in the left-hand corner of the room from the entrance, and I immediately, as I recall it, told Nicholas approximately the following: that his imperial relatives and close associates both inside the country and abroad had tried to free him and that the Soviet of Workers' Deputies had decreed that they be shot. He asked: 'What?' and turned to face Aleksei. Right then, I shot him and killed him on the spot. He didn't manage to turn to face us to get an answer. Now, instead of order, chaotic shooting began. The room was very small, but still everyone could have entered the room and performed the shooting in an orderly way. But, apparently, many shot across the threshold, and the bullets began to ricochet, since the wall was made of stone.

Moreover, the firing intensified when those being shot began to scream. It took a great effort on my part to stop the shooting. A bullet from one of those shooting behind me whizzed by my head, and I can't remember whether it was the palm, hand or finger of someone else that was hit and pierced by a bullet.

When the shooting stopped, it turned out that the daughters, Alexandra Fyodorovna, the lady-in-waiting [actually, the personal maid] Demidova, I think, and also Aleksei were alive. I thought that they had fallen out of fear or perhaps on purpose and that was why they were still alive. Then we began to finish them off (I had earlier suggested that they be shot in the region of the heart so that there would be less blood). Aleksei remained seated, petrified, and I finished him off. They shot the daughters but nothing happened, then Yermakov set the bayonet in motion and that didn't help, then they were finished off by being shot in the head. Only in the forest did I discover what hampered the shooting of the daughters and Alexandra Fyodorovna.

Now that the shooting was over, the corpses had to be moved, and it was rather a long way. How could they be carried? Here someone thought of stretchers (they didn't think of it at the proper time). They took harness beams from sleighs and stretched sheets over them, I think. Having checked that everyone was dead, we began to carry them. Then we realized that bloodstains would be everywhere. I immediately ordered that the stretchers be lined with available soldiers' blankets and that the truck be covered with them. I assigned Mikhail Medvedev to remove the corpses. He is a former member of the Cheka and, at present, an employee of the GPU (security police). He and Pyotr Zakharovich Yermakov were supposed to take the corpses and drive away with them. When the first corpses were taken away, someone, I can't remember who, told me that one of the men had appropriated some valuables for himself. I then understood that there were valuables among the things the family had brought with them. I immediately stopped the carrying of the corpses, gathered the men together, and demanded that the stolen valuables be handed over. After a certain amount of denial, two men returned valuables they had stolen. Threatening anyone who looted with execution, I dismissed these two and, as I recall, assigned comrade Nikulin to supervise the carrying of the corpses, having warned them that valuables were present on the bodies of those shot. I gathered together all the items containing objects that they had seized, in addition to the objects themselves, and sent them to the commandant's office. Comrade Filipp [Goloshchekin], apparently sparing me (as my health wasn't the best), warned me that I shouldn't go to the 'Funeral', but I was very worried about how well the corpses would be hidden. That was why I decided to go myself, and I did the right thing as it turned out; otherwise, all the corpses would certainly have fallen into the hands of the Whites. It is easy to see how they would have used this matter to their advantage.

Having ordered that everything be washed and cleaned up, we departed around 3 o'clock or a little later. I took a few people from the internal guard along with me. I did not know where they were planning to bury the corpses. As I said above, Filipp had apparently assigned this matter to comrade Yermakov, who took us somewhere near the Upper Isetsk factory (by the way, I think it was Pavel Medvedev who told me the same night that, when he was running the detachment, he saw comrade Filipp walking by the house the whole time and looking more than a little worried about how things would go there.) I hadn't been to these parts and wasn't familiar with them. About 1 or 2 miles or maybe more from the Upper Isetsk factory, we were met by a whole convoy of people on horseback and in light horse-drawn carts. I asked Yermakov who these people were, what they were here for, and he answered that these were the people he had prepared. I don't know to this day why there were so many. I heard only isolated shouts, 'We thought that you would deliver them to us alive, and now it turns out they're dead.' Then, I think, it was 2 or 3 miles farther on, the truck got stuck between two trees.

During this stop, some of Yermakov's people started to pull at the girls' blouses where they discovered the valuables. The stealing was starting up again.

Then I ordered that people be posted so that no one could come near the truck. The truck was stuck and couldn't budge. I asked Yermakov, 'And is the place chosen for them far?' he said, 'It's not far, beyond the railway embankment.' And, on top of being stuck between the trees, this was a marshy place. No matter where we went, it was swampy. I thought to myself, He brought so many people and horses; at least there should have been wagons instead of lightweight carts. But there was nothing to be done. We had to unload and lighten the truck; but even this didn't help. Then I ordered the bodies loaded on to the horse-drawn carts, since we couldn't wait any longer: dawn was coming.

Only when it was already beginning to be light did we reach the well-known 'clearing'. Peasants were sitting by the fire about 20 paces or so from the mine selected for the burial site, apparently having spent the night there after haymaking. Along the way, lone people could also be seen at a distance, and it became utterly impossible to continue working within sight of people. I have to say that the situation was becoming difficult and everything could have been ruined. I still didn't know then that the mine wasn't worth a damn for our purposes.

And then there were those cursed valuables. I didn't know then that there were rather a lot of them. The people that Yermakov had gathered weren't at all right for this sort of job, and there were so many of them, too. I decided that the people had to be gotten rid of. I immediately found out that we were about 1 or 2 miles outside the village of Koptiaki. A large-enough area had to be cordoned off, which I ordered done. I selected people and instructed them to surround a certain area. In addition, I sent people to the village to advise the villagers not to go anywhere, saying that Czechoslovaks were nearby, that our units had been brought here, and that it was dangerous. Then [I said] to send anyone they saw back to the village and, if nothing else worked, to shoot those who were stubbornly disobedient. I sent the other group of people back to the village, because they were no longer necessary.

Having done this, I ordered the corpses [unloaded] and the clothing removed and burned. That is, I ordered the things destroyed without a trace, and saw to it that any incriminating evidence was removed, in case someone were to discover the corpses. I ordered bonfires built. Things that had been sewn into the daughters' and Alexandra's clothing were discovered when the corpses began to be undressed; I can't remember exactly what was discovered on the latter or if it was simply the same sort of things as were sewn into the daughters' clothing. The daughters had bodices made up of solid diamonds and other precious stones that served not just as receptacles for valuables but also as protective armor. That was why neither bullets nor bayonets yielded results during the shooting and bayonet blows. No one is responsible for their death agonies but themselves, it has to be said.

There turned out to be about 18 pounds of such valuables. By the way, their greed turned out to be so great that on Alexandra Fyodorovna there was a simply huge piece of gold wire bent into the shape of a bracelet of around a pound in weight. All these valuables were immediately ripped out so that we wouldn't have to drag the bloody clothing with us. Those valuables that the Whites discovered when they excavated were undoubtedly part of the things that had been individually sewn into the clothing and that remained in the ashes of the fire when the clothing was burned. The next day, comrades gave me a few diamonds that they had found there. How could they have overlooked the other valuables? They had enough time to look. The most likely thing is that they just didn't think of it. By the way, some valuables are being returned to us through Torgsin stores, for it is likely that the peasants from Koptiaki village picked

The last Imperial family
of Russia.

Right: Tsar Nicholas II and
Alexandra in their earlier
years in St Petersburg.

The royal cousins bore such a strong resemblance that Tsar Nicholas II, to the left, was often confused with King George V and vice versa.

Kaiser Wilhelm II, the Emperor of Germany and King of Prussia during the First World War, also a cousin to Tsar Nicholas II, Tsarina Alexandra, as well as King George V.

Rasputin, surrounded by 'admiring women.'

Karol Yaroshinsky, the Russian point man for the banking scheme and benefactor to the Imperial family during their confinement in Siberia.

Anna Vyrubova, confidant of the Tsarina, and the contact in St Petersburg for the Brotherhood of St John of Tobolsk, the organisation in Siberia planning a rescue of the Imperial family.

Dressing as a nurse or nun was a common disguise for aristocratic women during the early days of the Bolshevik revolution.

Prince George Lvov, the first head of the Provisional Government after the abdication in 1917 of Tsar Nicholas II, attempted to gain permission for the Imperial family to go to England.

Alexander Kerensky, the second head of the Provisional Government, whom Lvov placed in charge of negotiating the Family's departure to England and who, after failing to gain British permission, sent the Family to Siberia 'to protect them from the first surges of the revolution'.

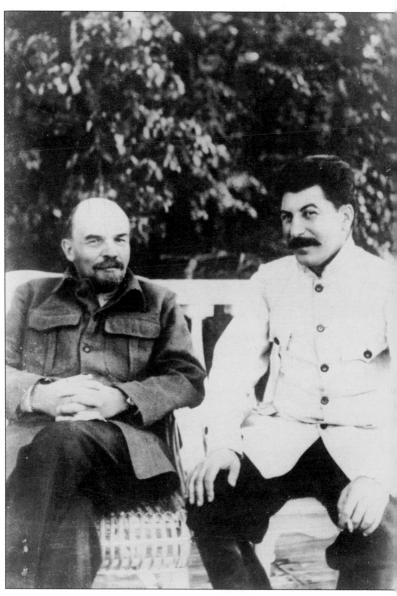

Lenin, on the left, groomed Stalin, on the right, to be one of his most able
administrators and later leader of the Soviet Union.

Leon Trotsky, one of the principal Bolshevik leaders and the head of the Red Army.

Charles Crane, President Wilson's advisor on Russian affairs and Thomas Masaryk's close friend, with the head of the Old Believers near Moscow.

Left: Thomas Masaryk, the first President of Czechoslovakia and close friend of American industrialist Charles Crane.

Below: President Woodrow Wilson, of the United States.

Mr William G. McAdoo, Secretary of Treasury and head of the United States Secret Service, and Mrs McAdoo, President Wilson's daughter.

Breckinridge Long, Third Under Secretary of State, who was in charge of the evacuation of important refugees.

David Lloyd George, the Prime Minister of Great Britain.

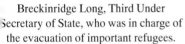

The Prince of Wales, Charles Evans Hughes (Secretary of State), the Duke of Connaught and Frank Kellogg seated at table, during a Pilgrim Society dinner in London.

The Ipatiev House in Ekaterinburg was the last place of imprisonment of the Imperial family; also called the 'House of Special Purpose'. Soon after the family's arrival in the spring of 1918 the Bolsheviks built a wooden palisade around the outside.

The room on the lower floor in the Ipatiev House where the Imperial family was alleged to have been murdered on 17 July 1918.

The living room of the Ipatiev House where the family met in the evenings and which the Czech Legion made their headquarters only eight days after the family vanished.

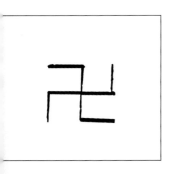

The reverse swastika, a Tibetan good luck symbol and the secret sign of the Brotherhood of St John of Tobolsk, who were attempting to rescue the family; found on the wall inside the Ipatiev House.

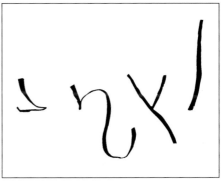

The strange writing when looked at in a mirror seems to spell Lysva, a town near Perm, where Count Beckendorf, Marshall of the Court and the head of Nicholas' court function's country estate was located.

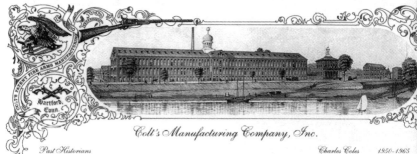

Colt's Manufacturing Company, Inc.

April 24, 1998

Dear Ms. McNeal:

Colt, by the means of this letter, is proud to authenticate the manufacture of the Colt firearm with the following serial number:

COLT MODEL 1911 AUTOMATIC PISTOL

Serial Number:	71905
Caliber:	.45/c
Barrel Length:	5"
Finish:	Blue
Type of Stocks:	Not Listed
Sold To:	United States Government
Shipped To:	Ordnance Officer
Address:	Fort Thomas, Kentucky
Date of Shipment:	April 30, 1914
Number of Same Type Guns in Shipment:	150

We trust you will find the historical information, retrieved from the original Colt shipping records, to be of interest.

Sincerely,

Kathleen J. Hoyt
Historian

Admiral Alexander Kolchak, the man under whom the investigation of the family's disappearance fell and the leader of the White forces until January 1920.

General Anton Denikin, later Sir Anton Denikin, a White military leader during the Russian Civil War.

Left: Certificate of origin for the gun described by Edvard Radzinsky, as the weapon Yurovsky used to kill the Tsar.

Czech Legion soldiers on the outskirts of Ekaterinburg in 1918.

Major Homer Slaughter, American liaison to the Czech Legion in Ekaterinburg in July 1918, who filed the Parfen Domnin report to United States Military Intelligence.

Sidney Reilly, who while working in British Intelligence also operated with numerous aliases including the Bolshevik, Comrade Relinsky.

The curious book *Rescuing the Czar* which was published in 1920 in San Francisco.

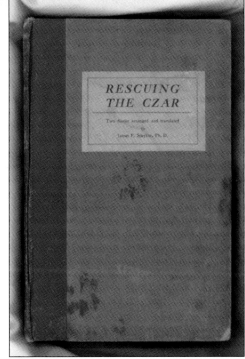

RESCUING
THE CZAR

Two diaries arranged and translated
by
James P. Smythe, Ph. D.

To the left is Mr and Mrs William Rutledge McGarry while on holiday
in Pebble Beach, California with Russian Consul General George Romanovsky
(circa 1920).

some valuables up after our departure. We gathered the valuables, burned the things, and threw the stark-naked corpses into the mine.

And here another muddle ensued. The water barely covered the bodies; what to do? We thought of blowing up the mine with bombs to cave it in. But nothing came of this, of course. I saw that we were getting nowhere with the burial and that the bodies couldn't be left as is and that everything had to be started all over again. But what to do? Where to put them? Around 2 o'clock in the afternoon I decided to go to town because it was clear that the corpses had to be extracted from the mine and transferred to a different place. Besides, even a blind man could find them with the place being so churned up. People had seen that something was going on there. I posted sentries and guards at the spot, took the valuables, and left.

I went to the Regional [Soviet] Executive Committee and told the authorities how badly things had gone. Comrade Safarov, and I can't remember who else, listened and had nothing to say. Then I found Filipp and pointed out the necessity of transferring the corpses to another place. Filipp summoned Yermakov, severely reprimanded him, and sent him to dig up the corpses. I simultaneously instructed him to take bread and dinner, as the men had been there almost 24 hours without sleep and were hungry and worn out. They were supposed to wait there until I arrived. It turned out not to be so easy to pull out the corpses, and we suffered rather a lot over it. We had set out late, and we fiddled with it all night.

I went to Sergei Yegorovich Chutskaev, then chairman of the [Yekaterinburg] City Soviet Executive Committee, to ask whether he perhaps knew of a place. He recommended some very deep abandoned mines on the Moscow highway. I got a car, took someone from the regional Cheka with me, Polushin, I think, and someone else, and we left.

About a mile short of the designated spot, the car broke down, so we left the driver to fix it and set out on foot, looked the place over, and found that it would do. The only thing was making sure there weren't extra, watchful eyes. Some people lived not far from there, and we decided we would go and remove them and send them to town. At the end of the operation we would free them; that was what we decided on. When we got back to the car, the car itself needed towing. I decided to wait for chance passersby. Some time later, some people were tearing along, driving a pair of horses. I stopped them, and it turned out that the boys knew me and were hurrying to get to their factory. They weren't very keen on it, but they gave the horses up.

While we rode, another plan came to mind; to burn the corpses. But no one knew how. It seems to me Polushin said he knew how, which was fine, since no one really knew how it would turn out. I still had the mines along the Moscow highway in mind and consequently decided to obtain carts to use for transport. Besides, in case of bad luck, I thought of burying them in groups in different places along the thoroughfare. The road leading to Koptiaki, which is next to the clearing, is clayey, so if they could be buried there without anyone seeing, not a living soul would ever guess. They could be buried and carts could be driven over [the site]. The result would be a rough pathway and nothing more. And so, three plans.

There was no form of transportation, no car. I went to the director of the military transport garage to find out if they had any cars. There turned out to be a car, but the director, whose surname I forget, later turned out to be a scoundrel, and I think they shot him in Perm. Comrade Pavel Petrovich Gorbunov was the garage director or deputy director, I don't remember exactly, and is currently the deputy [chairman] of the State Bank. I told him that I needed a car quickly. He said, 'And I know what for.' And he gave me the director's car. I went to Voikov, supply director for the Urals, to obtain gasoline or kerosene, sulfuric acid for disfiguring the faces, and a shovel. I obtained all of these. As deputy commissar of justice of the Ural region, I saw to it that ten carts without drivers were taken from the prisons. Everything was loaded up, and they left. The truck was directed to the same place, and I myself stayed to wait for Polushin, 'specialist' in burning, who had disappeared. I waited for him at Voikov's. Even though I waited until 11 o'clock at night, I didn't find him. Later they told me that he was on his way to me but fell from his horse, hurt his leg, and couldn't make it. I could have used the car again, but around 12 o'clock at night I mounted a horse with a comrade whose name I don't remember now and departed for the place where the corpses were. Misfortune befell me too. The horse stumbled, rose to its knees, and somehow fell awkwardly on its side, crushing my leg. I spent an hour or more lying down before I could mount my horse again. We arrived late during the night and went to work extracting [the corpses]. I decided to bury a few corpses on the road. We started digging a pit. It was almost ready by dawn when one comrade came up to me and said that, despite the ban on allowing anyone near, a person had shown up from somewhere, an acquaintance of Yermakov's, whom Yermakov permitted to remain at a distance. The person could see that people were digging around here since piles of clay were lying around. Although Yermakov assured us that this person couldn't see anything, other comrades started to illustrate, that is, to show, where the person had been standing and how he undoubtedly could not help seeing.

That was how this plan was ruined too. It was decided to fill in the pit. We piled everything on to the cart as evening fell. The truck was waiting in a spot where it was pretty nearly guaranteed that it would not get stuck (the driver was Liukhanov, the worker from the Zlokazov factory). We headed for the Siberian highway.

Having crossed the railway embankment, we loaded the corpses into the truck again and quickly got in. We had been struggling for two hours, so it was getting close to midnight, and I decided that we had to bury them somewhere around here because at this late hour it was certain that no one at all could see us. I had sent for railroad ties to be brought to cover the place where the corpses would be piled, so there was only one person who might see a few of the men – the railroad night watchman. I had in mind that if anyone found the ties, they might guess that they were put down to let a truck pass through.

I forgot to say that during that evening or, more precisely, during the night, we got stuck twice. Having unloaded everything, we got out, but then we got hopelessly stuck a second time. Two months ago, I saw a picture of these ties as I leafed through the book by Sokolov [the White army commander], Kolchak's investigator for exceptionally important cases. There it was noted that the railway ties were put down at that spot to let a truck drive through. So, having dug up a whole area, they never thought to look beneath the ties.

I have to say that we were all so devilishly exhausted that we didn't want to dig new graves, but, as always happens in these cases, two or three began doing it and then others joined in. We immediately lit fires, and while the grave was being readied, we burned two corpses, Aleksei and, apparently, Demidova, instead of Alexandra Fyodorovna, as we had intended. We dug a pit by the spot where they were burned, piled in the bones, evened it over, lit another big fire, and covered all traces with ashes. Before putting the rest of the corpses in the pit, we poured sulfuric acid on them, then we filled in the pit, covered it with railway ties, drove the empty truck over them, tamped the ties down a little, and were done with it. At

5 or 6 o'clock in the morning, we gathered everyone together, explained the importance of what we had accomplished, warned everyone to forget about what they had seen and never speak of it to anyone, and left for town. The boys from the regional Cheka who had lost track of us – comrades Isai Rodginsky, Gorin, and someone else – arrived when we had already finished with everything.

I left with a report for Moscow on the night of the 19th. It was then that I gave the valuables to Trifonov, member of the Third Army's Revolutionary Council. I think Beloborodov, Novoselov, and someone else buried them in a basement in the earthen floor of a worker's house in Lysev. In 1919, when a Central Committee commission was on its way to the liberated Urals to establish Soviet power there, I was also coming there to work. The same Novoselov, together with someone else whose name I can't remember, extracted [the valuables]. N. N. Krestinsky, who was returning to Moscow, took them with him. In 1922–1923, when I worked in the republic's State Depository putting the valuables in order, I remember that one of Alexandra Fyodorovna's pearl strands was valued at 600,000 gold rubles.

In Perm, when I was sorting through things that had belonged to the former imperial family, a number of valuables – more than a wagonload – were again discovered, hidden in things down to their underwear.

There are numerous inconsistencies and several contradictions between the two accounts. Yurovsky admitted reading Sokolov's book some time between its publication and his speech in 1934, for he made mention of the book in his lecture. When most of the contradictions between the Note and the speech are compared, in every case, the revision has the effect of bringing Yurovsky's story more into line with the evidence presented by Sokolov.

These instances can be quickly summarised: in 1920 there are no pets in the 'murder room'. But Sokolov allegedly found the body of Jemmy, Grand Duchess Tatiana's dog, at the bottom of the mine where the remains were first destroyed in part. So in 1934, Yurovsky recalls that the victims entered the room carrying 'various little things – pillows, little bags, and so forth – and, I believe, a little dog.'[1] Could a barking dog be overlooked in the midst of the carnage? Or are we to believe that someone was designated to shoot straight for the heart of a dog that Yurovsky doesn't even remember in his first telling of the sordid details? Once again, Yurovsky was clearly reciting bits of the Sokolov report.

In the 1920 Note, Yurovsky first learned on 16 July that the family was to be executed. But Sokolov demonstrated that Goloshchekin had discussed the fate of the Family with the Ural Soviet much earlier. Accordingly, in 1934, Yurovsky states that 'around 10 or 11 July, Filipp [Goloshchekin] told me that Nicholas would have to be liquidated and that it was necessary to prepare for this.'[2] If, in fact, the team led by Yurovsky had almost a week to prepare for the night in question, why was it such a debacle? The order of execution that Yurovsky says he read to Nicholas also varies. According to the Note, the family was shot 'in light of the fact that their relatives in Europe were continuing their aggression against Soviet Russia'. In the speech, Yurovsky recalls telling Nicholas 'that his imperial relatives and close associates both inside the country and abroad had tried to free him and that the Soviet Workers' Deputies had decreed that [the family] be shot'.

The change is small but significant. Yurovsky appears once again to be borrowing from information he had been fed. For in the intervening years, evidence had come to light that pointed to an intricate international alliance that plotted to rescue the Romanovs. Other smaller inconsistencies exist. In the Note, for instance, Yurovsky says that Alexandra was wearing 'a whole pearl belt made of several strands sewn into cloth'. He makes no mention of this belt in 1934, but obviously uses Sokolov's information. He recalls for the first time 'a simply huge piece of gold wire bent into the shape of a bracelet of around a pound in weight'. In 1920 Yurovsky says he left the shallow mine at 'around 10 to 11 o'clock in the morning'. When the party later needed railroad ties to ease their passage over the boggy ground and to cover the common grave, they are readily available. In 1934, Yurovsky does not leave the mine until 'around 2 o'clock in the afternoon', and later he has to send for the railroad ties – which are used only for the burial. In both the 1920 and 1934 accounts it is worth noting that there never was an explanation for the wood that was used to 'burn' the bodies. The Koptiaki forest is swampy and burning enough green wood in the summer to dispose of at least eleven bodies is hardly conceivable. And the fact is that the only combination that will rapidly attain the 2000 degrees needed to destroy bodies by fire is a combination of rubber and diesel fuel. Even commercial crematoria cannot completely destroy bodies, for, in the end, they must grind up the remaining bones and teeth.

Certainly, some of the discrepancies can be attributed innocently enough to an unreliable memory. After fourteen years it should not be expected that Yurovsky would recount the story word for word, or that he would not be tempted to embellish the narrative when addressing a gathering of those who were on the front lines during the initial revolutionary struggle.

But Radzinsky and others believe that Yurovsky composed the Note in 1920 and kept a copy of it. The very copy that was later given to Ryabov by Yurovsky's son. Since he obviously could have consulted his copy when preparing his speech, deteriorating memory is hardly a viable excuse for the differences.

Of course, Yurovsky was presumably the only individual in attendance at the gathering in 1934 who knew of the existence of the 1920 Note, let alone its content. Consequently, he did not have to fear that someone would ask him to explain the discrepancies. Still, we have to ask: why would Yurovsky change important details of the story in 1934? The answer, I think, is clear: there was quite a history of the Soviet government feeding from information taken from White sources to account for the end of the Romanovs. As we shall see, when we compare Pavel M. Bykov's *The Last Days of the Romanovs* and Yurovsky's account, both Yurovsky and Bykov appear merely to have recycled Sokolov's material that came to light when a Bolshevik named Gruzenberg broke into Sokolov's lodgings in Berlin in 1921. When in the next chapter we examine how this strange chain of events occurred, it will become clearer how minor alterations appeared in Yurovsky's 1934 account that differed from the facts described in his original Note.

One known account could explain all the contradictions recorded in the different testimonies. Published in 1920, well before Sokolov's or Bykov's accounts were known, *Rescuing the Czar* describes a scene where, after realising the family had vanished, a couple of Bolsheviks are angrily demanding of each other the whereabouts of the Romanovs. Charles James Fox, the British intelligence agent, is portrayed as being huddled with the family in a tunnel under the Ipatiev House that connects to the British consulate, when he overhears the Bolshevik guards in utter confusion concocting lies to cover the disappearance of the family. *Rescuing the Czar* further maintains that Fox successfully spirited the

Romanovs out of the Ipatiev House through the cellar to the British consulate via the tunnel. Did the family escape? Or is Sokolov's version that they were all shot by eleven or twelve assassins, then destroyed completely by fire and acid, the true one? As we shall see, all the factions had enormous motivation to plant their own version of the night of 16/17 July 1918.

What seems apparent is that for several years after the disappearance of the family neither the Bolsheviks, nor the Allies, or various White factions could furnish conclusive evidence that the Romanovs had been murdered or had survived. Yet it is evident that both the Bolsheviks and their adversaries wanted the world to accept the fact that the family had been murdered. War makes strange bedfellows indeed. And we shall see how intertwined all these protagonists will prove to be.

CHAPTER 13

Tsar and Family Destroyed Without a Trace

Straining Credibility

On 7 February 1919, Nicholas Sokolov took over Sergeyev's investigation for the Whites. Although preliminary narratives regarding Sokolov's findings were placed in both British and United States archives in August 1920, just one month after the publication of *Rescuing the Czar*, many years would pass until his full report, *Judicial Enquiry into the Assassination of the Russian Imperial Family*, was published posthumously in 1924. And it would tell a different story from the ambiguous reports of its predecessors.

Sokolov, aided by Captain Paul Bulygin, the former head of the guard of the Empress Marie, Nicholas II's mother, was mandated to carry on a lengthy investigation under less than perfect conditions. Both he and Bulygin would conclude that all seven Romanovs had died. Burned and covered with acid would be Sokolov's official diagnosis in the early 1920s regarding the disappearance of the family and his conclusion would be accepted by the world at large. That is, until the putative bones of the family buried in St Petersburg in July 1998 were discovered.

Sokolov did have access to several sources of fresh evidence that his predecessor purportedly did not examine. Just before Judge Sergeyev turned over the investigation, his office received a batch of telegrams that had been left behind by the Bolsheviks. Most of the messages were banal and insignificant. But one telegram in particular has become the single most controversial piece of evidence in the entire investigation. The plausibility of the case for or against the execution of the Imperial family can easily turn on how one understands the message and accounts for the strange circumstances surrounding it.

> Decoded, the message reads: 'Inform Sverdlov family suffered same fate as head. Officially family will die in evacuation.'[1]

It was sent at 9 p.m. on 17 July 1918, not even twenty-four hours after the alleged execution, and signed by Alexander Beloborodov, the chairman of the Ural Regional Soviet. It was addressed to Lenin's secretary, Nicholas Gorbunov, who was to communicate the message to Sverdlov – precisely the same extremely small inner-circle-within-the-inner-circle that had directed all the activities regarding the Imperial family. It reflects the same information about the survival of the family members that was contained in the Parfen Domnin account delivered by the nun from the Ekaterinburg monastery to Major Homer Slaughter. We do not know if Slaughter ever shared the Domnin account with any of the investigators. What we do know is that if he did, it was never listed as a piece of evidence in the official report by Sokolov.

And we also know that because of the timing and the source, Sokolov focused his attention on the telegram immediately. When, after a bizarre delay of over nineteen months, he finally learned of its contents, he made it the crowning element of his murder hypothesis. He took it to be a straightforward admission, accidentally left behind by the hastily retreating Bolsheviks, that Nicholas, as well as the entire family, had been executed.

But as John O'Conor pointed out in *The Sokolov Investigation*, this interpretation requires one to ignore completely the striking and unusual wording of the message, which Summers and Mangold have nicely characterised as its 'almost literary quality'. If the Bolsheviks simply wanted to acknowledge that the deed had been done, why not just say so? Why say 'suffered same fate' rather than 'also executed'? Why refer to an 'official' explanation? And why use the future tense, 'will die', if the family were already dead? O'Conor suggested that the decoded message still contained code words, so that 'suffered same fate as head' might mean, for example, that the entire family had been transferred to Perm by train. While he agreed with Sokolov that the Bolsheviks had been negligent in leaving the telegram in the Ekaterinburg post office, he took it to be the exact opposite of a cold-blooded confession of guilt.[2]

In *The File on the Tsar*, Summers and Mangold undertook a meticulous analysis of the telegram and its history. Their surprising but quite compelling conclusion was that the telegram was not a Bolshevik text at all but was, rather, fabricated and planted in the post office by the White Russians' military command. Noting the manner in which Sokolov finally managed to get the telegram decoded, Summers and Mangold argued that the investigator must have participated in the deception. Between February 1919 and late August 1920 Sokolov made three attempts to have the telegram deciphered, sending it in turn to code breakers at White Russian headquarters, to a specialist at the Ministry of Foreign Affairs, and to the office of General Maurice Janin, the Frenchman who was in August 1919 the commander-in-chief of the Allied forces in Siberia. In every case, Sokolov later wrote, 'The results were pathetic.'

It took a chance encounter with an old acquaintance for Sokolov finally to learn what the telegram said:

When I reached Europe [having been forced out of Omsk by the Bolshevik advances in 1919], I had the good luck to meet a Russian whom I had known long since to be particularly competent. Before the revolution he had worked in the government code department for many years. I gave him the telegram on 25 August 1920. He returned it to me deciphered on 15 September.[3]

Summers and Mangold identified this Russian as Lieutenant A. Abaza, an assistant naval attaché at the White Russian embassy in London. Why had Abaza succeeded where the others failed? It does not seem logical that Sokolov just happened upon Abaza. More likely Abaza was set up to furnish Sokolov with the successful decoding of the telegram when the intelligence community felt the timing was right. So Abaza had a significant advantage, as Sokolov noted: 'When giving this telegram to [Abaza] . . . I told him, to make his work easier, that he would probably find in it the words: "family" and "evacuation". This man, being endowed with exceptional faculties, and with considerable experience in the business, managed to decipher the message.'[4]

To understand these 'exceptional faculties' it is necess. understand the background of Abaza. Lieutenant Aleks. Alexeevich Abaza was the son of Vice Admiral Aleksei Michaelovic. Abaza and had been attached to the guard-Equipage (the Imperial Russian Marines).[5] Abaza's father had interesting ties to British intelligence because of his past relationship with Sidney Reilly. Reilly had been in the employ[6] of Moisei Akimovich Ginsburg (Gintsburg), also known as 'Ginzburg Port-Arturski' (Port Arthur Ginsburg).[7] They had worked together in Maritime Construction and Insurance from 1906 through to 1914. Ginsburg visited Reilly in America in 1915. One of Ginsburg's partners was the Russkoe Lesopromysh-lennie Tovarishchestvo (Russian Lumber Company).

The 'Bezobrazof clique' owned the lumber company. This entity, with the backing of the Imperial Court, had attempted to gain control of timber and other concessions in Manchuria in the early 1900s. The head of the group, A. M. Bezobrazof, was assisted in this venture by his first cousin, Admiral A. M. Abaza, and the Tsar's first cousin, Grand Duke Alexander Michaelovich,[8] who was also a friend of Sidney Reilly's.[9]

The involvement of another member of the clique, V. M. Vonliarliarskii, is of special interest since he is the man who claimed to have introduced Karol Yaroshinsky to banking scheme operative Hugh Leech in 1917. It was the Sidney Reilly–Yaroshinsky–Leech relationship that formed the core of the banking scheme early in 1918.[10]

Later in Sidney Reilly's diary,[11] written while he was in captivity in the Lubianka Prison in Moscow in 1925, the name Abaza appears along with Kobylinski and Kovalski [*sic*]. These three names are all found in the pages of the history of the Romanov investigations: Abaza, the man who decoded the telegram – and as we shall see, an equally intriguing, if not the same, telegram is identified in *Rescuing the Czar* – Kobylinsky, in charge of the family in Tobolsk, and Kovalski, the name of the man whom the British agent Charles James Fox was supposedly reporting to during the escape of the family portrayed in *Rescuing the Czar*.

As Summers and Mangold pointed out, Sokolov's remarkable ability to predict the key contents of the message 'strains credibility to the breaking point'. Why, in particular, would he have guessed that it contained the word 'evacuation', when his expectation was that the message somehow communicated that the family had died?

There is, however, an additional question. As Summers and Mangold carefully establish, the code in which the message is written (the 'polyalphabetical substitution system') was neither new nor particularly sophisticated. They consulted a historian of codes who stated directly that it seems 'out of the question that either the White Russians or the French would not have been able to decipher the telegram in 1919'.

The 'exceptional faculties' attributed to Abaza should therefore not have been required; even without knowing that the telegram contained 'family' and 'evacuation', any competent cryptologist should have been able to provide the decoded message. But then, if the telegram was planted by the Whites to 'assist' Sokolov's case (with or without his knowledge), why did they not provide the deciphered message to him in February 1919? Why did it take him an additional nineteen months, great personal effort and some luck finally to learn what it said? This is the question that Summers and Mangold had pondered.

In contrast to all the attempted explanations to date, one is compelled to conclude that the White Russian and Allied officers to whom Sokolov submitted the telegram could and did have it deciphered – and then decided to feign ignorance for the sole purpose of denying Sokolov access to the decoded message.

If the telegram did not originate with the Whites or the Bolsheviks, then what was its source and meaning? Again, it makes one ask if the book *Rescuing the Czar* harbours some of the answers. It was published in early July 1920, nearly three months before Sokolov received the deciphered telegram and four years before it was first made public in his book. *Rescuing the Czar* closes with the translation of a letter found in a diary. The translator's remark: 'Written in ungrammatical Russian, bearing many orthographic mistakes, this document seems to be a fragment of a report, by some unidentified co-operating agent, to his unrevealed superior.'[12]

The author of the letter claims to be a member of the guard detachment at the Ipatiev House. He records that in early July a 'new man . . . took command of the guards'. That would be Yurovsky. In the early morning hours of 17 July the author is at his post across the street from the Ipatiev House. Hearing shots, he runs to the house and eventually gains entry, finding 'complete commotion'. He reports: 'The family disappeared – it is true; there was no trace of them.' Some time later, 'the Soviet representatives arrived. Then', says the author, 'a resolution was made that the prisoners had been taken away and shot, and they sent a wire to Moscow.'[13]

Was this wire the famous telegram? If so, then we have at last a satisfactory explanation for the bizarre wording of the message. It is neither a clumsy attempt (as Sokolov believed) to avoid saying 'we've killed them', nor a clever attempt (as O'Conor argues) to avoid saying 'we've hidden them'. It is, rather, the direct transcription of the utter confusion, disorder and fear that reigned among those in Ekaterinburg who knew only that the Imperial family had disappeared and that they would have to account for it. Quite understandably, their first reaction is to avoid saying anything specific: 'family suffered same fate as head' could mean, as the various interpretations show, practically anything. Their second reaction is to buy time: 'family will die in evacuation' – hoping that the family would soon be found and the promise of that future tense can be realised.

In addition to the telegrams, Sokolov had other pieces of evidence to explore. The testimony of three Red guards who had been on duty at the Ipatiev House on the night of 16/17 July and who had been captured by or surrendered to the White Russians. Philip Proskuryakov, Anatole Yakimov and Pavel Medvedev all maintained that they had not taken part in the execution, although Medvedev did claim that he had been in the room shortly after the shooting and had seen the bodies of all of the victims. The three testimonies contradicted each other regarding some of the central facts, such as when and how many shots were heard and how the bodies were removed from the house.

In the 'murder room' Sokolov found three more bullet holes (or thirteen more, if Eliot's account of Sergeyev's tally is accurate), additional graffiti and considerably more bloodstains. Given the extraordinary care with which Nametkin, Sergeyev and others had scrutinised the scene over the course of some six months – Sergeyev even had large parts of the wall and floor removed and carted off for microscopic analysis – Sokolov's discoveries of the bullet holes are rather implausible. Unless the new evidence appeared in the house after Sergeyev's last visit.

Initially, Sokolov's team was able to work a similar kind of forensic magic at the Ganin Pit. From 23 May to 17 June 1919 a team of soldiers and experts were constantly at the site. They again pumped water from the mine shaft, combed through the area inch by inch and passed the topsoil through sieves. Between 6 June and 10 July an extended area of twenty hectares around the mine was subjected to a methodical search, with rows of men moving slowly through the marshy forest, plunging iron bars into the ground every few feet.

The most impressive discovery was a complete set of metal stays from six corsets (accounting for the four Romanov women and the two female servants). Sokolov points out that the corsets were burned, but otherwise there is not a notation specifying any other damage – i.e. no bullet holes or dents. Oddly, not one of these stays had been noticed by previous investigators. The search also turned up a few bones, but experts could only say that they 'could not exclude the possibility that they were human'. Material from the Soviet archives now seems to confirm that they probably were the remains of one or more large animals slaughtered for a meal.[14]

The results were otherwise disappointing. In all, the numerous investigations since July 1918 had turned up some sixty-five small items, mainly buttons, buckles, the remnants of burned cloth and jewellery, nearly all of which were recognised as belonging to the family. Yet in the end, the upper section of Dr Botkin's dentures, a bit of skin and a single fingertip (which Sokolov thought he could positively identify as the Tsarina's) were the only human remains found. This after months of painstaking inspection of the place where eleven bodies, or twelve if we believe Yurovsky, were supposed to be buried.

In late June 1919, shortly before the Whites were driven from Ekaterinburg by a resurgent Bolshevik army, there was one breakthrough. The body of Jemmy, the Grand Duchess Tatiana's dog, was found at the bottom of the mine shaft. Sokolov and the White officials took this discovery to be conclusive evidence of the murder of the entire family, but they also recognised that it was necessary to explain why the dog was so strangely well-preserved. Sokolov's strategy was to argue that the body had been frozen for most of the eleven months it had lain in the mine. Consulting meteorological records and veterinary pathologists, Summers and Mangold demonstrated conclusively in 1976 that Sokolov's hypothesis could not be correct. It is simply not possible that the dog had been in the mine since 17 July 1918, because summers in Siberia are hot. It seems somehow fitting that Jemmy's body, once celebrated as *prima facie* evidence for the murder of the Romanovs, must rather be accepted as compelling proof that some (if not much) of the evidence gathered by the investigators was fabricated or planted. The intriguing question of how Jemmy's body got into the mine nearly a year after the disappearance of the Romanovs or why Yurovsky did not remember the dog in his 1920 Note remains unanswered.

The Sokolov Report, intended to be the first rendering by the White investigators of the events of 16/17 July 1918, after the misleading press releases of the Bolsheviks, was actually scooped by an article published by Pavel Bykov in Russia in 1921. The astonishing similarity of these two chronicles was later explained when it became known that a Bolshevik by the name of Gruzenberg had broken into the Berlin home where Sokolov was in residence.[15] According to Paul Bulygin, Gruzenberg absconded with the notes of the preliminary report on the death of the Imperial family. These notes mysteriously surfaced in Prague, Czechoslovakia, before landing in the hands of Bykov in Russia. When Bykov published the revision of his book in 1926, it bore all the markings of the final Sokolov Report.

Why would Gruzenberg and the Soviets go to such lengths to discover what Sokolov and Bulygin were in the process of preparing for world consumption? And who was Gruzenberg? The man most likely to have engaged in this burglary was Michael Gruzenberg, a Chicagoan and 'journalist'.[16] By 1921, Gruzenberg had already lived a most unusual life and would go on to play yet another role as a revolutionary in China.[17] A close confidant of Lenin, he has frequently been confused with Alexander Gumberg, who had served as secretary to Raymond Robins, the American in charge of the American Red Cross effort in Russia in the spring of 1918 when he and Lockhart had been negotiating with Trotsky.[18] Military intelligence files of the United States, Britain and France[19] followed Gruzenberg closely.

In May 1918 Gruzenberg had been summoned by Lenin via personal courier to come immediately to Russia. Wasting little time, he sailed to Russia with great haste and special privileges.[20] When he presented himself at customs on 8 June, the customs officials were instructed to allow his departure from the United States without the customary procedures.[21] Consequently we shall never know the full content of his parcels. More astonishing was what happened when Gruzenburg, after journeying from America, first arrived in Switzerland. A telegram was sent on 31 August:

Secstate Washington
3 p.m.

576 For Sisson [Edgar] Compub [the propaganda arm of the United States government] from Palmer

Michael Gruzenberg of Chicago presented letter of Compub with his photograph signed by Irwin. [Assistant to George Creel, head of US propaganda]. Said Irwin sent him to prepare for a visit of special mission to Russia but had also talked with Creel. Left Monday night for Petrograd after opening account here. Naturally under no circumstances will I advance funds without cable authorization but suggest representatives be supplied directly . . .

[Sheldon] Whitehouse[22]

The propaganda divisions both in the United States and England often served as 'soft money' channels to handle payments for secret operations. In late August 1918 Gruzenberg, an avowed Bolshevik, would seem an unlikely courier of unexplained US funds. Later it was established that the United States had bought documents that purported to prove that the Soviets were under the control of the Germans. These came to be known as the Sisson Papers, but because of the time-frame, the funds transported by Gruzenberg do not appear to be linked to that transaction. The August 1918 financial transaction, handled by an operative close to Lenin, proved to be another unexplained payment to Lenin in 1918, the first being the money that was paid out of the banking scheme.[23]

The fact that it appears that Michael Gruzenberg was sent on a mission to Berlin in order to appropriate Sokolov's notes is witness to the importance the Bolshevik leadership attached to the documents. Once the notes were back in Russia, what the world would accept from both Nicholas Sokolov, who had been employed by the White Russians under the influence of the Allies, and Pavel Bykov, the official Soviet historian and member of the Ural Soviet, was that the entire family had disappeared in the early morning hours of 17 July 1918.

However, Bykov does part company with some of his predecessors. For example, on the number of assassins Sokolov says eleven or twelve, Yurovsky states twelve and Bykov says four. Both Bykov and Sokolov say that after the execution Yakov Yurovsky led his men to the Koptiaki forest with the bodies. Sokolov says the bodies were burned and covered with acid. Bykov says only that they were burned – destroyed without a trace. Later some recorded Bolshevik testimony would claim to have burned them all and 'cast their ashes to the wind'.

The following is the entire account by Bykov, namely the version that appeared in a book published in 1935 by Paul Bulygin, Nicholas Sokolov's assistant in the investigation, and Alexander Kerensky, the man who had been responsible for the family's relocation to Siberia. This abridged text contains the essence of the official Soviet history that Bykov first published in 1921, after gaining access to Sokolov's material. It would for many years represent the Soviet interpretation of the last months of the Imperial family.

THE LAST DAYS OF THE LAST TSAR[24]
by
P. M. Bykov
Chairman, Ekaterinburg Soviet

Even as early as the beginning of winter, 1917, there began to appear in the St Petersburg Press, and particularly in the capitalist papers, various articles about the life of the Romanov Family in Tobolsk and the gathering round them of counter-revolutionary elements.

A series of malicious false rumours of the ex-Tsar's escape put the All-Russian Central Executive Committee on its guard – and with it the local Soviets, particularly the Ural Regional Soviet. Such fragmentary news as came from Tobolsk, forced one to conclude that both Russian and – even more so – the foreign counter-revolutionaries were paving the way for the escape of Nicholas Romanov and his family, and the restoration of his rule with the aid of his crowned relatives abroad and the adherents of the old regime at home.

Incidentally, that prominent reactionary, Bishop Hermogen, was already in Tobolsk to meet the Romanov Family when they were transferred there. He settled down to the work of causing more trouble over the Tsar's person . . .

Mysterious officers, living under false passports, began to gather in Tobolsk, ostensibly 'to recuperate'. One of them, Ravevsky, visited Hermogen and handed him a letter from the former Empress Maria. . . .

The question of transferring the Romanovs from Tobolsk to a more reliable locality and of taking immediate precautions against the escape of Nicholas Romanov, was raised at one of the February meetings of the Ural Regional Soviet . . . At the same time negotiations were entered into with the All-Russian Central Executive Committee and also directly with its chairman, J. M. Sverdlov. The Ural Soviet stressed the necessity of transferring Nicholas Romanov to Ekaterinburg.

Meanwhile, in order to have reliable information about the true position in Tobolsk, and to prepare the ground for the transfer of the ex-Tsar's family to Ekaterinburg, three comrades were sent to Tobolsk by the Ural-Soviet. They were Avdeyev (a worker at the Zlokazovsky works), Hokhriakov [Khokhriakov] (a sailor) and Zaslavsky (a worker at the Nadezhdinsky works). Their mission was to ascertain the general atmosphere, to disseminate Communist propaganda, and to influence the local Soviet.

These comrades left for Tobolsk early in March, under false passports and without disclosing the true object of their journey, as we had reasons to mistrust both the Tobolsk Soviet and the units that looked after the Romanov family, because these were still composed of Kerensky's guards, who did not wish to have anything to do with the Bolsheviks, as a matter of principle.

Soon the Ural Soviet emissaries were in Tobolsk and settled down to work, keeping in touch with Ekaterinburg by means of special messengers. The Soviet at Tobolsk was composed of Mensheviks and S.R.s [Socialist Revolutionaries]. There was no Communist organisation.

The Romanov family, living in the former Governor's Residence, was allowed a considerable measure of freedom: they could correspond freely with the outside world, received food supplies from outside, and so forth . . .

The comrades who came from Ekaterinburg soon organised Communist propaganda among the soldiers, including the special units that guarded the Romanovs, as well as among the workers of such undertakings as existed in the town. Within ten days, Hokhriakov was elected vice-president, and soon afterwards president of the local Soviet. This enabled the Ural Soviet to establish a closer connection with Tobolsk, because hitherto it had not been possible to make full use of the telegraph, as important messages were generally held up, or had their meaning twisted.

Meanwhile there arrived at Tobolsk an independent detachment from Omsk, headed by Demianov and sent by the West-Siberian Soviet; at the same time other parties were sent out from Ekaterinburg to various points near Tobolsk, such as Tiumen,

Golyshmanovo, etc., and the Ural Soviet also sent reliable Red Army men one by one from various points into Tobolsk itself, so that presently they formed a considerable force which was at Hokhriakov's disposal.

The gathering in Tobolsk of these various parties, who kept their true aims secret, was causing definite uneasiness among the troops that guarded the Romanovs, among the respective members of the Ekaterinburg and the Omsk detachments, and particularly, of course, amongst the counter-revolutionary elements in Tobolsk. . . .

The strained relations between the Omsk and Ekaterinburg parties finally ended in the arrest of Hokhriakov, who was accused of intriguing, and it was only a telegraphic conversation with the Ural Soviet confirming that he had special powers in the matter, that saved him from being shot.

All this time the Ekaterinburg authorities were earnestly discussing with the All-Russian Central Executive Committee (in Moscow), the question of transferring the Romanovs. The committee which was in charge of the matter was strengthened by the addition of Goloshchekin, the Military Commissar of the Region, which made it possible for them to enlist the help of the Army in organising the transfer.

At last, after repeated approaches from the Ural Soviet (supported by the Western-Siberian Soviet), the All-Russian Central Executive Committee announced that the former Tsar and his family would be moved to the Ural Region, for which purpose it would send its own representative Yakovlev.

In spite of the obvious necessity for co-operation with the Ural Soviet, Yakovlev did not appear in Ekaterinburg, and presently it was discovered that he had gone to Tobolsk via Chaliabinsk and Omsk with a posse of workers from the Simsky and Miniarsky works.

The roads were becoming impassable owing to the melting of the snows, and there was not time to waste over moving the Romanov family. It was decided to transfer first of all, Nicholas Romanov, his wife Alexandra, and their daughter Maria and the physician Botkin, leaving the other members of the Family and the retinue of ladies-in-waiting and attendants until the first steamers. The ex-Prince Dolgorukov was also included in the first party that left Tobolsk.

The nature of the preliminary preparations for the journey, which were started before ever Yakovlev arrived, made the Romanovs realise that there was to be a drastic change in their condition, so they left Tobolsk very reluctantly and with many protests.

The journey from Tobolsk to Tiumen was accomplished without a hitch, except for the fact that, from the start, the Ural men began to be suspicious of Yakovlev, who took the business of guarding Nicholas into his own hands – according him exceptional honours, not admitting anyone into his presence, and so forth. The Ural men, therefore at their own risk, laid an ambush near the village Yovlevo (where they were to cross the River Tobol) intending to attack the party at the first sign of treason on Yakovlev's part.

In Tiumen, the Romanovs were put on a special train, and Yakovlev, by virtue of the special powers conferred upon him by the All-Russian Central Executive Committee, installed himself in the telegraph office, cleared the line, and began direct telegraphic conversations with the Kremlin. The outcome of these conversations soon became apparent.

The Ural Soviet received a telegram that the train had left for Ekaterinburg, but this was followed by a telegram stating that the Commissar Yakovlev's train, carrying the Romanov family, had passed Tiumen station at full speed in the direction of Omsk.

At a secret session of the Ural Regional conference of the Communist party (which was in progress at the time), Goloshchekin presented a report concerning the developments in connection with the transfer of the Tsar and his family from Tobolsk. The conference decided to insist on having the Romanovs brought to revolutionary Ekaterinburg. This resolution was communicated to the All-Russian Central Executive Committee and to the Executive Committee of the party.

A small force was immediately dispatched from Ekaterinburg by special train, to apprehend Yakovlev and bring him back to the Ural Region. Simultaneously, reliable comrades in Omsk were approached by telegraph and it was agreed not to let the train go on to Siberia: to blow it up, if necessary.

On approaching Ishim, Yakovlev stopped the train in the open country and permitted the Romanovs to take a walk 'in the sun', after which the journey towards Omsk was resumed. He never got to Omsk, however, but went back to Ekaterinburg when he heard of the 'welcome' that was being prepared for him. . . .

The Ekaterinburg Soviet decided to imprison the Romanovs in the Ipatiev House. The owner of the mansion was evicted and subsequently it was surrounded with a light fence to screen it from inquisitive eyes.

On its arrival at the 'house of special purpose', as the Ipatiev mansion was termed in Soviet circles, the Romanov family was received by the House Superintendent, Comrade Avdeyev.

It transpired that their personal effects had not been searched, either at the time of arrest, or in Tobolsk. They were asked forthwith to open the small suitcases they brought with them.

Nicholas did so without a murmur. Alexandra, however, announced that she would not have her belongings searched. She started an altercation with the superintendent.

Nicholas began to pace excitedly up and down the room and remarked, rather loudly: 'Perfectly damnable! So far we have had polite treatment and men who were gentlemen, but now . . .'

Romanov was thereupon asked to remember that he was no longer at Tsarskoe Selo but in Ekaterinburg, and if he was going to act in a provocative manner, he would be isolated from his family, and on a second offence – given forced labour.

Both Alexandra and Nicholas realised that they were not going to be trifled with, and submitted to the demands of the House Superintendent.

The Ipatiev House is two storied and the lower floor is partly below the ground level, owing to the steep slope leading to the Voznesensky Avenue; this was occupied mainly by stores, offices and kitchens. The Romanovs were allotted five rooms on the upper floor, where they were kept under semi-prison conditions.

Romanov's son and his other daughters, who were brought from Tobolsk in May, were likewise imprisoned in the Ipatiev House.

Though not resorting to any particular reprisals against the prisoners, or introducing strict prison discipline, the Regional Soviet kept the house strongly guarded, and the prisoners were always under the vigilant observation of the Red Guard, a detachment of which was stationed in one of the buildings that faced 'the house of special purpose'.

Nicholas Romanov, who was, in general, idiotically indifferent to all that went on around him, took the house regulations very calmly. He tried, at first, to engage the sentries in conversation; but when this was forbidden him, he did not persevere.

Not so Alexandra. She seized every opportunity to protest against the conditions imposed upon her by the regulations and insulted the guard, as well as the officials representing the Regional Soviet.

The family's meals were brought from a Soviet soup-kitchen, the best in the town; each prisoner was allowed two 'dinners' a day. The family had an oil-stove at its disposal for warming the meals.

The prisoners were allowed a daily walk in the little garden belonging to the house, where they could do manual work, the necessary tools being placed at their disposal. They themselves chose the time for their walk.

The House Superintendent did not interfere in the private life of the prisoners, who were allowed to dispose of their time as they liked.

At Easter-time the Romanovs expressed a desire to go to church. This was refused to them, but a clergyman was allowed to visit the house and hold a service. Easter cakes, Easter pudding and eggs were also ordered for the Romanovs.

No 'parcels' of any kind were allowed 'from outside'. Particularly insistent with their food offerings were the nuns of a near-by convent, who brought baskets of all kinds of pastries and cooked foods for the Romanovs almost every day. These were invariably given by the superintendent to the guards.

No sooner was Nicholas transferred to Ekaterinburg than monarchists of every description began to gather there: beginning with half-witted old ladies, countesses and baronesses, nuns and clergy, and ending with representatives of foreign powers.

Free admission to the Ipatiev House was limited to a very narrow circle of people and to members of the Ural Regional Soviet. Permission to visit Nicholas could only be given by the All-Russian Central Executive Committee.

For this reason the ceaseless attempts of various persons to get in touch with Nicholas were invariably unsuccessful. Nevertheless, the monarchist hangers-on continued to take all the available hotel accommodation, and, incidentally, were very busy writing letters, especially on Imperial birthdays and similar occasions. . . .

It was beginning to be quite obvious, even to the population at large, that the monarchists at Ekaterinburg were building up an organisation for the release of the ex-Tsar; so that the Regional Soviet had to face the possibility of an unorganised, spontaneous attempt by the workers to lynch the ex-Tsar and the clique that gathered around him. The indignation of the proletariat over the scarcely concealed preparations for a counter-revolutionary act was so great that the workers of the Verkhne-Isetsky Works had definitely fixed a date for the lynching – the May Day demonstrations. In order to prevent such an unorganised outburst, the Regional Soviet was forced to arrange for one of its members to be on duty day and night. Subsequently, the connection between certain representatives of the Red Cross and the Czecho-Slovaks was indeed proved.

Prominent counter-revolutionaries and suspicious characters continued to flock to Ekaterinburg, as they formerly did to Tobolsk, and their aim was still to engineer plots and to liberate Romanov and all his relatives.

With the approach of the Front nearer to Ekaterinburg, the local counter-revolutionary 'loyalist' officers also began to try and get in touch with the Tsar's family, assiduously corresponding with Nicholas Romanov, and particularly with his wife, who was more active and irreconcilable.

The following is one of the letters which passed between the prisoners and the conspirators who were trying to engineer a rising in Ekaterinburg in June to liberate the Romanovs:

> The hour of liberation is at hand and the usurpers' days are numbered. Slav armies are daily advancing nearer Ekaterinburg. They are only a few miles from the city. The critical moment is approaching and there is danger of bloodshed. The time has come. We must act.

> Your friends, [runs another letter] no longer sleep, and hope that the long awaited hour is at hand.

Who were these men, then, who were trying to snatch the dethroned criminals out of the hands of the people? Who were the men who had the interests of the Tsar's family so much at heart?

Most of the intercepted letters written by Romanov's well-wishers outside were signed with the word 'Officer'; and one even ended thus: 'One of those who are ready to die for you – An Officer of the Russian Army . . .'

The question of executing Nicholas Romanov and all those who were with him, was settled in principle early in July.

The practical details of the execution were left to the Soviet Presiding Committee. The sentence was carried out on the night of the 16th to 17th July. On the 18th July, at a meeting of the Presiding Committee of the All-Russia Central Executive Committee, its chairman, J. M. Sverdlov, announced that the former Tsar had been shot.

After a full discussion of the circumstances which prompted the decision of the Ural Regional Soviet to have Romanov shot, the Presiding Committee of the All-Russian Central Executive Committee approved this decision.

When the Presiding Committee of the Regional Soviet signed the death sentence of Nicholas Romanov and his family, the Czecho-Slovak lines were already near and the counter-revolutionary hordes were converging towards Ekaterinburg simultaneously from two directions: from Cheliabinsk and along the West Ural Railway.

It was essential to hurry with the execution. All arrangements in connection with the execution and the disposal of the corpses had been left to a tried revolutionary who had already been under fire on the Dutov (Orenburg Cossacks) front – Peter Zakharovich Ermakov, a worker at the Verkhne-Isetsky Works.

The members of the Romanov family were informed that they must go down from the upper story, where they lived, to the basement. About ten o'clock in the evening the entire Romanov family – namely, the former Tsar Nicholas Alexandrovich, his wife Alexandra Feodorovna, his son Alexis, the daughters, the family physician Botkin, the Heir-Apparent's under-tutor and a former lady's maid who had remained in the family – went downstairs. They were all in ordinary indoor attire, as they generally went to bed at a much later hour.

In one of the basement rooms they were asked to line up against the wall. The House Superintendent, who was at the same time the official representative of the Ural Soviet, read out the death-warrant and concluded by saying that all their hopes were vain – they must die.

This unexpected pronouncement left the prisoners dumbfounded; the Tsar alone had time to say, interrogatively, 'So we are not to be taken anywhere?'

The condemned persons were then dispatched with revolver shots. . . .

Only four men were present at the execution and they were the people who were shooting.

About one o'clock at night the corpses of the persons executed were taken into the country to a wood near the Verkhne-Isetsky Works and the village Palkino, where they were burnt the next day.

The shooting passed unnoticed, in spite of the fact that it took place almost in the centre of the town. The shots were not heard owing to the noise of a lorry which stood outside the house during the execution. Even the sentries who guarded the house from outside did not know about it, and continued their regular duties for two more days.

The announcement that the execution had taken place was published in the local Press on the 23rd July. . .

The first thing the White Generals did when they took possession of Ekaterinburg, in the summer of 1918, was to start searching for the corpses of the Romanov family.

The Official Investigator for Cases of Exceptional Importance to the Omsk Regional Court, Sokolov, was instructed to conduct an investigation, and the result of his labours was the dossier 'Concerning the murder of the deposed monarch, Emperor Nicholas Alexandrovich and his family'.

He considers that about two hundred people were involved in this 'crime', as he calls it. Needless to say, most of them were in no way connected with the shooting of the Romanov family and were only dragged in by the investigator to make it a good, lengthy case.

White Guard newspapers and all sorts of money-grubbers published for the benefit of the public the most fantastic stories concerning the life of the Romanov family in Ekaterinburg and their execution.

There were even a number of romancers who were trying to persuade the public that the Romanov family, complete with Nicholas, had been smuggled out of Ekaterinburg.

The search of the neighborhood where the bodies were destroyed, which was undertaken by the military authorities, produced no results, except for the finding of a few precious stones and golden trinkets.

The origin of these is as follows. The Romanovs were executed in ordinary dress. When it was decided to burn the corpses, they were first undressed. Certain articles of their clothing (which was afterwards burnt) were found to conceal sewn-in jewellery. It is possible that some of these valuables were dropped by the finders, or thrown into the fire with the clothes.

That was all the White Guard searchers could find, in spite of the fact that they had commandeered Red Army prisoners and peasants of the village Koptiaki to help with the work. They even brought a steam engine from the Verkhne-Isetsky works to pump the water out of 'suspected' abandoned mines!

General Diterichs, who was appointed by Kolchak to direct the investigation, was finally compelled to announce that the Romanov family had been shot and the corpses had been destroyed without a trace . . .

It was not the Tsar and his family alone that met their death in the Ural Region. Nicholas Romanov's brother, Michael Alexandrovich – with whose aid in February, 1917, the capitalists attempted to save the monarch by transferring to him the Imperial Crown – was shot in Perm about the middle of July.

About the same time, in Alapayevsk, were shot the Grand Dukes Sergius Mikhailovich, Igor Constantinovich, Constantine Constantinovich and Ivan Constantinovich. The bodies of the latter were found by the White Guard Secret Service and received a full-dress burial in the crypt of the Alapayevsk Cathedral.

It is noteworthy that the official Soviet announcements at the time did not give the full text of the resolutions concerning the execution of the members of the Romanov family. Only the execution of the former Tsar was announced, whereas the Grand Dukes, according to our Press, were supposed to have escaped, or been carried off – kidnapped – by persons unknown. A similar announcement was published concerning the wife, son and daughters of Nicholas, who were supposed to have been transferred 'to a safe spot'.

This was not due to any vacillation on the part of the local Soviets. The actual historical facts are proof that our Soviets – the Regional Soviet and those of Perm and Alapayevsk – acted with courage and decision, when once it was decided to extirpate all who were near to the Tsarist throne.

Moreover, now that we can regard these events simply as historical facts in the development of the Workers' Revolution, we must admit, that in shooting the Tsar and in acting on their own initiative and at their own risk as regards the other Romanovs, the Ural Soviets were not unnaturally anxious to keep the execution of the family and the Grand Dukes in the background.

This enabled the Monarchists to talk of the escape of certain members of the family.

It was not until the winter of 1918 that the Regional Soviet dispersed some of these doubts by publishing an official declaration that Michael Romanov had been shot.

Of all the assertions in Bykov's account, one of the most troubling is the statement: 'The shots were not heard owing to the noise of a lorry which stood outside the house during the execution.' He says 'even the sentries who guarded the house from outside' did not hear shots. This is rather implausible. The hail of shots in the basement room would have resonated and the cries of the victims would have been impossible to muffle so that guards just outside the house could not hear . . . that is, unless it never happened as he professes and the family left the house by other means and subsequently met a different fate.

Even though the versions of Sokolov and Bykov were refuted by excellent forensic analyses conducted by both John O'Conor,[25] who published *The Sokolov Investigation*, and Anthony Summers and Tom Mangold, who authored *The File on the Tsar*, parts of Bykov's and Sokolov's versions still survived for seventy years – that is, until the bones of the 'Christian victims of the Revolution' were found in the forest. Ultimately, when the DNA testing was conducted and the 'funeral' held, the world at large finally had unknowingly refuted another critical part of the claims made by Sokolov and the 'official historian of the Soviets', Bykov.

And so it goes. Burned . . . shot by only four assassins, twelve assassins, etc. etc. Bykov excuses the Ekaterinburg Soviet for not taking credit immediately. He should have been a man in the know, for he was the head of the Ekaterinburg Soviet at the time and as such would be expected to have had first-hand knowledge and all the details of the deliberate execution of the Tsar and his family, especially how many executioners were present. It is normal to have discrepancies in the recall of facts that are considered to be of little consequence. But for proud revolutionaries, the number of men who would eventually lay claim to participation in such a momentous event hardly seems to fall into that category. Just another lapse, or a failure to co-ordinate?

For decades to come, after the family vanished, each time the Romanov name was uttered in some circles, participants would faithfully retell one of the versions that had been spun over the years by those who had ulterior motives. Even now the search for the truth has been made more difficult because of the countless obfuscations and half-truths. The burden of proof from a legal perspective has certainly not been met and, unfortunately, the bar has been lowered for the historical standard. Some academics have confidentially shared that working on the 'Romanov case' has been perceived among their peers as a 'career killer'.

PART FOUR

In Search of the Truth

CHAPTER 14

San Francisco 1920

'A matter of great importance to the nation'

The year 1920 seems to have been almost as intriguing a year in the Romanov saga as 1918. While I had become acquainted with *Rescuing the Czar*, after having read Guy Richards's book, *Hunt for the Czar*, I was anything but persuaded about its validity. But finding the San Francisco Russian consul Romanovsky[1] linked to shipments of arms and gold enticed me to press on and ascertain whether there was a relationship between, on the one hand the movement of arms and gold and, on the other hand attempts to gain the release of the family as Radek had intimated.

In fact, the complicated links between the Americans, British, Czechs, French, Germans, Japanese and Bolsheviks that we have seen in the earlier sections of this book definitely included people and events in San Francisco in 1920 who themselves had been involved in the Russian situation in 1918. San Francisco was an embarkation and exit port for Russian émigrés, as well as the departure point for the shipping of munitions and money for the con-tinuing fight then being waged by White General Wrangel in the south of Russia.

During the time that I was studying the Russian consulate files, a body of work came to my attention that admirably explored the arms shipments in America. William Clarke's book, *The Lost Fortune of the Tsars*, attempted to follow the trail of numerous arms shipments to Vladivostok from San Francisco on ships including the *Thomas*, the *Sheraton* and the *Sherman*.[2] When we recall the 23 May 1918 meeting at which Radek informed Lenin and the other participants that a ship called the *Thomas* would be involved in bringing shipments of arms for Masaryk's Czechs, the San Francisco activities and personages gain even more significance. These intriguing arms transactions were very complex, obscure and difficult to track. The trading of arms and money involved the National City Bank, the House of Morgan, Kuhn & Loeb, and others. Equally intriguing is that these same firms were the ones that were owed staggering Russian war debts and especially worthy of note here is the National City Bank that Radek maintained was involved in the trading of arms to the Czechs for Nicholas.

Upon further investigation of the San Francisco Russian consulate records, I found additional documents that led to the conclusion that George Romanovsky, one of the 'translators' of *Rescuing the Czar*, was even more deeply implicated in these shipments than Clarke mentions in his book. And, as we shall see, he may also have been implicated in attempting to bring a substantial portion of the tsarist gold reserve to America.[3] This new-found information also prompted me to explore what now appeared to be a reasonably clear connection between high-level government officials in the United States in 1918 and the Romanovs' fate.

Clarke's book mentions Gretchen Haskin, who, with her husband, David, had assisted Guy Richards in researching his first book, *The Hunt for the Czar*. David's father, Henry Haskin, had been responsible for the printing of *Rescuing the Czar* in the spring and summer of 1920. Gretchen's and David's contributions were invaluable, since they furnished additional documents that helped me to accomplish a complete and thorough analysis of the book and the individuals who had agreed to 'translate and compile' the diaries that comprise the curious book *Rescuing the Czar*.

The account laid out in *Rescuing the Czar* presented evidence that the Tsar and his family had escaped. The name of the author, James P. Smythe, actually was the nom de plume of William Rutledge McGarry, a narrator of British war films, and George S. Romanovsky.[4] In a contract executed on 10 March 1920 McGarry and Romanovsky agreed to 'arrange and prepare for publication the manuscript for a book entitled *The Prisoners of Tobolsk*', the original name of *Rescuing the Czar*.[5] On 18 March, from the Fairmont Hotel in San Francisco, Romanovsky returned the signed agreement to McGarry, 'With my best regards to Mrs McGarry and yourself'. It is apparent from the agreement that neither man wrote the book: they had only agreed to 'arrange and prepare' the manuscript.[6] The book was delivered to its 'translators' on 21 July 1920.

For the most part, *Rescuing the Czar* consists of the diaries of two men: one a British intelligence operative and the other a Russian nobleman posing as a Bolshevik. Its description of the last days of the family is remarkably different from any other published version that had been made available to the world prior to *Rescuing the Czar*'s debut. It proposed quite a different outcome: the successful removal of the family from the Ipatiev House by the British intelligence agent Charles James Fox who 'claims to be an American' but says he was 'born in Paris'. Fox's diary, which comprises the first part of the book, also covers his infiltration of the Bolshevik guard in Ekaterinburg one week prior to the events of that July summer night in 1918.

In *Rescuing the Czar*, Charles James Fox alleges that the family were extricated from an underground tunnel by the British and taken into the British consulate, where they were secretly removed and hidden in Russia for a couple of weeks before being taken to Turkistan. Then, due to troubles in India, which was their intended destination, they travelled through Tibet where, with the aid of lamas, at the behest of the Dalai Lama, they were guided on to China. They are supposed to have ended their flight in Chungking. Charles James Fox states that upon arrival in Chungking he turned them over to the commander of a British gunboat where they embarked on a trip down the Yangtze river to Woosung, twelve miles from Shanghai.

The diary alludes to ships dressed with holiday flags and infers it was the holiday season – December 1918. Curiously, this date corresponds to the December 1918 telegram referencing the 'family seven times'. Fox's final notes reveal the interaction he had with the commander of the gunboat:

> With his code word still ringing in my ears to be repeated to one man at Berlin, to another man in England, another in Japan, and to a dignitary in Italy, the mission I have undertaken shall have been successfully discharged, so far as history and public policy is concerned . . .[7]

Rescuing the Czar indicates that the Imperial family's ultimate destination was Ceylon, where they supposedly arrived on an unnamed man-of-war accompanied by a wealthy tea merchant.

The second diary contained in *Rescuing the Czar* chronicles an unknown nobleman's activities as Alexei Syvorotka, a monarchist disguised as a Bolshevik. Formerly a member of the Tsar's inner circle and St Petersburg society, he was forced to leave his home with very little money or assurances for his future well-being. After sending his wife away to what he thought would be safety, he learns she was shot by the Bolsheviks and, as a result of his despair, he is finally persuaded to join in an attempt to rescue the Imperial family. Assuming the identity of a Bolshevik, he makes his way to Tobolsk where he hovers close to the Romanovs and through his eyes we gain insight into the activities of the guards who were in charge of the family. We also are acquainted with numerous people secretly laying plans to save them.

Frequently, he alludes to his friend the 'Baroness B.' who, we come to understand, was also a member of St Petersburg society. Syvorotka's diary portrays his life as a Bolshevik, and reveals that he and the Baroness were co-operating with an English intelligence team to extricate the family. In the final pages of *Rescuing the Czar* Syvorotka is wounded and it is unclear whether he survives or not.

Because of its unorthodox portrayal of the last days of the Romanovs, historians and political scientists have in the past dismissed *Rescuing the Czar* as nonsense and indeed, many aspects of the book remain bewildering. Was it a complete fabrication and/or a product of disinformation planted by the Americans, the British or the Soviets? What could be gained by any government from its publication? In fact, as we shall see in chapter 15, numerous governments had an interest in the publication of *Rescuing the Czar*. Even more intriguing is the question of why this account of a purported rescue of the Tsar and his family was destined to all but disappear from circulation by 1921.

It is worth spending some time examining the rather fascinating backgrounds of the two so-called 'translators' who supposedly concocted this tale, as their backgrounds make clear the fact that this book must have come from very high-level and well-informed sources indeed. As mentioned earlier, McGarry had previously been employed as a narrator of British war films.[8] His correspondence for the year 1917 yields insight into his war efforts. He was cited in both the San Francisco *Herald* and the San Francisco *Chronicle* as giving lectures at the Tivoli Opera House, the Hotel St James and the Palace Hotel on the Mesopotamian Campaign.[9] McGarry's work for

British war propaganda efforts in America fell under the direction of Sir William Wiseman, a confidant of Colonel House, President Woodrow Wilson's de facto Secretary of State. When the United States entered World War One, we saw that Wiseman operated as the head of the SIS/MI1c (British intelligence) section in New York. McGarry's activities eventually placed him in a position of influence with people such as a relative of his wife, John Temple Graves, who was close to President Wilson.[10] In McGarry's *Who's Who in America* listing in 1926–7, he is publicly connected to the publication of *Rescuing the Czar* for the first time and also is credited with having written *Berlin to Baghdad*, the story of the Kaiser's railroad. What is glaring in this entry is that it does not mention McGarry's wartime activities or the fact that he worked for the American Department of State. A later biographical sketch, researched by his children with the aid of his personal correspondence, further revealed that he had at one time been attached to the American embassies in St Petersburg, Paris and Berlin. These last details lead us to an interesting anomaly in McGarry's life story. Some investigation was conducted about him in the late sixties by Guy Richards and others while preparing Richards's book, *Hunt for the Czar*. The National Archives in Washington, DC reported the following statement dated 21 August 1969:

> According to the Passport Office of the Department of State, McGarry first filed an application in June, 1923. He stated at the times [*sic*] that he was a journalist by profession, that he planned to travel various parts [*sic*] of Europe for possibly two years, and under oath that he had never filed an application or been issued a passport previously. A duplicate of this application and the attached oath (File No. 306531, dated June 11, 1923) can be provided upon request by the Passport Office, Department of State, Washington, D. C. 20520.[11]

A copy of passport application number 306531, filed in 1923 requesting passports for both McGarry and his wife Emily Graves McGarry, indicated that McGarry was making his first trip abroad. McGarry, who was by then fifty-one, noted that he and his wife were going abroad for the purpose of 'study and recreation'. On the face of it, all this seems in order, except for the fact that the *San Francisco Examiner* on 29 April 1919, carried:

S.F. AUTHOR WEDS WIDOW IN SECRET

A romance that started a year ago in Australia resulted on Friday night in the marriage of Mrs. Emily Graves Strong, widow of a wealthy New York Attorney and William Rutledge McGarry, San Francisco author and traveler. The marriage here was in secret and the couple had gone from the city on a month's honeymoon by auto through the Santa Cruz Mountains before McGarry's friends learned of it. Both are well known in California. Mrs. McGarry formerly lived in Los Angeles and is the daughter of W. L. Graves, Los Angeles banker. McGarry upon his return from the Orient a year ago became one of the founders of the *Pan-Pacific Magazine*, of which he is now the consulting editor.[12]

Someone in the passport office had obviously been mistaken about McGarry's background. In fact, he had evidently been a globetrotter long before 1923 and had apparently already fostered high-level contacts in the Far East. His personal correspondence reveals that in late 1917 he was involved in negotiating a contract with Japanese industrialist, Jiuju G. Kasai, for delivery of Mexican steel.[13] Interestingly, while his correspondence is relatively voluminous before 7 May 1918 and after the following November, it is scant during the period from May to November. But in November J. G. Kasai furnished McGarry with a letter of introduction for Viscount Ishii, Japanese ambassador to America.[14] Finally, Kasai addressed McGarry as 'My Dear General' and on 29 January 1919 wrote a note inviting Mr and Mrs McGarry to Japan for a 'honeymoon' trip.[15]

McGarry's trading was not limited to steel, for on 20 June 1919 he wrote to George Romanovsky, in response to a request from Romanovsky about bringing in an amazing $315 million in gold. McGarry explained that 'the gold should not be brought in direct, but under the aegis of a purchasing commission, the Russian Government transmitting the bullion with authority to deposit it against letters of credit in local banks'. Then again, on 20 September, he received a letter from the National City Bank in New York regarding the 'Far Eastern gold' and the arrangements of credits against it. It now seems apparent that McGarry and Romanovsky were closely connected to the Kolchak government that was then in possession of the Tsarist gold as well as being the government conducting the investigation of the presumed murders of the Tsar and his family. It is strange that the two men who would be responsible for arranging and translating the book that proclaimed that the Tsar and his family had survived were also the men to whom the Kolchak government appeared to have turned to secure their letters of credit for purchasing and shipping of their much needed armaments to continue their fight against the Bolsheviks.

George Romanovsky, the other man associated with *Rescuing the Czar*, as well as the armaments and gold, was in July 1920 serving in San Francisco as acting consul general of the Provisional Government of Russia (the only Russian government officially recognised by the United States – the Bolshevik government would not be recognised until 1933). He had held the same position in Chicago[16] and while there had married a prominent Chicagoan, Goldie Biankini. Her father, a Chicago physician, served as the head of the Jugo-Slav Society in America as well as the head of the Slav Liberty Loan Organisation.[17] It has been rumoured but never substantiated that Goldie Biankini was the niece of Thomas Masaryk, who would become the first president of Czechoslovakia and who was also the man we have seen closely connected to Charles Crane and the activities of the Czech legions in 1918 in Siberia. Whether Masaryk was that closely related to the consul general or not, it is well documented that the Romanovskys entertained many other notables of their day and from his personal correspondence it is suggested that he had close links not only to the Tsar's court but also to former members of the Provisional Government of 1918. Outstanding among those were Mr and Mrs Vladimir Baranofsky who visited the Romanovskys. When the Baranofskys arrived in California in the spring of 1918, quite a stir ensued. The *San Francisco Examiner* reported:

> Mme. Vladimir Baranofsky, who was a patient at one of the sanatoriums for the past several weeks, has been taken to her home and is fast recuperating. Mr. Baranofsky is the brother-in-law of the former leader, Kerensky.[18] Mme. Baranofsky is a particularly handsome young woman and from her striking resemblance to one of the daughters of the former czar of Russia, was mistaken for the Grand Duchess Tatiana. Mr. and Mrs. Baranofsky were frequently seen about town with Admiral Bosse, with whom they crossed the Pacific. This officer was at the head of the Russian Navy and was the friend and advisor of the czar for years, and this fact exaggerated the rumor of the attractive young woman's identity. She,

however, merely smiles at the idea and says very complimentary things about the young daughter of the czar whom she knows very well.[19]

Ironically, the man who would 'author' part of a book professing that the family lived was now host to the brother-in-law of Kerensky who had attempted to transfer the family to England but instead had been forced to relocate them to Siberia, thereby unintentionally leading them to their presumed deaths in 1918. Shortly after the visit of the Baranofskys, Romanovsky was granted a promotion at the request of the Russian embassy in Washington. He was officially recognised as consul general by letter from the Department of State to the Russian ambassador.[20]

Almost simultaneously with the Baranofskys' arrival, McGarry and Romanovsky received a shipment of copies of *Rescuing the Czar* that had been printed by the California Printing Company at Romanovsky's request. A flurry of activities surrounded the book's arrival including the possibility of a film deal based on the book's assertions that the family did not die. But the most astounding activity was when McGarry requested that Major Samuel White, Office of the Judge Advocate, War Department in San Francisco, contact William G. McAdoo for him. McAdoo, the former Secretary of Treasury (the US Secret Service in 1918 reported to Treasury) and son-in-law of President Woodrow Wilson, was requested by White to meet McGarry on

a matter of great importance to the nation.[21]

Shortly after White's letter of 20 August requesting the meeting, McGarry, in turn, posted a letter on 25 August to Romanovsky stating that: '. . . you may send me my half viz. $2000.00 less any additional expenses that may be incurred between now and September 15th in care of William G. McAdoo, 120 Broadway, New York.'[22]

McAdoo responded to White on 13 September that he would 'be delighted' to meet McGarry upon his arrival 'in this city'.[23] What was the 'matter of great importance to the nation' that prompted McGarry suddenly to leave California and make the long trip to the east coast of America? Unfortunately the text of White's letter regarding a 'matter of great importance to the nation' is not in the

McAdoo papers, only the response to White's initial request is still of record. The substance of the meeting between McGarry and McAdoo remains unrevealed. But it certainly seems to have had a tremendous impact on McGarry, for shortly thereafter he wrote another telegram to a friend who was assisting in the sale of the book's rights for serialisation and film, and instructed him to 'withdraw all offers for sale'.[24]

CHAPTER 15

Politics, Intrigue and Provenance

San Francisco 1920

Whose interest would be served by the withdrawal of *Rescuing the Czar*, thereby effectively censoring the portrayal of survival contained within its somewhat flamboyant pages? In order to determine not only the true provenance of the book, but also the individuals or organisations responsible for its emergence and rapid disappearance, it is essential to examine what at first seemed to be coincidences and interconnections that over time piled on top of one another. It is important to note that some names and incidents appear only in both *Rescuing the Czar* and Homer Slaughter's 'Parfen Domnin' report. The suggestiveness of these coincidences is emphasised by the fact that Slaughter's military intelligence report containing the reference to Parfen Domnin and his role during the last days of the family's confinement in Ekaterinburg, was not of record until nine months after *Rescuing the Czar*'s publication.

McGarry later stated that he and Romanovsky received the book, not from a Lieutenant Butler, as the book indicated, but from a friend of Queen Marie of Romania.[1] The Queen was a close relative of both Nicholas and Alexandra. The Canadian, Joe Boyle, who had run a rescue mission to save the Romanian family when it was threatened by the Germans, could have been the conduit for the book. Boyle, as we recall, also attempted to persuade Nicholas's mother to leave the Crimea with him.[2] Joe Boyle had also negotiated a treaty with the Bolsheviks for Romania and is said to have saved the Romanian jewels and archives when he extricated them from Moscow.[3] He also worked alongside an American military attaché, Captain William Smythe.[4]

Boyle is reputed to have been among the last to have seen Nicholas alive in Ekaterinburg. Queen Marie of Romania stated that before she and her daughter nursed him back to health after a stroke in late 1918, he had been involved in the most secret and hazardous missions of the war.[5] Did Smythe, Boyle's attaché, give McGarry and Romanovsky the book? Hence the nom de plume James P. Smythe? Yet, another real possibility for the book finding its way into the hands of McGarry and Romanovsky was through Gavin McNab, who had been charged with the duty of escorting the Romanian family, including the Prince of Romania, through San Francisco in 1919.

We now know from Charles Crane's letters that he too was in San Francisco in May of 1920, on his way to China in his new role as ambassador when he stopped off to see Gavin McNab, the same man who had also taken care of Prince Arthur while he stayed in San Francisco on his mission to Japan in 1918. Crane wrote to McNab rather cryptically from his ship that he was worried about the upcoming election (autumn of 1920) and that they (the Democrats) 'have the cards that the Republicans can either play or discard as they must'.[6] Since Crane was in San Francisco in late May when Henry Haskin said he was taking proofs to George Romanovsky, was Crane or Gavin McNab the mysterious person in the room with Romanovsky correcting the book that Haskin said he never saw?

After McGarry's meeting with McAdoo in Washington he wrote in a letter to Romanovsky that he was angry with the shipping company of 'McNab and Smith' which had shipped the remaining books to McGarry under his real name. In another correspondence he said he was going to get after 'the company'[7] for breaking the sale of *Rescuing the Czar*. Surely a shipping company could not have broken the sale of *Rescuing the Czar*. So the enigmatic 'company' remains just that – another cryptic phrase in this inexplicable chain of events. However, in light of all the new evidence it certainly appears that McGarry and Romanovsky were the front men for something called 'the company', a term which suggests that there were more people involved behind the scenes directing the fate of the book. Most assuredly McGarry believed the story conveyed by *Rescuing the Czar* and maintained to his dying day that the

Romanovs were rescued. He even showed his family two letters he had in his possession which he called the 'My Dear Fox' letters. Supposedly the letters were written from Tsar Nicholas and Kaiser Wilhelm to the mysterious Fox thanking him for his participation in the release of the family and further for maintaining their 'state secret'. McGarry's family believed in the legitimacy of the two expressions of gratitude. Copies of these letters are still in the hands of Barbara Finlayson, his granddaughter.[8]

In an effort to understand the complex machinations behind the book's publication additional research in the archives of several countries was pursued, and as a result, I have managed to find and identify numerous individuals mentioned in *Rescuing the Czar* who were unknown in the West prior to its publication in 1920 and who, even now, have only recently come to light since the opening of the Soviet archives. Events, too, hitherto described only in *Rescuing the Czar* and otherwise unknown, have finally been corroborated, thereby adding to the legitimacy of the book.

A thorough analysis of the book reveals that it contains the names of obscure Bolshevik officials, such as Hokhriakov (Khokhriakov), Kaganitsky, Dutzman and numerous others, who were absolutely unknown to the West in the spring and early summer of 1920. The remarkable detail of events that took place in the spring of 1918 and the following weeks leading up to July only became public knowledge after the publication of *Rescuing the Czar*. On 31 July 1920 an article by G. G. Telberg, a former minister of the Kolchak government, which had become the primary governing faction in Siberia after the fall of Ekaterinburg entitled 'Last Days and Death of the Russian Emperor and His Family, Told in Official Documents' appeared in the *Saturday Evening Post*. By comparison, *Rescuing the Czar* included more details and obscure personages than did the Telberg article. However, interestingly, *Rescuing the Czar* had already been 'translated and assembled', printed, bound and delivered one week prior to the *Post* article. Also, *Rescuing the Czar* mirrors many events that we now know had really taken place, but which, in 1920, could only have been known of by someone who was on the ground at the time. If not, then only someone who had been thoroughly briefed as to the actual details, which were unknown in the West in May or June 1920, could have concocted the book.

Let us further consider that in *Rescuing the Czar*, a reference is made to Parafine Domino, who is described as one of the Tsar's valets.[9] This certainly is an allusion to the Parfen Domnin mentioned in Homer Slaughter's report sent to military intelligence in December 1918. Slaughter, as we know, says he received a manuscript from Domnin, passed on to him by American Consul Palmer via a nun from a convent who had been delivering eggs and milk to the family. As we have also seen, it is the same Parfen Domnin account that Carl Ackerman recited for his December 1918 article for the *New York Times* suggesting that only Nicholas had died. Later Ackerman in his book published in 1919 once again mentioned Parfen Domnin and he also maintained in that same book that the Czechs were bent on rescuing the Tsar.[10] In *Rescuing the Czar*, Fox says, 'I must get rid of this old valet, Parafine Domino, who makes a nuisance of himself hovering around my prisoner like a hawk . . .' Could this reference have been cobbled together from Ackerman's article and book? Certainly it is likely, but the reference to Parafine Domino is not as troubling as the significance that both Slaughter and Ackerman seem to have placed in the credibility of the Domnin account that Slaughter received from the nun via Consul Palmer. The fact that he eventually sent it to Washington where it still resides in the intelligence archives is intriguing since we now know that both Ackerman and Slaughter were intelligence operatives.[11] Why would they give credence to the existence of a man named Parfen Domnin, had he never existed? Moreover, in Ackerman's correspondence a curious document caught my attention which seems to indicate that both Slaughter and Ackerman took additional steps to confirm the Parfen account of the last days of the family in Ekaterinburg. It is an unsigned report, presumably written by Ackerman to his superior, detailing a meeting he had had with one of the nuns at the monastery in Ekaterinburg. When he questioned her about the last days of the family at the Ipatiev House, he reported that she said she had been requested to bring to the house fifty eggs as well as ink and paper on the night before the family disappeared. This comment regarding the paper and ink will become particularly significant when we review the last pages of *Rescuing the Czar*. For an unknown intelligence operative indicates that 'P.D.', presumably Parfen Domnin, was asked to recopy a document that had been fabricated to convince the world that the Tsar died, 'on different paper and with different ink'. Is it simply a coincidence that whoever created the pages of *Rescuing the Czar* would have known that a nun at the monastery in Ekaterinburg would mention to Ackerman that she had been requested to bring paper and ink on 15 July?

Even more compelling, given the involvement of the nun, is that Sidney Reilly at this time was dealing not only with the Church but also with all the men mentioned in the Parfen testimony given to Slaughter. In fact, the efforts of these same men were not only definitely linked to those of Sidney Reilly, who as we know was on a 'special secret mission', but they had been supported by the Allies' two-track policy via the banking scheme.

While in Russia Reilly frequently masqueraded as Relinsky the Bolshevik, and on many occasions he would list his profession as 'engineer'. The Parfen Domnin account refers to 'engineer Ilinsky, and Ekhart's tunnel'. The Chief of Staff of the Baltic White forces, who were also supposed to be acting in conjunction with Savinkov's uprising, was Otto Ekkert, who may have been the man the Domnin manuscript was referring to when it cited 'Ekhart's tunnel' and the engineer Ilinsky could well have been a typographical error meant to be Relinsky. Perhaps it is really only coincidence, but Domnin's report has many parallels to the real events of 1918.

In conclusion, the Parfen Domnin report covered in chapter 9, when read thoroughly, does indicate it was written by someone who knew about the intricate politics at work in Russia in the summer of 1918. That the Czechs were advancing on Ekaterinburg to help save the Tsar now seems feasible and the Domnin document argues that position. The allusion to numerous Russian generals and Savinkov being part of an Allied scheme to incite reprisals and overthrow the Bolsheviks is now an indisputable fact. And the presumed authentic letters between the Tsar and loyal soldiers that passed back and forth in June at the Ipatiev House now can be considered more real than speculative. In summary, even with its badly constructed grammar and atrocious spelling, the Parfen Domnin account conveys a surprisingly accurate picture of what we now know was the political and military reality playing itself out in a chaotic fashion, far from the public view in remote areas of Siberia in the summer of 1918.

Does *Rescuing the Czar* reveal in an allegorical fashion something that others did not know? Was Domnin's role, with the help of Ackerman and Slaughter, to feed the story that the Tsar died, but not necessarily the Tsarina and the children in the hopes that after the overthrow of the Bolsheviks, if the political climate allowed, an announcement could be made that like the other Romanov 300 years before, the Tsar had to die to live? If so, what could have happened to the family after the last night in the Ipatiev House?

When we recall that *Rescuing the Czar* said the family were taken through Turkistan, it led me to probe whether Slaughter was active in that area. In fact, Tashkent, in Turkistan, is mentioned in his intelligence reports filed around 24 July 1918, where he made reference to 'our (US) consul in Tashkent'. The interesting point about this is that Tashkent was not a regular consular city in July 1918.[12] However, as we have already seen in chapter 9, the United States had quietly moved Roger Tredwell to Tashkent after he had been intricately involved with Robert Bruce Lockhart and the Bolsheviks in March 1918 while the Allies were executing the two-track policy. Why was his presence necessary in Tashkent at this time?

A British officer had reported Tredwell as having died around the same time Tredwell mysteriously left for Tashkent. However, unfortunately for the United States State Department, a quite clearly alive Tredwell, in the company of Colonel Frederick Bailey, British intelligence operative stationed in India, was arrested in October 1918 by the Bolsheviks. A French citizen and a Russian translator were also arrested with them. Their arrest caused quite an incident.[13] Were Tredwell and Bailey handling the logistics for an out for the Tsar and his family and the onward journey that would eventually go through Tibet to China? In *Rescuing the Czar* there is reference to waiting for the India officer. While Colonel Keyes, who ran the banking scheme, was from the Indian army, so too was Bailey and there are several intriguing facts about the latter that are worth knowing.

Bailey spoke numerous Tibetan dialects and had made two solo treks across Tibet. In 1924 he wrote a book called *Mission to Tashkent*, which was censored several times by the British government and not allowed to be published until decades later.[14] The book, in its final form, actually appeared to be an attempt to obfuscate what really occurred in Tashkent in 1918. Indirectly, this gives even more credibility to *Rescuing the Czar*. In fact, Bailey practically replicates the route that *Rescuing the Czar* indicated the family utilised in their exit from Siberia. Furthermore, he alludes to having been responsible for bringing out very important refugees whom he cannot name.

In a further effort to ascertain the validity of *Rescuing the Czar*'s assertions, particularly regarding the India officers and the tea merchant who escorted the family to Ceylon on a British man-of-war, I gained access to the list of tea planters in Ceylon in 1918. It was then cross-referenced with any known intelligence operatives in Russia in 1918, as well as any individuals who might have functioned in some capacity in Russia in 1918. The findings may not be conclusive, but there are at least two intriguing surnames germane to men in northern Russia who had roots in Ceylon – Keyes and Webster. In researching the Keyes family in Ceylon, I found a Captain A. J. H. Keyes who had been a member of the Ceylon garrison in 1918. But unfortunately, at this time it remains unclear whether Colonel Terence Keyes and Captain A. J. H. Keyes were related. In Russia there were two notable Websters: Captain Valentine Webster, who was quite wealthy and a friend of Jonas Lied's, the very man who confided in his diary about being approached by British intelligence to participate in a rescue attempt and who was being paid through the Hudson's Bay Company by Henry Armitstead, also the man who was supervising the building of the house in Murmansk. But by 1918 Valentine Webster, the man whom Jonas Lied mentions in his book as being someone with whom he had done business in Siberia prior to the war, was dead.[15]

While Valentine Webster may not be the Webster *Rescuing the Czar* might have been referring to, another Webster was involved in the extremely fluid events of 1918. When Sidney Reilly needed to move money around at a fast pace for fear of losing the funds that were needed to operate the various intelligence missions he was conducting, he sent Lieutenant Laurence Webster, a British passport officer, to the American Embassy to pick up the money that had been placed there, presumably under the care of Consul DeWitt Poole (the man later implicated in the so-called Lockhart plot). Little has survived to enlighten us about Laurence Webster since as a British passport control officer, his files are still not available to the public.

However, according to Captain George Hill, one of Mansfield Cumming's Secret Service agents in Russia in 1918, Laurence Webster was knowledgeable about Sidney Reilly's affairs. And it seems Webster was more than just a passport control officer – he was also a member of naval intelligence and seems to have had connections with the Ukraine that was also the location of Yaroshinsky, Crane and Masaryk in Kiev just prior to the implementation of the banking scheme. As a passport control officer and a member of naval intelligence, Webster was one of the men connected to Captain Cromie of the British Mission, killed during the supposed Lockhart plot. The Bolsheviks arrested Webster on 5 August. In September he was involved in attempting to pay off a blackmailer who made it known he would expose numerous MI1c operations. Whether Lieutenant Laurence Webster was a member of the tea merchant Captain Valentine Webster's family remains unclear.

Who would have made arrangements for the journey outlined in *Rescuing the Czar*? Other curious details from the book can now be verified and shed light on the possible identity of the nobleman Alexei, the other diarist in *Rescuing the Czar* and the man who possibly organised the logistics of the escape. Alexei often mentioned his wife Maroussia in his diary. He wrote that he was concerned about his wife's friendship with a woman he called 'The Baroness B'. Two Baronesses come to mind. One is Baroness Budberg, who was Bruce Lockhart's, as well as the novelist Maxim Gorky's, mistress. However, the most likely candidate appears to be the Baroness Buxhoeveden, who had volunteered to accompany the family into exile. However, due to illness 'Isa', as she was called by the family, had been forced to stay behind and finally became a part of the Imperial suite three months later in Tobolsk.[16] Yet when she attempted to take up residence with the family in the Ipatiev House in Ekaterinburg, her request was denied by the local authorities. Consequently, as far as we know, she was never allowed into their presence again. One puzzling aspect of the Baroness's life in Siberia remains unclear. Why was she not arrested like numerous others in the entourage of the Imperial family? Eventually, the United States authorities aided her departure from Russia, for there is a visa application index card for her in the archives in Washington, DC. Unfortunately the corresponding file is not of record.[17]

In the twenties the Baroness penned several literary tomes while she was living at Windsor where she remained for the rest of her life as a guest of the British royal family. Attempts by researchers to view her private papers have proved fruitless. However, her books recounted her experiences at the Russian court, as well as her trials and tribulations in Siberia. One of them defends Alexandra, and the Baroness draws a picture of a warm, loving woman who had been much maligned.

Rescuing the Czar also states that Baroness B was close to

Madame Vyrubova – the woman who was in league with Yaroshinsky and Soloviev in their rescue attempts.[18] In Alexei Syvorotka's diary he notes that he had been told that Maroussia had been shot and now, feeling he had nothing to lose, joined the intriguers. Even though the Baroness B had pressed Alexei many times before, he had always refused to become a part of the intrigues since: 'Heaven knows what the baroness has become since her peculiar conduct with the Vassilchikov and her permanent whisperings to Madame Vyrubova and the rest of the gang.' But apparently Baroness B was successful because, after learning about his wife being shot, he then had assumed the name Alexei Syvorotka and had become involved in the plot outlined in *Rescuing the Czar* to save the family. A careful reading of *Rescuing the Czar* reveals that in the end Alexei will also be duped. Someone who was not present at the scene could hardly have conveyed the details of his experiences as a Bolshevik as convincingly as 'Syvorotka' did. For example, he recounts in vivid detail his infiltration of a meeting, disguised as a Bolshevik, where Khokhriakov and Kaganitsky were discussing the fate of the family. This same scenario would be reported later in numerous books published well after 1920.

So, who could the real 'Alexei' have been? Charles Crane's friend, Rostovstov, curiously enough, also had a wife named Maroussia. She had indeed known Madame Vyrubova and Baroness Buxhoeveden. Count Rostovstov had been the vice-president of the Aero Club formed in St Petersburg in 1909.[19] Shortly thereafter Sidney Reilly was asked to join and soon became a 'leading spirit of the club'.[20] In a letter to Crane, by a friend of Rostovstov, it is stated that it is feared that Maroussia had been shot.[21]

Crane received in December 1917, a letter from his friend and former secretary to Alexandra, Count Rostovstov, in which Rostovstov confirmed to Crane that he had completed the instructions Crane had left prior to leaving St Petersburg for England only weeks before. The letter describes the number of telegrams Rostovstov has sent at Crane's behest. He opened a substantial bank account at National City Bank on Crane's instructions, as well as disposing of curiously large amounts of money given to him by Crane to pay a jeweller. And among other items of business he had also sent money to Dashy-Sampiton, of the Bouriat (Buryat) National Committee, who was to deliver a present to the Dalai Lama.[22] The Bouriat National Committee was comprised of two factions: one led by Sampiton was not only anti-Bolshevik but also pro-monarchy and in league with Ataman Semenov, while the other was pro-Bolshevik. That Crane would be supporting the far-off Bouriats in Siberia at exactly the time plans were being laid to rescue the family is puzzling unless he was, as evidence suggests, the point man involved in laying the trail by which they were to attempt to escape. Furthermore, if he were playing that role it would help to explain why he would send money to the Dalai Lama because, unless it is another coincidence, the book *Rescuing the Czar* speaks of the 'Lamas' who led the family through Tibet. In light of the assertions of *Rescuing the Czar*, Crane's cryptic letter now appears to have been outlining steps to be taken to aid the escape of unknown persons through the Bouriat territories of Siberia to Tibet and most likely on through China if it became necessary.

The same letter, from the Tsarina's financial secretary Rostovstov also referred to 'the pilgrims', 'Miss Schneider' and 'money to Ella for fuel'. There was a Miss Schneider who had been a member of the Imperial family's entourage, and during that period Alexandra's sister, Grand Duchess Elizabeth – 'Ella' – was actually in need of money for fuel.[23] It now seems that we can at least consider that Rostovstov who appears to have been the financial point man for the escape could possibly have been the nobleman referred to as Syvorotka in *Rescuing the Czar* as well. And also that he had sent money to the Dalai Lama to aid in the evacuation of the family by the lamas as *Rescuing the Czar* says.

The countryside from Ekaterinburg through northern Turkistan was at that time in the hands of friendly forces. After the trek to Chungking, as *Rescuing the Czar* stated, the family could have boarded a British gunboat, since there were twelve in the China theatre, and headed downriver to Woosung, where Fox maintains the family were to embark for Japan.

If in fact, *Rescuing the Czar* was not just an allegorical portrayal of real events, the correspondence of McGarry and Romanovsky never indicated that to be the case. In their correspondence they openly talked about publishing the book in order to embarrass Lloyd George in his 'trying times with the Irish'. And Romanovsky in a letter to a friend stated 'when our day comes I will go to Ireland and kiss her revered green ground' as if Ireland somehow would play a role in this return to a non-Bolshevik driven Russian. The tone of the letters between Romanovsky and his friend could lead one to feel that in some way Ireland would have something to do with a restoration. Later, when some copies of *Rescuing the Czar* had been shipped under the name of Rutledge rather than McGarry, McGarry wrote a cryptic letter to Romanovsky, stating: 'You will notice the Bull made by the R. R. addressing the notice to one Wm. Rutledge – instead of to me as it should have been. That Bull lost me some money and you also . . . Notwithstanding this I did and do yet intend to get after the Company for breaking that sale for us.'[24]

Just two months before, on 22 November 1920, only five months after *Rescuing the Czar* was first published, McGarry wrote to Romanovsky:

Now that England has Nicholas in India –
– and Wells in Moscow –
– and the Bolsheviki bottled in a treaty –
– What is she going to do with the prisoners of Tobolsk? –
I have not heard whether they escaped via Los Angeles or are still marooned in the Monadnock [the building where the books had been stored].

This letter is certainly fascinating. Its implication is that Britain (she) was behind the book originally called *Prisoners of Tobolsk*, but published as *Rescuing the Czar*. In Richard Deacon's *The British Connection, Russia's Manipulation of British Individuals and Institutions* he points to a connection between Sidney Reilly and McGarry. He also thought that *Rescuing the Czar* might have been Soviet disinformation, but after an exhaustive investigation of Romanovsky and McGarry there is not one scintilla of evidence linking either man knowingly to a Bolshevik conspiracy. However, it seems quite plausible that the book could be linked to certain officials in the British government. When McGarry spoke enigmatically of 'Bull' he may have been alluding to Sir William Bull, the noted Unionist who first introduced Reilly to Churchill. McGarry also belonged to the Union League of New York and had business associates in common with Sidney Reilly.

Recently, in *Churchill and the Secret Service* by David Stafford, it was revealed that Sir Henry Wilson, the Ulster-born chief of the Imperial General Staff was so:

. . . convinced of the gravity of the crisis facing the British Government that he frequently fantasized about a coup d'État to get rid of Lloyd George on the grounds that his tolerance for Krasin [head of Soviet delegation in London during trade treaty negotiations] and his misdeeds could only have a sinister interpretation. Churchill saw Wilson several times a day that month.[25]

Churchill was not a fan of the Bolsheviks and Wilson had begun to think of Lloyd George as a traitor.[26] Was Reilly, who had been in the Far East just prior to July 1920 and on his way back from the Orient via San Francisco, once again active on behalf of the British Secret Service? And was the publication of *Rescuing the Czar* intended to embarrass or put pressure on certain government officials, such as Lloyd George who was resistant to the partitioning of Ireland? For if it became known that the head of a government sensitive to labour had, in fact, worked to bring out a relative of the King – and one who had, no less, been branded as unsympathetic to the workers – it could have had disastrous consequences for Lloyd George and his party. And, further, did the Irish partitioning issue somehow become tangled in the Russian web? Strangely, in 1920 Carl Ackerman, the State Department 'special agent' who had been deeply involved in the Romanov saga, was again acting as a courier – but this time between Lloyd George and Eamon de Valera in the negotiations pertaining to the partitioning of Ireland.[27] We should remember that it was Ackerman who first filed the report that he received from Homer Slaughter about Parfen Domnin. Ultimately, regardless of who was responsible for the publication of *Rescuing the Czar* or what their motives were, its final pages contain a compelling narrative that now has, as we have seen, collateral corroboration for its account of the last night in the Ipatiev House.

However, over the years, *Rescuing the Czar* has been dismissed as too bizarre to be taken seriously. Some believe it was a money-making scheme on behalf of McGarry and Romanovsky since they were expecting a movie deal as a result of the publication of the book, while others believed it was black propaganda. While we may never know who actually was behind this effort it is now more than ever difficult, if not impossible, to toss it aside for it may hold one of the keys to the Romanov riddle.

CHAPTER 16

Coming Full Circle

Fact as Fiction and Fiction as Fact

As compelling as the new facts are, there are some who will continue to embrace the sealed results of the Commission in Russia regarding the DNA tests on the remains found in the forest near Koptiaki as the final word on the fate of the Romanovs. Yet the newly discovered documents reveal that there were several complex operations mounted in 1918 to save the Romanovs and that perhaps one may have succeeded, at least in part.

In the allegorical work *Rescuing the Czar*, Fox describes the moment he and the Tsar, while still in the tunnel, overheard the guards' surprise when they came in and realised the family had vanished:

> Then my 'prisoners' returned to the mouth of the entrance. There we heard a horrible row ... we could hear, quite distinctly, a sullen voice saying ... now I order you to explain the whereabouts of the PRISONERS ... what did he do with the bodies?. . . he's lying! . . . burned![1]

Is this the moment that the story which was spread around the world was concocted? If *Rescuing the Czar* has any validity it indicates that in the final hours once again different plots to rescue the family collided – one being engineered by the German General Staff and the other involving a lone British Secret Service agent, the man we know as 'Charles James Fox', who claims to have infiltrated the Ipatiev House guard. The epilogue of *Rescuing the Czar:*

242

Translator's note.

With paragraph 55 ends the diary of Syvorotka. [the Russian nobleman]. Among his documents, however, has been found the following letter, not in his characteristic handwriting, but in that of someone else, bearing directly upon the incidents narrated by the diarist. Written in ungrammatical Russian, bearing many orthographic mistakes, this document seems to be a fragment of a report, by some unidentified co-operating agent, to his unrevealed superior. It is deemed necessary, therefore, for purposes of clearness, to append this document, as I find it among the literary remains of Al. Syvorotka:

... four or five days after your departure, I gave the story to P.D.; he took it to the E****; the latter made but a few corrections in it, and P.D. copied it, – as you ordered: with different ink, and on different paper.[2]

This notable entry at the end of *Rescuing the Czar* identifies P.D. who only appeared in one other book, Carl Ackerman's *Trailing the Bolsheviki*, as Parfen Domnin, the name of the valet also found in the intelligence report of Major Homer Slaughter and the *New York Times* article by Ackerman. E**** is the Emperor. The implication of this passage is that the Emperor reviewed the story of his own death in a manuscript that had been brought to him by Parfen Domnin, and 'made but a few corrections'.

What is certain is that the 'authors' of the curious diaries/ manuscript given to McGarry and Romanovsky knew about the character who first came to the attention of United States Military Intelligence via Homer Slaughter's report. Yet this latter source is unlikely since the report had only been in the hands of General Graves at the time and was not made of record until after the publication of *Rescuing the Czar*. It would seem the only other obvious way for the 'authors' to have known about the Parfen Domnin character was through Carl Ackerman's *New York Times* story and subsequent book *Trailing the Bolsheviki*.

But then there is that eerie comment, '*he took it to the E****; the latter made but a few corrections in it, and P.D. copied it, – as you ordered: with different ink, and on different paper.*' As mentioned earlier in chapter 9, a report still exists in Ackerman's papers, which recalls a meeting with the nun who had been taking food from the monastery. From the following remarks it could be considered that the nun may have been an aristocratic woman masquerading as a churchwoman. The report says: 'We were shown to the room of the head sister where we met a woman well past middle age but still very well preserved and active and ready to tell what she knew of the Czar.' Later Homer Slaughter stated in his official report that the nun at the monastery had little to add to the Parfen Domnin account. To Slaughter it may well have appeared that she did not have anything more to reveal. Except that in the unpublished report found in the Ackerman papers, on the meeting with the nun it is further stated:

> 21 November 1918
> . . . On second July old style (15 July new style) the sister was asked to bring paper and ink, which was taken on the third (16 July). On the second (15 July) she was asked to bring for the next day fifty eggs beside the milk, which was done . . .

What is interesting about this entry is that neither Ackerman's article in the *New York Times* nor Slaughter's intelligence report make any mention of the fact that the nun told them about the request for paper and ink in addition to food supplies. Moreover, nor does the testimony contained in the Sokolov report, and repeated in John O'Conor's book, note that the nun was requested to bring paper and ink to the house in the days before the family vanished, though it does mention the fifty eggs. The fact that the reference to the need for paper and ink just prior to the family's disappearance only appears in *Rescuing* and the nun's unpublished interview seems uncanny. Can this be another unlikely coincidence?

The unknown agent continues:

> The fourteenth passed quietly. The new man who took command of the guards and his assistant, assembled the men and organized a meeting; Syvorotka was present. Some of the people spoke of the 'hidden treasury'; some spoke of the People's Tribunal; some insisted upon a wholesale killing, – for the loyals and the Czechs are rapidly approaching, and from everywhere come rumors about uprisings. Finally it was decided to try the Family immediately.[3]

In this passage we get an insight into someone who seems to have been on the ground at the time that the fate of the family was being decided. In a telegram sent to Sverdlov on 16 July, at 5.50 pm, with a copy to Lenin there is a discussion of a trial:

> For military reasons the trial agreed upon with Filipp (Goloshchekin) cannot be put off; we cannot wait. If your opinions differ, then immediately notify without delay.
>
> Goloshchekin and Safarov

This telegram is supposed to have been received at 9:22 pm in Moscow. The narrator in *Rescuing the Czar* continues:

> The next day we were busy with the trucks; towards evening all of them were in shape including the Number 74-M in which you ordered the change of magneto, and ready to move. So you see – we have done what you ordered, and if all happened so that we could not foresee, it was not my fault, nor Syvorotka's, nor Philip's.
>
> All the day of the 16th the investigation continued, and the Commissaries asked for the E**** twice; once four men went to Ipatiev's; their conduct was outrageous. At eight in the evening I was on my post in the red house, the wires were working fine and Philip answered. Nachman's place answered too.[4]

The Nachman referred to by the commentator could be Nachman Steinberg, who reported the suppression of the Left Socialist Revolutionaries (LSR) when the split between the LSR and the Bolsheviks had occurred ten days earlier in July. Nachman Steinberg described the arrest of all those who had taken part in the insurgence, which had culminated in the assassination on 6 July 1918 of Count von Mirbach, the German ambassador to Lenin's government.

As mentioned earlier, Lenin feared reprisals from Germany. Nachman Steinberg's personal account of these events further illuminates the real fear Lenin had of the Germans during July 1918.[5] Steinberg was from Ufa, the location towards which, as we shall see, *Rescuing the Czar* says some of the conspirators were headed after they realised that their effort to take the family had failed. And Steinberg was also close to Savinkov and the leaders of the Socialist Revolutionaries, who were attempting to overthrow the Bolsheviks, and as such either he or someone in his family would have been an ideal candidate to assist in the plot to save the family.

Is this Nachman the Nachman who appeared in *Rescuing the Czar*? Furthermore, in *Trotsky and the Jews,* Nachman Steinberg is described as an accidental revolutionary when it is stated that, 'Trotsky and Steinberg clashed on the crucial question of the use of terror. Steinberg's "liberal weakness" was not entirely to Trotsky's liking.'[6] Later, in Trotsky's book on Lenin he defined Steinberg as follows: 'The Left Social-Revolutionary Steinberg, whom a curious wind had driven into the revolution and even into the Council of People's Commissars'.[7] As a result of the way in which even Trotsky speaks of Steinberg, failing any other candidate that may come to light, it can be suggested that Lenin, who was at cross purposes with Trotsky regarding the Romanovs, may have asked Steinberg to participate in the effort to free the family since it appears that he was anything but ruthless and bloodthirsty. The epilogue continues describing the events of that July night:

At nine I signalled to the Ipatiev's, and Princess waved 'all well', but could not continue for a Red came to the window and shut it with a baynoet [*sic*]. It had already begun to get very dark, so I phoned again to Philip and Syvorotka and asked them whether they had orders to start. I was told that they had not heard anything from the house. I decided to wait a little longer and then to phone to Tikhvinsky to inquire whether or not the Nun was on her place, so I could go and investigate why S-y did not start. At ten I called up, but the phone was dead. While I was waiting for some movement about the house, Philip himself came and said that S-y had ordered him to remove the trucks away out of the city. Philip refused to do so, and tried to reach me by phone but it was out of order, so he left Syvorotka in charge and came to ask me personally. While we were trying to digest what all of this meant and what should be done, a movement began in the house; lights flickered in the windows and shortly afterwards, we distinctly heard the report of a revolver. As this looked bad we both left and ran across the place, but the Reds would not let anybody in. Already there were about fifteen men trying to break down the fence. The inside guards resisted and some shots were exchanged. The assailants were Reds, asking for 'a treasury' and some of them were asking for the Family as it was rumored that they had already been killed.[8]

Here we learn that 'Philip' and his unknown companion had

apparently been waiting in the garage to receive a phone call about the movements of the trucks but that these trucks were then ordered out of the city. However, 'Philip' refused to do as instructed.

The nun who was interviewed by Ackerman and Slaughter also made mention of a truck: 'This sister refuses to believe that the Czar or any other member of his family have been killed, and thinks they were taken out of the city in the truck she saw standing in the yard on the third (16 July new style)'. It is very interesting to note that when Yurovsky recounted his memory of the events of that night in both his testimonies in 1920 and in 1934, he alluded as well to the fact that the trucks were late in arriving and that Filipp Goloshchekin, the man Yakovlev said was the only man in the Urals who did not want to see the family die, was pacing outside the Ipatiev House.

And is it possible that the S-Y who seems to have had an important role was Sheremetevsky, the White officer who later led the investigators to the 'remains'? Continuing through the eyes of our unknown conspirator:

> Seeing that nothing could be done from this side I went to the rear and squeezed in, for Ch. was there and he let me do so; but he said that he had heard shots inside and that he thought all was finished, and said also that Leinst and three others went to search in Syvorotka's home – they evidently don't know that all was taken out yesterday.[9]

Syvorotka, or Alexei, the Russian nobleman disguised as a Bolshevik, related in his diary that he had been indoctrinated into a plot to save the Imperial family by a Baroness B, who was a friend of Anna Vyrubova, the Tsarina's confidante. Little Markov, in his book, says he himself was in league with Boris Soloviev, who as we have seen was referred to, along with Sidney Reilly, as Karol Yaroshinsky's assistant. Additionally, Soloviev was the head of the Brotherhood of St John of Tobolsk, which had been founded to rescue the family. The fact that Karol Yaroshinsky, who had been deeply involved with the Allies' banking scheme was at the same time the financial benefactor to the family, implies that he may have, through Soloviev and Reilly, been a member of the Brotherhood of St John of Tobolsk. What is of record is that Soloviev was frequently communicating with Anna Vyrubova at that time.

According to *Rescuing the Czar*, Baroness B and two other individuals, a member of British intelligence named Stanley, together with an unnamed man from the 'San Francisco' area, had planted telegraphic equipment in Syvorotka's home.

The 'Ch.' spoken about most probably is Sergei Yegorovich Chutskaev, who was chairman of the Ekaterinburg City Executive Committee. In 1920 and 1934, Yurovsky mentions Chutskaev as the individual who recommended some very deep mines on the Moscow highway to be used as a place to dispose of the bodies. Statements of this sort by Yurovsky are interesting because in his 1934 speech to the 'old Bolsheviks', he stated that he was told on 10 July to begin preparations for the execution of the family. Why then, on the day after the purported executions, would he receive advice from Chutskaev regarding the disposal of the bodies? Our narrator continues:

In the house I found complete commotion. The family had disappeared, and no one knew where or how. Pytkan was shot in the stomach and in the throat and I saw him lying on the floor in the room. Khokhriakov and his men were shaking the rest of his life out of him, asking where the E. and the jewelry were, but all that Pytkan could say was 'they were taken away'. No one could make out what really had happened and who had shot him; some said that they went away in trucks, yet, in the evening, some that a detachment sent by the Soviet took them secretly out, some said aeroplanes. All were wrong, for Philip had just come back and the trucks were in place, no one came into the Ipatiev's house as I was on guard, and there had been no aeroplanes since six o'clock. Pytkan was almost dead when Khokhriakov finally got from him that the family had been shot and taken away – and then he began to expire. Later the German appeared and chased us all away, – he sent for his assistant, but they could not find him.[10]

Perhaps we should revisit the testimony of Pavel Medvedev, which has long been extremely controversial. He supposedly switched sides and joined the Whites when he mysteriously disappeared soon after having given the only eyewitness account to the death of the Romanovs. It was stated that he died from typhus, even though great pains had been made to protect him from the disease: he had been moved by the Whites to a hospital that was virtually free of infection as he was about to be re-interrogated by Sokolov. Medvedev, who was on guard at the Ipatiev House the night in question, stated that after the change of guard on 10 July 1918, Yurovsky had an assistant described as being twenty-six to twenty-seven years old, blond and someone whom Medvedev did not know.[11] Additionally, paralleling another statement made by the unknown narrator, Medvedev also says some fifteen men came running to the house on the night he said the murders occurred. Medvedev's testimony became important indeed because it was recorded by Sokolov as the only eyewitness testimony he had and consequently it was touted as the smoking gun that confirmed once and for all time that the Romanovs had died that fateful summer night in Ekaterinburg.

In addition to querying whether this unknown new assistant could have been Charles James Fox – the man that no one can find who appeared at the Ipatiev House out of nowhere, it is also worth questioning whether Medvedev could be the unknown conspirator appearing in the last pages of *Rescuing the Czar*. One intriguing fact which seems to link the two men is that both Medvedev and the man whose report we are reading seem to be very familiar with the Sysert area. Sysert was in fact Medvedev's home and the narrator of *Rescuing the Czar* implies that it was where logistics to gain custody of the family had been taking place. Similarities between the testimony of the key eyewitness at the Ipatiev House to the family's purported demise, and the report of the man speaking through the pages of *Rescuing the Czar* appear to be another incidence of alleged fiction having a basis in fact.

The name Khokhriakov is also contained in the fading pages of *Rescuing the Czar* and is worthy of additional attention. As we have seen this was an unknown name in the western world at the time of the publication of *Rescuing the Czar*. Pavel Danilovich Khokhriakov, whom we first met during the Yakovlev episode, was a sailor in the Baltic Fleet. He was also briefly the chairman of the Tobolsk Soviet, where Nicholas, Alexandra, and Maria had been separated from the rest of the family and moved to Ekaterinburg. After Yakovlev's attempt to remove the family to 'Moscow or wherever' it was Khokhriakov who was instructed to transfer the rest of the family and the Romanov suite to Ekaterinburg. It is said he died on 17 August 1918, within a month of the family's disappearance, a victim of the Civil War.[12] And *Rescuing the Czar* also refers to his colleague Kaganitsky, whom Syvorotka refers to as being 'from Ural, I guess'.[13] It has only recently become widely known that an Isaak Yakovlevich Koganitsky, also a resident of Tobolsk, in the Urals, had been sent by the Moscow Party Committee to keep an eye on the Imperial household.[14]

So how could a book printed in 1920 in America have contained the correct names of minor officials who were virtually unheard of in the western world until recently and were certainly not known in San Francisco in the spring of 1920? Unless, of course, the diaries in *Rescuing the Czar* are valid or, at the very minimum, constructed by someone with enough detailed inside knowledge of the events surrounding the Imperial family to perpetrate an enduring and plausible yarn. Down through the decades, rumours have floated among members of various intelligence communities that the brief life of *Rescuing the Czar* – before it was pulled after McGarry's visit to McAdoo – may have cost the lives of some British, American and other Allied nations' agents. That assertion has never been confirmed.

But why was this book linked in any way to William McAdoo, who had a cabinet position in World War One under Woodrow Wilson and was his son-in-law, no less? Was McAdoo still assisting his father-in-law? Wilson was not as active as he had been in 1918, due to a stroke he had suffered in 1919 while on a tour across the United States to promote the Treaty of Versailles and his vision of the League of Nations.

Our narrator continues:

> The family disappeared, – it is true; there was no trace of them. I continued to look everywhere up to the time that the Soviet representatives arrived, having been ordered to arrest all people who were with the family, and commenced searching for the bodies. The whole place was surrounded by Reds, and all were ordered out, but nothing was there. Then a resolution was made that the prisoners had been taken away and shot, and they sent a wire to Moscow.[15]

The previous extract reminds us of the infamous wire to Moscow. In 1924, when Nicholas Sokolov's official investigation was published, the world first learned of the telegram decoded by Abaza (the associate of Reilly's) that was purportedly sent in reference to the execution of the Tsar and his family. This telegram said:

Tell Sverdlov entire family suffered same fate as head. Officially family will perish in evacuation.[16]

Much has been made of this telegram, which was already examined in detail earlier in this book. However, what is interesting about the telegram referenced in *Rescuing the Czar* is that it is the only known record of a telegram, apart from the above telegram itself, sent regarding the family. Should the sentence 'sent a wire to Moscow' that appeared in *Rescuing the Czar* be viewed only as another coincidence? Or, were the wires portrayed in both *Rescuing the Czar* and the Sokolov Report, the content of which was supposedly unknown until Abaza decoded the mysterious telegram for Sokolov in late 1920, in fact one and the same telegram?

And stranger still, in Sokolov's assistant Bulygin's notes in the Hoover Institute is an intriguing mention of the Red Army leader Trotsky's 'hairbrush' found in the Ipatiev House.[17] Had another struggle for the family between the Lenin and Trotsky factions come to a head and had Charles James Fox, if he existed, arrived just in time to extricate the Romanovs?

Certainly, the final days of the Romanov family appear to have been cloaked in lies and the truth, even today, remains elusive. One example of these contradictions lies in the fact that Trotsky maintained later, while living in exile, that he was away from Moscow during the period from early July 1918 to some time after Ekaterinburg fell to the Czech Legion and the Whites. But making any sense of his actions on the night in question still remains difficult since, contrary to his own account of his whereabouts, recently released documents in the Soviet Archives recounting the meeting of the Sovnarkom, in Moscow, on 18 July 1918 show him present.

Let's return to the epilogue of *Rescuing the Czar*:

I only know that inside the house they killed two people and nobody else, anyhow. Pytkan and Kramer were dead; Kramer probably had been shot from a distance – the bullet was in his head. There were no more than two men killed, I know it; so you may feel sure, when you hear that all were killed in the house that it is a lie. Somebody must have been burning things in the stove long before – maybe in the daytime or the early evening; the stove was almost cold, – the Reds got something out of it, I did not see what it was. When I understood that the whole family had been taken away, dead or alive, or had somehow disappeared, and that there was nothing for us to do, I took Philip and we rushed back to Syvorotka. The trucks and the chauffeurs were all gone. In the garage we found Syvorotka tied with a rope and shot in the spine, and bleeding from scratches and other wounds.[18]

It is interesting to note that in the 1934 speech that Yurovsky made to the old Bolsheviks, he spoke of returning to Ekaterinburg from where he was attempting to bury the Imperial family, and trying to locate a car or truck and not having either available to him. Yurovsky finally made arrangements for another car and he also said that the commandant of the garage was a scoundrel who irritated him since they did not have any cars. He further stated this scoundrel was later shot in Perm. So again there is a ring of truth, or at least of mysterious coincidence, in what our narrator says. Then we are told:

From the appearance of the garage we understood that there had been a struggle, but he (Syvorotka) could not speak comprehensively; all we got from him were moanings, separate phrases and words like 'treason', 'run away', 'leave me die here', etc., etc., – he was decidedly raving and very weak. We helped him as best we could and came back to the city at about five in the morning and Philip went to Nachman's. They both reported that shortly after two o'clock, three of the trucks passed on the highway to Sysertsky Works. Some people were in them, and the Nachmans thought it was our affair, for the rumors had already reached them that the family had disappeared or had been executed. This Sysertsky direction is more or less correct for I know from Syvorotka that supplies were lately being sent continuously with him to Tubiuk. This way also went Syvorotka's woman.

S-y and all the rest left, – some people say in the evening, some early in the morning of the 17th.

Maybe something could be told by Syvorotka if he ever survives his wounds, and if the Reds do not find him and finish him before they leave, for he is under suspicion. He still is unconscious, and has fever. All Philip and I know is that either all our organization has failed to succeed, or we were all betrayed and sold, or that you intentionally detracted our attention from the truth.

This letter will be given to you by Mrs. Nachman who is going tonight to Ufa. As soon as the Reds leave Ekaterinburg we will both follow, – we are hiding now, – and will report on the facts that we witnessed and the rumors we heard.[19]

The 'Sysertsky direction' is not only the location of Medvedev's home but was where the Baroness B, and her compatriots were alleged to be going. The S-y mentioned here once again could have been the mysterious Sheremetevsky, who had been the Tsar's aide-de-camp and had married a Dehn, one of the relatives of Lily Dehn, who was also part of the group led by Anna Vyrubova and Soloviev. As noted previously, that a Sheremetevsky conveniently hid in the village of Koptiaki and just happened to draw the attention of the Czechs to the remains of the family in the woods as proof that they had been murdered has, in my view, always been suspect.

Was the Mrs Nachman who was 'going tonight to Ufa (the home of Nachman Steinberg)' with the report in her possession related to the accidental revolutionary Steinberg perhaps sent by Lenin to Ekaterinburg to work with Filipp Goloshchekin, reportedly the only Bolshevik in the Urals who did not want the family killed? Were they to assist in a plot to extricate the family and trade them to the Allies or Germany, and were they in the end as puzzled at the family's disappearance as everyone else?

The lingering question remains. With a house under observation, how could the Bolsheviks have shot and removed the bodies of at least eleven people without anyone observing the flurry of activity? That is unless the activity described in *Rescuing the Czar,* which was considerably less, commenced after the family had been extricated through a tunnel leading to the British Consul's house.

And all the recent evidence – the bribes and the payments through the Allied banking scheme – suggests that Lenin was holding the family as hostages for the purpose of bringing financial gain to his revolution. Is it conceivable that Nicholas's and Alexandra's cousins, King George V and Emperor Wilhelm, who was at that time frequently at cross purposes with his own General Staff, may have tired of the endless negotiations and failed exchange attempts? As a result, they may have surreptitiously agreed to remove Lenin's bargaining chips once and for all. With the assistance of a small number of high-level government and Church officials, in arranging for Charles James Fox to save the family, they may have turned the tables on Lenin. While this could at least be feasible it seemed there was probably more waiting to be found.

While the family's removal via a tunnel may have in the past sounded far-fetched, it now seemed to be a scenario that deserved to be examined further. I attempted to do just that.

I returned to the United States State Department records after reviewing the background of intrigue revealed by my research. Suddenly people and events that had at first seemed unrelated now appeared to be connected in a surprising fashion. Additional analysis of both old as well as some new files indicated that from June 1918 to the end of the year there was unusual movement of many United States and British diplomats. Their activities in China were intense, including negotiations for platinum in Russia at precisely the same time that not only British Consul Thomas Preston and American Consul Henry Palmer, but also Alexander Beloborodov and Chaya (Filipp) Goloshchekin were concentrating on the same issue.

On 12 June, the very day that Preston was wiring that the Bolsheviks were removing the gold and platinum from Ekaterinburg, another wire was sent from Shanghai to the U S State Department to the effect that the negotiations for the sale of Russian platinum were temporarily delayed.[20] Considering that *Rescuing the Czar* portrayed that Woosung was the destination of the escaping Romanovs, the knowledge possessed in Shanghai relative to gold and platinum, if these were indeed the code words for the Tsar and his family, is not surprising since Woosung, the family's destination, was just 12 miles from Shanghai.

However, that information about the status of the gold and platinum in Russia was being handled by Major Homer Slaughter's former West Point roommate is rather more surprising since Captain Cutrer had only recently been moved to Shanghai. Cutrer had come into Siberia with Slaughter and is the same man that Slaughter's wife enigmatically said in a letter to Slaughter's mother was to accompany Homer while he 'stands-in' for a Bolshevik.

There was also a State Department Special Agent, Charles Denby, in China who had been assigned from at least 13 June onward. He was communicating as well with United States naval intelligence to which he sent a cryptic message on 16 July. Denby was close to Wilson and in contact with Paul Reinsch, the American ambassador to China who had been hand-picked by Charles Crane.[21] Paul Reinsch, who had suddenly returned home in the summer of 1918, came back to China in September in the company of Crane.

They then both made an unexplained visit to Yokohama, Japan, at the end of September.[22]

Were they there to iron out last-minute hitches regarding the rescue mission? Why did Crane go on to China where the British representative, Sir John Jordan appears to have paved the way for him? Crane did not return from Shanghai until just before Christmas 1918.

John Crane, Charles's son, who served as the private secretary to Thomas Masaryk, stated in an unpublished manuscript that his father went on a 'secret mission' to China for President Wilson in the autumn and winter of 1918.[23] There seems to have been little else but the Romanov trek as described in *Rescuing the Czar* that would have placed Crane along the Yangtze river in the very places leading to Woosung at the same time as the book described as the route to freedom for the family. When we remember that Crane sent a gift to the Dalai Lama via Count Rostovstov and that Crane had been in the vicinity of the Bouriat Ataman Semenov forces in China where Soloviev also ended up, we must consider, even more carefully, his role in the entire Romanov affair. What else would have demanded the presence of this man in China, just one step ahead of the itinerary outlined in *Rescuing the Czar* in a country to which he was not yet accredited as an ambassador? Then – the startling series of telegrams beginning with one sent from Siberia by General William Graves on 29 December 1918:

TELEGRAM RECEIVED
PLAIN CODE
Department of State
December 29, 1918

Secretary of State
Washington

General Romanovsky has just informed me that he thinks Russians will have to abandon to family east of Baikal as it is impossible for them to do anything against family powers now here; that family will not permit them to use any force against Semenoff and at the same time will permit Semenoff to arrest Government railroad men and interfere with all their plans; that Russia will have to trust the United States to force family to carry out honestly their agreements or the matter will have to be settled when Russia gets a stable Government; that there is no use talking to family as Russians can put no dependence on what they tell them; that General Horvath the other influential Russian in the east is vacillating and will take no Decisive stand against the family. Following from Intelligence officer Verkneudinsk this date 'Representative Semenoff arrived here last night with soldiers and machine guns put all public officials under arrest and his own men in their places. Family withdrew guards which had been promised'. This supports Romanovsky statement that Semenoff allowed to do as he pleased without interference.[24]

Then came the rapid 'urgent' response.

> TELEGRAM RECEIVED GREEN
> FROM LONDON
> Dated Dec 30, 1918
> Recd, Jan 3, 1919, 4:16 pm.
> Secretary of State
> Washington.

Urgent.
Department's December 30, 6 pm. Through Paris. Near the end verify 'family' used seven times: family powers, the family, to force family, etc. Reply promptly. DAVIS.[25]

What tangled webs. The telegram originated on the 29th utilised the 'Plain code', which meant it contained a code within a code. The code used on the 30th, 'Special Green', was the highest ranking American code, used only for matters of greatest secrecy. 'Special' also indicates that when the message was deciphered, the resulting text would still conceal the true message that was being sent.

The next telegram in this series was written several weeks later:

> TELEGRAM SENT
>
> Department of State
> Washington
> 'Special'
> CIPHER
> January 20, 1919.
> AMEMBASSY (American Embassy)

PARIS – LONDON

Your/unnumbered/December/30th,/Word/QUOTE/
family/UNQUOTE/ is used/in/original (confidential) telegram/from/
General/Graves/apparently/to cover/reference to/Japan./
    Signed by: Polk
    Acting.[26]

Taken at face value, and substituting the word 'Japan' for 'Family',
in the 29 December telegram as Polk suggested, does not produce an
acceptable result, especially in the sentence ending with 'stand
against the family'. Although the decoded message might ostensibly
be about the Japanese, the hidden message is definitely not. On no
other occasion I could find, nor in any published codebooks did the
word Japan refer to 'family'. Besides, in the context of this message,
'family' would have to mean both Japan and Japanese. United States
codes invariably used different code words for the nominative and
the adjective, and the code word was drawn from the same root.
Thus, if the root for anything to do with Japan was 'family', the
word used for Japanese would be something like 'familial', or even
'familiar'. The same word would never be used for different
derivatives.

Furthermore, the text is contrived because of the frequent and
unusual use of the word 'family'. If this message was meant to be
taken at face value, then the pronouns 'their' and 'they' would seem
to make more sense.

The fact that Polk did not clearly understand the inference of the
telegram and that it took him almost three weeks to guess at the
meaning of 'family' in the telegram of 29 December is understandable since his position regarding Russian affairs was not one of
a man who was well informed. During the evolution of the two-track
policy regarding Russia and the banking scheme, his colleague
William Phillips, in the State Department, had expressed his
frustration about how he felt both he and Polk were being omitted
from the most important policy decisions:

. . . neither Polk nor I have seen it [regarding the policy to be adopted
in south Russia in the first half of 1918], although both of us are
handling the Russian situation. It is too absurd.[27]

As we have seen, the timing of the telegram to London is made significant by the presence there of Woodrow Wilson on the evening of 30 December and according to United States Secret Service agent Will Starling's diary, the very night the President and Mrs Wilson were dining at Buckingham Palace with the King and Queen.[28]

The operations regarding the fate of the Imperial family were a matter of the greatest concern to both men. By contrast, the obstructive activities of the Japanese and Ataman Semenov in far-off Siberia were hardly reasons for sending a telegram marked secret and urgent at the time the president and King George were together for an extended period of time. But the two leaders would need to know that the whole family had reached safety, and since there were seven members of the Romanov family – Nicholas, Alexandra, Olga, Tatiana, Maria, Anastasia and Alexei – the reference, 'Urgent, verify family seven times' gains more weight.

Throughout the research for this book, I have frequently encountered the same formats: small interconnected circles of people who knew and could trust each other absolutely, records that are missing and actions by these trusted few that would not pass through official channels, thus leaving little or no trace of what was done.

While some have dismissed *Rescuing the Czar* as fiction, designed to make money, the facts seem to keep colliding with this 'fiction'. The route sketched out based upon *Rescuing the Czar* to Turkistan, and on to Tibet under the guidance of representatives of the Dalai Lama, a route that ultimately ended in Chungking, China, where Fox handed over the family to the care of the British navy – an itinerary that does make sense.

Indeed, unaccountably, one of the Royal Navy gunboats captained by a Lieutenant Hall in the Far East in 1918 is missing its logs for this period.[29] There is no obvious reason for this disappearance: the war was over, none of the gunboats was sunk and China Station had been a remarkably quiet one. This, together with the presence in China of Charles Crane, Wilson's point man on a secret mission along the Yangtze seems more than peculiar.

That a Hall was commanding a gunboat has also continued to intrigue me since, as we saw in chapter 6, Jonas Lied said that he was invited to Admiral Hall's house to discuss the rescue of the Imperial family and Lied said Hall's daughter was present. In *Rescuing the Czar* the commander asked Charles James Fox if he would like to meet his sister, who shortly thereafter appeared at the door of the gunboat. Was this Hall related to Admiral Hall? To date the relationship remains unclear but the similarity of these two independent accounts is another striking coincidence.

As I continued to pursue other naval records for the China theatre, my attention was drawn to the logs of HMS *Kent*, the ship William Clarke's book identified as being one of the vessels later utilised to transport goods belonging to the Imperial family. The *Kent*, having been stationed in the Indian Ocean for most of 1918, was called out on 31 August 1918 for duty in China.

If one follows the chronology in *Rescuing the Czar*, it would be approximately at the time *Kent* was called out that Fox confided to his diary that what should have been a relatively short trip through the Trans-Caspian to Bombay and on across the peninsula (to Ceylon – present day Sri Lanka) had now, because of civil disobedience that had led to disturbances, prevented their journey to Bombay. As a consequence they were forced to go 'halfway around the world.' HMS *Kent* arrived in Singapore on 21 September 1918. It then left Singapore on 5 October and arrived in Hong Kong on 10 October, where it is noted to have carried out equipment trials until 20 December 1918. On 21 December it weighed anchor and sailed to Shanghai, arriving on Christmas Day 1918.

Four days later, on the very day that the telegram from General Graves using the code word 'family' seven times was sent to America, England, France and Rome, HMS *Kent* slipped up the coast to Woosung, a journey of only twelve miles from Shanghai, where it docked for one day. Strangely enough *Rescuing the Czar*'s presumed time line places the family in Woosung at almost exactly the same time.[30] *Kent* then sailed to Nagasaki, Japan, which it ultimately departed on 1 January 1919[31] for Vladivostok. Is it merely yet another coincidence that Charles James Fox noted that when the family arrived in Chungking and were turned over to the commander of the British gunboat, it was the holiday season? By all calculations it took approximately seven days to travel downriver from Chungking to Woosung, thereby indicating the family's arrival around Christmas.

Further, the records of HMS *Kent* show it was once again called to perform a special duty when it loaded twenty-nine cases of the Imperial family's personal goods some time prior to 15 March 1919. This mission was kept extremely quiet as the telegrams indicate:

Telegram: Blair, Vladivostok to WO Sent: 15:45 9.2.19
Rec'd.: 16.00 10.2.19 NR1042: Feb 9.

Following dated Feb. 5th received from General Knox. Some eight tons of personal belongings of the family are being sent down to Vladivostok. Some of these things are of national as well as material value . . . Admiral K. [Kolchak] said if possible he would like them for greater security to be placed on board the Kent.[32]

In the margin the following remark is written with a thick blue pencil:

No need to publish this. C. [Cumming, head of MI1c and the same man who paid Armitstead and Lied through the Hudson's Bay Company for work in Northern Russia some eight months earlier.][33]

Then follows from the King's secretary, Stamfordham:

From: Buckingham Palace, 8.3.19. [Handwritten note]
The King hopes that officer in command of HMS Kent will be instructed to keep these cases in safe custody as they may contain property of the utmost value to the Imperial Family.[34]

Soon after, the Commodore of *Kent* got instructions from London:

From: London [presumably Admiralty]
To: British Warship, Vladivostok
Date: 15th March, 1919

It is understood you have now twenty cases on board containing personal property late RUSSIAN IMPERIAL FAMILY. These should be retained by you in safe custody pending further instructions. 1746[35]

Then followed a reply:

From: Commodore HMS 'Kent', Vladivostok
To: Commodore, Hong Kong for Admiralty
Date: 21 March, 1919

31. For Admiralty. Following telegram received 15 March for London, [presumably Admiralty]: – (Begins) It is understood you have now 20 cases on board containing personal property of late

RUSSIAN IMPERIAL FAMILY. These should be retained by you in safe custody pending further instructions. 1746 (Ends}. These cases 29[sic?] in number have been received.[36]

And finally:

> From; HMS Kent at Vladivostok, 31 March, 1919.
> . . . Upon the application of General Dieterichs and the High Commissioner [most likely British Commissioner Miles Lampson] I consented to receive on board for safe custody 29 cases containing personal property of the late Imperial Family. It would appear it is desired that these cases should finally be deposited at the Russian Embassy in London, but Admiral Kolchak has on request consented to send a formal request stating what has ultimately to be done with the articles. This is not yet to hand but authority to hold the cases pending further instructions has been received from London. (See enclosure 1)[37]

Enclosure 1 was the previous response confirming the twenty-nine cases and not twenty that had been loaded aboard. According to the logbook of HMS *Kent* on 22 March, the ship discharged eight ratings (people) to S.S. *Penza* for passage to Hong Kong. And there is never any further mention of the twenty-nine cases of goods belonging to the Imperial family. William Clarke's book says these twenty-nine cases turned up in England much later.

Robert Wilton, who was being paid by the Foreign Office and who had had his infamous conversation with Joseph Lasies about the fate of the family, was told that the boxes contained only old pokers and junk. Wilton then spread the word that the boxes were just filled with dusty nonsensical trash. But somehow Clarke confused these twenty-nine cases with the hundred or so cases that were later shipped from the Crimea belonging to the Dowager Empress, Marie, Nicholas's mother, and her entourage.[38]

It still remains puzzling how eight tons of goods, pokers or not, could have been sent from Ekaterinburg after the Bolsheviks had at least seven days to ship the Imperial family's goods to another location. And it seems they would not have taken time, since they thought they were under siege, to stuff trash in boxes to be later found and shipped to England. Some local people did indeed loot the contents of the shed in the rear of the Ipatiev House but eight tons amounting to twenty-nine cases is an average weight of over 500 pounds per case. Far too heavy, one would have thought to have been carried off in a hurry. Even if the Whites had recaptured all the items belonging to the Imperial family, how were they discreetly taken out of Russia during these contentious times, unless someone in the Bolshevik hierarchy co-operated in their removal?

Only weeks after the HMS *Kent* telegram, telegram 111 dated 10 April 1919 'from Admiral Kolchak to Lieutenant General Dieterichs', ordered that the general be charged with the

> ... further inquiry into the effects and documents of the late Imperial Family, without in any way impeding the investigations now in process ... I authorise you to assemble the various articles in the passenger – and goods – wagons and the company kitchen under your command and to have a sentry on guard, but only within the war zone. If expenses are incurred in connection with the assembly and safe-keeping of the things, the accounts are to be presented to me.

The document is marked 'Secret'. Why this effort if HMS *Kent* had already secretly made its way out of Russia, less than three weeks before, with eight tons of the family's belongings? Why would Kolchak seemingly not know about the shipment of the initial twenty-nine cases that were secretly in transit in March? Unless the family had been taken out by the *Kent* in January and therefore the *Kent* had returned to collect their personal belongings.

One man who may have known the whole story relative to the Imperial family was Breckinridge Long. At the bottom left of the 'Family' telegram of 30 December are Long's initials. We have seen how involved he was in the attempt to save the family from the very beginning; he ran his own secret service, 'known only to the president'; he recruited Jerome Barker Landfield; he was responsible for looking after British Foreign Secretary Balfour as well as Prince Arthur of Connaught and for the secrecy surrounding his presence in the United States; he was in constant contact with Sir William Wiseman of British intelligence; he dealt with the political aspects of the negotiations over the loans to China and the Chinese Eastern Railway; he reported directly to the President and was the President's right-hand man when anything sensitive needed to be handled. Even when he was brought back by President Franklin Roosevelt during the Second World War, he was again made responsible for 'the safety of influential refugees'.

That this telegram should have been passed to him therefore comes as no surprise. He was probably the first man in the United States who would have needed to know what had happened to the family. Could Long, having been involved from the outset, be the man further to confirm that the rescue mission was a success? He may have done this on 17 and 18 January 1919. On the evening of the 17th Long met Mr Debuabi, a representative of the Japanese embassy. Debuabi followed up the next day with a hand-delivered letter to Long confirming that the 'seven points' enumerated in the memorandum handed by the American ambassador in Tokyo to Viscount Uchida on 9 January 'are well understood by the latter'.[39]

The letter, dated 18 January 1919; bore the letterhead of the Imperial Japanese embassy in Washington. In Long's handwriting he noted, 'Handed me by Mr. Debuabi of the Jap. Embassy. BL'. Yet, it was not stamped in until 13 February 1919. And it was finally filed on 13 April 1921.[40] Why was it filed two years and two months later? The significance of the letter may have been lost on his successor, as Long had resigned by then. The letter is supposed to have referred to the plan for supervision of the Chinese Eastern Railroad and the Trans-Siberian Railway. Breckinridge Long was shepherding the negotiations of the Chinese Eastern Railway in 1918 and 1919, thereby making its correspondence the perfect vehicle for messages regarding the seven members of the Romanov family.

So the 'family' telegram may have informed Breckinridge Long that the completed rescue had occurred as planned and that the family were in the hands of the Japanese. Polk's statement of 20 January 1919 that 'apparently' 'family' meant Japan may now be seen in a new light.

Returning again to the allegorical account in *Rescuing the Czar,* Fox said that he was to whisper the code word that would eventually pass to men in England, Berlin, Japan and Italy that he had been successful in the removal of the family. There is no doubt that the leaders of many other nations apparently unconnected to the plans concocted by Germany and the Allies to secure the release of the Romanovs were concerned for the safety of the family. Even the Vatican seems to have played a role. In *The Lost Fortune of the Tsars,* William Clarke reported that Alfonso XIII of Spain had sought help for the Imperial family from the Pope. Alfonso was married to a Battenberg princess who was a first cousin to Alexandra. When England's Queen Mary, King George's wife, urged Alfonso to help, he asked if George approved. She replied, 'George away, Telegram sent with knowledge of the Foreign Office'. On 6 August King Alfonso sent a letter to Princess Victoria, a sister of Alexandra's, that he had begun negotiations to save 'Empress and girls as Tsarevich think is dead'. Alfonso communicated with the Kaiser, and by the end of August 1918, he had received a promise of help from Berlin. Pope Benedict XV and the King of Denmark all supported Alfonso's efforts. The Pope's secretary of state, Cardinal Gaspari, committed that the Holy See was ready 'to provide, if needed, the finance of the lady's maintenance and proper style'.[41] The last known report seems to have been around 28 October 1918 and at that time it appeared that the hopes for the family's survival were dashed.[42]

Yet at this time in America, William G. McAdoo was to receive a cablegram from White General Tcherep Spiridovitch who was staying at the Savoy Hotel in London. The General's wire was of the utmost importance. For in it he said to McAdoo:

Having important state secret submit please order permission travel Washington.[43]

Later when the General was ill in 1921 in Bellevue Hospital in New York City, he listed Mr McAdoo as his 'best friend'. What state secret did he possess? What is interesting is that he had been a part of a contingent of Russian officers who had taken a death oath both to rescue and protect the Tsar and his family. Did he know that the final attempt to save them had been successful? Or was he vaguely aware that McAdoo was most likely to know about the 'state secret' as well? Unfortunately, his information never became of record for some dismissed Spiridovitch as a man of straw. Was he? Or was it the same state secret spoken of in *Rescuing the Czar*? Unfortunately he died a suspicious death when a gas oven supposedly leaked in his New York apartment in the 1920s at around the same time as Yaroshinsky was stabbed with a poison needle at the Paris Opera and Savinkov jumped out of the window in the Lubianka prison, where Sidney Reilly also disappeared shortly thereafter.

On 6 December another report that should be considered legitimate once again mirrored events in *Rescuing the Czar*. The report emanated from Charles Crane's friend Nelson Page, who was the American ambassador in Rome. Page wired the State Department:

> For your confidential information. I learned that in highest quarters here it is believed that the Czar and his family are all alive.

The timing is almost perfect for a message to have arrived in Italy, since if the family had been brought out in some fashion or another as *Rescuing the Czar* portrays, Charles James Fox says that the code word was 'to be repeated to one man at Berlin, to another man in England, another in Japan, and to a "dignitary in Italy".' Given Charles Crane's secret activities along the Yangtze, it might not have been difficult to send an initial message regarding the family in the first part of December once they had reached the vicinity of Chungking where they were to board a British gunboat. Then after the trip down river to rendezvous with HMS *Kent* which only weighed anchor in Woosung for one day on 29 December, the telegram confirming 'family seven times' could have been relayed to Vladivostok and on to Washington and London, to confirm their safe arrival. Hence, 'Urgent, confirm family seven times . . .'

Did the family really make it to Woosung as related in *Rescuing the Czar?* And did they sail away to a reasonably secure environment and new home in Ceylon, after the gunboat brought them to safety as *Rescuing the Czar* asserts? Was that the reason HMS *Kent* was called out of the Indian Ocean, during the war, merely to run sea trials just outside Hong Kong until it received the order to proceed to Woosung for only one day, then slip up the coast to Japan?

Perhaps we have not totally come full circle. Does the evidence indicate that the allegorical account told in *Rescuing the Czar* demonstrates that the Imperial family could have been brought to safety out of Russia by a small international team? There is certainly intriguing evidence to support it. Even if *Rescuing the Czar* does not hold all the answers, it does stand as a roadblock to complete acceptance of the traditional view of the night of 17 July 1918.

If nothing else, *Rescuing the Czar* may be the Rosetta Stone that has given us a glimpse into the world of intelligence activity and secret diplomacy that sometimes shapes the destinies of nations. In this case, the impact on Russia of this activity remains unclear. Still it is interesting to note that three men, who decades later would be the leaders of their countries, played significant roles in their respective governments in 1918 – Churchill, Director of Munitions; Stalin, one of Lenin's most able administrators; and Franklin Delano Roosevelt as Under-Secretary of Navy for the United States – and each was connected to events in Russia during this time-frame.

In the paperback edition of *The File on the Tsar,* Summers and Mangold note that:

> Pressed on the matter (of the Romanovs' fate) in the House of Lords, Lord Goronwy-Roberts made two curious remarks. Asked whether he was absolutely satisfied that three daughters of the Tsar are not still alive, he replied: 'No. Nor do I think anybody else is absolutely satisfied about that.' He also suggested that this book, 'The File on the Tsar', be placed with official material on the case in the Public Record Office.

How many other members of the House of Parliament shared his opinion remains unknown. But in America there was one man who also gave indications he too was not satisfied.

President Roosevelt piqued my interest, when I learned that in the 1930s he had told an aide that he had a mystery story whose ending he could not solve and that he had wanted to write for years but had never had time to undertake the task. His aide responded that if the President would share his storyline with him he would engage six writers to work out the ending for the President. The aide subsequently invited the best mystery writers in America to take part and commissioned them to contribute to a book called, *The President's Mystery Story.* Roosevelt provided them with the beginnings of a tale about a Russian man who was wealthy, well-known and wanted to disappear with enough of his fortune to live on, but be perceived as dead. His story's character seemed to mirror that of the Tsar. The President appeared genuinely intrigued by the thought that a man could die but continue to live and he wanted the writers to explain what would happen to a man who falsified his own death. Why would Roosevelt have conjured up such a yarn unless he was puzzling over something about which he had some first-hand knowledge but had lost the track?

Under what circumstances did the family vanish and who was responsible for their disappearance? At the present not one of the explanations examined in this book, including the recent DNA analysis, can categorically be stated as the entirely conclusive account of the disappearance of the Romanovs. But what can be asserted with certainty is that the true historical account has yet to be completely constructed.

What seems feasible is that the Allies did indeed work diligently to construct a method of funding anti-Bolshevik activities through the secret banking scheme established under Major Terence Keyes in Siberia, with the objective of overthrowing the Bolsheviks and potentially re-establishing a constitutional monarchy. Moreover the very men who were central to these efforts – Karol Yaroshinsky, Boris Soloviev and Sidney Reilly were all connected, at a time when Yaroshinsky was the financial benefactor to the family during the last days of their captivity in Tobolsk and Ekaterinburg. These men were also involved with Henry Armitstead and Jonas Lied, who had been paid through the British Secret Service for activities in Northern Russia that included building a house that appears to have been for the Tsar, which was stocked with supplies in increments of seven. This trail also led to the failed April and June attempts to gain the freedom of the family after what seems to have been a ransom paid to Lenin for their release. At the same time the Germans also appear to have engaged in their own bidding war for the Romanov family. Further, the story told by the Parfen Domnin document regarding the planned overthrows and the Czech Legion's attempt to advance on Ekaterinburg also has more than a ring of truth.

But did the family survive? Did one of the factions succeed in taking control of the family and were they taken to Lysva as the symbols found on the wall, in addition to the symbol of the Brotherhood of St John of Tobolsk (see plate section) would indicate? Did they subsequently meet their fate in the Perm/Lysva area, where in 1919 some obscure Bolsheviks were accused of the murder of the Imperial family and were summarily executed? We know practically nothing about this episode and therefore cannot adequately weigh it, as the event quickly and with little investigation disappeared from the pages of history.

Or did the family actually disappear by being evacuated through the tunnel and escape for a time via the route in *Rescuing the Czar*?

If they did, one thing is certain, the sightings all but dry up by the 1930s. The long arm of the communist red terror, as we have seen, very effectively hunted down and destroyed its enemies if it could locate them. For this reason the British Secret Service kept the identitites of its intelligence operatives in Russia sealed for years for fear that a brutal death would await them if they could be found. Would not the authorities have had no less, but even more concern for the Romanovs?

What can categorically be stated to have come from this research has been the deconstruction of the notion that King George V and his close allies did nothing to try to save the Tsar and his family. It is now also certain that they made attempts, albeit unsuccessful ones, to overthrow the Bolsheviks and give Russia the breathing space it deserved to determine whether it wanted a return to Tsardom in the form of a constitutional monarchy.

The real story of the Romanovs' fate remains tied up in the heretofore unknown machinations of the people and situations that seem to have collided on that summer night in 1918 in Siberia. That more of the real story can be pieced together has been the purpose of this book and my hope is that more information will come forward after the publication of this work that will continue to shed light on this mysterious chapter of twentieth-century history. It may be too much to hope that the respective governments and churches will aid in completing the picture. It may, of course, be impossible for their current leaders to come forward, for there is a chance they really do not know about the Romanovs' state secret because, in fact, the knowledge of its true outcome may have died with their predecessors.

Epilogue

Charles Crane continued to work for the Democratic party and remained close to Woodrow Wilson. His philanthropic endeavours were immense. When the greatly esteemed British historian, Bernard Pares, wrote *A History of Russia* in 1928 he dedicated his work to 'The Honourable Charles R. Crane' and called him 'The Unfailing Friend of Russia'. But Crane was destined never to receive the recognition he so deserved and he became merely a footnote to history.

Count Rostovstov spent some time in a Bolshevik prison. Charles Crane eventually learned that Maroussia, Count Rostovstov's wife had not died. Charles Crane and his son John visited the Count for the last time in 1921 when Crane had just completed his tour of duty as ambassador to China. Just after Crane left Russia, many of those whom he had visited were shot. While Count Rostovstov was not shot as a result of Crane's visit he, like Crane, became obscure. He is never mentioned in any of the books that the Baroness Buxhoeveden wrote describing the life and times of the Tsarina, even though he was Alexandra's financial secretary and obviously close to her and the family. However, the Baroness did mention him in a letter in 1936 when she wrote, 'Rostovstov is dead.'

Pavel Bulygin, whom the Dowager Empress sent to assist Nicholas Sokolov in his investigation about the family, attempted to publish a book regarding his Ekaterinburg experience. His papers in the Shinkarenko Collection at the Hoover Institute at Stanford University indicate he blamed Kerensky and Miliukov (Charles

Crane's close friend) for 'attempting to stop the publication of the book' (his book) in the early twenties. Yet in 1935 he finally brought out his book in tandem with Kerensky, although many intriguing items that were first mentioned in his earlier outline never found their way into his final manuscript. Bulygin speaks of Baronovsky (the man in the Romanovsky household in San Francisco in 1920) and Krivoshein (the man who brought Yaroshinsky into the Allied banking scheme) in his notes but they are curiously absent in any depth in his later book. He attempts to blame Boris Soloviev for some role in the death of the family but is told by Semenov that Soloviev is innocent. In Bulygin's book he says Soloviev then left for Shanghai where it is said he purchased tickets for the daughters of the Imperial family. Also, Soloviev was said to be in possession of a money voucher to be paid by the Russo-Asiatic Bank – the bank that was later at the base of a dispute involving members of the banking scheme and the East China Railroad, as well as some American government officials.

There is no record of what became of the **Brotherhood of St John of Tobolsk**. Marina Grey, the author and daughter of General Denikin (later Sir Anton Denikin), under whom the Romanov execution investigation fell, states firmly that she believes Soloviev was purposefully discredited by Sokolov and Bulygin.

Homer Slaughter returned to the United States and was promoted to the General Staff. He later taught at West Point Military Academy. According to his son, he became visibly disturbed at the mention of the name Nicholas Sokolov.

Carl Ackerman sought to book passage to India the second week in January 1919, at the same time as Breckinridge Long indicated that the seven points had been turned over to the Japanese Ambassador, but could not find an available ticket until March. We do not know his reason for seeking to go to India as the first two sheets of the three-page correspondence are missing from his papers. We also do not know if he ever made his way to India. But what we do know is that he was involved in the negotiations regarding the partitioning of Ireland when he acted as intermediary between Lloyd George and Eamon De Valera in what appears to have been his final quasi-governmental assignment. In his article, 'The Irish Education of Lloyd George, he enigmatically stated that during the course of his assignment he had sought the advice of an internationally known figure whom he could not name. He subsequently became the head of the School of Journalism at Columbia University.

Colonel Ralph Van Deman was charged late fees by the Library of Congress for keeping out a book on 'Punjabi Grammar', which he had checked out in April of 1918, prior to his secret mission in Europe. Later he was promoted to general and came to be called the 'Father of US Intelligence'. In the early 1920s he and Colonel Wigham (the man who removed the Prince Arthur of Connaught file pertaining to July 1918) travelled to India together.

Karol Yaroshinsky died in near poverty in 1928, after giving away the remainder of his fortune to found Lublin University, the largest Jesuit university in Poland. His last years were spent in pain as a result of a poison needle having been jabbed into him at the opera in Paris at almost the same time as Sidney Reilly disappeared in the Soviet Union. There were also attempts to discredit him but at his funeral, almost as if from nowhere, nearly a thousand people appeared to honour him. But there was no widow among them – he never married. According to his family, before the Revolution he had fallen in love with one of the Tsar's daughters, a feeling which seemed to have been unrequited. But nevertheless his role in the final months of the family's confinement was of paramount significance.[1]

Sidney Reilly is supposed to have died in the Lubianka prison in Moscow in 1925. When the diary he kept in prison was released, numerous names that had been associated with the last days of the Romanovs were all clustered together as if to indicate that he had been interrogated about them in the same session. Interestingly, the name Kolvalsky appears and it was a Kolvalsky to whom Charles James Fox of *Rescuing the Czar* said he was reporting while on his mission. I located a Vladimir Ivanovich Kolvalsky who proved to be a colleague of Count Rostovstov's when they were both serving as state councillors.[2] Reilly also noted the names Voikov and Kobylinsky, both of whom were with the family in exile in Tobolsk. Additionally he spoke of Abaza.

This Abaza was almost certainly the same man who finally decoded the famous Sokolov telegram stating 'officially the family will die during evacuation'. Reilly had gone to Russia to look for his associate and friend, 'the Doctor' Savinkov, who had been lured back to the Soviet Union through a Bolshevik device called 'The Trust', which was designed to snare past leaders and either 'turn' them or kill them. As mentioned before, Savinkov had been in league with Reilly in the summer of 1918 and had helped plan and instigate the uprisings in July of that same year. Savinkov supposedly was rehabilitated by the Bolshevik leadership, but then became depressed and killed himself, much like Charles Crane's former son-in-law, Jan Masaryk, is supposed to have done by jumping out of a window as the Communists invaded Czechoslovakia three decades later.

'**Charles Fox**' seems to have existed only as a code name listed in 1919 in the Bureau of Investigation and military intelligence files as the code name for the head of the British Secret Service in America. He is alternatively called C. M. James or Captain A.W. James:[3] 'Captain A.W. James. It is the understanding of the Bureau that this individual is head of the British Secret Service force in the United States, that he has assumed the alias of Charles Fox, and receives reports from his various operatives, at Box 1232, City Hall Station, New York City.'

Could it be that after his mission he was sent on to America to head up British intelligence agents in the United States? There are indications that Captain James was a British passport control officer and unfortunately the files of these men, even today, remain closed. One day if the records of British passport control officers are made available, we may finally learn enough to determine whether he was the real Charles James Fox and if there was actually a man who played a role in the lives of the Romanovs that resembled the story told in *Rescuing the Czar*. Another Charles James Fox, an American newspaper man lived in Tientsin, China in 1918 and was friendly with Carl Ackerman but there is no evidence that he was in Siberia in July 1918, nor that he spoke Russian.

Anna Vyrubova became a nun and wrote about her days with the Imperial family. She maintained that one day she received a card from a woman who surreptitiously placed it in her hand. She said the woman indicated it was from someone she loved and the person wanted her to know that all was well. She said it looked like a much older picture of the Tsarina, but for fear of reprisal she did not act on the information. At the time Anna was still in the Soviet Union.

Baroness Buxhoeveden finally got out of Russia in 1919. In the United States there is a visa listing for her in the index of the 811.111 files[4], but no file remains of record. The Baroness was the only significant participant in the Ekaterinburg drama who refused to be interviewed by Nicholas Sokolov regarding the family's disappearance. She lived the remainder of her life with the royal family of England. After her voluntary exile with the family she was not allowed into the Ipatiev House. Her activities in Russia after that are unclear. She wrote a heartfelt book about Alexandra Feodorovna entitled, *The Life and Tragedy of Alexandra Feodorovna, Empress of Russia, A Biography*. It attempted to dispel much of the rumour and innuendo surrounding her. The final lines of Baroness Buxhoeveden's book are the Tsarina's last diary entry and then she says: 'The final curtain falls on the life of a great and noble character – a woman whose love for her husband and his country and whose trust in the mercy of God were stronger than fear of death.'

Then she adds an enigmatic line: 'Three hours later the dark tragedy of Ekaterinburg *is believed to have occurred . . .* ' (author's italics).

Appendix

DNA testing, while supposedly irrefutable evidence, can in fact be considerably flawed. Far from proving the identity of the putative Romanov bones, it raises further questions. To comprehend why DNA has its limitations it is necessary to understand the basics of human genetics and the complicated, somewhat mysterious technique of 'identifying' a given human being from a DNA profile.[1]

The process of DNA analysis can be conducted using either nuclear or mitochondrial DNA. Generally, nuclear DNA testing is more discriminating but more time-consuming; it characterises DNA fragments by their size, sequence, or both. It also requires a larger and fresher evidence sample from which to extract a relatively large amount of DNA. Mitochondrial DNA (mtDNA) compares fewer genetic loci, and mtDNA testing is inherently less discriminating than nuclear DNA.[2] It is, however, a powerful tool for exploring what is called maternal relatedness. Unlike nuclear DNA, the mother contributes all mitochondrial DNA. So a given individual should have the same mtDNA as his/her mother, as his/her full siblings, as his/her mother's mother and so on, all the way back through the maternal lineage. The mitochondrial identity is also effective 'sideways': maternal aunts and their children, as well as all their maternal ancestors and descendants, should have the same mtDNA.

This very basic overview is sufficient to introduce the first problem with the Romanov DNA testing: the putative Romanov remains were subjected to mtDNA testing. Dr William Shields, genetics expert at the State University of New York in Syracuse, New York, remains sceptical of the use of mitochondrial DNA testing to establish identity, continually arguing that the high incidence of random matches may be enough to warrant extreme caution in concluding identity on the basis of a match:

> The problem is not only that mtDNA typing uses a very small fraction of an individual's DNA, but even within this small fragment, there is a limited amount of variation between individuals. Of the more than 600 base pairs in a typical mtDNA sample, only about 100 of them exhibit any variation. It is easy to see that if only 100 of the sites vary, and there are only four possibilities for each of them (C, T, A, G), you have a finite number of possible combinations. When you look at the few databases produced (I think there are approximately thirteen hundred individuals among ethnic groups where the sequences have been produced to the degree where they can be used in a database), the possibilities are even more finite than expected. For example, in the original FSS database (in Great Britain) four out of the 100 individuals are identical to each other. They are not relatives in any way, at least not in any immediate sense. In addition, there are a couple of additional instances in which two different unrelated individuals are identical. Overall what I have discovered by analyzing the available databases is that about 30% of the individuals in a database match at least one other person at every base in the tested sequence.[3]

While Dr Shields's findings may be controversial, he feels confident that they are accurate.

It is not entirely clear which local population one would ideally want to check to establish such incidence of random matches for the Tsarina. As early as 1993, Dr William Maples noted that the relevant population should be German, since both Alexandra's and Philip's ancestors were German. Moreover, the high rate of inter-marriage between the royal houses of Europe prior to World War One would obviously introduce further uncertainties and deviations into the equation. Dr Shields found it curious that the Forensic Science Service (FSS) laboratory at Aldermaston in England did not double check the match between Alexandra and Prince Philip by matching her 'daughters' to him as well (the mtDNA should be identical for all of them).

The United States Armed Forces DNA Identification Laboratory (AFDIL) had in fact been contracted to supplement tests conducted by the British Home Office's FSS laboratory in 1993. Working with Russian DNA expert Pavel Ivanov, Dr Peter Gill and the FSS team had first used nuclear DNA testing to explore the familial relation among the remains (and so to sort out those belonging to the Romanovs' doctor and others reportedly killed and buried with the family in 1918).

They then matched the mitochondrial DNA of the presumed Tsarina to that of a living maternal relative, Prince Philip. Yet a similar attempt to match the DNA of the presumed Tsar to two maternal relatives provided mixed results. At one genetic position the Tsar's DNA exhibited a perplexing result: it contained both thymine and cytosine bases. Normally, only one base is present at a given position. Some scientists, including the respected American forensic anthropologist Dr William Maples, charged that the results indicated the tests' sample had been contaminated.

Gill's team, however, concluded that the Tsar exhibited what was then thought to be a rare condition called 'heteroplasmy', in which a person can carry more than one mitochondrial DNA sequence. Seeking to quell the ongoing controversy over the authenticity of the remains, the Russian government authorised the exhumation of the Tsar's brother, Grand Duke George, in 1994. The United States AFDIL team, led by Lieutenant Colonel Victor Weedn and Ivanov, was able to show that a sample purported to be from George exhibited a heteroplasmic condition at the same position.

This result was cause for a double celebration: it turned heteroplasmy, usually a grave liability for DNA forensic analysis, into an asset and used it to help establish identity. With the earlier results that supported familial relation the AFDIL tests seemed to put to rest further questions about the remains of the five Romanovs. (A fourth daughter and the Tsarevich Alexei were missing, reputedly because their bodies had been burned to ash in 1918.) 'Beyond any reasonable doubt,' declared Ivanov at the 1995 press conference, 'the remains are those of the Tsar Nicholas and his family.' However, based upon the fact that mtDNA only establishes a maternal link, the heteroplasmy simply proved a maternal link that, as we have seen, many members of the population may have shared, particularly any maternal relatives of the Romanovs. Dr Shields further pointed out that the fact that the heteroplasmy showed up as C greater than T in one set of the purported fraternal bones and T greater than C in the other set does not rule out the possibility that the sample might have come from the same person, both samples from 'Nicholas' or both samples from George could have exhibited either combination.

Some supposed Romanov remains were in fact submitted to an additional test conducted by Dr Erika Hagelberg at Cambridge University in Britain. It simply confirmed the heteroplasmic anomalies found by the FSS.

So the problem remains: the raw data from other tests conducted over the years has yet to be released to the Russian Expert Commission Abroad, even though they have repeatedly requested it. They want to submit the results to the scrutiny of what they consider to be a truly independent commission. Until such time, the results must be deemed inconclusive.

Characters

Ackerman, Carl – American Journalist for *The New York Times* and Saturday Evening Post, intelligence courier

Alexandra – the Tsarina, wife of Nicholas II

Alexeev – White Army General

Alexei – the heir apparent

Archangel – town in Northern Russia

Armitstead, Henry – Hudson's Bay employee in charge of constructing house in Murmansk, operated out of Archangel, member of Trade Mission in June

Baggage – the Romanov family

Balfour, Arthur – British Foreign Secretary

Beloborodov, Alexander – Chairman of the Ural Regional Soviet

Bolsheviks – members of the radical left party led initially by Lenin, also known as Reds, later as communists

Botkin, Dr. Eugene – the Tsar's physician, imprisoned with the Imperial family

Boyle, Joe – Canadian, in charge of a sanitary train used to take the Romanian Royal family out of the reach of the Germans

Brest-Litovsk Treaty of, 3 March 1918 – the treaty that ended the hostilities between the Bolshevik Government and Germany

Buchanan, Sir George – British Ambassador in Petrograd

Bulygin, Captain Pavel – former Palace guard, sent by the Dowager Empress to investigate the disappearance of the Imperial family in Ekaterinburg

Bykov, Pavel M. – Bolshevik Russian Historian, Author of *The Last Days of the Romanovs*

Cheka – Secret Police of the Bolshevik Government

Chemodurov, Terenty – the Tsar's manservant and perhaps Parfen Domnin

Connaught, Prince Arthur – Cousin of King George V, Nicholas II, and the Tsarina, called back by King George V to go on a special mission to Japan in May 1918

Crane, Charles – Multimillionaire Industrialist, President of Crane Plumbing, friend and foremost advisor to President Wilson on Russia

Crane, Frances Leatherbee – daughter of Charles Crane, married Jan Masaryk, son of Thomas Masaryk, first president of Czechoslovakia

Crane, John – son of Charles Crane, Private Secretary to Thomas Masaryk

Crane, Richard Teller – son of Charles Crane, Secretary to the American Secretary of State, Robert Lansing, Later, United States' first Ambassador to the new Czechoslovak Republic

Dalai Lama – Spiritual Leader of the Tibetan people

Dashy-Simpiton – one of the leaders of the Buriat (Buryat) National Committee

Davis, John – American ambassador in London

Demidova, Anna – the family's chambermaid, imprisoned with the Imperial family

Diterikhs, General – Russian, commander of the Czechs advancing from Vladivostok

Dolgorukov, Prince Alexander – Russian Monarchist who was close to the family

Domnin, Parfen – the alleged Tsar's valet, most likely Terenty Chemodurov, the known manservant to the Tsar

Dowager Empress Marie – the Tsar's Mother

Duke of Leuchtenberg – maintained that some members of the Imperial family survived, (one time Aide de Camp to the Emperor)

Ekaterinburg, Siberia (in the Ural Mountains) –final place of imprisonment of the Imperial family

Eliot, Sir Charles – British High Commissioner for Siberia

ELOPE – a British Force sent to Northern Russia

Ermakov, Peter – Military Commissar of the Upper-Isetsk near Ekaterinburg

Fox, Charles James – An agent who claimed to be an American and who allegedly wrote one of the two diaries contained in '*Rescuing the Czar*'

Francis, David – American ambassador to Russia, hand picked by Charles Crane

Goloshchekin, Filipp – Regional Commissar for War in the Ural

Grand Duchesses Olga, Tatiana, Maria and Anastasia – the daughters of the Tsar and Tsarina

Grand Duke Michael – the Tsar's brother

Greene, Sir Conyngham – British Ambassador in Japan

Groves, Major William Peer – British Intelligence Officer, Royal Air Force, who maintained to his children that the family escaped to Japan

Hesse, Grand Duke of – the Tsarina's brother

House, Colonel Edward – Special Advisor to President Wilson, de facto Secretary of State

Ipatiev House – the final place of imprisonment of the Imperial family, also called the House of Special Purpose

Kaiser – Wilhelm II of Germany, Nicholas and Alexandra's first cousin

Kerensky, Alexander – minister of Justice in the Provisional Government, later its Head

Keyes, Terence, Colonel – one of the original members of the banking scheme

King George V – the King of England, first cousin of Nicholas and Alexandra

Kobylinsky, Eugene, Colonial – in charge of the family in Tsarskoe Selo and later in Tobolsk

Kolchak, Admiral Alexander – Head of the White Army, proclaimed himself as the Supreme Ruler of all the Russias caught and executed by the Bolsheviks in January 1920

Koptiaki – village and forest near Ekaterinburg where the putative remains of the Romanovs were found

Landfield, Jerome Barker – married Princess Lobanoff-Rostovsky, American fluent in Russian, attended graduate school in Petrograd, first American to own mining claims in the Ural Mountains, and first to cover the Urals on a horse to map the mountains, explored Siberia, urgently called into service upon arrival of Prince Connaught in America in May, 1918 by Breckinridge Long, Third Under Secretary of State

Lansing, Robert – United States Secretary of State

Lasies, Joseph – French Officer, Deputy and Journalist, visited Ekaterinburg in early 1919 and did not believe the Imperial family had been murdered the 'way it was described'

Leech, Hugh – one of the original members of the banking scheme

Lied, Jonas – Norwegian businessman in Siberia who was approached by British Intelligence to work on a plot to rescue the Imperial family and was paid through the Hudson's Bay Company by Henry Armitstead

Lindley, Francis, Sir – British Charge d'Affaires in Russia and original member of banking scheme

Lloyd George, David, Prime Minister – Leader of the Coalition Government in Britain

Long, Breckinridge – Third Under Secretary of State, Colonel House stated Breckenridge Long ran his own State Department known only to the President, Long served as a courier between Colonel House and President Wilson

Lord Reading – British Ambassador to the United States

Masaryk, Jan – son of Thomas Masaryk, Minister of Foreign Affairs

Masaryk, Thomas – Leader of the National Movement to free the old Kingdom of Bohemia from the Austro-Hungarian Empire, close friend of Charles Crane, first president of Czechoslovakia

McAdoo, William G. – Woodrow Wilson's son-in-law, Head of the Treasury Department during WWI, to which the American Secret Service reported

McGarry, William Rutledge – American Agent also employed by the British Government for war propaganda films, author of *From Berlin to Baghdad*, one of the compilers of *Rescuing the Czar*

McNab, Gavin – Lawyer in San Francisco, in charge of Wilson's re-election Campaign in the West, host of Prince Arthur of Connaught and the Romanian Royal family

Medvedev, Pavel Spiridonovitch – guard at the Ipatiev House

Miliukov, Paul – Foreign Minister of the Provisional Government

Murmansk – town in Northern Russia close to the Artic Circle, the town Nicholas wanted to go to after his abdication

Nicholas II – the last Tsar of Russia

Polk, William – Acting Secretary of State

Poole, Major-General Sir Frederick – British Commander of the Allied Forces in North Russia

Preston, Thomas – British Consul in Ekaterinburg

Prince Lvov – Head of the first Provisional Government, replaced by Kerensky

Provisional Government – the first government that came to power after the February Revolution of 1917 and the Tsar's abdication

Radek, Karl – Bolshevik leader who had returned to Russia from Sweden with Lenin influential in Soviet Foreign Policy

Rasputin – the peasant monk who held sway over the Imperial household because of his enigmatic ability to cure the illness of the heir apparent

Reilly, Sidney – sometimes known as the 'Ace of Spies' – British intelligence operative who was born in Russia

Rescuing the Czar – book printed in July 1920 portraying survival of the Imperial family

Revolution of February 1917 – forced the Tsar's abdication

Robins, Raymond – American Red Cross official also known as 'Redbreast'

Romanovsky, George Sergeyevich, – Russian Consul in San Francisco and one of the 'compliers and translators' of *Rescuing the Czar*'

Rostovstov, Count James – the Tsarina's Personal Secretary, handled the family's finances and close friend of Charles Crane

Savinkov, Boris – Social Revolutionary leader of failed July uprising 'the doctor' and close friend of Sidney Reilly

Schiff, Jacob – Financier Partner of the House of Kuhn and Loeb Banking Institution

Sergeyev, Judge Ivan – one of the investigators of the disappearance of the Imperial family

Slaughter, Major Homer – an attaché to be assigned to Romania but was assigned to Ekaterinburg in 1918, later filed intelligence report regarding Parfen Domnin

Smythe, James P. – Pseudonym of the 'authors' of *Rescuing the Czar*

Sokolov, Judge N.A. – official investigator of the murder of the Imperial family assigned by the White Army

Soloviev, Boris – head of the Brotherhood of St. John of Tobolsk and Yaroshinsky's assistant

Stalin – Successor to Lenin as head of the Soviet Union

Sussanin, Ivan – rescued and created a false death for the first Romanov, of the Romanov line when he was in danger

Sverdlov, Yakov – Chairman of the Central Committee and in charge of the family in their final days in Ekaterinburg

SYREN – a British Force assigned to Northern Russia

Tobolsk, Siberia – the second place of imprisonment of the Imperial family

Tredwell, Roger – American Consul operating out of St. Petersburg, Moscow and Tashkent

Trotsky, Leon – Minister of War for the Bolshevik Government, founded the Red Army

Tsarskoe Selo – the palace where the Imperial family were first placed under house arrest

Urquhart, Leslie – businessman in Siberia who was a member of the June Trade Mission with Henry Armitstead

von Mirbach, Count Wilhelm – German Ambassador in Moscow, murdered in early July 1918.

Voska, Emanuel – Czech Agent who organized intricate spy organization operating in US, Russia, and Europe

Vyrubova, Anna – close friend of the family who was working with the Brotherhood of St. John of Tobolsk

White, Samuel – go-between for William Rutledge McGarry and McAdoo on a 'matter of great importance for the nation'

Wilson, Woodrow – President of the United States in 1918

Wilton, Robert – Journalist for *The Times* in London, Intelligence Operative

Wiseman, Sir William – Head of the British Secret Intelligence Service MI1c in the United States

Yakovlev, Vassily Vassilievitch – Commander under Lenin's Government, assigned to remove the Imperial family from Tobolsk to 'Moscow or wherever'

Yaroshinsky, Karol – Russia's point man on the banking scheme, friend and benefactor of the Imperial family

Yeltsin, President Boris – First Secretary of the Region Committee of the Communist Party and later President of Russia

Yurovsky – Head of the team who purportedly murdered the Imperial family, supposed author of the infamous 1920 'Yurovsky Note'

Yusupov, Felix – leader of the plot to successfully murder Rasputin

Bibliography

Primary Sources

The U.S. Department of State Papers Relating to the Foreign Relations of the United States 1917, Supplement 2, The World War, Volume I, Washington, D.C., United States Government Printing Office, 1932

The U.S. Department of State Papers Relating to the Foreign Relations of the United States 1918, Washington, D.C., United States Government Printing Office, 1930

The U.S. Department of State Papers Relating to the Foreign Relations of the United States 1918, Supplement 1, The World War, Volume II, Washington, D.C., United States Government Printing Office, 1933

The U.S. Department of State Papers Relating to the Foreign Relations of the United States 1918, Supplement 2, The World War, Washington, D.C., United States Government Printing Office 1933

The U.S. Department of State Papers Relating to the Foreign Relations of the United States 1919, Volume II, Washington, D.C., Supplement United States Government Printing Office, 1934

The U.S. Department of State Papers Relating to the Foreign Relations of the United States 1920, Volume I, Washington, D.C., United States Government Printing Office, 1935

The U.S. Department of State Papers Relating to the Foreign Relations of the United States 1920, Volume II, Washington, D.C., United States Government Printing Office, 1936

The U.S. Department of State Papers Relating to the Foreign Relations of the United States 1921, Volume II,

Washington, D.C., United States Government Printing Office, 1936

The Kaiser's Secret Negotiations with the Tsar, The American Historical Review, Volume XXIV, October 1918 to July 1919, London, Macmillan and Co. Ltd.

Order of Battle of the United States Land Forces in the World War: American Expeditionary Forces: General Headquarters, Armies, Army Corps., Services of Supply and Separate Forces, Volume I, Center of Military History, United States Army, Washington, D.C., 1988

India Office File, Russian Banks, NSS EUR file 131/21 Affidavit of Colonel Terence Keyes, *Russian Banks*, 5/3/1928

3 March, 1918: The Peace Treaty of Brest-Litovsk, World War I Document Archive, ttp://www.lib.byu.edu/~rdh/wwi/1918/brestlitovsk.html

Germany and the Russian Revolution in Russia, 1915 – 1918, Document 71, p. 70, The State Secretary to the Foreign Ministry Liaison Officer at General Headquarters, telegram 1610, A5 3640, 29 September 1917

Testimony of Crown Princess Cecile of Prussia – Germany, Court Record of Anderson v. Duchess Christian Ludwig of Mecklenburg, Hamburg Court of Appeal, Volume XXIV, p. 4696; Prince Ferdinand of Schoenaich Carolath, Volume XXXI, p. 5826; Prince Dmitri Galitzin, Volume XXXVII, p. 6955; Princess of Thurn and Taxis, Volume XVIII, p. 3658; Baroness Marie Pilar von Pilchau, Volume VII, p. 299; Colonel Dmitri von Lar-Larsky, Volume I, p. 186; Fritz von Unruh, Volume XX, p. 3932

Admiralty, London to British Commander in Chief, Mediterranean, 1 November 1918, 103z, Broadlands Archives

Archives of the Central Committee at the Kremlin, Dossier – 'The Peace of Brest-Litovsk,' Series 75, Folder 1

Army Officers War Records of Deaths, 1914–1921, Death Certificate File SA054008, Application PSR B 002746

German Foreign Office Draft, A. S. 1356 & A.S. 27476

United States National Archives – USNA

USNA, Record Group (hereinafter referred to as RG) 59, file 861.77/611a

USNA, RG 165, Office Chief of Staff, Military Intelligence, War Department, file 9728–469–38

USNA, RG 165, Office Chief of Staff, Executive Division, Military Intelligence Division, War Department, file 164-39

USNA, RG 59, file 124.543/51a, 14 August 1917

USNA, RG 165, Office Chief of Staff, Executive Division, Military Intelligence Division, War Department, file 2355–339–1, 17 February 1918

USNA, RG 59, file 103.93/335, 9 May 1918

USNA, Quartermaster Corps, Form 928, 20 May 1918–7 July 1918

USNA, RG 59, file 861.6343/45, 12 June 1918

USNA, RG 59, file 103.96/880, 16 July 1918

USNA, Microfilm Publications M587, List of US Consular Officers, 1789–1939, Roll 19, 24 July 1918

USNA, RG 165, file 184-96.1, 24 July 1918

USNA, RG 59, file 861.6343/60, 29 July 1918

USNA, RG 59, file 103.9302/95a, 7 September 1918

USNA, RG 59, file 123R 271/83, 25 September 1918

UNSA, RG 59, file 861.00/3139, October 1918

USNA, RG 38, Office of Naval Intelligence, file 21010-3241, 11 October 1918

USNA, RG 59, file 861.00/3545, 30 December 1918

USNA, RG 165, Office Chief of Staff, Executive Division, Military Intelligence Division, War Department, file 9944–A–178, 1919

USNA, RG 59, file 103.9302/123e, 11 January 1919

USNA, RG 59, Microfilm Publications M316, Records of the Department of State Relating to Internal Affairs of Russia and the Soviet Union, 1910–1929, file 861.77/672, 18 January 1919

USNA, Visa Files 811.111/20583, 17 February 1919

USNA, RG 59, Robert C. Bannerman file

USNA, RG 59, Jerome Barker Landfield personnel file

USNA, RG 165 file 119.2/88

USNA, RG 165, War Department, Military Intelligence Department, file 9944–D–12

USNA, RG 165, Office Chief of Staff, Executive Division, Military Intelligence

USNA, RG 59, Consul Ray personnel file

USNA, RG 59, Consul Roger C. Tredwell personnel file 123T71

USNA, RG 59, file 861.00/2983; 861.00/7456; 861.00/8173; 861.00/8174

USNA, RG 165 War Department, Military Intelligence Division, file 184–123–1

USNA, RG 165, Office Chief of Staff, Military Intelligence Division, War Department, file 9728-469-44-39x; 9728–469–38; 9728–469-29; 9728–469–30
USNA, RG 59, file 861.51/727, 4 March 1920
USNA, RG 59, file 702.6111/135, 7 July 1920
USNA, Microfilm Publications M1486, Records of Russian Consulates 1862-1922, Roll 153
USNA, RG 59, file 702.6111/155, July 1920
USNA, RG 59, file 811.111

Public Record Office – PRO
PRO FO 800/205 30 March 1917
PRO FO 800/205 6 April 1917
PRO FO 371/3020, December 1917
PRO ADM 53, Ships' Logs, 1918
PRO WO 33/96, Telegram 59154, 28 May 1918
PRO WO 106/1151, June and July 1918
PRO FO 371/3342, 10 June 1918
PRO GFM 6/139, A 26851, 22 June 1918
PRO FO 371/3234, 1 July 1918
PRO FO 175/16/60212, Telegram 369, 2 July 1918
PRO WO 33/902, 4 August 1918
PRO WO 374/19738, 27 August 1918
PRO FO 337/87, 9 September 1918
PRO WO 374/19738, 24 September 1918
PRO ADM Telegram to Rear Admiral, Archangel, 8 October 1918
PRO FO 371/3350, 26 November 1918
PRO FO 371/3977A, 9 February 1919
PRO ADM 116/1878, 15 March 1919
PRO ADM 1/8938, 22 March 1919
PRO FO 380/21 Telegram 69, 31 May 1919
PRO FO 380/21 Telegram 60, 26 June 1919
PRO FO 175/16/60212, Banking scheme file
PRO FO 371/3342
PRO FO 371/3977A/60669
PRO FO 395/31807
PRO FO 395/62607
PRO FO 395/184
PRO WO 106/1234
PRO WO 95/4960

PRO T1/12258
PRO T160/635
PRO ADM 53/45614, HMS Kent

Hudson's Bay Company Archives – HBCA

HBCA AFG RG 26/4/3, 10 May 1916
HBCA RG 22/26/5/6
HBCA AFG RG 22/26.101, 16 November 1917
HBCA RG 22/4/2, February 1918
HBCA RG 22/5/103, FO 67, 21 May 1918
HBCA RG 22/4/2, 25 June 1918
HBCA RG 22/5/103, FO 67
HBCA AFG RG 26/10/6, 25 September 1918

Manuscripts

The Papers of Carl W. Ackerman, Manuscript Division of the United States Library of Congress

General Bandholtz's Diary

Joe Boyle Papers, Canadian National Archives, MG 31 H159, Volume 1.

Chartwell Papers, Churchill College, Cambridge, U.K.

Crane, Charles Papers, Bakmetieff Collection, Special Collections, Columbia University, New York, New York

The Unpublished Manuscript of John Crane in the possession of Thomas Crane, Charles Crane's grandson

The Richard Teller Crane Papers, Manuscript Division of the Library, Georgetown University, Washington, D.C.

The David Francis Papers, The Diplomatic Papers of David Francis, U.S. Ambassador to Russia, 1916-1918, Bethesda: University Publications of America

The Papers of Henry Haskin and the California Printing Company, in possession of David Gretchen Haskin

Hoare Papers, Cambridge University Library. Cambridge, England.

Kilgour Collection, Houghton Library, Harvard University, Cambridge, Ma.

The Papers of Jerome Barker Landfield, Department of Special Collections and Manuscript Division of the University of Chicago Library

The Papers of Robert Lansing, The Manuscript Division of the United States Library of Congress

The Papers of Breckinridge Long, The Manuscript Division of the United States Library of Congress

The Papers of William G. McAdoo, The Manuscript Division of the United States Library of Congress

The Papers of William Rutledge McGarry in possession of Judge McGarry, his grandson and notes in possession of John Bescoby-Chambers

Nicholas II to George V, Central Museum of the October Revolution, Moscow, Fond 601, Opus , Ye.khr, 1219

Queen Marie of Romania Papers, The Manuscript Division of Kent State University

Shinkarenko Papers, Hoover Institution of War, Revolution and Peace, Stanford University, Palo Alto, Ca.

Steinberg, Nachman, The Events of July 1918 n.d., 10VXX692, Hoover Institution of War, Revolution and Peace, Stanford University, Palo Alto, Ca.

Anthony Summers Collections, in the possession of Anthony Summers

The Papers of Woodrow Wilson, The Manuscript Division of the United States Library of Congress

Newspaper Sources

Germans Lost 60,000 by Crossing Marne, *The New York Times*, July 20, 1918

Kerensky – His Failure as Showing the Way to Help Russia, *The New York Times*, July 20, 1918

Ex-Czar of Russia Killed by Order of Ural Soviet – Nicholas Shot on July 16 when it was Feared that Czechoslovaks Might Seize Him, *The New York Times*, July 24, 1918, p. 1, 8

English Pity for Ex-Czar, *The New York Times*, July 23, 1918, p. 4

Army Mobilization Begun by Bolsheviki, *The New York Times*, July 25, 1918, p. 11

Former Czar's Son Dead, *The New York Times*, July 25, 1918, p. 3

Says Italy has Berlin Peace Offer, *The New York Times*, July 26, 1918, p. 5

Balfour Says Balkan People will be Free, *The New York Times,* July 26, 1918, p. 5

Lloyd George Pays Tribute to Hoover, *The New York Times,* July 26, 1918, p. 5

Lenin Threatens to Fight Allies, *The New York Times,* July 26, 1918, p. 6

Denies Ex-Czarina's Plea, *The New York Times*, July 27, 1918, p. 3

Kerensky not Coming to America, *The New York Times*, July 27, 1918, p. 3

Ex-Czar's Family Safe, *The New York Times,* July 28, 1918, p. 5

Starzhevskaia, Olga, Dimitrievna, *Izvestiia, Biography and Testimony*, December 1, 1918

Russia's 'A List' Begs Off Attending Czar's Funeral, *New York Times*, June 18, 1998

The New York Times October 7, 1915

The New York Times March 24, 1917

San Francisco Herald August 5, 1917

The New York Times, March 12, 1918

San Francisco Examiner April 28, 1918

The Times 27 January, 1919

San Francisco Examiner April 29, 1919

Sunday Times, 12 July 1998

The International Times, 19 November, 2000

Secondary Sources

Ackerman, Carl W., *'The Irish Education of Mr. Lloyd George'*, Atlantic Monthly Volume CXXIX, January-July 1922, Boston and New York, The Atlantic Monthly Company

Ackerman, Carl W., *Trailing the Bolsheviki – Twelve Thousand Miles With The Allies In Siberia*, New York, Charles Scribner's Sons, 1919

Alexandrov, Victor, *The End of the Romanovs*, London, Hutchinson, 1966

Andrew, Christopher, *Her Majesty's Secret Service, The Making of the British Intelligence Community,* New York, Viking, Penguin, Inc., New York, 1986

Baerlein, Henry, *The March of the Seventy Thousand*, London, Leonard Parsons, 1926

Baker, Ray Stannard, *Woodrow Wilson – Life and Letters War Leader April 6, 1917–February 28, 1918*, New York, Greenwood Press, 1968

Balfour, Michael, *The Kaiser And His Times*, New York and London, W.W. Norton & Co., 1972

Belisle, Olga, *Eyewitness in Tobolsk*, Vernon B.C. Canada, Canho Enterprises, 1982

Bokhanov, A.N., *Delovaia Elita Rossii,* 1914 god Moscow, 1994

Botkin, Gleb, *The Woman Who Rose Again*, New York, London, Edinburgh, Fleming H. Revell Company, 1937

Bromwell, Will and Billings, Richard N., *So Close to Greatness – A Biography of William C. Bullitt*, New York, Collier Macmillan Publishers, 1987

Brook-Shepherd, Gordon, *Iron Maze, The Western Secret Services and the Bolsheviks*, Pan Books, London, 1998

Brown, Louis Edgar, *New Russia in the Balance How Germany's Designs May be Defeated and Russian Democracy Preserved*, Reprinted from the *Chicago Daily News*, Hartford, Connecticut State Library

Buckmaster, Maurice J., *They Fought Alone – The Story of British Agents In France*, Long Acre, London, Odhams Press Limited, 1958

Bulygin, Captain Paul, *The Murder of the Romanovs – The Authentic Account, Including The Road to Tragedy by Alexander Kerensky,* Westport, CT, Hyperion Press, Inc., New York, McBride and Company, 1935

Buxhoeveden, Baroness Sophie, *The Life and Tragedy of Alexandra Feodorovna, Empress of Russia, A Biography*, London, New York, Toronto, Longmans, Green and Company, 1928

Buxhoeveden, Baroness Sophie, *Before the Storm*, London, Macmillan & Company, 1938

Buxhoeveden, Baronese Sophie, *Left Behind, Fourteen Months in Siberia During the Revolution, December 1917–1920*, London, New York, Oxford, Oxford University Press, 1993

Capek, Karel, *President Masaryk Tells His Story,* New York, G. P. Putnam's Sons, 1935

Chernow, Ron, *The House of Morgan*, New York, Simon & Schuster, 1990

Churchill, Winston S., *The Unknown War, The Eastern Front*, Toronto, The Macmillan Company of Canada, 1931

Clarke, William, *The Lost Fortune of the Tsars,* New York, St. Martins Press, 1996

Conquest, Robert, *Stalin – Breaker of Nations*, New York, Penguin Books, 1992

Courtney, W.L. 'Trotsky in Ekaterinburg', *The Fortnightly Review*

– Volume CVIII New Series July to December 1920, London – Chapman and Hall Ltd., New York – Leonard Scott Publication Company, 1920

Crawford, Rosemary and Donald, *Michael and Natasha-The Life and Love of Michael II, the Last of the Romanov Tsars*, New York, A Lisa Drew Book/Scribner, 1997

Creel, George, *The German – Bolshevik Conspiracy – War Information Series Issued by The Committee On Public Information,* No. 20, October 1918

Degras, Jane, (ed.), *Soviet Documents on Foreign Policy, Volume I, 1917–1924, Issued Under the Auspices of the Royal Institute of International Affairs,* Geoffrey Cumberlege, London, New York, Toronto, Oxford University Press, 1951

Danelski, David J. and Joseph S. Tulchin, (eds.), *'The Autobiographical Notes of Charles Evans Hughes',* Cambridge Massachusetts, Harvard University Press, 1973

Dupee, F.W., (ed.), *The Russian Revolution – The Overthrow of Tsarism and the Triumph of the Soviets from the History of the Russian Revolution* by Leon Trotsky, New York, Toronto, London, Sydney, Auckland, Anchor Books/Doubleday, 1989

Epstein, Edward Jay, *Dossier – The Secret History of Armand Hammer*, New York, NY, Toronto, Doubleday 1996

Ferro, Marc, *Nicholas II – Last of the Tsars,* New York, Oxford, Oxford University Press, 1991

Fic, Victor M., *The Collapse of American Policy in Russia and Siberia, 1918,* Boulder, East European Monographs, 1995

Fleischhauer, Ingeborg and Benjamin Pinkus, *The Soviet Germans – Past and Present*, London, C. Hurst & Company, 1986

Fogelsong, David S., *America's Secret War Against Bolshevism, US Intervention in the Russian Civil War 1917–1920,* Chapel Hill & London, The University of North Carolina Press, 1995

Francis, David R., *US Ambassador to Russia Under the Czar, the Provisional Government and the Bolshevists – Russian From the American Embassy*, New York, Charles Scribner's Sons, 1921

Frothingham, Helen Losanitch, Matilda Spence, (ed.), *Mission for Serbia – Letters from America and Canada 1915–1920,* New York, Walker and Company, 1970

Gerhart, Ann Garcia, *The United States and The Problem of Russia at the Paris Peace Conference*, Bryn Mawr College, Submitted to the Department of History for Honors, 1956

Gilbert, Martin, *Atlas of Russian History, From 800BC to the Present Day*, New York, Oxford, Oxford University Press, 1993

Gilbert, Martin, *Atlas of the First World War*, Weidenfeld-Nicholson, London, 1994

Gill, Peter, et all, 'Identification of the Remains of the Romanov Family by DNA Analysis', *Nature Genetics*, 6, 1994

Gilliard, Pierre, *Thirteen Years At The Russian Court*, New York, Arno Press & *The New York Times*, 1970

Glad, Betty, *Charles Evans Hughes and the Illusions of Innocence – A Study in American Diplomacy,* Urbana and London, University of Illinois Press, 1966

Goldhurst, Richard, *The Midnight War – The American Intervention in Russia, 1918–1920*, New York, St. Louis, San Francisco, Toronto, Dusseldorf, Mexico, McGraw Hill Book Co.1978

Goldman, Emma, *My Further Disillusionment in Russia, Chapter VIII*, New York, Doubleday, Page and Company, 1924 (http://www.pitzer.edu/~dward/Anarc. . .chives/goldman/further/mfdr_8.html)

Graves, William S., *America's Siberian Adventure 1918–1920*, New York, Peter Smith, 1941

Great Soviet Encyclopedia, *A Translation of the Third Edition, Volume 4*, New York, Macmillan, Inc., London, Collier-Macmillan Publishers, 1973

Grey, Marina, *Enquête Sur Le Massacre Des Romanov,* Paris, Librairie Academique Perrin, 1987

Grey, Marina, *Des Romanov,* Criterion, Paris, 1991

Harris, John, (ed.), *Farewell to the Don, The Russian Revolution in the Journals of Brigadier H.N.H. Williamson*, New York, The John Day Company, 1971

Heller, Mikhail and Aleksander Nekrich, *Utopia in Power – The History of the Soviet Union From 1917 to the Present,* New York, Summit Books, 1986

Holubnychy, Lydia, *Michael Borodin, and the Chinese Revolution 1923–1925*, Ann Arbor, Michigan: published for East Asian Institute, Columbia University by University Microfilms International, 1979

Hopkins, J. Castell, *The Canadian Annual Review of Public Affairs*, Toronto, The Canadian Annual Review, Limited, 1919

Hopkirk, Peter, (ed.), *Bailey, F. M., Mission to Tashkent*, Oxford, Oxford University Press, 1992

Hughes, Charles Evans, (eds. David J. Danelski and Joseph S. Tulchin), *The Autobiographical Notes of Charles Evans Hughes*, Cambridge, Massachusetts, Harvard University Press, 1973

Israel, Fred L., (ed.), *The War Diary of Breckinridge Long-Selections from the Years 1939–1944* Lincoln, University of Nebraska Press, 1966

Janin, General, Maurice *Ma Mission En Siberie 1918–1920,* Paris, Payot, 1933

Kelly's Handbook to Titled Families & Who Was Who

Kennan, George F., *Russia Leaves the War, Soviet American Relations, 1917-1920, Volume I,* Princeton, New Jersey, Princeton University Press, 1956

Kennan, George F., *The Decision to Intervene, Soviet-American Relations 1917-1920*, Princeton, Princeton University Press 1958

Kennan, George F., *Russia and the West, Under Lenin and Stalin*, Boston and Toronto, An Atlantic Monthly Press Book, Little Brown and Company, 1960

Kennedy, K. H., *Mining Tzar, The Life and Times of Leslie Urquhart*, Boston, Allen & Unwin, 1986

Kerensky, Alexander, *Russia and History's Turning Point*, New York, Deuell, Sloan and Pearce, 1965

Kerensky, Alexander, *The Road to the Tragedy*, Westport, Conn. Hyperion Press, Reprint 1997

Kerensky, A., *La Verite sur le Massacre des Romanov,* Paris, Payot, 1936

Kettle, Michael, *The Allies and the Russian Collapse March 1917–March 1918,* Andre Deutsch, 1981

Kettle, Michael, *The Road to Intervention, March–November 1918, Volume II*, London and New York, Routledge, 1988

Kettle, Michael, *Sidney Reilly, The True Story of the World's Greatest Spy*, New York, St. Martin's Press, 1983.

Kotypin-Wallovskoy, Peter, Schereatow, Alexis, Prince, and Magerovsky, Eugene, The Russian Expert Commission Abroad – *Open Letter to the President of Russia, Memorandum 3*, Connecticut, Stratford, 18 January 1998

Krymov, Vladimir, *Novoe Russhoe Slovo, Koporyi Vse Znal (The Man who Knew Everything)*, 8 April 1956

Krymov, Vladimir, *Portrety Neobychnykh Liudei*, Paris, 1971

Kurth, Peter, *Tsar – The Lost World of Nicholas and Alexandra*, Boston, New York, London, Little Brown and Company, 1995

Lansing, Robert, *War Memoirs of Robert Lansing, Secretary of State,* Indianapolis, New York, The Bobbs-Merrill Company, 1935

Lasies, Joseph, *La Tragedie Siberienne,* Paris, L'Edition Francaise Illustree, 1920

Lehovich, Dimitry V., *White Against Red; The Life of General Anton Denikin*, New York, W.W. Norton & Company, Inc.1974

Levykin, Alexei K., (compiled by), *Nicholas II (Nikolai Alexandrovitch) 1868-1918 Emperor of All Russia 1894–1917,* St. Petersburg Times, The Times Publishing Company Index Page sptimes.com, 1995

Lied, Jonas, *Return to Happiness,* New York, Macmillan and Company, 1943

Lieven, Dominic, *Nicholas II – Twilight of the Empire,* New York, St. Martin's Press, 1996

Lincoln, W. Bruce, *Red Victory*, *A History of the Russian Civil War*, New York, London, Toronto, Sidney, Tokyo, Simon & Schuster, 1989

Lincoln W. Bruce, *Romanovs, Autocrats of All the Russias,* New York, London, Toronto, Sydney, Auckland, Anchor Books, Doubleday, 1981

Link, Arthur S., (trans./ed. with assistance of Manfred F. Boemeke), *The Deliberations of the Council of Four (March 24-June 28, 1919)-Notes of the Official Interpreter, Paul Mantoux, to the Delivery to the German Delegation of the Preliminaries of Peace,* Supplementary Volume to the *Papers of Woodrow Wilson*, New Jersey, Princeton University Press, 1919

Lockhart, Robin Bruce, *Ace of Spies*, London, Hodder & Stoughton, 1967

Long, Breckinridge, *The War – An Address by Breckinridge Long*, *Third Assistant Secretary of State* – Before The City Club, St. Louis, January 19, 1918

Luckett, Richard, *The White Generals, An Account of the White Movement and The Russian Civil War,* New York, Viking Press, 1971

Markov, Sergeiv Vladimirovich, *How We Tried To Save the Tsaritsa*, London and New York, G.P. Putnam's Sons, 1929

Masaryk, Thomas, *The Making of a State* – Memories and Observations 1914–1918, New York, H. Fertig, 1969

Massie, Robert, K. *'Dreadnought'* – *Britain, Germany and the*

Coming of the Great War, London, Pimlico, 1993

Massie, Robert K., *The Romanovs-The Final Chapter*, New York, Random House, 1995

Massie, Robert K., *Nicholas and Alexandra,* New York, Athenuem, 1967

Maylunas, Andrei and Mironenko, Sergei, *A Lifelong Passion, Nicholas and Alexandra, Their Own Story,* New York, London, Toronto, Sidney, and Auckland, Doubleday, 1997

Medava, Joseph, *Trotsky and the Jews*, Philadelphia, Pa., The Jewish Publication Society of America, 5732/1972

Niessel, Hemi-Albert, General, *Le Triomphe des Bolsheviks et La Paix de Brest-Litovsk, Souvenirs 1917-1918*, Paris, Plon, 1940

Null, Gary, *The Conspirator Who Saved the Romanovs*, New Jersey, Prentice-Hall, Inc., 1971

O'Conor, John F., *Translator of Sections of Nicholas A. Sokolov's The Murder of the Imperial Family,* New York, Robert Speller and Sons Publishers, Inc., 1971

Occleshaw, Michael, *The Romanov Conspiracies – The Romanovs and the House of Windsor*, London, Orion Books Ltd., 1994

Pares, Bernard, *My Russian Memoirs*, New York, AMS Press, 1969

Parliament of Great Britain, *The Evacuation of North Russia 1919,* London, His Majesty's Stationary Office, 1920

Perman, Dagmar Horna, President Wilson and Charles Crane: Russia and the US Declaration of War, 1917, *Peace and Change*, Volume II, No. 2, 1974

Pipes, Richard, *Russia Under the Old Regime,* London, New York, Victoria, Toronto and Auckland, Penguin Books, 1974

Pipes, Richard, *The Russian Revolution,* New York, Vintage Books, a Division of Random House, 1990

Pipes, Richard, *Russia Under Bolshevik Regime*, New York, Vintage Books, a Division of Random House, 1994

Pipes, Richard, *A Concise History of the Russian Revolution*, New York, Vintage Books, A Division of Random House, 1995

Pipes, Richard, *Three 'Whys' of the Russian Revolution*, New York, Vintage Books, a Division of Random House, 1995

Pipes, Richard, *The Unknown Lenin, From the Secret Archives*, New Haven and London, Yale University Press, 1996

Radzinsky, Edvard, (trans. by H.T. Willetts), *Stalin,* New York, Toronto, Sydney, Aukland, Doubleday, 1996

Radzinsky, Edvard, *The Last Tsar, The Life and Death of Nicholas*

II, New York, Doubleday, 1992

Rall, Hans, *Wilhelm II: eine Biographie,* Graz, Styria, 1995

Reed, John, *Ten Days That Shook the World*, London, Penguin Books, 1966

Reilly, Sidney and Bodadilla (Reilly), Pepita, *Britain's Master Spy, The Adventures of Sidney Reilly, A Narrative Written by Himself, Edited and Completed by his Wife*, New York and London, Harper & Brothers Publishers, 1933

Richards, Guy, *The Hunt for the Czar,* Garden City, New York, Doubleday, 1970

Richards, Guy, *The Rescue of the Romanovs,* Old Greenwich Connecticut, The Devin-Adair Company, 1975

Roberts, Kenneth, *I Wanted to Write*, New York, Doubleday and Company, Inc., 1949

Roberts, Priscilla, *Jewish Bankers, Russia, and the Soviet Union, 1900–1940: The Case of Kuhn and Loeb and Company,* American Jewish Archives Journal, 1999

Robertson, William, Sir, Field Marshal, *Soldiers and Statesmen,* Vol. I, London, Cassell and Co., 1926

Romanov, B.A., *Kontsessiia na Yalu, Russkoe Proshloe*, 1 (1923)

Service, Robert, *Lenin – A Political Life, Volume 3 – The Iron Ring*, Bloomington and Indianapolis, Indiana University Press, 1995

Seymour, Charles, *The Intimate Papers of Colonel House-Into the World War,* Boston and New York, Houghton Mifflin Company, Cambridge, The Riverside Press, 1928

Sharp, William Graves, *The War Memoirs of William Graves Sharp – American Ambassador to France 1914–1919*, London, Constable & Co. Ltd., 1931

Slizberg, G. B., *Dela Minuvshikh' Dnei*, Volume 3 (Paris, 1934)

Smith, George, *The Dictionary of National Biography – 1922–1930*, London, Oxford University Press

Smythe, James P., *Rescuing the Czar*, California Printing Company, San Francisco, 1920

Sokolov, N. A., *Enquête Judiciaire Sur l'Assassinat de la Famille Imperiale Russe*, Payot, Paris, 1924

Spence, Richard, *Sidney Reilly in America 1914-1917*, Intelligence and National Security Volume 10, January 1995, London, Frank Cass, 1995

Spence, Richard, *Sidney Reilly's Lubianka Diary*, 30 October/

4 November 1925, *Revolutionary Russia*, Volume 8, 2, December 1995

Stafford, David, Churchill and the Secret Service, Woodstock and New York, The Overlook Press, 1997

Steinberg, Mark D. and Vladimir M. Khrustalev, *The Fall of the Romanovs – Political Dreams and Personal Struggles in a Time of Revolution*, New Haven and London, Yale University Press, 1995

Stewart, George, *The White Armies of Russia, A Chronicle of Counter – Revolution and Allied Intervention,* New York, Russell and Russell, 1970

Strakhovsky, Leonid I., *Intervention at Archangel, The Story of Allied Intervention and Russian Counter – Revolution in North Russia 1918–1920,* New York, Howard Fertig, 1971

Sugrue, Thomas, *Starling of the White House*, New York, NY, Simon & Schuster, 1946

Summers, Anthony and Tom Mangold, *The File on the Tsar*, London, Victor Gollancz Ltd., 1976

Sylvester, Albert James, *Life with Lloyd George, The Diary of A. J. Sylvester, 1931–1945,* Macmillan, London, 1975

Temperley, H.W.V., (ed.), *A History of the Peace Conference of Paris, Volume I,* London, Henry Frowde and Hodder & Stoughton, Published under the auspices of the British Institute of International Affairs, 1920

Temperley, H.W.V., (ed.), *A History of the Peace Conference of Paris, Volume VI,* London, Henry Frowde – Oxford University Press, Hodder & Stoughton, 1924

Travis, Frederick F., *George Kennan and the American – Russian Relationship 1865–1924*, Athens, Ohio University Press, 1990

Trewin, J.C., Tutor to the Tsarevich: *An Intimate Portrait of the Last Days of the Romanov Family, compiled from the papers of Charles Sidney Gibbs*, London, Macmillan, 1975

Trotsky, *My Life,* New York, Pathfinder Press, 1970.

Trotsky, Leon, *The Russian Revolution, The Overthrow of Czarism, and the Triumph of the Soviets*, New York, Anchor Books, 1989

Tucker, Robert C., *Stalin As Revolutionary – A Study in History and Personality, 1879-1929,* New York and London, W.W. Norton & Co., 1973

Tyler-Whittle, Michael Sidney, *The Last Kaiser: A Biography of*

Wilhelm II, German Emperor and King of Prussia, London, Heinemann, 1977

Ulam, Adam B., *The Bolsheviks, The Intellectual and Political History of the Triumph of Communism in Russia,* New York, The MacMillan Company, London, Collier-Macmillan Limited 1965

Venner, Dominique, *Les Blancs et Les Rouges,* Paris, Pygmalion, 1995

Viereck, George Sylvester, *The Kaiser on Trial,* New York, The Grey Stone Press, 1937

Viereck, George Sylvester, *The Strangest Friendship in History, Woodrow Wilson and Colonel House,* New York, Liveright, Inc., Publishers, 1932

Von Laue, Theodore H., Jacob and Francis Hiatt, *Why Lenin? Why Stalin? – A Reappraisal of the Russian Revolution 1900–1930,* Second Edition, Philadelphia, New York, Toronto, J.B. Lippincot Company, 1964

Vopicka, Charles J., *Secrets of the Balkans,* Chicago, Rand McNally & Company, 1921

Vyrubova, Anna Alexandrodna, *Memories of the Russian Court,* New York, Macmillan, 1923

Ward, Colonel John, *With the 'Die Hards' in Siberia',* New York, George H. Doran Company, 1920

Warman, Roberta M., *The Foreign Mission 1916–1918,* Garland Publishing, Inc., 1986 (The University of London, PHD Thesis), 1982

Weber, Ralph E., *The Final Memoranda*: *Major General Ralph H. Van Deman, USA, Ret., 1865-1952, Father of US Military Intelligence,* Wilmington, Delaware, SR Books, 1988

West Point Military Academy Biographical Sketches, West Point Military Academy Library, West Point, New York

White, John Albert, *The Siberian Intervention,* Princeton, New Jersey, Princeton University Press, 1950

Wick, Ned Elvin, *Service in Siberia,* South Dakota, Fenwynn Press, Inc., 1975

Wieczynski, Joseph L., (ed.), *The Modern Encyclopedia of Russian and Soviet History,* Gulf Breeze, Florida, Academic International Press, 1979

Wilhelm II, The Kaiser's Memoirs, (trans. by Thomas R. Ybarra), New York and London, Harper & Brothers Publishers, 1922

Wilton, Robert, *The Last Days of the Romanovs, From 15 March,*

1917, Part I, The Narrative, Part II, The Depositions of Eye-witnesses, London, Thorton Butterworth Limited, 1920

Zhivotovsky, Lev, Dr., *Annuals of Human Biology, Journal of the Society for the Study of Human Biology*, Volume 26, 6, November/December 1999

Notes

Introduction

1 'White Russian' evolved into a generic term used to describe any member of various disparate groups who opposed the Bolsheviks.

2 *New York Times*, 18 June 1998, 'Russia's "A List" Begs Off Attending Czar's Funeral'.

3 *Sunday Times*, 12 July 1998.

4 The legal process of discovery involves the relinquishing by all parties to their opponents of any requested documents and working notes relevant to the case.

5 Interview with Dr Marcia Eisenberg.

6 Various statistical models are used to arrive at such probability ratios; 'frequency tables', for example, indicate the frequency with which an observed genetic sequence occurs in the population as a whole. These probabilities are usually expressed as a percentage or a ratio, indicating, say, that 99.9 per cent of the given population has been ruled out as the source of the DNA at the crime scene, or that there is only a one in two million chance that the evidence sample would come from an unrelated individual at random. Such probabilities are certainly impressive, but they also indicate that there is some chance, however small, of a random or coincidental match. Since genetic variations are inherited, the patterns are not evenly distributed across the human population as a whole: a variation that is very rare among Caucasians may be relatively common among African-Americans or Japanese. The trial of a minority

defendant can easily be prejudiced if a probability calculated from a population-wide DNA database does not reflect the incidence of the variation among his or her specific ethnic group if other members of this group are alternative donors of the evidence. To date, however, little is known about the distribution of genetic variations among ethnic sub-populations, let alone among the increasing number of interracial individuals.

7 Interview with Dr William Shields.
8 Ibid.
9 Zhivotovsky, Dr Lev, *Annals of Human Biology, Journal of the Society for the Study of Human Biology*, vol. 26, no. 6, November/December 1999, pp. 569–77.
10 Massie, Robert K., *The Romanovs, The Final Chapter*, Random House, New York, 1995, p. 32.
11 Appeared in the Russian *Moscow News*, as cited in Robert Massie's, *The Romanovs, The Final Chapter*, on p. 35.
12 Gill, Peter et al, 'Identification of the Remains of the Romanov Family by DNA Analysis', *Nature Genetics* 6, 1994.
13 Russian Expert Commission Abroad, Open Letter to the President of Russia, Memorandum No. 3, 18 January 1998.
14 Shields, op. cit.
15 Ibid.
16 Ibid. Because the samples (even in the case of nuclear DNA) are so small and the lab procedures so exacting, mtDNA sequencing is extremely susceptible to incidental contamination and, therefore, unreliable results. The published report of the AFDIL tests of the putative Romanov remains contains a note on 'contamination avoidance'. The disclaimer provided a chilling litany of the lengths that DNA laboratories must go to in an attempt to preclude contamination. Dr Shields estimates that, in United States DNA labs as a whole, at least fifty per cent of the so-called negative controls (the samples that are not supposed to contain any DNA) end up producing DNA sequences.
17 Zhivotovsky, op. cit.
18 Ibid., p. 574.
19 Ibid., p. 571.
20 Ibid., p. 569.

Chapter 1

1 Pipes, Richard, *The Russian Revolution*, Vintage Books, A Division of Random House, Inc., New York, p. 262.
2 Ibid., p. 265.
3 Maylunas, Andrei and Mironenko, Sergei, *A Lifelong Passion, Nicholas and Alexandra, Their Own Story*, Doubleday, New York, London, Toronto, Sidney and Auckland, 1997, p. 532.
4 Lincoln, W. Bruce, *Red Victory, A History of the Russian Civil War*, Simon & Schuster, New York, 1989, p. 33.
5 Churchill, Winston S., *The Unknown War, The Eastern Front*, The Macmillan Co. of Canada, Toronto, 1931, pp. 377–80.
6 Ibid., pp 545–6.
7 Ibid.
8 Ibid. p. 547.
9 Ibid.

Chapter 2

1 Pipes, Richard, *The Unknown Lenin: From the Secret Archive*, Yale University Press, New Haven and London, 1996.
2 Ibid., p. 15.
3 Pipes, Richard, *A Concise History of the Russian Revolution*, Vintage Books, A Division of Random House, New York, 1995, p. 118.
4 The State Secretary to the Foreign Ministry Liaison Officer at General Headquarters, Telegram No. 1610, AS 3640, 29 September 1917, in Z. A. B. Zeman, *Germany and the Russian Revolution in Russia 1915-1918*, Document no. 71, p. 70.
5 Pipes, *The Russian Revolution*, op. cit., p. 411.
6 Ibid., p. 616.
7 Testimonies of Crown Princess Cecile of Prussia-Germany court record of Anderson v. Duchess Christian Ludwig of Mecklenburg, Hamburg Court of Appeal, vol. XXIV, p. 4696; Prince Ferdinand of Schoenaich Carolath, vol. XXXI, p. 5826; Prince Dmitri Galitzin, vol. XXXVII, p. 6955; Princess of Thurn und Taxis, vol. XVIII, p. 3658; Baroness Marie Pilar von Pilchau, vol. VII, p. 299; Colonel Dmitri von Lar-Larsky, vol. I, p. 186; Fritz von Unruh, vol. XX, p. 3932.
8 Public Record Office (hereinafter PRO) Foreign Office (hereinafter FO) 337/87 message from British Consul, Christiania, to Lord Hardinge of Penshurst, 9 September 1918.

9 *New York Times*, 24 March 1917.

10 Venner, Dominique, *Les Blancs et les Rouges*, Pygmalion/Watelet, Paris, p. 65.

11 Roberts, Priscilla, 'Jewish Bankers, Russia, and The Soviet Union, 1900–1940: The Case of Kuhn and Loeb and Company', *American Jewish Archives Journal*, www.huc.edu/aja/97–1.htm.

12 *New York Times*, 7 October 1915.

13 PRO War Office (hereinafter referred to as WO) 33/96, telegram 59154, 28 May 1918.

14 Perman, Dagmar Horna, 'President Wilson and Charles Crane: Russia and the US Declaration of War, 1917', in *Peace and Change*, vol. II, no. 2, 1974, pp.18/28.

15 Charles Richard Crane papers, Bakhmeteff Archive, Rare Book and Manuscript Library, Columbia University, Charles R. Crane to Cornelia Smith Crane, Moscow, 31 July 1888.

16 Charles R. Crane Papers, op. cit., Charles R. Crane to Cornelia Smith Crane, 7 May 1894.

17 Clarke, William, *The Lost Fortune of the Tsars*, St Martin's Press, New York, 1995, p. 23.

18 Charles R. Crane Papers, op. cit., Charles R. Crane to his daughter Josephine, 12 July 1917.

19 Charles R. Crane Papers, op. cit., Charles R. Crane to Cornelia Smith Crane, 7 May 1894.

20 Charles R. Crane Papers, op. cit., Charles R. Crane to Cornelia Smith Crane, 3 May 1894.

21 Charles R. Crane Papers, op. cit., Charles R. Crane to Cornelia Smith Crane, 7 May 1894.

22 Charles R. Crane Papers, op. cit., Letter to William E. Smith from Secretary to Empress Alexandra, 13 Marh 1904.

23 Clarke, op. cit., p. 41.

24 Picher, Charles Crane to Josephine, 25 July 1917.

25 Ibid.

26 PRO FO 800/205, memo from A.J. Balfour to Sir Arthur Davidson, no. 77, 6 April 1917.

27 Ibid.

28 Robertson, Field Marshal Sir William, *Soldiers and Statesmen*, vol. 1, p. 313.

29 PRO FO 800/205, Lord Stamfordham to A. J. Balfour, 30 March 1917.

30 Ibid., folio 88.

31 Ibid., folio 82.

32 Correspondence of Nicholas II and George V, Central State Museum of the October Revolution, Moscow. Fond no. 601, opus no. 1, Ye.khr. No. 1219.

33 *The US Department of State Papers Relating to the Foreign Relations of the United States*, 1917, Supplement 2, pp. 459–61.

34 1919 Correspondence Sent, PRO FO 380/21, Gaisford to Lord Curzon, telegram 69, 31 May 1919 and PRO FO 380/21, Gaisford to Lord Curzon, telegram 60, 26 June 1919.

35 Admiralty, London to British Commander-In-Chief, Mediterranean, 1 November 1918, 103z, Broadlands Archive.

36 Ibid., Commander Turle, R.N. to Commander-In-Chief, HMS *Superb*, 22 November 1918.

37 Copy of letter from the Marchioness of Milford Haven to Mrs R. Chrichton, her lady-in-waiting, Anthony Summers collection.

38 Kerensky, Alexander, *The Road to the Tragedy*, Hyperion Press, Westport, Conn., reprint 1997, p. 107.

39 Radzinsky, Edvard, *The Last Tsar, the Life and Death of Nicholas II*, Doubleday, New York, 1992, pp. 196, 199.

40 Kerensky, *The Road*, op. cit., p. 118.

41 Radzinsky, op. cit., pp. 299–300.

42 Memorandum EWT to Breckinridge Long, 5 March 1918. Collections of the Manuscript Division, Library of Congress.

43 Lincoln, Bruce W., *Romanovs, Autocrats of All the Russias*, Anchor Books, Doubleday, New York, 1967, p. 609.

44 *New York Times International*, 19 November 2000.

45 Depicted in Andrew, Christopher, *Her Majesty's Secret Service, The Making of the British Intelligence Community*, Viking Penguin Inc., New York, 1986. 'Hidden hands' was a pseudonym utilised to convey intelligence activities. A graphic depicting the concept was displayed on a 1918 New Year's card for MI5. Illustration plate between pp. 270–1.

Chapter 3

1 Trotsky, Leon, *The Russian Revolution, the Overthrow of Czarism, and the Triumph of the Soviets*, Anchor Books, New York, 1989.

2 Steinberg, Mark D. and Khrustalëv, Vladimir M., *The Fall of the Romanovs*, Yale University Press, New Haven, Ct, 1995, p. 161.

3 Pipes, *The Russian Revolution*, op. cit., p. 435.

4 Ibid., pp. 440–67.

5 Steinberg and Khrustalëv, op. cit., p. 164.

6 Ibid., p. 173.

7 Ibid., p. 174.

8 Ibid., p. 189.

9 Ibid.

10 Ibid., p. 171.

11 Trotsky, *The Russian Revolution*, op. cit.

12 Ibid.

13 Steinberg and Khrustalëv, op. cit., pp. 176–80.

14 Ibid

15 Goldhurst, Richard, *The Midnight War, The American Intervention in Russia, 1918–1920*, McGraw Hill, New York, 1978, p. 3.

16 Ibid, p. 7.

17 Gilbert, Martin, *Atlas of World War I*, Weidenfeld & Nicolson, New York, Oxford University Press, 1994, p. 104.

18 Richard Teller Crane Papers, Manuscript Division of the Library, Georgetown University, Washington, DC, box 2, folder 24, Omsk via Peking, 18 December 1918.

19 Ibid.

20 United States National Archives, College Park, Maryland, (hereinafter referred to as USNA), Record Group (hereinafter referred to as RG) 59, File 861.77/611a.

21 Hudson's Bay Company Archives (hereafter HBCA), Winnipeg, Manitoba, file RG 22/5/103. FO. 67.

22 Richard Teller Crane Papers, to Richard Crane from Charles Crane, 30 October 1917.

23 HBCA, op. cit., file RG 22/26/5/6.

24 PRO Admiralty (hereinafter referred to as ADM) telegram 662. To: RA (Rear-Admiral), Archangel, 10 August 1918.

25 Interview with Barbara Kelcey.

26 Sylvester, Albert James, *Life with Lloyd George: The Diary of A. J. Sylvester, 1931–45*, Macmillan, London, 1975, p. 106.

27 Clarke, *The Lost Fortune*, op. cit., pp. 23, 41, 101, 222, 263, 264.

28 Capek, Karel (recounted by), *President Masaryk Tells His Story*, G. P. Putnam's Sons, 1935, p. 224.

29 Charles R. Crane Papers, op. cit., unpublished manuscript of Charles R. Crane's son John, who was Thomas Masaryk's secretary for ten years.

30 HBCA, file no. RG 22/5/103. FO. 67.
31 Kennan, George F., *Soviet American Relations, 1917–1920*, vol. I, *Russia Leaves the War*, Princeton University Press, Princeton, New Jersey, 1956.
32 Foglesong, David S., *America's Secret War Against Bolshevism, US Intervention in the Russian Civil War, 1917–1920*, University of North Carolina Press, Chapel Hill, N.C., 1995, p. 101.
33 Gilbert, *Atlas Of The First World War*, op. cit., p. 235.
34 Foglesong, op. cit., p. 95.
35 Ibid., p. 97.
36 Ibid., pp. 87–8.
37 Ibid.
38 Ibid.
39 Ibid., p. 89–90.
40 Ibid.
41 Ibid.
42 Ibid.
43 Ibid., p. 90.
44 Ibid., p. 91.
45 Ibid., p. 90.
46 Ibid., pp. 92–3.
47 Ibid., p. 94.
48 Ibid., p. 95.
49 Ibid., p. 94.
50 USNA War Department, file 9728–469–38.
51 Ibid.
52 USNA, RG59, file 861.51/727, 4 March 1920, Bakmetieff to Polk.
53 Foglesong, op. cit., p. 100.
54 Ibid., p. 101.
55 PRO FO, 175/16/60212.

Chapter 4

1 PRO FO, 371/3020, 4006, December 1917.
2 Roberts, op. cit.
3 Ibid. Note: While in America, Trotsky was not a Bolshevik but became one shortly after his return to Russia.
4 Ibid.
5 Spence, Richard B., *Intelligence and National Security*, vol. 10, no. 1, *Sidney Reilly in America, 1914–1917*, January 1995,

Frank Cass, London, p. 92.

6 Ibid.

7 Krymov, Vladimir, *Novoe Russhoe Slovo, Koporyi Vse Znal (The Man Who Knew Everything)* 8 April 1956 and Krymov, Vladimir, *Portrety Neobychnykh Liudei*, Paris, 1971, p. 74.

8 Chartwell Papers, Churchill College, Cambridge, UK, Russian Economic Affairs, 1919, folio no. CHAR1628, Sinclair, Archibald to Mr Tilden-Smith, 11 November 1919.

9 Trewin, J. C., *Tutor to the Tsarevich: an Intimate Portrait of the Last Days of the Romanov Family, Compiled from the Papers of Charles Sidney Gibbes*, Macmillan, London, 1975, pp. 88–91.

10 Maylunas and Mironenko, op. cit., p. 545.

11 Grand Duke Alexander Michaelovich wrote regarding Yaroshinsky: 'The years of youth of Yaroshinsky were surrounded with mystery, nobody could define his nationality. He spoke Polish, but the rumour circulates that his uncle is an Italian Cardinal who occupies a high position in the Vatican. He arrived to St Petersburg when he already was the owner of a big estate which he earned as a result of a sugar business in the south of Russia.'

12 USNA, War Department file 16439.

13 Wilton, Robert, *The Times*, London, 1923.

14 Lord Curzon memo regarding Yaroshinsky.

15 USNA Chief of Staff, Executive Division, Military Intelligence Branch, FN. 164–39, Washington.

16 Grey, Marina, *Enquête sur le Massacre des Romanov*, Librarie Académique Perrin, Paris, 1987, p. 70.

17 Bokhanov, A. N., *Delovaia elita Rossii*, 1914 god, Moscow, 1994 (*Business Elite of Russia*, year 1914).

18 Grey, op. cit., Marina Grey was the daughter of General Denikin (one of the White Russian generals intended to be supported by the banking scheme as well as being one of the generals who will be mentioned in an intriguing report regarding a Parfen Domnin – report filed by Major Homer Slaughter, appears in the War Department Intelligence files).

19 Vyrubova, Anna Alexandrovna, *Memories of the Russian Court*, 1923.

20 HBCA, AFG 26/4/3, letter of Henry Armitstead, 10 May 1916. Henry Armitstead was a cousin of Baron Serge Kroff, one of the members of the Tsar's court and another relative, Princess

Orussoff. Additionally, Armitstead had been close to his 'old friend' N. W. Sweginzeff, 'my link with the Court party of which he is a prominent leader and as a master of ceremonies and as persona gratissima with the dowager Empress, of good influence'.

21 Romanov, B. A., *Kontsessiia na Yalu, Russkoe Proshloe*, 1 (1923), pp. 87–108.

22 USNA, RG 38, Office of Naval Intelligence (ONI) files, 21010–3241: Chief Yeoman Bond to H. H. Hunnewell and Abel I. Smith, re: Reilly and Weinstein Case, 11 October 1918. Note: The following is noted in the file regarding Reilly, the Grand Duke (who was married to Nicholas II's sister, Zenia) and Mr Samuel Vauclain, Vice-President of Baldwin Locomotive Works: A Mr Vauclain had run into contact with Reilly when he was in Petrograd during the first year of the war. Vauclain went to Russia to arrange for some contracts . . . while there found that his hardest competitor was Reilly . . . Vauclain said that there was no doubt that Reilly had tremendous political backing in Russia at the time which led right to the office of the Grand Duke (Alexander) Michaelovich.

23 Maylunas and Mironenko, op. cit., p. 544.

24 Ferro, Marc, *Nicholas II, Last of Tsars*, Oxford University Press, New York, Oxford, 1991, p. 227.

25 PRO FO 175/16/60212.

26 India Office File, Russian Banks, MSS Eur. F. 131/21. Affidavit of Colonel Terence Keyes, 5 March 1928.

27 PRO FO 175/16/60212 op. cit.

28 Hoare Papers, Cambridge University Library, part II, box 3, file 4a.

29 PRO FO 175/16/60212, op. cit., telegram 411, 2 October, 1918.

30 PRO FO 175/16/60212, op. cit.

Chapter 5

1 PRO FO 175/16/60212 op. cit.

2 Ibid.

3 Ibid.

4 Ibid.

5 PRO FO WO 33/96, telegram 59154, 28 May, 1918.

6 PRO FO 175/16/60212, telegram 369, 7 February 1918, op. cit.

7 PRO FO 175/16/60212, op. cit.

8 PRO FO 371/3342, op. cit.

9 PRO FO 175/16/60212, op. cit.
10 PRO T160/635.
11 Francis, David, *David Francis' Papers, The Diplomatic Papers of David Francis, U. S. Ambassador to Russia, 1916–1918*, Bethesda: University Publications of America, Reel 8, 17 March 1918.
12 Ibid.
13 Goldhurst, op. cit., p. 3.
14 Pipes, *The Unknown Lenin*, op. cit., p. 43.
15 Ibid., p. 45.
16 Kettle, Michael, *The Road to Intervention, March–November 1918*, vol. II, Routledge, London and New York, p. 83.

Chapter 6
1 Steinberg and Khrustalëv, op. cit., p. 386.
2 Maylunas and Mironenko, op. cit., p. 607.
3 Ibid.
4 Grey, op. cit., p. 70.
5 Markov, Sergeiv Vladimirovich, *How We Tried to Save the Tsaritsa*, G. P. Putnam's Sons, London and New York, p. 79.
6 Ibid.
7 Ibid., pp. 153 and 173.
8 Ibid., pp. 160–78.
9 Maylunas and Mironenko, op. cit., pp. 582–3. Letter from Valia Dolgorukov to his brother Pavel Dolgorukov, 14 August 1917.
10 HBCA, series AFG FN RG22/26.1016, 26/10/6. Outlays in connection with building of House in Murmansk, 16 November 1817–25, 1 September 1918.
11 Steinberg and Khrustalëv, op. cit., p. 333.
12 Summers, Anthony and Mangold, Tom, *The File on the Tsar*, Harper & Row, New York, 1976, pp. 255–8.
13 HBCA biographical sketch of Charles Vincent Sale. Sale was formerly a prominent businessman in Japan whose trading company also represented Baldwin Locomotive Works, the same Locomotive company that Sidney Reilly represented.
14 Ibid.
15 Summers and Mangold, op. cit., p. 256–7.
16 Hall had met the Tsar in Russia in 1914 while a guest at Tsarskoe Selo Palace and he was extremely close to Mansfield Cumming ('C'), the head of MI1C.

17 Summers and Mangold, op. cit., p. 257. Grand Duke Michael Michaelovich was the brother of Sandro, who had married Nicholas's sister Zenia.

18 Ibid., p. 258.

19 Ibid., p. 258.

20 Ibid.

21 HBCA, RG22/4/2.

22 HBCA, RG22/5/103 FO 67.

23 Ibid.

24 Biography and testimony of Olga Dimitrievna Starzhevskaia, Secretary/worker in the Administrative Office of the All-Russian Central Executive Committee (VTsIK), *Izvestiia*, 1 December 1918, p. 2 (263/527) and issue of 30 November 1918.

25 USNA, Robert C. Bannerman's file, confidential file 215, RG59.

26 Biography and Testimony of Olga Dimitrievna Starzhevskaia, op. cit.

27 This statement was made by Xenophon Kalamatiano, an American accused of spying in the Soviet Union.

28 Steinberg and Khrustalëv, op. cit., p. 229.

29 Ibid.

30 Ibid., pp. 235–7.

31 Ibid., p. 234.

32 Markov, op. cit., p. 194.

33 O'Conor, John F., *The Sokolov Investigation of the Alleged Murder of the Russian Imperial Family*, New York, Robert Speller & Sons, Publishers, inc., 1971.

34 Steinberg and Khrustalëv, op. cit., p. 245.

35 Ibid., p. 245.

36 Ibid.

37 Ibid., p. 246.

38 Ibid.

39 Ibid., pp. 246–8.

40 Ibid.

41 Ibid., p. 249.

42 Ibid., p. 249.

43 Ibid., pp. 250–1.

44 Ibid., p. 251.

45 Ibid., pp. 251–2.

46 Ibid., p. 252.

47 Ibid., pp. 253–4.

48 Ibid.

49 Ibid.

50 Kurth, Peter, *Tsar, The Lost World of Nicholas and Alexandra*, Boston, New York, and London, Little, Brown, and Company, 1995.

51 Radzinsky, op. cit., pp. 257–8.

52 Steinberg and Khrustalëv, op. cit., p. 185.

53 Russian consulate files, Record Group 261: Records of the former Russian Agencies, Microfilm 1486, Records of Imperial Russian Consulates in the United States, 1862–1922.

54 *See* Kerensky A. F., op.cit., Wilton R., *The Last Days of the Romanovs*, Bulygin, P. *The Murder of the Romanovs*, and Buxhoeveden, Baroness Sophie, *The Empress of Russia* and *Left Behind*.

55 USNA, Robert C. Bannerman, op. cit.

Chapter 7

1 USNA, Jerome Barker Landfield's personnel file, RG59, Breckinridge Long to Gavin McNab.

2 Ibid., Jerome Landfield to Breckinridge Long, 31 August 1917; Breckinridge Long to Mr Landfield, 17 October 1917.

3 Ibid., Breckinridge Long to Gavin McNab, 21 May 1918.

4 Israel, Fred L., ed. *The War Diary of Breckinridge Long*, University of Nebraska Press, Lincoln, pp. xiv and 106.

5 *New York Times*, 5 October 1919.

6 Papers of Jerome Barker Landfield, Department of Special Collections and Manuscript Division of the University of Chicago Library.

7 *Kelly's Handbook to Titled Families* and *Who Was Who*.

8 Warman, Roberta M., *The Foreign Office 1916–1918*, Garland Publishing Inc., 1986 (University of London, Ph.D. thesis, 1982), pp. 28–41, 75–199, 82–286.

9 Archives of the Central Committee at the Kremlin, dossier – the peace of Brest-Litovsk, series 75, folder 1, cited in Alexandrov, Victor, *The End of the Romanovs*, Little Brown, Boston, 1967, p. 74.

10 On 11 May the new German ambassador to Moscow, Count Wilhelm von Mirbach, reported that he had approached the People's Commissars and had been assured 'the German princesses will be treated with every consideration' and would

not be subjected to unnecessary petty annoyances or threats to their lives.

11 USNA, Quartermaster Corps, form 938, Report of Expenditures of the US Army Transport *Thomas* and Report of Passengers and Freight Transported During Voyage, Part Voyage 63–71, 20 May 1918–7 July 1918.

12 Ibid., p. 74.

13 Von Kuhlman, State Secretary to von Grunau, PRO GFM 6/139, A 26851, 22 June 1918.

14 Radzinsky, op. cit., p. 134.

15 USNA, Jerome Barker Landfield, op. cit.

16 Crawford, Donald and Rosemary, *Michael and Natasha*, Scribner, New York, 1997, p. 350.

17 USNA, Jerome Barker Landfield, op. cit., 21 and 25 May 1918.

18 Reilly, Sidney and Bobadilla (Reilly), Pepita, *Britain's Master Spy, The Adventures of Sidney Reilly, A Narrative Written by Himself, Edited and Completed by His Wife*, Harper & Brothers Publishers, New York and London, 1933.

19 Foglesong, op. cit., p. 119.

20 Foglesong, op. cit., p. 115.

21 Masaryk, Thomas, *The Making of a State*, H. Fertig, 1969, pp. 277–8.

22 PRO WO 106/1151, Nominal Roll of Officers, 'Syren' and 'Elope' Forces, June and July 1918. Note: Some of these men maintained they were sent to rescue the Tsar but it was, until now, only hearsay.

23 Charles Crane Papers, op. cit., Charles Crane to Tumulty, 30 May 1918.

24 Ackerman, Carl W., *Trailing the Bolsheviki – Twelve Thousand Miles With The Allies in Siberia*, New York, Charles Scribner's Sons, 1919.

25 USNA, RG59, file 103.93/335. US Legation, Berne, to Department of State, 9 May 1918.

26 USNA, RG59, file 103.9302/95a.

27 USNA, RG165, file 184-96.1, Major H. H. Slaughter to Chief, Military Intelligence Bureau, Report on trip into Siberia and Russia, 19 May to 15 September 1918, War Department.

28 Ibid.

29 Weber, Ralph E. (ed.), *The Final Memoranda, Major General Ralph H. Van Deman, USA Ret., 1865–1952, Father of US*

Military Intelligence, Scholarly Resources Inc., Wilmington, Delaware, 1988, p. 43.
30 Ibid.
31 Ibid., pp. 54–55.
32 Ibid.
33 Masaryk, op. cit.
34 USNA, file 119.2/88.
35 USNA, War Department, Executive Division, Military Intelligence Branch, file 184–95–1.
36 PRO FO 395/31807; 395/62607; PRO FO 395/184 61784.
37 PRO WO 374/19738.
38 Death Certificate file no. SA054008/Application Number PSR B 002746. An extract from an Entry in the Army Officers War Records of Deaths, 1914–1921.
39 Kennan, George F., *Soviet-American Relations, 1917–1920, The Decision to Intervene*, vol. II, Princeton University Press, 1958, p. 408.
40 PRO WO 106/1234 – This file contains a notation regarding 'k193' – perhaps Jones's agent number.
41 PRO WO 33/902, no. 83, from Captain Steveni, Vladivostok, to Director of Military Intelligence, 4 August 1918.
42 West Point Military Academy biographical sketch, West Point Military Academy Library, West Point, NY.
43 PRO FO 371/3234, Political. Japan. Files 6083–9874, No. 198/99, 1 July 1918.

Chapter 8

1 Summers and Mangold, op. cit., pp. 259–60.
2 Lied and Urquhart had been friendly before the revolution as is evidenced by Urquhart's diary entry in August 1916: 'I also met my friend Jonas Lied at the hotel and had quite a long talk with him', and Urquhart further stated that Lied has asked him to sail with him on his yacht.
3 Kennedy, K. H., *Mining Tsar, The Life and Times of Leslie Urquhart*, Allen & Unwin, Boston, 1986, p. 316.
4 HBCA, op. cit., C.V. Sale's personnel file.
5 The identity of Lambert and his relationship to another Lambert mentioned in William Clarke's *Lost Fortune of the Tsars* on page 188 as Manager of the Hong Kong and Shanghai Banking Corporation is unclear. The B. C. Lambert in Hong Kong was

apparently involved in shipping some Tsarist gold that had fallen into the hands of the Czech Legions to India in early 1920.

6 HBCA, op. cit., RG 22/4/2.
7 Steinberg and Khrustalëv, op. cit., p. 310.
8 Ibid., p. 350.
9 Ibid., p. 320.
10 Maylunas and Mironenko, op. cit., p. 632.
11 Luckett, Richard, *The White Generals*, Routledge & Kegan Paul, London and New York, 1971, p. 166.
12 PRO FO 175/16/60212, op. cit.
13 Kennedy, op. cit.
14 Sinclair, Archibald, op. cit., p. 258.
15 PRO WO 33/96, op. cit. Telegram 59154, 28 May 1918.
16 Memorandum in possession of Dr Richard Spence's collection.
17 PRO FO 175/6, no. 117.
18 Papers of Anthony Summers.
19 Maylunas and Mironenko, op. cit., p. 545.
20 German Foreign Office draft AS 1356.
21 Ibid, A 27476.
22 Summers and Mangold, op. cit., pp. 281–2.
23 Ibid.
24 Ibid., p. 293.
25 Sokolov, N. A., *Enquête Judiciaire sur l'Assassinat de la Famille Impériale Russe*, Payot, Paris, 1924, pp. 310–11.
26 Pipes, *The Unknown Lenin*, op. cit., pp. 6, 42–5.
27 PRO WO 95/4960.
28 PRO FO 371/3342, no. 6, 10 June 1918.
29 USNA file 861.6343/45.
30 PRO T1/12258.
31 USNA, War Department, file 9944–D–12.
32 O'Conor, op. cit., p. 31.
33 Ibid., p. 212.
34 Steinberg and Khrustalëv, op. cit., p. 387.
35 O'Conor, op. cit., pp. 68 and 212.
36 Ibid., pp. 68–9.
37 Romanov researcher David Haskin (the son of Henry Haskin, the man who owned the printing company that printed *Rescuing the* Czar) was the first to decipher these symbols.
38 Diary of Will Starling, entry for 25 July 1918, US Secret Service Archive.

Chapter 9

1 Gilbert, *Atlas Of The First World War*, op. cit., p. 104.
2 HBCA, op. cit., RG 22/5/103.FO.67.
3 Ibid.
4 Foglesong, op. cit.
5 USNA, op. cit., file 861.77/611a.
6 Summers and Mangold, op. cit., Sverdlov's statement, *Sokolov*, Russian edition, cited in chapter 25, p. 53.
7 Ibid.
8 Ibid., p. 84.
9 Ibid., pp. 85–6.
10 Ibid., p. 272.
11 Ibid., p. 271.
12 PRO WO 374/19738.
13 Kennedy op. cit.
14 USNA, Military Intelligence Division, Office Chief of Intelligence, War Department, file 2355-339-1.
15 Ibid.
16 USNA, op. cit., RG165, file 184–96.1. Major H. H. Slaughter, to Chief, Military Intelligence Bureau, Report on trip into Siberia and Russia, 19 May–15 September 1918.
17 USNA, op. cit., file 184–96.1.
18 USNA, op. cit., file 184–96.1
19 USNA, RG59, file 123 T71/191.
20 USNA, RG59, file no. 123 T71/107.
21 USNA, op. cit., file 184–96.1
22 USNA, RG59, files 861.00/2983; 861.00/7456; 861.00/8617; 861.00/8174.
23 Ibid.
24 Papers of Carl Ackerman, Manuscript Division of the United States Library of Congress, Washington DC. According to the original draft of Parfen Domnin, Ackerman edited and wired his story from the Hotel Wagon Lits in Peking. The document is undated.
25 Maylunas and Mironenko, op. cit., p. 625.
26 Ibid. p. 626.
27 Summers and Mangold, op. cit., p. 310.
28 Ibid.
29 Buxhoeveden, Baroness Sophie, *The Life and Tragedy of Alexandra Feodorovna Empress of Russia,* Longmans, Green

and Co., London, New York & Toronto, 1928, Chapter VII, The Coronation, 1896. p. 66.

30 USNA, op. cit., RG59, file 103.93/335.
31 USNA RG59, file 124.543/51a.
32 USNA, RG59, file 103.9302/123e, 11 January 1919.

Chapter 10

1   Sokolov Investigation of the Assassination of the Russian Royal Family, Kilgour Collection, Houghton Library, Harvard University, Cambridge Ma.
2   Summers and Mangold, op. cit., p. 67.
3   Radzinsky, op. cit., p. 366.
4   Summers and Mangold, op. cit., p. 67.
5   Buxhoeveden, *The Life And Tragedy*, op. cit., p. 267.
6   Maylunas and Mironenko, op. cit., p. 545.
7   Summers and Mangold, op. cit., p. 130.
8   Ibid., p. 69.
9   Ibid., p. 132.
10 Ferro, op. cit., p. 259.
11 Steinberg and Khrustalëv, op. cit., p. 353.
12 Ibid., p. 390.
13 Kathleen Holt, Colt Company, Hartford, Conn., 1998.

Chapter 11

1   *New York Times*, 12 March 1918.
2   Richard Teller Crane Papers, op. cit., Prince George Lvov to Charles Crane, 12 October 1918, mailed on 4 December 1918.
3   Maylunas and Mironenko, op. cit., p. 550.
4   Summers and Mangold, op. cit., p. 94.
5   *The Times*, 27 January 1919.
6   USNA, op. cit., RG165, file 184–96–1
7   Lasies, Joseph, *La Tragédie Sibérienne*, L'Edition Française Illustrée, Paris, 1920, p. 156.
8   Ibid.
9   Ibid.
10 Steinberg and Khrustalëv, op. cit., pp. 351–6.
11 Radzinsky, op. cit., p. 376.
12 Ibid.
13 Massie, *The Romanovs*, op. cit., p. 116.
14 Radzinsky, op. cit., p. 377.

15 Steinberg and Khrustalëv, op. cit., p. 351.
16 Zhivotovsky, op. cit., p. 571.
17 An N.N. Pokrovsky is mentioned in *A Lifelong Passion*, by Andrei Maylunas and Sergei Mironenko as a devoted subject of the Tsar who served as Foreign Minister under the last Tsarist regime and an M. Pokrovsky was cited in the banking scheme files in the PRO as 'had been Assistant Minister of Finance as well as Foreign Minister'. Additionally the banking scheme papers call him one of the 'soundest and most honourable representatives of the old regime'.
18 The only other Tikhomirov to be found was Lev Tikhomirov, the ultra-conservative former revolutionary who had served in the Duma.
19 Steinberg and Khrustalëv, op. cit., p. 356.

Chapter 12

1 Steinberg and Khrustalëv, op. cit., p. 358.
2 Ibid., p. 357.

Chapter 13

1 Summers and Mangold, op. cit., p. 107.
2 O'Conor, op. cit., p. 62.
3 Summers and Mangold, op. cit., p. 110.
4 Ibid., p. 111.
5 Ves Peterburg, 1912.
6 Krymov, Vladimir, *Portrety Neobychnykh Liudei*, Paris, 1971, pp. 78–9.
7 Sliozberg, G.B., *Dela Minuvshikh' Dnie*, vol. III, Paris, 1934, pp. 293–8.
8 Romanov, B.A., op. cit., pp. 87–108.
9 USNA, op. cit., file 21010–3241, 11 October 1918. Note: The following is noted in the file regarding Reilly, the Grand Duke (who was married to Nicholas II's sister, Zenia) and Mr Samuel Vauclain, Vice-President of Baldwin Locomotive Works: 'Mr Vauclain had run into contact with Reilly when he was in Petrograd during the first year of the war. Vauclain went to Russia to arrange for some contracts . . . while there found that his hardest competitor was Reilly . . . Vauclain said that there was no doubt that Reilly had tremendous political backing in Russia at the time which led right to the office of the Grand Duke

Alexander Michaelovitch.'
10 PRO FO 175/16/60212.
11 Spence, Richard, 'Sidney Reilly's Lubianka Diary, 30 October/
    4 November 1925', *Revolutionary Russia*, vol. 8, 2, December
    1995, pp. 179–94.
12 Smythe, James P., *Rescuing the Czar*, California Printing Co.,
    San Francisco, Ca, 1920, pp. 264.
13 Ibid., p. 267–8.
14 Steinberg and Khrustalëv, op. cit., pp. 362–3.
15 Kerensky, *The Road To Tragedy*, op. cit.
16 USNA, file 9728–469–30.
17 Holubnychyu, Lydia, *Michael Borodin, and the Chinese
    Revolution 1923–1925*, Ann Arbor, Michigan. Published for
    East Asian Institute, Columbia University by Microfilms Inter-
    national, 1979.
18 USNA, op. cit., file 9728–469–44–39X–(41).
19 Ibid.
20 Ibid., file 9728–469–38.
21 Ibid., file 9728–469–29.
22 Ibid.
23 Ibid.
24 Kerensky, *The Road To the Tragedy*, op. cit., pp. 137–52.
25 O'Conor, op. cit.

Chapter 14
1 USNA, RG59, file 702.6111/135, 7 July 1920.
2 Clarke, op. cit., p. 231.
3 National Archives Microfilm Publications, M1486, Records of
   Russian Consulates 1862–1922, Roll 153, San Francisco
   Consulate, Box 83.
4 Copyright application dated 23 July 1920 stating the publication
   date as 22 July 1920; copyright affidavits received 28 July 1920,
   in the papers of William Rutledge McGarry.
5 Correspondence of William Rutledge McGarry, contract
   between George Romanovsky and William Rutledge McGarry,
   10 March 1920.
6 Ibid.
7 Smythe, op. cit. p. 115.
8 San Francisco newspaper.
9 Notes of John Bescoby-Chambers, on the private papers of

William Rutledge McGarry, Chesterfield, Derbyshire, England.

10 Woodrow Wilson Papers, United States Library of Congress, Manuscript Division, Letters of John Temple Graves to President Wilson; McGarry family correspondence in the possession of the McGarry family.

11 Haskin Papers, op. cit., 21 August 1969.

12 *San Francisco Examiner*, 29 April 1919.

13 Notes of John Bescoby-Chambers, actual letter.

14 Ibid., actual letter.

15 Ibid.

16 USNA, RG59, file 702.6111/55.

17 *San Francisco Examiner*, 28 April 1918.

18 Kerensky, Alexander, *Russia and History's Turning Point*, Deuell, Sloan and Pearce, New York, 1965, p. 271.

19 *San Francisco Examiner*, 28 April 1918.

20 USNA, op. cit., file 702.6111/135.

21 Notes of John Bescoby-Chambers, op. cit.

22 Haskin Papers, op. cit., 25 August 1918.

23 William G. McAdoo Papers, op. cit., 13 September 1918.

24 Notes of John Bescoby-Chambers, op. cit.

Chapter 15

1 Notes of John Bescoby-Chambers, op. cit.

2 Joe Boyle Papers, Canadian National Archives, MG31 H159, vol. I, and *The US Department of State Papers Relating to the Foreign Relations of the United States*, 1917, Supplement 2, pp. 459–61.

3 PRO FO 371/3350, 26 November 1918, Report from Captain George Hill.

4 General Bandholtz's diary.

5 Queen Marie of Romania, Manuscript Division, Kent State University.

6 Charles Crane Letters, op. cit., 1920.

7 McGarry Family Letters, custody of John Bescoby-Chambers.

8 Ibid.

9 Smythe, op. cit., p. 258.

10 Ackerman, *Trailing the Bolsheviki*, op. cit., pp. 86–87, and p. 101.

11 USNA, op. cit., RG165, file 184–123.

12 USNA, List of US Consular Officers, 1789–1939, Microfilm

587, Roll 19, 136.

13 USNA, RG59, General Records of the Department of State.

14 Bailey, F.M. (ed. Peter Hopkirk), *Mission to Tashkent*, Oxford University Press, 1992, p. 9.

15 Lied, Jonas, *Return to Happiness*, Macmillan and Company, New York, 1943.

16 Clarke, op. cit., p. 38.

17 USNA, RG 59, file 811.111.

18 Smythe, op. cit., p. 132.

19 Amanach de St Petersbourg, 1913–14, p. 454.

20 Reilly, Sidney and wife, op. cit.

21 Charles Crane Letters, op. cit., 1920.

22 Ibid., Count James Rostovstov to Charles Crane, December 1917.

23 Ibid.

24 Papers of William Rutledge McGarry.

25 Stafford, David, *Churchill and the Secret Service*, Overlook Press, Woodstock and New York, 1997, p. 99.

26 Ibid.

27 Ackerman, Carl W., 'The Education of Lloyd-George', 1922.

Chapter 16

1 Smythe, op. cit., p. 75.

2 Ibid., pp. 254–5.

3 Ibid.

4 Ibid.

5 N. Steinberg, *The Events of July 1918*, n.d., 10VXX692, Hoover Institution of War, Revolution and Peace, Stanford University.

6 Medava, Joseph, 'Trotsky and the Jews', The Jewish Publication Society of America, Philadelphia, 5732/1972, p. 102.

7 Trotsky, *The Russian Revolution*, op. cit., p. 102-103.

8 Smythe, op. cit., p. 266.

9 Ibid., 266–7.

10 Ibid.

11 Radzinksy, op. cit., p. 382.

12 Steinberg and Khrustalëv op. cit., pp. 385–6.

13 Smythe, op. cit., p. 238.

14 Steinberg and Khrustalëv op. cit., pp. 216–7.

15 Smythe, op. cit., pp. 267–8.

16 Steinberg and Khrustalëv op. cit., p. 71.

17 Shinkarenko Papers, Hoover Institute, Palo Alto, Ca.

18 Smythe, op. cit., pp. 268–9.

19 USNA, RG 59, file 861.5343/45, 12 June 1918

20 USNA RG 59, file 861.6343/45, 29 July 1918.

21 USNA RG 59, file 103.96/880, July 16, 1918, and 123R271/83, September 25, 1918.

22 Ibid.

23 The unpublished Papers of Charles Crane, in the possession of Thomas Crane, son of John Crane.

24 USNA, op. cit., file 861.77/611a.

25 USNA, RG 59, 861.00/3545.

26 Ibid.

27 Fogelsong, op. cit., p. 89.

28 Diary of Will Starling, op. cit.

29 PRO ADM 53, Ship's Logs.

30 PRO ADM 53/45613.

31 PRO ADM 53/45614.

32 FO 371/3977A – 25632 – Fate of the Russian Royal Family

33 Ibid.

34 Ibid.

35 PRO ADM 116/1878.

36 Ibid.

37 Ibid.

38 PRO, ADM1/8938 & PRO FO 371/3977A/60669.

39 USNA, RG59, Microfilm 316, Records of the Department of State Relating to Internal Affairs of Russia and the Soviet Union, 1910–1929, file 861.77/672, Message from Imperial Japanese Embassy, Washington, to Breckinridge Long, 18 January, 1919.

40 Ibid.

41 Clarke, op. cit., pp. 89–91.

42 Ibid.

43 USNA, RG 59, file 861.00/3139.

Epilogue

1 Interview with Dino Yaroshinsky in Glasgow, Scotland, where he is a physicist at the university and his father in Paris where he works as a sculptor.

2 Blitz

3 USNA, RG165, Office Chief of Staff, Military Intelligence, file 9944-A-178.

4 USNA, Visa Files 811.111/20583, Baroness Buxhoeveden 17 February 1919 and another very difficult to read record on 8 (?) February: 'British Ambassador desires diplomatic visa for leaving Yokohama Feb. 20.'

Appendix

1 DNA (deoxyribonucleic acid) is composed of long strings of chemical building blocks called nucleotides. Each nucleotide consists of a sugar molecule (deoxyribose), a phosphate unit, and one of four nitrogen compounds called bases: adenine (abbreviated A), cytosine (C), guanine (G) and thymine (T). Because of certain chemical affinities in a specific individual, A always matches with T and C always matches with G – these complementary units forming the 'base pairs' for that individual. Mitochondrial DNA (mtDNA profiling involves a process called sequencing that isolates segments of DNA and identifies the different base sequences in a given sample. The first step in the forensic analysis is to extract human DNA from the given tissue sample – bone, hair, blood, even buccal cells from inside the mouth. In some recent cases the DNA was extracted from saliva residue on cigarette butts or from a fingerprint left on a glass. This DNA is then amplified or xeroxed via PCR (Polymerase Chain Reaction). The lab then runs three samples through the sequencer: the target sample (say, the suspect's blood), the evidence sample (blood from the crime scene) and a control sample, containing no DNA, to guarantee the integrity of the test. In mtDNA profiling the sequences from the target and evidence samples are then compared to see whether, at a given position in the DNA string, they 'match' (C for C, A for A etc.) or differ, which is called an 'exclusion'. If they are different at a sufficient number of base pairs the conclusion will be that the individual who contributed the target sample could not have been the source of the evidence

sample.

2 mtDNA testing sequences genetic material from the mito-chondria, the so-called energy engines of the cell. It is faster and can be carried out with as little as a single cell. The process of PCR allows a lab technician to 'amplify' pieces of the DNA molecules in the cell, making millions or billions of copies in a matter of hours.

3 Shields, op. cit.

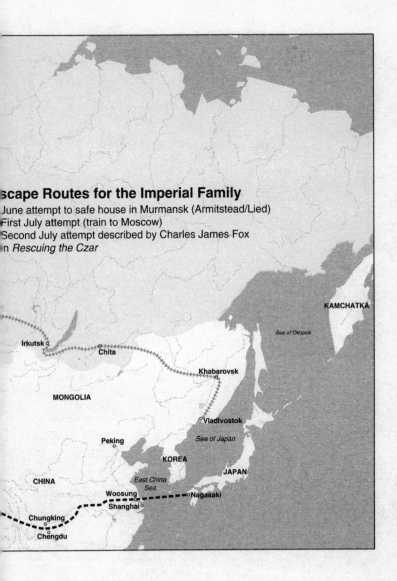

scape Routes for the Imperial Family

June attempt to safe house in Murmansk (Armitstead/Lied)
First July attempt (train to Moscow)
Second July attempt described by Charles James Fox
in *Rescuing the Czar*

Index

Abaza, Lt. Aleksandr Alexeevich 200-
202, 250
abdication of Nicholas II 20, 22
abuse of power by Bolsheviks 56
accounts
disposal of bodies by Yurovsky
179–181
evidence for fate of Nicholas II
135–157
execution at Alapayevsk, Pavel Bykov
216
implausible nature of, Yurovsky at
Ekaterinburg 181
last days of Imperial family,
documented details 146–154
last days of Imperial family, Slaughter
report 145–154
last days at Tobolsk 207–209
last days of Tsar, Pavel Bykov on
207–217
last farewell of Tsarina Alexandra
150–151
Lvov as witness to execution of
Imperial family 168
manipulation and obfuscation on fate of
Imperial family 166–183
Medvedev on events at Ekaterinburg
181–182
messages of help for Imperial family
(June 1918) 117–119
noise of shooting at Ekaterinburg, Pavel
Bykov 217
number of assassins 206
official version on demise of Imperial
family 136
relocation of Imperial family from
Tobolsk 82–95
report on visit to Ipatiev House
(October 1918) 139–140
Slaughter's note on last days of Czar
153–154
stylistic resemblance, 'Yurovsky Note'
and Domnin story 178
summary of Yakovlev's activities
(April 1918) 88–89
supplement from Historical Society of
Ekaterinburg 152–153
testimony excised from Sokolov's
published report 161–162
unpublished report on last days at
Ekaterinburg, Carl Ackerman
243–244
variations between 'Yurovsky Note'
and 1934 speech 177–178,
184–197
'Yurovsky Note' on fate of Imperial
family 170–176
Yurovsky's 1934 speech 184–194
Ackerman, Carl W.
action as spy 109–110

belief in credibility of Domnin story 233

Czech Legion, plans to snatch Czar 108–109

Domnin story, publication of 155–156

epilogue on 270–271

foreign agents in Ekaterinburg, reference to 145

papers of 318

story on death of Tsar revealed by 146

touting story of death of Tsar 166

unpublished report on last days at Ekaterinburg 243–244

advance on Ekaterinburg, Czech Legion 146

Alexandra, Queen 30, 31–32

Alexandra, Tsarina
   see also Imperial family
   after the execution 151–152
   allegations of spying 33, 36
   DNA match to Prince Philip 6
   last days at Ekaterinburg 148
   last farewell of 150–151
   overprotective of Alexei 18
   Rasputin, rumours of undue influence over 16, 17
   reluctance to leave Russia 75
   remains confirmed as a match 2
   secret relocation to Tobolsk 37
   smuggled note from 58–59
   tensions in royal circles 19
   thanks to Yaroshinsky 60

Alexeev, General 21, 48, 50–51, 53

Alexei II, Patriarch, Russian Orthodox Church 3

Alexei, Tsarevich
   see also Imperial family
   after the execution 151–152
   Andeyev and provision of milk and eggs for 126
   haemophilia of 17–18, 93, 118
   premonition of father's execution 147
   putative skull of 9
   secret relocation to Tobolsk 37
   welfare a prime concern 20

Alfonso XIII, King of Spain 263–264

allegorical revelation, Rescuing the Czar 234

allied
   agents in Ekaterinburg 141, 145, 213
   backing for Savinkov 71
   complicity with Bolsheviks 13

Allied Supreme War Council 43

ambush plans of Ekaterinburg Soviet 85

America's Secret War Against Bolshevism (Foglesong, D.) 52

Anastasia, Grand Duchess 9, 37, 60
   see also Imperial family

Andropov, Yuri 8

announcement of death of Tsar 138–139

Armitstead, Henry
   connection to Jonas Lied 78
   influence at court of Tsar 310–311
   Murmansk rescue attempt 116–117
   questioning banking scheme relevance 67
   'trade mission' of 113
   working for British Secret Service 79–80
   Yaroshinsky link 60

arms shipments
   to Czech Legion 221–222
   Reilly and 102–103
   San Francisco and 221–222

Atlas of the First World War 44

author's scepticism on Rescuing the Czar 221–223

Avdeyev, Alexander 88, 125–126, 130, 211

Avdonin, Alexander 7, 8, 176–177

Bakmetieff, Boris 54

Baldwin Locomotive Company 117, 321

Balfour, Arthur 31, 78, 99

banking scheme,
   Bolshevik overthrow as objective 267

banking scheme, Charles Crane and 49

banking scheme, difficulties 64

banking scheme, England as sponsor 54–55, 58, 61–2

banking scheme, involvement of Reilly 58

banking scheme, Keyes as controller 55

banking scheme, Keyes' dealings 62, 63

banking scheme, misunderstandings 61–2
banking scheme, scrutiny and disastrous
    consequences 65
banking scheme, secret plans 64–71
banking scheme, Yaroshinsky as front
    man 58, 178
Baranofsky, Vladimir 227–228
Barker, Sir Francis 78–79
'Baton Mission' to Japan 100, 114–115
Beloborodov, Alexander 87, 89–91, 129,
    161, 199
Berlin to Baghdad (McGarry, W.R.) 225
Berzin, Reinhold 124–125
Bezak, Fyodor 126
Bezobrazof, A.M. (Bezobrazof clique)
    201
Bolsheviks
  abuse of power by 56
  allied complicity with 13
  banking scheme and 66
  British relationship with 50
  characterisation of events at
      Ekaterinburg flawed 7–8
  combined operation against 106
  co-operation in safety of Imperial
      family 68
  counter-revolution against, Allied
      funding for 39
  Czech revolt against 108
  destabilisation of Romanovs by 16
  driven from Ekaterinburg 131
  expediency ruling actions of 127
  first uprising planned against 71
  freedom for imprisoned leaders 41
  funded by Germany 24
  gains in power of 29
  German common interest with 23
  international banking support for 25–26
  knowledge of banking scheme 63
  machinations of propagandists 21
  negotiations with Germans 126
  neutralisation of, only temporary 40
  progress of 'armed insurrection' 42
  repudiation of 'foreign debts' 50,
      107–108
  Romanov financial position, enquiries
      into 28

  Schiff's change of attitude towards 57
  Zionist support for overthrow of 26
Bonch-Bruevich, Vladimir 81–82, 88
Botkin, Eugene 37
Bouriat National Committee 238, 255
Boyle, 'Colonel' Joe 35, 230–231
Brest-Litovsk, Treaty of 66, 101, 108, 123
British allowed into Murmansk 127
*British Connection, Russia's Manipulation
    of British Individuals and Institutions*
    (Deacon, R.) 240
British diplomatic acid 170
British propagandism in America 224–225
British refuge for Nicholas II, opposition
    to 33
British relationship with Bolsheviks 50
Brusilov, General Alexei 40, 51
Buchanan, Sir George 31–34, 36
bullet holes in execution room 163, 203
Bulygin, Pavel
  aide to Sokolov 198
  Dowager Empress' link to Sokalov
      investigation 123
  epilogue on 269–270
  respect for Yakovlev 96
  theft of notes on death of Imperial
      family 205
Buxhoeveden, Baroness Sophie
  'Baroness B' 237
  epilogue on 272–273
  rejection of attempt to join Imperial
      suite 237
  respect for Yakovlev 96
  Sheremetevsky mystery 160
  Tsarina's lady-in-waiting 37
Bykov, Pavel
  account of last days of Tsar 207–217
  account inconsistent with Yurovsky's
      171, 183
  number of assassins 206
  Sokolov Report scooped by 205
  version of events refuted by forensic
      analysis 217

Calthorpe, Vice-Admiral 35
Calypso, HMS 36
Cambridge University 62

Cecil, Lord Robert 52, 54
Central Committee *see* Sverdlov
Ceylon 223, 235–6
chaos and fear 15–21
Chemodurov, Terenty Ivanovich 154–155, 159
Chicherin, George 103, 124
China 223, 254, 255, 258, 259
Chinese Eastern Railroad 37, 263
Churchill and the Secret Service (Stafford, D.) 240–241
Churchill, Winston S. 241
Chutskaev, Sergei Yegorovich 248
Civil War in England 312
Clarke, Sir W.H. 67, 113
Cocker, Mark 9
collapse of Imperial Germany 164–165
collision of rescue plots 242–243
combined operation against Bolsheviks 106
Comrade Relinsky (Reilly) 97, 160–161
Connaught, Prince Arthur of 100, 105, 111, 114, 115
Cornell University 99
Cossacks 50, 54
Crane, Charles
  banking scheme 49
  behind-the-scenes operator 137
  Bouriats, support for 239
  China, presence in 258
  correcting *Rescuing the Czar*? 231
  Czech Legion, efforts on behalf of 106–107
  Czech Legion, and extraction of Imperial family 104
  England, visit to 46, 48
  epilogue on 269
  knowledgeable on Russian affairs 26–27
  link to plans for Bolshevik overthrow 47–48
  Masaryk as intelligence source 112
  misgivings on Russia 30
  National City Bank director 109
  refinement of America's Russian strategy 50
  Russian associations of 28–30, 38

tipper of scales in favour White Russians 53
Creel, George 54
Crimea 21
Crosby, Oscar 51–53
Cumming, Mansfield 80, 117
Czech Legion
  advance on Ekaterinburg 146
  arms shipments to 221–222
  driving Bolsheviks from Ekaterinburg 131
  extraction intentions (of Imperial family) denied 112
  spontaneous nature of revolt debatable 114
  uprising and objectives of 110–111
Czechoslovakia 13, 104, 144–145, 205

Dalai Lama 238, 239
Davidson, Sir Arthur 31
Dehn, Captain D.V. 160
Dehn, Lily 76, 160, 253
Demidova, Anna 37
Denby, Charles 254–5
Derevenko, Dr. Vladimir 159
Digby-Jones, Captain Kenelm 113–14, 141–2, 144–5
diplomacy, invisible 39–63
disappearance of Imperial family 130–1, 135–6, 196, 198–218, 250–3
discovery of remains at Ekaterinburg 6
dismissal as fiction, *Rescuing the Czar* 258
diversity of versions of fate of Imperial family 138–41
DNA
  circumspection regarding evidence 5–6
  description of 325–6
  identification problems with 5
  incidental contamination of mtDNA sequencing 304
  inconclusive nature of test results 12, 277
  problems with Romanov tests 274–277
  process of analysis 274
  protocol for testing 3–5

Index

remains confirmed as a match 2
results of testing announced 10
soundness of testing a concern 3
statistical models and 303–304
testing in England 9
Tsarina match to Prince Philip 6
Zhivotovsky, concern on studies 11
DNA Identification Laboratory, U.S.
    Forces (AFDIL) 2, 4, 276
Dolgorukov, Prince Valia 37, 77, 126
Domino, Parafine 232–3
Domnin, Parfen Alekseivich 146–54,
    232–3, 243

Edward VII, King 30–31
Egerton, Sir Edwin 99
Eisenberg, Dr. Marcia 4
Ekaterinburg
    allied agents in 141, 145, 213
    bullet holes in execution room 163, 203
    Buxhoeveden's attempt to join Imperial
      suite rejected 237
    centre of allied activity 145
    danger zone for Imperial family 86, 91,
      98
    dimensions of execution room 162–3
    discovery of remains at (1979) 6
    fall of 158, 232, 251
    gold and platinum, status of 254
    implausible nature of Yurovsky account
      181
    imprisonment of Lvov in 167
    infiltration by Fox 131
    investigatory change in 165
    Medvedev account, contrast with
      Yurovsky's 181–2
    message to Petrograd Soviet concerning
      'measures to be taken' 41
    noise of shooting, Bykov's account 217
    official version on demise of Imperial
      family 136
    officials lacking funds for DNA testing
      9
    remains unearthed 2
    report on visit to Ipatiev House
      (October 1918) 139–40
    search for Romanov remains 8

Slaughter involvement in area of 143
supplement from Historical Society of
    152–153
testing remains from 5
Trotsky and 251
tunnel to British consulate 196–197,
    253–254
'Yurovsky Note' on events at 170–6
Ekaterinburg Soviet
    ambush plans of 85
    control of Imperial family, effects of 98
    demands to control Imperial family
      82–83
    excused by Bykov 217
    Goloshchekin critical of 82–83
    guard change at Ipatiev House 125
    Imperial family and Yakovlev both
      targets of 92–93
    innuendo implying threat to Imperial
      family 41
    militancy of 77
    participation in last days of Tsar 209
    plans to keep Imperial family from 130
    radical view of 96
    rogue nature of 115
Eliot, Sir Charles 114, 139–142, 163
Elizabeth, Grand Duchess 239
England
    American two-track policy and 53
    links to Tsar 13
    reaction to revolution in Russia 22–23
    refuge for Imperial family 30–31
    risks in supporting White Russians 54
    royal approval for rescue attempt
      263–264
    sponsor of illegal banking scheme
      54–55, 58, 61–62
enigma of history, search for truth 1–14
Enquéte sur le Massacre des Romanov
    (Grey, M.) 310
epilogues
    Ackerman, Carl W. 270–271
    Bulygin, Pavel 269–270
    Crane, Charles 269
    Fox, Charles James 272
    Nicholas II 152
    Reilly, Sidney 271–272

Rescuing the Czar 242–243, 244, 245,
  246, 247, 248
Rostovsov, Count 269
St John of Tobolsk, Brotherhood of 270
Slaughter, Homer 270
Vyrubova, Anna 272
Yaroshinsky, Karol 271
Ermakov, Pyotr 179–180, 182
Ersberg, Elizaveta 37
escape routes of Imperial family 328–329
escort change for Imperial family 90
Europe, unrest spreading across 32–33
extortion
  bidding war in 127–129
  bids for 'gold and platinum' 116–131

fear and chaos 15–21
Fedorov, Professor Sergei Petrovich 20
The File on the Tsar (Summers, A. and
  Mangold, T.) 7, 8, 78, 161–162, 200,
  217, 266
The Final Memoranda (Weber, R.E.) 111
Finland 42
Foglesong, David 52, 53, 105
Forensic Science Service (FSS), British 4,
  10, 275, 277
Fox, Charles James
  arrangements for saving Imperial family
    253–254
  diaries of 223
  epilogue on 272
  on guards' surprise at disappearance of
    Imperial family 242
  infiltration of Ekaterinburg guard by
    131
  invisibility of 249
  note added to document on last days of
    Czar 155
  note on arrival of Imperial family at
    Chungking 259
  portrayed as rescuing Imperial family
    196
  royal thanks for 232
France 13, 22–23, 53
Francis, David 27, 29
Frederick III, King of Prussia 31
French Revolution 31

Galitzin, Prince 28
Ganin Pit 160, 203–204
Gendrikova, Anastasia 37
George V, King
  censorship by 47
  close personal relationship with
    Nicholas II 34
  concerns for safety of Imperial family
    37
  Connaught as link to Emperor of Japan
    100–101
  deconstruction of notion of inertia of
    268
  enquiries on welfare of Imperial family
    34
  Imperial family, familial relationships
    30
  liberation of Imperial family,
    motivation for 135
  meeting with President Wilson 137–138
  name change to Windsor 33
  protection of foreign sovereigns, record
    on 34–36
  public opposition to Romanov refuge in
    Britain 33–34
  reluctance (in secret) to reject help for
    Tsar 13
  royalty, view on the impermanent
    nature of 31
  support for Landfield 99–100
  Tsarina responding to message from
    59
Germany
  American aid against 52
  Bolshevik common interest with 23
  collapse of Imperial 164–165
  interconnections with Imperial family
    30–31
  Lenin's policy towards 101
  links to Tsar 13
  offers of safety from 124
  promise of help in rescue 264
  reaction to revolution in Russia 22–23
  Russian bank nationalisation and 62–63
  threat to Northern Russia 42
  undermining Provisional Government
    25

Gibbes, Charles Sidney 37, 59
Gill, Dr. Peter 10, 276
Gilliard, Pierre 20, 37, 41, 75
Ginsburg, Moisei Akimovich 201
Glebov, Father Boris 3
Golitsyn, Andrei 10
Goloshchekin, Philip (Chaya)
  alleged orders to liquidate Imperial
    family 195
  critical of Ekaterinburg Soviet 82–83
  disappearance of Imperial family 253
  Lenin, working with 104
  spreading story of death of Imperial
    family 162
  Sverdlov, direct response to 90
  trucks, late arrival of 247
  Ural District Military Commissar 161
  Yurovsky conversation with 183
Gorbunov, Nicholas 129, 199
Gorshkov, Fidor Nikitin 159
Graves, General William 255
Graves, John Temple 225
Greene, Sir Conyngham 115
Groves, Major William Peer 122–123
Gruzenberg, Michael 54, 205–206
Guchkov, Alexander 29, 40
Gumberg, Alexander 205

haemophilia of Tsarevich Alexei 17–18,
  93
Hagelberg, Dr. Erika 277
Haig, Field Marshal Sir Douglas 33
Hall, Sir Reginald 78
Harper, Professor Samuel 27
Harris, Ernest 45
Haskin, Gretchen and David 222
Helphand, Alexander Israel (Parvus) 23
Hesse, Alice of 30–31
Hesse, Grand Duke of 25
heteroplasmy 276
Hewins, Ralph 79
historical enigma, search for truth 1–14
Hoare, R.H. 62
Hoare, Sir Samuel 62
Hokhriakov, Pavel 77
hopes of survival of Imperial family
  158–65

house arrest at Tsarskoe Selo 36
House, Colonel (special adviser to
  President Wilson) 52, 53, 98–9
Hudson's Bay Company 79–80, 97
Hudson's Bay Company, archives of
  46–7, 49, 77
Human Biology, Annals of 11, 178
The Hunt for the Czar (Richards, G.) 7, 8,
  221, 222, 225

Imperial family
  ancestry of menservants of 155
  'baggage', as code for 84–86, 89
  bidding war for 127–129
  Bolshevik co-operation on safety of 68
  Bykov account of last days of 207–217
  Central Committee split on 101
  Ceylon as ultimate destination 223
  code words for 128–129
  concern of George V and President
    Wilson 258
  conflicting views on fate of 13
  Crane and the 27
  deteriorating living conditions of
    (Tobolsk) 78
  diplomacy, motivations for 'hidden
    hands' 38
  disappearance forever 130–131,
    135–136, 250–253
  disappearance straining credibility
    198–218
  diversity of versions of fate of 138–141
  Ekaterinburg as danger zone for 91, 98
  escape operation planned 116
  escape routes mapped 328–329
  escape scenario for 122
  escort change for 90
  familial relationships 30, 31
  Fox allegation of flight to China 223
  future of, on agenda 39
  guards' surprise at disappearance of 242
  HMS *Kent* and transport of belongings
    259–262
  hopes of survival of 158–165
  insistence on remaining in Russia
    119
  investigations into fate of 158–163

irregularity of DNA evidence at Ekaterinburg gravesite 10–12
last days of, documentary details 146–154
Lenin's assurances on safety of 103–104
loyalty of Yaroshinsky towards 60
manipulation and obfuscation on fate of 166–183
messages of help (June 1918) 117–119
monarchical restoration, reactions to possibility 44–45
Moscow's attempts to move to safety 90–92
multinational attempts at rescue 136–137
Murmansk, safe house plans 46
official version on demise of 136
pawns of Lenin 13, 101, 103, 125, 253
plan for motor boat rescue from Tobolsk 79
pressure on Lenin to protect 123–124
proliferation of flawed versions of disappearance 217–218
proliferation of stories of murder of 165
real story, unfinished business 267–268
recorded accounts of relocation of 94
regime crumbling around 16
reinstallation considerations 44–46
relocation to Tobolsk 37
Roman confirmation of survival 264–265
rumours of survival 138
search for remains of 164
secrecy on salvation of 135–136
seldom mentioned in British records 34
survival possibility reported 139–140
targets of operation 'Elope' 106
Tashkent, exit from Siberia through 235
train movements and the 129–130
Vatican concern for 263–264
verification sought on (December 1918) 45–46
victims of the Russian Revolution 1
waiting and uncertainty a torture for 119
'Yurovsky Note' on 170–176

impoverished nature of revolution in Russia 13
India 43, 235, 240
international interest 22–38
investigations, first steps 158–165
invisible diplomacy 39–63
Ipatiev House see Ekaterinburg, Imperial family
Ireland 241
Ivanov, Pavel 2, 11, 276
Izvestiya 138

Japan
    'Baton Mission' to 100, 114–15
    concern for safety of Tsar 37
    Connaught visit in secrecy 114
    Imperial family in? 262–3
    intervention in Siberia 69
    links to Tsar 13
    McGarry's influence in 226
    reaction to revolution in Russia 22
    unexplained visits to 255
Joffe, Adolf 103

Kachurov, Michael 7
Kalamatiano, Xenophon 121
Kaledkin, General Alexis 48, 50–51, 54
Kara Sea 79
Kasai, Jiuju G. 226
Kelcey, Barbara 47
Kennan. George 48
Kent HMS 259, 265
Kerensky, Alexander
    see also Provisional Government
    fall of 42
    government of 29
    Imperial relocation arrangements 37
    military failure of 40
    offensive against Germany ordered by 39
    poor judgement of 40
    Provisional Government Justice Minister 31
    sanctuary in England, questions on responsibility for 36–37
    tactical mistake by 40–41
Kettle, Michael 62

Keyes, Sir Terence
  banking scheme controller 55
  banking scheme dealings 62, 63
  banking scheme difficulties 64
  banking scheme misunderstandings
    61–2
  Bolshevik involvement of 67
  Bolshevik overthrow, objective of
    banking scheme 267
  Boslheviks and banking scheme 66
  Indian/Ceylonese background 235–236
Keynes, John Maynard 52
Keyes, Captain A.J.H. 236
KGB 8
Kharitonov (the cook) 37
Khokhriakov, Pavel Danilovich 83, 84,
    238, 249
Kiev 126, 236
Kobylinsky, Col. Eugene 41, 75, 76–77,
    82, 155, 201
Koganitsky, Isaak Yakovlevich
    (Kaganitsky) 250
Kolchak, Admiral Alexander 45, 165, 227,
    232, 260–261
Koltypin-Wallovskoy, Peter 10, 12
Koptiaki, reported burial site 173,
    175–176, 195, 206, 242, 253
Kornilov, General Lavr 40, 41, 51
Korostovzoff, Lt-Commander 35
Kosarev, Vladimir 85, 86, 91
Krivoshein, M. 61, 64
Kuhn and Loeb, Bankers 25–26, 222
Kuhn, General 114
Kutuzov, Alexander 162

Lab Corporation of America 4
Landfield, Jerome Barker 98, 99, 100,
    104–106
Lansing, Robert 51–52
  'larrabee' code 113
  Lasies, Joseph 169–170, 261
  Last Days of the Romanovs (Bykov,
    P.M.) 196
  The Last Tsar, The (Radzinsky, E.) 164
Leech, Hugh 58, 66
  legitimacy of *Rescuing the Czar* 232
Lenin, Vladimir Ilyich
  allegations of German complicity 40
  assurances on safety of Imperial family
    103–104
  awareness of Trotsky's allied
    negotiations 70
  call for 'armed insurrection' 42
  cash demands by 66, 68
  checkmated by Ekaterinburg Soviet 96,
    97, 120
  concerns at German ties 23–24
  Ekaterinburg Soviet, telegram from
    87
  extortion, bidding war in 127–129
  fear of German reprisals 245
  Imperial family as bargaining counters
    125, 253
  nationalisation of banks 55, 63
  order for protection of Imperial family
    125
  parallel intrigues of 127
  payments to 206
  personal steps to ensure safety of
    Imperial family 124–125
  pressure to protect Imperial family
    123–124
  protective of Imperial family 103–104,
    125
  Reilly (Comrade Relinsky) as liaison to
    British 81
  rise of 42
  Romanovs as pawns 13, 101, 103
  working with Goloshchekin/Sverdlov
    104
Les Blancs et les Rouges (Venner, D.)
    26
Leuchtenberg, Duke of 25
Lied, Jonas
  diary extracts 78
  friendship with Urquhart 316
  meeting at Vickers Company 79
  Murmansk rescue attempt 116–117
  pioneer of Siberian trade routes 79
  rescue attempt participation 236
A Lifelong Passion (Maylunas, A. and
    Mironenko, S.) 320
Lindley, Sir Francis 65–66, 68, 113, 116,
    121

Lloyd George, David 31, 32, 43, 47, 239, 241

Lobanoff-Rostovsky, Princess Louba 99

Lockhart, Robert Bruce 68, 69–70, 71, 121, 235

Long, Breckinridge
    Connaught, meeting with Prince Arthur of 100
    knowledge of Imperial story 262–263
    Landfield, promoting services of 98, 104
    secret arrangements for Connaught visit to Japan 114

The Lost Fortune of the Tsars (Clarke, W.) 221, 263, 316–317

Ludendorff, General Eric 70

Lvov, Prince George
    commitment to continuation of war with Germany 22
    fears for Imperial safety 36
    Imperial relocation arrangements 37
    imprisonment in Ekaterinburg 167
    misinformation promotion 166–169
    negotiation, safe passage for Romanovs to England 31
    resignation of 29, 40
    witness to execution of Imperial family 168

Lysva 130, 267

Magerovsky, Eugene 10

Makarov Construction Company 47, 77

Makarov, Eugene 77

Maklakov, Vasilii Alekseevich 17

Mangold, Tom 7, 155, 159, 162, 199–201, 217

Maples, Dr. William 9, 275, 276

maps
    activities of Yakovlev/Moscow (April 1918) 88–89
    disposition of forces (1917–18) xiv–xv
    escape routes of the Imperial family 328–329

Marie, Dowager Empress 30–31, 35–36, 122–123, 261

Marie, Grand Duchess 37, 60
    see also Imperial family

Marie, Queen of Romania 230–1

Markov, Sergeiv Vladimirovich ('Little Markov') 76–77, 83, 247

Marlborough, HMS 35

Marye, George T. 27

Masaryk, Thomas
    behind-the-scenes operator 137
    Crane, relationship with 107
    Czech Legions and extraction of Imperial family 104
    Czech Legions, remote control of 102
    Czech Legions, withdrawal negotiations 108
    denial of intention to extract Imperial family 112
    intelligence source 111, 112
    Landfield, thanks to 106
    negotiations for safety of Czech Legions 66
    obfuscation by 112
    planning Bolshevik overthrow 48
    Romanovsky link 227

Matveyev, Pavel 88, 129–130

McAdoo, William G. 51, 228, 231, 250, 264

McGarry, William Rutledge (James P. Smythe) 222, 224–226, 228, 230–232, 239–241

McNab, Gavin 98–99, 100, 104, 114, 231

Medvedev, Pavel 159, 182, 203, 248–249

Meinertzhagen, Richard 9

Mensheviks 42, 208

Michael and Natasha (Crawford, R. and D.) 104

Mikhailovich, Grand Duke Alexander (Sandro)
    see also Imperial family
    American visitors whilst under house arrest 104–105
    execution at Alapayevsk, Bykov's account 216
    meeting with Jonas Lied 78
    regency proposed for 20
    Reilly backed by 311, 321
    Reilly close to 61
    Yaroshinsky, writing on 310
    tensions in royal circles 18–19

Milford Haven, Marchioness of 35
military failure of Alexander Kerensky 40
Miliukov, Paul 26, 32, 40
Milner, Lord Alfred 52
Mirbach, Count Wilhelm von 24, 124, 127, 245, 314
Mission to Tashkent (Bailey, F.) 235
monarchical restoration, reactions to possibility 44–45
Murmansk
  Armitstead in charge of house assembly operation 79
  Armitstead's concern and frustration 117
  British allowed into 127
  central to plans for rescue of Imperial family 49
  failure of second rescue attempt 123
  ideal protective location 60
  Makarov Construction Company in 77
  military protection for 67
  Moscow knowledge of activities at 70
  plan to deliver Imperial family to 97
  plans for safe house in 21
  'safe house' construction in 58–59, 67–78
  trade mission to 116–117
My Life with Lloyd-George 1931–45 (Sylvester, A.J.) 47

Nagorny, N.G. 37
Nametkin, Alexander 158–9, 162
National City Bank 109, 222
nationalisation of banks 55, 63
negotiations
  Bolsheviks with Germans 126
  safe passage for Romanovs to England 31
  safety of Czech Legions 66
  Trotsky with allies 68–70
Nevolin, Aleksander 92
New York Times 108, 109, 144–6, 155–6, 233, 243–4
Nicholas II, Tsar
  see also Imperial family
  abdication of 20, 22
  attempted Japanese assassination of
    37–38
  British refuge for, opposition to 33
  close personal relationship with George V 34
  criticism, unrelenting of 16
  demands to Alexeev 21
  epilogue on 152
  evidence for fate of 135–157
  German negotiations with 25
  hearing of 'the Revolution' 42
  house arrest at Tsarskoe Selo 36
  Japanese difficulties for 37
  last days of, documentary details 146–154
  loyal ally against Germany 30
  maternal relatives bones (in Ekaterinburg gravesite) 10–12
  military actions, following closely 39
  overprotective of Alexei 18
  Rasputin\Tsarina 'relationship', tacit approval of 17
  remains confirmed as a match 2
  reputation damaged by massacres 15
  reviewing his own death story 243
  rumours of death of (June 1918) 124–125
  skull lacking wound indication 11–12
  tensions in royal circles 19
  Trotsky's show trial demand 101
Nicholas, Grand Duke 16
Nikolaevna, Olga 99
Nikolsky, Ensign Alexander 77–78

Occleshaw, Michael 10
O'Conor, John 7
Olga, Grand Duchess 37
Omsk PSG (Provisional Siberian Government) 110
Omsk Soviet 77, 82–83, 85–86, 88, 89
Oxford University 9

Page, Walter Hines 52, 53
Palmer, Henry 128, 254
Pankratov, Vasily 41
Parvus *see* Helphand, Alexander Israel
Pavlovich, Duke Dmitrii 17
Perm 7, 11, 129–130, 182

Persians 50

Petrograd Soviet
  establishment of 20
  foreign intervention, attitude towards 32
  Lenin and call for 'armed insurrection'
    42
  message from Ekaterinburg Soviet
    concerning 'measures to be taken' 41
  vulnerable to German advance 68

Philip, Prince, Duke of Edinburgh 3, 6,
  275

Phillips, William 52, 53

Pichon, Stephen 168

Pipe, Dr. Richard 23

Pipes, Richard 17

plans
  delivery of Imperial family to
    Murmansk 97
  Masaryk and Bolshevik overthrow 48
  motor boat rescue 79
  protection of Imperial family from
    Ekaterinburg Soviet 130
  safe house in Murmansk 21
  Savinkov and secret uprising 105

Pokrovsky, M. 178, 320

Pokrovsky, N.N. 61, 64

Poole, DeWitt 49, 53, 54–55, 105, 121,
  236

Poole, General Frederick 64–66, 106, 113,
  121

Popov, Professor Vyacheslav L. 11

Portraits of Extraordinary People
  (Krymov, V.) 58

premonition of father's execution,
  Tsarevich Alexei 147

The President's Mystery Story (Roosevelt,
  F.D.) 266

Preston, Sir Thomas 128, 129, 141, 254

The Prisoners of Tobolsk (McGarry, W.R.
  and Romanovsky, G.) 222, 240

progress of 'armed insurrection'
  Bolsheviks 42

proliferation of stories
  disappearance of Imperial family
    217–218
  murder of Imperial family 165

Proskuryakov, Philip 203

protocol for DNA testing DNA 3–4

Provisional Government
  see also Kerensky, Alexander
  Bolshevik coup against 23
  diplomatic relations with 28–29
  house arrest decision by 36
  inclusion of aristocratic leaders 22
  negotiating safe passage for Romanovs
    31
  new government formed 40
  protective of Imperial family 39
  U.S. support for 25–26

Purishkevich, Vladimir Mitrofanovich 17

Radek, Karl 101–103, 107, 109

radical stance of Ekaterinburg Soviet 96

Radzinsky, Edvard 36, 94, 176, 182, 196

Rasputin, Gregory 16, 17, 18

reaction to revolution in Russia 22–23

Reading, Rufus Daniel Isaacs, Marquess
  of 26

refutation by forensic analysis, Sokolov
  version of events 217

Reilly, Sidney
  arms dealing 102–103
  Baldwin Locomotive Company
    representative 117
  banking scheme involvement 58
  behind-the-scenes operator 137
  captivity in Lubianka 201
  Comrade Relinsky, operating as 97,
    160–161
  Domnin report, mention in 234
  epilogue on 271–272
  McGarry, connection to 240
  memoirs and 'doctor' reference 105,
    130
  Mikhailovich, link with 61
  noted in US Office of Naval
    Intelligence files 311, 321
  party to two-track policy 120–121
  personnel file irregularities 143
  return to Russia of 57
  role in Murmansk attempt 120
  St. Petersburg Aero Club, leading spirit
    of 238
  secret mission on banking scheme 65

travel pass 'not to be bothered' 121–122
Vickers Company representative 79
Reinsch, Paul 44–45, 254–255
remains confirmed as a match 2
Remington Arms Company 58, 102, 107
repudiation of 'foreign debts' by
    Bolsheviks 50, 107–108
reputation of Nicholas II, damage to 15
Rescuing the Czar (Smythe, J.P.)
    allegorical revelation 234
    appearance in United States of 157
    collision of rescue plots 242–243
    compromise of allied agents by 250
    Czech Legion, plans to snatch Czar 109
    detailing survival of Imperial family 28
    disappearance of Imperial family 196,
        250, 251–252, 252-3
    dismissal as fiction 258
    Domnin, mentioned in 146
    Domnin, residence at Ipatiev House 155
    Ekaterinburg centre of allied activity
        145
    epilogue of 242–243, 244, 245, 246,
        247, 248
    escape of Imperial family through
        cistern (tunnel) 131
    escape route, sensible nature of 258
    escape scenario 122
    escape story 267
    first mention in *Hunt for the Czar* 8
    legitimacy of 232
    Makarov Construction Company 47, 77
    McGarry to Romanovsky, 'Nicholas in
        India' 240
    names of obscure Bolshevik officials
        contained in 232, 250
    provenance of 230
    roadblock to acceptance of traditional
        view 265
    as Rosetta Stone 265–266
    Sokolov report publication and 198
    state secrets 264–265
    stylistic resemblance to 'Yurovsky
        Note' and Domnin account 178
    Syvorotka, tied and shot 252
    validity, author's scepticism on
        221–223

    'wire to Moscow' 250–251
    withdrawal of 228–229, 230, 231
    'Yurovsky Note' and publication of 177
Revolution in Russia
    breathless pace of 39
    impoverished nature of 13
    spreading unrest through Europe 33
    unpredictability of 22
Revolutionary Committee *see* Petrograd
    Soviet
Richards, Guy 8, 225
Riezler, Kurt 24
The Road to Tragedy (Kerensky, A.) 36
Robertson, General Sir William 33
Robins, Raymond 69–70
Rodzianko, Michael 61
rogue nature of Ekaterinburg Soviet 115
'Romanov bones' view of history 2–3
The Romanov Conspiracies (Occleshaw,
    M.) 9
Romanov dynasty, 300 year reign of 15
Romanov, Prince Michael 11
Romanovsky, George Sergevich 95,
    221–222, 226–227, 228, 230–231,
    239–241
Roosevelt, President Franklin D. 266
Root Commission 29
Rostovstov, Count
    Crane banking instructions
        accomplished 238, 239
    Crane host 48
    epilogue on 269
    financial secretary to Imperial family
        27, 119
    resident in Turkistan 28
Rothchilds, Bankers 25
royal moves, new plans 98–115
rumours
    death of Nicholas II (June 1918)
        124–125
    survival of Imperial family 138
Russian Academy of Sciences 4
Russian Governmental Commission 2, 5,
    10
Russian Orthodox Church 2, 35, 122
Russo-Japanese War (1904–5) 15, 26, 28
Ryabov, Geli 7, 8, 9, 176–177

Safarov, Georgy 87, 89, 90
Sale, Charles Vincent 78, 80, 117, 312
Samara, Komuch in 110
Samoilov, Alexander 162
San Francisco
  arms shipments through 221–222
  McGarry cited in newspapers 224
  nationally important matters 221–229
  politics, intrigue and provenance
    230–241
  Russian consular records in 222
  Russian consulate at 95
  Russian émigrés and 221
San Francisco Examiner 225–226,
  227–228
Saturday Evening Post 108, 109, 156, 232
Savinkov, Boris
  allied backing for 71
  betrayal of 130
  Bolshevik overthrow effort 106
  Kerensky aide 40
  part of allied scheme to oust Bolsheviks
    234
  planning secret uprising 105
  Socialist Revolutionary leader 245
Scherbatow, Prince Alexis 10
Schiff, Jacob 26, 57, 109
Schneider, Ekaterina 37
searches for Imperial remains 8, 164,
  203–204
secret plans, banking scheme 64–71
Sednev, Ivan 37
Semenov, Ataman 69, 238, 255, 258
Sergeyev, Ivan 159, 162–163, 165, 169,
  170
Sheremetevsky (S-y, the mysterious)
  159–161, 247, 252, 253
Shields, Dr. William 5, 6, 11, 274–275,
  276–277
show trial demands of Trotsky 82
Siberian Bank 64, 67
Siberian intervention 43
Siberian trade routes 79
Siberian Trading Co. Ltd. 79
Siemonoff, Peter 27–28
Simsky Gorny district 86, 91
Sinclair, Archibald 58, 120

Sisson Papers 206
Slaughter, Major Homer
  deeply involved in Ekaterinburg area
    142–144
  documented details, last days of
    Imperial family 145–154
  Domnin report 230
  Domnin story, publication of 155–156
  epilogue on 270
  gold and platinum, status of 254
  records required by Congress 156–157
  reference to 'larrabee' code 113
  report from 243, 244
  report on Domnin story to military
    intelligence 232–3
  report on Palmer as trusted consul 128
  statement on Russian government
    structures 110
  Tashkent, activity in 235
  Turkistan communications of 144
  Van Deman, reporting to 111
Smith, Thomas 27
Sokolov, Nicholas
  access to fresh evidence 198–199
  bullet hole count by 163
  characterisation of events
    fundamentally flawed 7–8
  decoding Beloborodov telegram 200,
    250–251
  Dowager Empress and endeavours of
    123
  full report published posthumously 198
  Kilgour Collection, Harvard University
    Library 319
  last official investigator 7
  number of assassins 206
  search for remains 203–204
  testimony excised from report of
    161–162
  theft of notes for report 205, 206
  version of events refuted by forensic
    analysis 217
  Yurovsky's 1934 speech compared to
    report of 194–195
The Sokolov Investigation (O'Conor, J.) 7,
  8, 199, 217
Soloviev, Boris 59, 76, 83, 160, 247, 253

Index

Spiridovitch, General Tcherep 264

Spring-Rice, Dominick 56–57, 67

St John of Tobolsk, Brotherhood of
    epilogue on 247, 267, 270

St. Petersburg 3, 27

St. Petersburg Aero Club 238

Stalin, Joseph 70–71, 104, 108, 184

Starkov, Ivan 161

Starling, Will 131, 258

Starzhevskaia, Olga Dimitrievna 81

State Department Records 254

statistical models and DNA testing
    303–304

Stavka [at Mogilev) 19, 20

Steinberg, Nachman 245, 246, 253

Summers, Anthony 7, 155, 159, 162,
    199–201, 217

Summers, Maddin 50

Sussanin, Ivan 155, 156

Sverdlov, Yakov (Chairman of Central
    Committee)
  announcement of death of Tsar
    138–139
  Beloborodov telegram, controversial
    evidence of 199–200, 250–251
  direct response to Ekaterinburg Soviet
    90
  direction to Omsk Soviet to assist
    Yakovlev 86–87
  Goloshchekin/Safarov telegram to 245
  instructions to take Imperial family to
    Ekaterinburg 90–91
  knowledge of Reilly's position 81–82
  Lenin, working with 104
  relationship with Yakovlev 95
  sibling coincidences 96–97
  support for Yakovlev 84–86, 90–91

Sysertsky, direction of 252, 253

Syvorotka, Alexei 224, 237–238,
    243–245, 247, 252

Tashkent 235

Tatiana, Grand Duchess 37, 204, 227–228
  see also Imperial family

Tatishchev, General 37

Tchayeff, S.N. 67

telegraphic communications

controversial evidence 199–203,
    250–251

Ekaterinburg Soviet/Sverdlov on
    disposition of Imperial family 88

Goloshchekin/Safarov to Sverdlov 245

Lenin order for protection of Imperial
    family 125

startling series of 255–258, 259

'wire to Moscow' 250–251

Yakovlev/Sverdlov en route from
    Tobolsk 84–86, 90–91

tensions in Imperial circles 18–19

Tereshchenko, Michael 36

Thomas (US cargo ship on Pacific circuit)
    102, 221

The Times 96, 169

Tiumen 85, 89, 90–91

Tobolsk
  first attempt to secure Imperial family
    75–97
  last days of Tsar at 207–209
  relocation of Imperial family to 36–37
  smuggled note from 58–59

Tolstoy, Count A.A. 169

trade mission to Murmansk 113, 116–17

La Tragédie Sibérienne (Lasies, J.) 169

Trailing the Bolsheviki (Ackerman, C.)
    243

Trans-Siberian Railway 15, 28, 114, 169,
    263

transportation of Imperial belongings
    259–262

Tredwell, Roger 68, 69–70, 143–144

Tribune, HMS 35

Trotsky, Leon (Lev Davidovich
    Bronstein)
  banking finance for 26
  description of Steinberg 246
  Ekaterinburg and 251
  negotiations with allies 68–70
  removal plan of? 104
  renunciation of foreign debt, call for
    101
  return from America 39
  show-trial demands of 82, 101

Trotsky and the Jews (Medava, J.) 246

Tsarist war debts 44

Tsarkoe Selo 21, 36, 75
tunnel to British consul's Ekaterinburg
    house 196–197, 253–254
Turkistan 28
Turle, Commander A. 35

Ullman, Richard 116
United States
    background stance by 53
    financial support against Bolshevism
        52–55
    'hidden hand' revealed 51
    knowledgeability on Russian affairs
        26–27
    links to Tsar 13
    Long and the whole Imperial family
        story 262–263
    refinement of Russian strategy 50
    State Department Records 254
    support for Provisional Government
        25
    two-track policy of 53–54, 68
University of Chicago 27
University of New York at Syracuse 5,
    275
University of St. Petersburg 99
unpredictability of revolution in Russia 22
Ural Regional Soviet 87, 89, 149–150,
    208–209
Urals, power struggle in 82
Urquhart, Leslie 67, 116, 120

Van Deman, Major-General Ralph H. 111,
    112, 271
Varakushev, Alexander 162
Vasiliev, Father 76
Vatican concern for Imperial family
    263–264
Vauclain, Samuel 321
Venner, Dominique 26
Victoria, Princess 31
Vladivostok 15, 102, 221, 259–260
Volkov, Alexander 37
Vologda 120, 131
Vonliarliarskii, V.M. 61, 201
Voska, Emanuel 107, 111, 112
Vyrubova, Anna

co-conspirator with Soloviev 76
    epilogue on 272
    escape group participant 253
    escape strategies 160
    Tsarina's confidante 247
    Yaroshinsky note to 60
    Yaroshinsky/Soloviev rescue
        participation 237–238

Webster, Captain Valentine 236–237
Webster, Lieutenant Laurence 236–237
Weedn, Lieut. Col. Victor W. 2, 276
Westinghouse Company 28
White (anti-Bolshevik) Russians
    banking system utilised for support of
        137
    Beloborodov telegram and 199–203
    objection to confirmation of remains'
        authenticity 2
    Sokolov appointed by 7
Who's Who in America 225
Wilhelm II, Kaiser
    Imperial family, familial relationships
        31
    liberation of Imperial family,
        motivation for 135
    pressure on Lenin for safety of
        Princesses 24
    reluctance (in secret) to reject help for
        Tsar 13
Wilson, General Henry Hugh 43
Wilson, President Woodrow
    Connaught as perfect conduit from
        George V 100
    Crane as adviser to 27
    meeting with King George V 137–138
    policy towards Russia 25, 26
    Provisional Government, support for
        (and concerns) 29–30
    refinement of America's Russia strategy
        50
    sensitivity of Russian plans 52
    special relationship with J.B. Landfield
        99
Wilson, Sir Henry 240–241
Wilton, Robert 96, 261
Wilton, Thomas 169–170

Index

Wiseman, Sir William
  British intelligence head in U.S. 52
  British propagandist in America
    224–225
  Long as courier for 99
  Masaryk as intelligence source 111, 112
  Yaroshinsky connections 120
withdrawal of *Rescuing the Czar* 228–229,
  230, 231
World War I 13, 32

Yakimov, Anatole 159, 203
Yakovlev, Vassily
  accused of treason 87
  Bykov account of Tsar's last days
    209–210
  death of 95
  direct link to Lenin 96–97
  emphasis of dangers at Ekaterinburg 86
  epic nature of service to his country 95
  fear of ambush by Ekaterinburg Soviet
    84–85
  final warning on dangers at
    Ekaterinburg 91
  life subsequent to relocation débacle 94
  Matveyev, service with 129–130
  'mission of special purpose' by 71, 83
  pressure for haste in relocation from
    Tobolsk 93
  protection for Imperial family en route
    from Tobolsk 82–84
  relationship with Sverdlov 95
  respect accorded to 96
  summary of activities (April 1918)
    88–89
  support for assertions of 92
  Sverdlov, complete trust in 90
  treatment in later books 96
Yaroshinsky, Karol
  banking scheme front man 58, 178
  banking scheme scrutiny, disastrous
    consequences 65
  banking/financial background 59
  behind-the scenes operator 137
  epilogue on 271
  implementation of bank takeovers 62–3
  loyalty to Imperial family 60
  meeting 'trade mission' members
    119–120
  political flak from London 61
Yeltsin, Boris 3, 8, 10
Yuriev, A.M. 70
Yurovsky, Yakov
  account of disposal of bodies 179–181
  appearance in 1979 of 'Note' 9
  additions to 'Note' 12
  aiming instructions of 163
  character in stark contrast to Andeyev
    126
  confusion in 'Note' on number
    executed 178–179
  deep mine disposal of remains 248
  fabrication of 'Note' 177
  firing-squad leader 7
  Imperial family, new head of guard 125
  implausible nature of account of events
    at Ekaterinburg 181
  Medvedev account (of events at
    Ekaterinburg) contrasted 181–182
  number of assassins 206
  provenance doubt, Colt 45 used by 164
  speech, 1934, of 184–194
  transportation problems of 252
  variations between 'Note' and 1934
    speech 177–178, 184–197
  'Yurovsky Note' 170–176
Yusopov, Prince Felix 17

Zaslavsky (Ekaterinburg Soviet) 82, 84
Zenia, Grand Duchess 18
Zhivotovsky, Dr. Lev 4, 11, 12, 178
Zionist activism 56

Also Available in Arrow Paperback

AMERICAN PIMPERNEL

Andy Marino

The incredible story of the American who saved more lives than Schindler – great scientific and artistic figures such as André Breton, Heinrich Mann, Marc Chagall and Max Ernst. This is one of the last great human interest stories of World War II.

Varian Fry was an outsider, a flawed man who was transformed by the advent of war in Europe, finding his purpose as the saviour of hundreds of people facing death under the Nazis. Marino traces the progress of a seemingly impossible rescue operation, revealing the charismatic personality of Fry and those who helped him. It is a story full of surreal and heart-stopping episodes; a novelist smuggled out of a concentration camp right under the noses of the guards; the 'secret' escape route up a mountainside in full view of the entire population of Cerbère

This is the first time his full, true story will be told, with the benefit of the author's access to archives and the cooperation of those who best knew Varian Fry.

HALL OF MIRRORS

David Sinclair

Hall of Mirrors is a fascinating insight into the single event which shaped the face of the modern world. If the Great War of 1914–18 was a tragedy, then the Treaty of Versailles was a complete travesty. Rather than sealing a guarantee for peace, stability and prosperity for a new and better world, the treaty ensured that the remainder of the twentieth century would see horror, brutality and suffering unparalleled in human history.

The treaty was engineered and manipulated by self-interested politicians with individual motivations and contrasting agendas. *Hall of Mirrors* reflects on how the representatives of America, Britain and France – Woodrow Wilson, David Lloyd George and Georges Clemeneau – deliberately ignored the possibility of finding a progressive international solution. Instead, driven by ego and personal vendetta, these statesmen stimulated a European future of faction, dispute and conflict. *Hall of Mirrors* is a fascinating story of destruction, delusion and greed, illuminating the personalities and politics involved in making the treaty. It is also a valuable and topical discussion on the political structures which enable indvidual character and will to dictate the course of history and culture.

'THIS IS BERLIN'

William L. Shirer

Before Britain and Germany went to war in 1939, Ed Murrow of CBS sent his star reporter William Shirer to report from Berlin on what was really happening in Hitler's Germany. And there Shirer stayed until December 1940, reporting on the war from within the Reich, battling against the censors and revealing to American and British audiences how Hitler, the SS, and his armed forces were conducting the war, and what it meant to live in a Nazi state. All through the campaigns leading to the fall of France, Dunkirk and the Battle of Britain, Shirer provided a unique and dramatic byline on history as it happened, and now his writings have been gathered together for the first time into a vivid, compelling and urgent narrative, one of the great first-hand documents of the Second World War.

OTHER TITLES AVAILABLE IN ARROW BOOKS